ADHAN OVER ANATOLIA

THE DIARY OF
AN AMERICAN MUSLIM

by
Marian Kazi

AMERICAN TRUST PUBLICATIONS

ADHAN OVER ANATOLIA

ADHAN OVER ANATOLIA

© American Trust Publications
7216 S. Madison Ave.
Indianapolis, Indiana 46227

Library of Congress Catalog Card No. 75-22575
ISBN 0-87141-054-0.
Manufactured in the United States of America

DEDICATION

To Jamal, Maryam and Nura, who bore with me throughout the seemingly endless months which were required for the preparation of this volume with a remarkable degree of patience, this book is lovingly dedicated, with the earnest prayer that the experiences which are recorded here will have left an indelible imprint on their young lives which will help them to be strong and committed Muslims in the years ahead.

TABLE OF CONTENTS

In the Name of God, the Compassionate, the Merciful

INTRODUCTION

Before the events narrated in this volume took place, my husband Selim, a Pakistani national settled in America, had spent considerable time planning for a year's study or research at some university in the Muslim world. An opportunity for such study presented itself during the academic year 1970-1971 at the Middle East Technical University in Ankara.

Prior to our visit to Turkey, we had had a very great interest in this part of the world in general. Turkey had particularly attracted our attention because close Turkish friends, in whom we had discerned certain unique and remarkable characteristics, had awakened in us a special interest in their country and culture. Pakistan, where my husband's closest relatives lived and where we ourselves had lived at one time, we knew already, but Turkey, Iran and the Arab world were all unknown to us at first hand. Thus, when this opportunity arose, we were happy to accept it not only because of the chance it afforded my husband to pursue studies in his area of special interest, but also because it promised to expand our knowledge and understanding of that part of the world where the majority of Muslims live.

Our interest in the Muslim world was one which precluded any nationalistic interest, one which was rather supranational. All people professing belief in the One God and in His prophet, Muhammad, peace be on him, were our brothers, their concerns were ours, and we belonged to their world although we might live thousands of miles distant from it. For several years both of us had been working actively with other Muslims in North America in an effort to make Islam better understood among both Muslims and non-Muslims, and indeed, I can say no less than that our lives were so totally bound up with our commitment to Islamic work and to our fellow Muslims that, apart from family and profession, it was our *raison d'etre.*

It is estimated that there are between one to two million Muslims living in North America at the present time. Of these, a large number are students from other countries residing here temporarily. Another large group includes immigrants, both those whose parents or grandparents settled here in the past as well as those who came more recently, a large percentage of whom are professionals, and it also includes increasing numbers of native Americans who are coming into the Faith, particularly those of African ancestry. To connect and co-ordinate all these Muslims and their varied activities, some nation-wide Islamic organizations have been established in recent years, and at the local level, many Islamic centers, mosques, associations, chapters, Islamic schools, youth camps and other activities have also come into being.

Now it is hardly fair to the non-Muslim reader to precipitate him abruptly into the world of Muslims and their way of life and thought without giving him some idea of the beliefs and practices of Islam. Briefly, then, Islam is neither an ideology, concept, faith nor practice; rather it is each and all of these, and much more. Belief in God and in His Prophet, Muhammad, who was the last in a long line of prophets, all of whom brought the same Divinely-revealed message concerning the existence and reality of the One God and man's relationship and responsibility to Him, is the first requisite. From this basic creed, the conceptions, injunctions and moral values of Islam are translated into a total orientation, a frame of reference, a criterion, a way of life and a commitment which considers even the most mundane acts to be worship of God if they are done in keeping with His injunctions and with the aim of pleasing Him. Islam, in short, is no Sunday religion, no part-time affair; it is the very sum-total of a Muslim's life as it is lived moment by moment with the consciousness of God.

Prophet Muhammad, peace be on him, was the means through whom God's final revelation was transmitted to mankind. Before the beginning of his mission in 612 A.C. (After Christ) during his fortieth year, he had been a man of completely upright character, spotless morality and integrity in the midst of a depraved pagan society. After the call to prophethood, this pure and blameless man, together with the small community of Muslims, faced continuous, active hostility and persecution simply because he called his fellow men to submit to God alone and to abandon their impure idolatrous worship and degraded way of life in exchange for a life of God-consciousness and righteousness. He was the leader of that group of God-fearing men and women who had accepted Faith, their connecting link with God, and the example for them and for Muslims of all times to follow.

The Divine revelation which was transmitted through him over a period of twenty-three years has been preserved exactly as it was revealed to him in the Holy Qur'an. This book is the first source of guidance, the standard and the criterion for Muslims and they are under obligation to follow its teachings. Besides this, many details concerning the actions and sayings of the Holy Prophet, peace be on him, have been preserved, and this *Sunnah* (practice) of the Prophet is the second source of guidance for Muslims, who must sincerely try to follow his example and injunctions as nearly as possible.

Islam differs from the other religions in that it has two aspects, both of which are essential and complementary, namely, the individual and the community aspect. Every Muslim has certain obligations to God and to other human beings which are carried out on an individual level. However, Muslims cannot function without a community, for many of their Islamic obligations can be carried out only through collective action; moreover, the community provides the atmosphere and the concrete practical situation which will help the individual Muslim to *live* Islam. Wherever Muslims reside, therefore, it is their duty to call together other Muslims in order to form a community which will carry out the observance of congregational prayers and other aspects of worship, the training and education of youth, the distribution of charity to the needy, the propagation of Islam, and which will provide the atmosphere, the concrete conditions, in which the individual Muslim can function as a Muslim even though he may be thousands of miles away from any center of Muslim population.

What, in actual practice, are a Muslim's obligations? These may be roughly classified into two aspects, namely, 'worship' (*ibadat*), and 'striving in the way of God' (*jihad fi sabeel Allah*). 'Worship includes prayers, fasting, obligatory and voluntary giving to the needy, pilgrimage to Mekkah once in a lifetime if possible, and also, in a broader sense, all the acts of one's daily life by means of which one satisfies the lawful needs of oneself or one's family or works toward the improvement of the society with the desire to obey God's laws and to please Him. Thus, for example, working to earn an honest living, caring for one's family and home, acquiring any sort of useful knowledge, helping one who is in difficulty or need, spending for one's lawful necessities, observing modest behavior and dress, and so on, are all considered as forms of worship of God if they are governed by what is called *taqwa,* that is, conscious- ness of God and of one's responsibility to Him under any and all conditions. 'Striving in the way of God,' on the other hand, relates to those aspects of a Muslim's individual and community life which are for the purpose of establishing God's law on earth, carry- ing forward the message of Islam, combating evil and injustice, establishing equitable and righteous political, economic and social systems, and so on, and it should begin in the heart of the individual Muslim in his striving to improve and perfect himself. For this world is the sphere of action which prepares the Believer for his ultimate goal, the world of the Hereafter, where he will be judged and recompensed according to his intentions and actions by his All-Wise Creator, Who is both Just and Merciful.

This is the dynamic principle of Islam. Why, then, it may justifiably be asked, are many of the Muslims of today so poor, backward and depressed if their religion is so dynamic and all- encompassing? Why are they politically and socially in such a state of ferment and turmoil? Why do they, in many cases, give the impression of being so spiritually and ideologically bankrupt?

Many among the so-called Muslims themselves, as well as

others, have attempted to answer these questions by laying the blame at the door of the religion itself, alleging that their miserable condition is due to it in one way or another. An honest and unbiased look at both the teachings of Islam and at the history of Muslims, however, will not bear out this allegation, for in early times Muslims were dynamic, intellectually active, possessed of a high standard of living and culture—characteristics fostered by the very dynamism of Islam—and above all, had a clear sense of direction and inner certainty. Today's distressing conditions are, on the contrary, rather due to the obvious fact that the supposed adherents of Islam are *not* following it, and that they have lost their sense of values, direction and clear moral imperative, to follow imported ideologies, ways of thought and patterns of life which have their genesis in conceptions and historical processes which are completely alien and antithetical to Islam, and which have no internal connection with the people who have so unthinkingly adopted them. Muslims today are, by and large, due to an inadequate or even non-existent Islamic education, profoundly unaware of the nature and significance of the religion which they profess, and which has been unable to fulfill its potential of changing their personal lives and transforming their societies *because they have never understood nor applied it..*

Thus there exists a critical state of stagnation in the realm of understanding and thought among Muslims. The dynamic principle of Islam has been lost sight of, and the basic obligatory acts such as prayer and fasting have been taken to be the totality of the religion, while morals, manners, cleanliness, orderliness, discipline, integrity and honesty, striving for social justice, utilizing earthly resources, attaining knowledge, developing human potential, and shunning what is forbidden have been forgotten or ignored. The Muslim indeed has such obligations of prayer and fasting, but they are certainly not the end of his Islam. Rather they are duties prescribed by God in order to make the Muslim always conscious of his responsibilities to his Sustainer, the source of strength and nearness to Him upon which he draws in order to strive toward what He has enjoined—essential and obligatory, indeed, but not sufficient; only the beginning rather than end of his practice of Islam.

Thus, among the numerous and very serious problems today afflicting the Muslim world, from North Africa to Indonesia, perhaps the greatest is precisely this terrible apathy concerning the most valuable, the most vital thing it possesses—the one thing, indeed, which can bind the peoples of this part of the world together and heal its festering wounds; the one thing which, if earnestly applied, could transform individuals and nations as it had done in the past. Perpetually torn apart by rivalries, political conflicts and every sort of divisive tactic from within and without, the Muslim world is the victim of its own appalling disunity which is exploited and encouraged from every side, failing to grasp the obvious fact that what is common is infinitely more important, meaningful and essential than the petty and selfish differences which divide it.

Today, however, the picture is not without a brighter side, for among a growing number of individuals here and there in this Muslim world, a clear consciousness of what is being lost and what, somehow, must be regained and re-established is being felt, and a movement toward Islamic revival is gaining momentum. But as in the first days of Islam, when the vested interests of the day stood with physical might and power against the flaming righteousness, spiritual strength and sublime purity of Islam and its exponent, Prophet Muhammad, peace be on him, so too in our time in the Muslim world, many of those in whose hands political and economic power rests, and whose main concern is to retain and consolidate that power, stand solidly opposed to any attempt at Islamic revival, their opposition taking various forms according to local conditions. In the majority of Muslim countries, there is little tolerance, if not open persecution, of those who speak in the name of Islam, calling the people to an upright way of life and the government to abandon its policy of religious, political and economic repression of the people. Although very few people in the Western world are aware of it, such attempts at Islamic revival have been systematically crushed with varying degrees of intensity by the governments of various nations. Thousands of devoted Muslims have been imprisoned, brutally tortured and killed in this effort during the past many years in such countries as Algeria, Ethiopia, Egypt, Turkey, Iran, Iraq, Indonesia, the Phillipines, Sudan, the Soviet

Union and Communist China. However, despite all the harsh measures which have been directed against the nascent Islamic movement and individual Muslims, the movement has not been destroyed nor weakened. Indeed, it is possible that all this persecution and repression have brought about further reawakening and have increased the commitment of Muslims to their cause; for truth cannot be crushed by material power, and those whose hearts are firm will continue to carry forward its indestructable message even though it lead them to their deaths.

To these difficulties are added the continuing problem with Israel, communist infiltration and revolutionary movements threatening many countries from within and without, aggression or threats of aggression against individual Muslim nations by their neighbors and the less obvious but equally strong pressures of 'friendly' nations, and above all, the shocking lack of unity and sincerity of leadership. These are the harsh realities of life for the Muslims of today. Under these conditions, the Muslim with a clear vision of Islam and dedication to its principles stands almost isolated in an ocean of powerful forces threatening him from every side. Although well aware of his individual powerlessness, it does not deter him, and he goes forward as well as he can, gathering around himself other dedicated Muslims whose goal—that of freeing mankind from domination by anything other than God and bringing it under the sovereignty of God alone—is the same, placing all his reliance upon his Lord, for he knows that all outcomes are with Him and that his personal responsibility is to make a sincere, earnest and intelligent effort to the best of his ability to make known the true message of Islam and to improve the state of his society and of the world.

The present volume, then, is an attempt to show some of the typical forces at work in a part of the Muslim world, both for and against Islam, as they come directly out of my personal experience. More specifically, this volume is a commentary on what I observed and on what happened to me and my family during the period between August 1970 and May 1971, in the course of our travels from the United States to Ankara, later to Pakistan and back to

Ankara, and in Turkey during the spring of 1971, with special emphasis on events and experiences which occured during our stay in Ankara, the diary which I kept throughout this period forming its base.

The diary was begun several months before we left for Turkey (see Chapter 1) purely for my private interest, as I have long found writing down my experiences and feelings a useful means of clarifying and comprehending events as well as my own reactions, and it was maintained throughout my absence from the United States. The possibility of using it as the basis of a book was in the back of my mind as I wrote, but it was not until we had returned from Turkey and I had re-read my notes and begun to clear away some of the unnecessary verbiage and personal details that I realized that what I had written had a clear direction and conveyed a distinct message, and that what I had felt and experienced throughout this trip might possibly have interest and meaning for others. I have tried as far as possible, despite the necessity of editing, to be true to the original experiences and to the understanding which I possessed at various stages, so that the reader could see everything with my eyes and mature in understanding with me. The factual material concerning political events in Turkey and Pakistan is accurate to the best of my knowledge, having been set down as it occurred and later verified as far as possible.

Scores of books have been written by Westerners who have spent longer or shorter periods somewhere in 'the East.' It is my sincere hope that this book will not be just another addition to this already vast collection, but rather a presentation which will be unique only because of one fact, namely, that although American by nationality, the author herself is a Muslim. Thus, in going to live in a Muslim country, even though in the beginning I could understand nothing of its language, I did not go, like any other American visitor, as an outsider looking in, but, as it were, to my own home, with an understanding of many of the elements of the environment and an access to the ways of thinking around me which would hardly be possible for a non-Muslim.

My main concern in writing this book has not been whether I have grasped or presented the contemporary scene in Turkey in entirety, something hardly possible in the limited period of time I spent there (the reader who is interested in the subject of Turkey or of Islam in Turkey may wish to utilize this volume merely as one source of information among many others, excerpts from some of which are found in the Notes at the end of this volume). My main concern is rather that whatever is presented here as part of an exceedingly complex picture should have been understood and presented correctly in relation to Islam, and I have tried to present the contrast between what Islam requires and what Muslims in practice do, an observation of which, unfortunately, often creates a very distorted image of Islam indeed. For Islam is not what individual Muslims or so-called 'Muslim' nations do or say or think, but an eternal, Divinely-ordained system, totally independent of and unrelated to whether those who call themselves Muslims follow it or not. Nevertheless, it is very easy for a non-Muslim—and even for those who have been born and raised as Muslims without very sound knowledge of their faith—to be confused by the practices of Muslims and led to feel that this *is* Islam.

Because the writer is a woman, there is also—rather naturally—considerable emphasis on what concerns women, namely, the conception of the Islamic society, the relations between men and women, the education of Muslim youth, and the role of the Muslim women in society, all matters of the greatest importance in today's Muslim world for the building of a sound Islamic society and for the future generations of Muslims.

If this book can render any contribution whatsoever toward a better understanding of Islam, of Turkey, of the contemporary Muslim world and the forces which are working for and against Islam for the concerned Muslim and non-Muslim reader, the purpose of writing it will have been amply fulfilled.

In conclusion, I ask Almighty God to accept this small effort, to forgive my unintentional mistakes, and to guide the community of Muslims and all others throughout the world who sincerely believe in Him to a return to those blessed eternal values which alone can give meaning to life and free mankind from the terrible disturbances and dilemmas which confront us today.

Marian Kazi
March 1973

GUIDE TO TURKISH PRONUNCIATION

The Turkish alphabet contains all the letters of the English alphabet excepting 'q,' 'w,' and 'x,' plus the following additional letters:

ı (undotted i), whose sound is approximately like that of 'u' in fur.

ö whose sound is like the *umlaut* 'ö' of German, as in *Österreich.*

ü whose sound is like the *umlaut* 'ü' of German, as in *über.*

ç 'ch' — for example, *çarşaf* is pronounced *charshaf.*

ş 'sh' — for example, *şalvar* is pronounced *shalwar.*

c 'j' — for example, Cemile is pronounced Jemile.

j pronounced like the 'g' in French; for example, the Turkish *jandarma* is pronounced like the French *gendarme.*

ğ a silent letter approximating the Arabic and Persian *ghayn* *(غ)*; for example, *ağabey* is pronounced *aahbey.*

Note on pronunciation of proper nouns — Due to the manner in which the transliteration of proper nouns has been standardized, it has unfortunately not been possible to phoneticize spellings of proper nouns in this book. For example, 'Selim' is the standard English spelling for a name which is pronounced Saleem, 'Rafiq' for Rafeeq, 'Tabriz' for Tabreez, etc., while 'Haleema' is the more common spelling for a name which could, in the above manner, be spelled 'Halima.' The reader is asked to use his imagination to remedy this defect as well as possible.

CHAPTER 1

IN ANTICIPATION

November 15, 1969: From today, the day on which the letter came making possible a year's study for Selim at the Middle East Technical University in Ankara, I have stopped living in the present and have begun to live in the future.

A succession of images of Turkey as I have put them together from all I have heard and read, and of ourselves in Turkey, came and went through my mind, mingled with feelings of joy, anticipation and some traces of anxiety. I could not understand how the children, with this before them, could be so calm and almost indifferent to the prospect, while I was continually turning over and over in my mind these glimpses of the future and all we have to do and to plan before it materializes.

For me Turkey has come to assume, since we have come to know our beloved Turkish friends, Enver and Emine the chief among them, a very special and beautiful character, centering around Istanbul. Pictures of Old Istanbul go through my mind—an ancient city, full of mementoes of history, with its vast, awe-inspiring mosques rising dome upon dome, built in a style which makes the heart bow in humility and reverence before God, for the love of Whom they were built. I seem to see a vision of dimly-lighted interiors, of shields bearing Arabic inscriptions, and the filigree of low-hanging lamps, their chains like spider-webs descending from the domes. I catch a glimpse of Islam as it had been understood and practiced in times gone by, the trace and echo of which still lingers, audible to our ears and visible to our eyes, exemplified by the qualities and characteristics of Turkish Muslims even today.

There is a quality about some of the Turks we have known which is special and remarkable—a warmth, a sincerity, a subtle, indefinable sweetness which makes them very dear. What can this Turkey be which has produced such unique qualities in some of its people? And now it seems to me that this same Turkey of the beloved friends and the great, awe-inspiring mosques is calling to me, pulling me toward itself, drawing me like a magnet . . .

What will happen to me, to us all, in Turkey? Will there indeed occur some sort of experience which will awaken what so many times seems like a spirit in need of revival, of refreshment, at times dried up and dumb within me, waiting for something to unlock and release its potentialities? Because of my firm belief that God Most High guides whom He wills to His light, and because I have continually prayed for that light, I am waiting for something to come to me through that Turkey which is drawing me on to itself. May the beneficient God bestow His help and guidance on me, my husband and our children, Jamal, Maryam and Nura, and may His mercy ever enfold us.

December 5: During the three weeks since I last wrote, Turkey and everything associated with our going there has been temporarily pushed into the background because of the many and diverse demands of the present, and I have had very little time and energy to feel and think about it. But at last today a letter arrived from Enver and Emine in Ankara in response to our letter informing them that we will be coming there in August—a letter long-awaited and much-desired, thus:

Dear Selim Agabey and Marian Abla,[*]

Esselâmün aleyküm. How wonderful to hear that you will be coming to Turkey! We could hardly believe your letter, and now we cannot find the proper words to express how happy we are! The days are passing very slowly. It is really hard to wait for August. Our minds are full of plans and dreams for your coming. *Inşallah*—God willing—it will be a good time for you all here.

---

[*] *Agabey, abla*—older brother, older sister. Terms of affection and respect used for older boys and men (and girls and women) who are not related, as well as for one's real older brother and sister.

Selim Ağabey, the tea kettle is on the stove and boiling, waiting for all of you. Mother is trying to learn a few words of English to talk to you all [probably the same words we are trying to learn to say to her in Turkish!]. She is so happy about your coming.

As you know, Turkey is not nearly as modern as America, but at the same time it is easy enough to live here, and *inşallah* you will find some other things to make you happy. We wish Turkey would be everything you want to find in a Muslim country.

Always remember that we are here waiting for you all. Allah guide and keep you all. With deep love to you and many kisses to Jamal, Maryam and Nura.

Enver-Emine

How unbelievable and wonderful to think of being together again with these friends for whom we have so much affection, something none of us could have hoped for the last time we met, this time in their own country! Is it really true, will it really come about? Oh, please God that nothing will happen to keep our plans and hopes from realization.

December 18: As I think ahead about Turkey, I try to compare the basic conceptions of a Muslim society with those which underlie contemporary Western culture.

In the modern West today, little effort is devoted to looking inward to the depths which lie beyond what is obvious and observable, which no man so far has fathomed and which, in this society, are not even generally assumed to exist except insofar as they can be explained in terms of modern behavioral sciences. By this I mean those depths which lie within the center of a human being, his soul, his *nafs.* Do the contemporary psychiatrists, psychologists and sociologists, those who to a large extent guide the thinking and behavior patterns of Western man today instead of the magicians, witch doctors or priests of former times, acknowledge the existence and importance of these depths, or is it all explained away in terms of mechanisms and dynamics of human adjustment, not going beyond what is obvious and apparent?

With this small place given to looking inward, because the material world is so much with us, so all-absorbing that the inward things very easily slip away from notice and are in fact not apparent at all, unless one makes an effort to cultivate an acquaintance with them, there is very little room for "*La ilaha illa Allah*"—There is no deity (in the sense of the One Who commands all one's devotion and obedience and Who is *the* Authority) except God—because most of us human beings are so absorbed with utterances of "There is no diety except Man." The call of "*Allahu Akbar*"—God is the Most Great—cannot be heard amidst the clamor of exclamations over the Most-Greatness of Man. Western man has become so intoxicated with the wonder of his own power and creativity, so enamored of and so utterly bound up with the gadgets and devices he has invented, from which he believes he derives his life and sustenance, that the obvious fact has escaped him that a Power beyond himself gives him these capacities and sustains him, and that the inventions upon which he relies so completely are themselves dependent on that sustaining Power. He imagines that he must be able to see, to handle, to measure and to analyze things in order to accept the fact of their existence, yet all the while his spirit as well as his faculties seem to be completely paralyzed in not perceiving that an unmeasureable, unanalyzable Being sustains everything which exists and keeps it functioning according to a determined law, a law which man can in many cases comprehend and analyze, and without which, on the other hand, he could comprehend and analyze nothing.

The capacity to believe in what is beyond man and the material world, to which the Holy Qur'an refers as *al-Ghaib*—the Unseen, the hidden or distant things—is a grace from God, I think: the grace of being able to accept the existence of a greater Reality than that which is within the perception of the senses, within analysis and definition by the limited capacities of men. In the West today, such a frame of reference is largely non-existent except in name. Thus, one searching for faith must continually struggle with the disbelief which is rather a cynical and desperate conviction that man is all and everything, that there is nothing beyond, and that even if there should happen to be it hardly matters, combined with a weary disillusionment with life—even with the material preoccupations which not so long ago seemed so bright and

meaningful—for which it knows of no better remedy than involvement in humanitarian concerns or cultural activities. The West has,
in the words of Muhammad Asad, assumed the non-existence of
God as a positive fact simply because it cannot *prove* His existence
empirically. As he says in his book, *Islam at the Crossroads:* *

> "As the intellectual and social atmosphere of old Rome was ut-
> terly utilitarian and anti-religious—in fact if not in open admission—
> so is the atmosphere of the modern West. Without having a proof
> against transcendental religion, and without even admitting the need
> of such a proof, modern Western thought, while tolerating and some-
> times even emphasizing religion as a social convention, generally
> leaves transcendental ethics out of the range of practical considera-
> tion. Western civilization does not strictly *deny* God, but has simply
> no room and no use for Him in its present intellectual system. It has
> made a virtue out of an intellectual difficulty of man—his inability to
> grasp the totality of life."

Western man once—not too long ago—did believe, indeed, but
when his beliefs failed to correspond with observed facts, instead of
purifying his beliefs and returning to their source, he discarded
them and lost this grace, substituting for them a reliance upon
man-made values and systems which have utterly alienated him
from his Creator, from the remainder of the natural world and from
his very self, and which he continues to allow to mislead him. Muslims, on the other hand, have always had before them a belief-
system and way of life which is in harmony both with what they
perceive and with their own inner natures, and because of this, although today many so-called Muslims have unthinkingly discarded
various elements of Islam in exchange for conceptions alien to it,
they basically retain the grace of *being able to believe* in a Being
beyond themselves and the material world, and this conception in
fact underlies the very structure and framework of their society.

---

* Arafat Publications, Lahore, Pakistan, 1955.

January 1, 1970: Today as I write, it is New Year 1970. A new decade has begun. Immediately after the past midnight, I heard various noises celebrating the start of a new year. Oh, why are there not those who make a noise in the dark night to tell man that his time and his rope are running out very fast, and that the beginning of a new year—an arbitrary marker of time—should be, if anything, an occasion for solemn reappraisal and self-scrutiny, to determine where we are going wrong and what can be done about it? Yes, there are indeed such voices being raised, but who hears them? Only those who are already engaged in self-appraisal, seldom those who are not! Can anything be more foolish and meaningless than to herald the coming of a 'new year' with the blaring of toy horns, the popping of fire-crackers, the drinking of liquor and feasting, when our world is in such terrible trouble from the irresponsible actions of human beings, and when its illness needs such a far-reaching and immediate remedy!

In a few days the children will be back in school after their Christmas holiday, and the usual routine will begin again; but this time with a difference, because the next few months will see the preparations for going to Ankara accelerating until the day comes when we will *insha'Allah* leave for a new world. I am thinking and thinking about it all, now in more practical terms: what to leave behind, how to store away all our personal belongings which are to remain here, what I should send ahead, what to take on the journey, what has to be brought to Turkey, how to manage everything, and most important, how to fit into the very short space of nine months all that I hope to do and to experience in that new world . . .

July 7: A midsummer evening. . . For the first time in months, I have leisure and concentration to sit down and write. Since I last wrote in winter, life has been very hectic and full, and my energies have been spent in an effort to do all that must be done before we leave for Turkey. Now let me pause for a moment and think: What lies before me and my family? What will come to us in the days that stretch ahead?

I hope that I may now have a little time and leisure to recover my scattered energies and may begin my journey with a peaceful mind and a whole heart. It will be, please God, a pilgrimage—the pilgrimage of one who is seeking to come closer to real understanding and to nearness to God. For I am going to a land where the sacred bonds of Islam have bound the souls of countless men and women to God Most High; a land where the upright servants of the Most Merciful have lived and labored in His way; a land where *"La ilaha illa Allah, Muhammadu Rasul Allah"*—There is no deity except God, Muhammad is the Messenger of God—has been known, heard, believed passionately and lived fully for the past ten centuries; and where, despite the veneer of westernization which has clouded the clear insight of people concerning the values of Islam, there still remains among the majority of them a clear conviction of the existence and power of God. Please God, a pilgrimage—to peace, to understanding, to inner certainty . . .

August 7: One week remains to us to live in this place.

During the last two or three weeks, we have been busy clearing the house and preparing for our trip. Several boxes containing personal effects were sent by mail to Ankara earlier, together with several parcels of books, including all the school books which the children would need for their respective classes in case we find that the school situation in Ankara is not workable; although Enver and Emine have sent us information on all essential matters, including the school and housing situation, after talking it over many times together, Selim and I came to the conclusion that we could decide nothing until we reach Ankara and can evaluate the situation for ourselves. I have packed and repacked the luggage for the journey, every day changing or adding something to it. There has been one invitation after another, and in his own particular way, each of our friends has contributed to our leave-taking by his kindness.

I did not believe, two or three months ago, or even as recently as a month ago, that this time would ever come—this time about which we have thought, hoped and planned for so long. Now it is one week ahead. Earlier I thought about our trip and our stay in Turkey in all its aspects, anticipating and trying to find solutions for the various problems which might arrise. Everything which we could take care of from here has been given due attention, and now all that remains is to look forward eagerly to what is ahead; we have made our plans and done our best, and the rest is with God. Yet in a sense I am only making the motions and performing the necessary actions which will enable us to go, and the time is coming by itself—as if I were on an escalator, standing still, but the top of the stairs were coming without my moving toward it.

A week from now, *insha'Allah,* we will be on a jet high above the earth, supported by God's mercy, and so in all our moves toward the goal of Ankara, He will be our Helper and Support. The past years of waiting for this opportunity, the recent months of trying to deal with a multitude of things in preparation will be over. We will be on the way; the time will have come.

Once again I ask myself what lies before us. A year from now, will I, re-reading these words, have encountered only those things which I expected and anticipated, or will there come to me, and to all of us, new, unexpected experiences which I cannot now forsee? What will it hold, this short, precious time in a corner of the Muslim world? Only God knows. I pray to Him to guide us to whatever is best, to give us strength to deal with whatever difficulties we may encounter, to show us His straight way, to increase our commitment and perfect our faith.

Section One

A NEW WORLD

CHAPTER 2

YUGOSLAVIA

August 14, 1970: So it has begun. We are sitting in a jet airliner bound for Chicago, our lunch eaten, our prayers—the shortened prayers of the traveler—said. Twelve-year-old Jamal is next to me, observing everything with keenest interest, and Maryam and Nura, who are nine and seven years old, are with their father across the aisle, chattering excitedly. This is the first time they have ever flown, and naturally it is one of the greatest experiences of their young lives.

So, unbelievably, the adventure of our lives has begun—what we waited, hoped, planned and prayed for so long: our first trip to the Muslim world as a family. Each child is now old enough to understand the fundamental differences between Muslim culture and that of the West, hopefully to absorb whatever is Islamic, and also to recognize whatever does not conform to that standard, even though it may be done by Muslims. Jamal, because of his age, will probably be able to derive the greatest benefit from the experience, but Maryam and Nura, will also, I hope, find many things which will open their minds and hearts to Islamic influences and values.

Even until yesterday I could not really believe in the reality of what lay ahead; it just did not seem to me that we were going any-where, although I was carrying out all the motions of going. When this morning came, however, I *had* to believe it at last. A number of close friends were at the airport to see us off; it was a difficult experience, and all the women, the children and I wept

very much. We were stepping away from those who are so dear
to us into an unknown adventure—difficult, yet joyous and
exhilarating at the same time. Still, long after the plane had left the
ground, we felt that pulling of our hearts in two opposite
directions, thinking of those who loved us whom we had just left,
and of what lay ahead.

I thank God for all His great blessings to us; may He help us
and guide us to all that is good.

August 15: When day broke this morning, after only two or three
hours of sleep, we saw the coast of France below, and later more
glimpses of France and then Switzerland. We landed in Zurich at
about noon (5 a.m. at home)—a small, pleasant airport with
courteous people. It was something like a dream to be down from
that height, setting our feet on Swiss soil for the first time.
Alhamdulillah—thank God—for a safe trip and a good beginning of
the journey.

August 18: Padova, Italy: I thank God with all my heart for this
most interesting trip and the chance to see this beautiful part of
the world, almost unknown to us. It was too much to ask, too
much to hope, and now it is really happening; at last it seems real
and completely wonderful! At times, as we have been driving in
Switzerland, Austria or Italy in our rented car, just as we drive on
trips at home—a seemingly ordinary, routine matter—it has crossed
my mind that I may never come this way again, that this is a
very brief, once-in-a-lifetime adventure, and that I should savor
every moment of it. And so I do!

The children needed several days of traveling to grasp the full
implications of the fact that they were no longer in America and
all the differences in conditions. They knew it as a fact, of course,
but it took time before their understanding and behavior were able
to adapt to all the changes. As we saw different places and the
language and environment changed, they began to grasp the
characteristics of the areas through which we were traveling, to get
an idea of the people and the sound of their language. On the
road they are well behaved, absorbed with what they are seeing,
sometimes playing, sometimes reading or sleeping. *Alhamdulillah*,
we are extremely happy and have seen many wonderful things and
enjoyed ourselves immensely.

August 29: I write in Peć in Serbia, Yugoslavia, in a government hotel, where we have a pleasant, modern two-room suite and a bedroom.

We came here from Rome in another rented car, driving up the Italian east coast to Trieste and down the Adriatic coast of Yugoslavia to Dubrovnik; there we turned inland to Montenegro and southern Serbia, our eventual destination Athens, from where we have reservations to fly to Istanbul on September 1. Our interest was to see some part of the Muslim areas of Yugoslavia. Selim is doing all the driving, and I am the co-pilot, reading the map.

Today has brought us out of the perimeter of Western Europe into the East. As we turned into the hinterland of south-eastern Yugoslavia, we traveled on narrow roads interspersed with small villages up to Kotor. At Titograd, which seemed in passing to be a drab industrial town, we ate lunch at a restaurant by the road. The area east of this is very poor, and the faces of many of the people are pinched with premature age and want.

Then in an inhospitable mountainous terrain, the houses changed into what the children named 'witchiepoohs,' quaint square buildings with pointed shingled or thatched roofs which looked for all the world like hats, with windows for eyes and a door for a mouth. Then came spectacular rocky canyons, and finally we left this terrain and continued on a very narrow, winding road—almost one-lane and very much patched—which, according to the map's legend, is classified as a 'major highway.' Selim sounded the horn around blind curves and moved over as much as possible when a vehicle came from the opposite direction; fortunately the traffic was very light. The countryside was green and hilly; we passed through many villages, an almost continuous population, with peasants and their beasts trudging along the road.

After this stretch of poor road, we stopped at a very small town where Selim hoped to find a cup of coffee; although the sky was heavily overcast and evening was approaching, we must continue driving as we needed to make more mileage that evening. Sixty kilometers away, according to the map, was another, larger town, Peć. We continued on our road expecting to reach there in the early evening.

However, the road soon turned abruptly into an unpaved dirt lane, very narrow and leading up, up, up, always with the little witchiepooh houses and their checker-board fields in the background, and occasional meager-looking peasants, sometimes with their animals. We saw that there were mountains—the Velika Strana range—all around and ahead of us, but as it was extremely cloudy and the higher elevations were shrouded in thick fog, we could form no conception of how high they might be nor where the road might lead.

The 'major highway' became even more steep and narrow, a one-lane, rutted track full of rocks. Evidently there had been recent rains, for I observed numerous small landslides along the inner side of the road. One blind curve followed another, our car on the outer side following an extremely steep cliff. Selim sounded his horn around every curve.

Now I began to be apprehensive as the road wound higher and still higher, night and fog closed in upon us, and there was no trace of human beings apart from the occasional primitive little houses with faces clinging to the steep slopes of the mountain, and once in a while a single peasant trudging along; it was difficult to imagine how people lived there under such hard conditions and climate. Very occasionally a car, bus or truck followed or passed us with difficulty from the opposite direction as we slowed to a crawl or stopped completely in the dark. The edge of the road was irregular and ragged, almost without warning signs, markers or guard rails as curve followed curve, and the slopes of the mountian-side were so precipitous that if—God forbid—the car should go over the edge (something which looked not entirely improbable to me from where I sat in the right front), it would be smashed, and we with it, into thousands of pieces, and perhaps the remains of it and us would be found only months later, after we had to all intents and purposes disappeared from the face of the earth.

There was ample time for all this to go through my mind as we
inched our way along that road at perhaps twenty-five kilometers
an hour in the near-darkness and thick fog. I made the children
laugh and I think they were largely unaware of the hazards, which
one could perceive only by close observation of the road and its
surroundings. And I ceased to worry myself, knowing that all was
in God's hands, now as at all times, that whatever He wants will
be and what He does not permit cannot be; I silently committed
our lives and souls into His keeping, concentrating on watching the
road and anticipating hazards, and occasionally reaching out a hand
to Selim to remind him that I was at his side. Later he said
that he had not been at all worried; there were no hazards, only
slow and tiring driving. Nevertheless he had to agree that it was
the worst and most dangerous road on which we had ever
traveled.

At the top of a mountain we went into a very dense fog,
passed a marker and began to crawl slowly down the other side;
the road was wet from the fog and everywhere I saw earth or
rock slides on the inner banks. It took what seemed an endless
time before we were down from that mountain and reached pavement again. Thank God for keeping us safe on this most
hazardous of all the roads of our journey!

The paved road now wound through what appeared in the
darkness to be very spectacular scenery, steep walls of white rock
intersected by a series of tunnels. At last, at last, we glimpsed
lights nearby; we had reached a roadhouse at the bottom of the
mountain. I entered hesitantly and found two men sitting inside,
of whom I asked the distance to Peć in primitive German,
"Peć? Ja, es ist nur fünf und-zwanzig kilometre," one of them
replied courteously, assuring me that it was a good road and that
the high mountains were behind us. Thus we continued to drive,
having in any case no alternative except to go on until we
reached a populated area with some accommodation for travelers.

At length we reached the edge of a town, and suddenly,
unbelievably, in a poor quarter where the houses had contiguous
walls, we glimpsed the slender minaret of a mosque in the dark.

We were among Muslims at last! Throughout our travels in Yugoslavia we had been looking for Muslim population, as it is scattered over many parts of it, but so far we had seen no mosques and had found it impossible to determine who was or was not Muslim from outward appearance or dress. But now at last we were unmistakably among our own people. Their habits and their language might be different, but they believed as we did and would surely respond to us as one of themselves, and if we had a chance to join them in prayer, their and our way of praying and the words we used would be identically the same, here as everywhere else in the Muslim world.

We drove on until we reached what seemed to be the center of the town, where we were very much astonished to find a very dense throng of young people dressed in Western clothing walking hand-in-hand or arm-in-arm—couples of the same sex, both boys and girls, and also couples of the opposite sex together—a very thick crowd, all going in the same direction in a long line. At first we could only suppose that it must be a political demonstration of some sort, and when later we grasped that this could hardly be the case, we were nevertheless at a loss to understand what it might be. The street was so completely blocked by these pedestrians that the car could hardly move, but when some in the crowd motioned us to drive through, the throng slowly parted before the car and we drove up to a government hotel. It had taken us three hours to go the last sixty kilometers!

Two boys, one of whom spoke some English, started talking to us in the parking area of the hotel, but we were so weary that we did not stay to speak to them. We took rooms and then went down to the hotel's restaurant for dinner. When we asked the desk clerk, who spoke fluent English, about the road we had just traversed, he was duly sympathetic but informed us that it was indeed the only road by which Peć could be reached from that direction. We also learned that the throng of young people had been merely the nightly promenade, the taking of air, by the youth of the town, and not a demonstration of any sort!

August 30: This morning when I looked out the window of the hotel room, I saw a beautiful and moving sight: the minaret of a mosque, framed like a picture in a circular opening in the wall of the hotel. We had arrived at last!

We breakfasted in the hotel and went out to see Peć. What had in the dark appeared to be a small, thriving metropolis (was it that road that had influenced our outlook?) was by daylight a poor little town. The weather was still dark and cloudy, with fog hanging on the higher elevations. Most of the people were in Eastern dress: women in *shalwaars,* the baggy trousers worn in many Muslim countries, of a type I had never seen before, shaped like a voluminous one-piece sack until they divided into two parts almost at the bottom; they wore veils or kerchiefs on their heads, and many of the men wore round caps of various types. Although everything was on a rather poor and shabby scale, nonetheless to me it was very picturesque and interesting.

When we went to the car, we found a blonde boy of about twelve years assiduously washing the windows. I did not know whether or not he was the same boy who had spoken to us the previous evening; in any case, he just kept on wiping the glass doggedly, ignoring the fact that he had already cleaned it several times over and that no one had requested this service of him. Then he spoke to us in broken English. A Muslim boy, of course, with three or four friends on hand to do the honors of the town! His name was Sharif, he said, but we did not learn the names of his companions, who spoke no English. "*Assalamu alaikum,*" we greeted them, happy for our meeting.

"*Wa alaikum salaam,*" Sharif responded at once, "Where you come from?"

"From America," Selim answered.

"Oh, America. I know. Many Muslims in America. My uncle live there. In New York is a *jam'i* (mosque)."

We were surprised at the extent of his information about Muslims in America and asked him about his studies. "I go to *madrasah* (school)," he informed us, but further communication concerning the details of his education totally broke down due to language difficulties on both sides.

From where we stood we could see the tall minarets of several mosques. "You have so many *jam'is* here!" I exclaimed.

"Yes, we have good *jam'is*. You like to see my *jam'i?*" Sharif asked eagerly.

Yes, we replied just as eagerly; we would be very happy to. Accompanied by his friends, he took us a short distance into a poor side-street paved with mud, where a small, simple, elderly mosque stood. It had a single, slender minaret with a tall pointed top and one balcony, similar to all the minarets we were to see in Yugoslavia and identical to the Ottoman-style minarets of Turkey, since this area had once been part of Ottoman territory. In front of it, surrounded by an iron fence, stood a group of old tombstones, some of them leaning at rakish angles, bearing Arabic inscriptions, typical of the Ottoman tombstones of Turkey. It was an old mosque, to be sure, but reasonably well-cared-for.

Sharif and his friends now took us inside. Some men came to the door of the building, enquiring, and in a few whispered words the boy sent them away. In an outer room were mats and benches undoubtedly for the use of pupils. Sharif then produced an enormous key from somewhere and with it unlocked the inner door of the mosque. The interior was clean and appealing, with simple painted decorations on the walls, a picture of one of the great Istanbul mosques, some Arabic inscriptions, and a sedate clock which audibly ticked away the seconds in the profound stillness.

"It is a beautiful mosque," we told the boys from our hearts. I took photos of the mosque from inside and outside, as well as of our friendly guides, thanking them warmly for showing it to us. We would have liked to see some of the other mosques we had glimpsed, but time was passing and we must return to the road, always keeping in mind that we must reach Athens the day after tomorrow for our flight to Istanbul.

Thus we returned to the car, the boys accompanying us and exchanging an occasional word about us with passing acquaintances. We could not think of offering money to our young guide who had cleaned the car's windows, but we asked Sharif and his friends if they liked ice cream. They were embarrassed and said, "No, no," but when we presented them each with an ice cream cone from a nearby shop and a bag of candy which I had in the car, there was no doubt that they were pleased. "We are very happy to meet you and to know about good Muslim

boys like you in Yugoslavia," Selim told them. "May Allah bless
you always." Waving goodbye, we drove slowly away, knowing
that we would never forget Sharif and his friends.

The mountains were behind us now. Skopje was the only major
city on our route before Athens, and we hoped to have time to
see something of its Muslm sections. We passed several small towns
with mosques of the same style as those of Peć. The roads were
full of carts laden with produce and peasants, both men and
women; the women wore picturesque clothing, their hair covered
with kerchiefs and many having the lower part of their faces
covered as well, and it was a pleasant, lively scene. We were
happy; we were among Muslims. Then suddenly, on a slight slope,
we caught sight of a good-sized rock in the middle of the road;
Selim had only time to decide that he must take it in the middle of
the car rather than swerve around it as there was other traffic nearby. As we went over it, there was a sharp grinding sound
as the car slowed nearly to a halt. It took only a moment for
Selim to realize that the transmission was damaged, with only third
and neutral gears remaining in working order.

Consternation! We had to reach Athens just forty-eight hours
from now; it was obvious that we could not continue very far with
only third gear, and repairs might be very difficult to manage or
take much time. What were we to do? We had passed a small
town some kilometers back and according to the map, another
larger one lay only a few kilometers ahead. If we could manage to
reach it, *insha'Allah* we would be able to find a reliable
mechanic there.

We drove on at a very much slowed pace and presently,
when we came to a hill crowded with wagons up ahead, the car
stalled and the engine died. Just at that time a tractor came up
behind us; Selim got out to signal its driver for help as I thumbed
through our tiny Yugoslavian dictionary to find the words for 'gear'
and other essential terms. Through the mediation of three
prosperous-looking Yugoslav gentlemen in business suits who drove
up behind us just then in a shiny black Mercedes, the owner
of the tractor helpfully towed the car to the top of the hill,

and then the three men brought us to a garage at the next town, Prizren, explaining our situation to an efficient-looking master mechanic who spoke a bit of English. However, he said that he could do nothing with the car until the next morning, since his shop would close for the day within half-an-hour, its hours 6 to 2; he would keep the car there and call us at the town's hotel the following morning when it was ready.

There was nothing to be done except to make the best of the situation. Our luggage was put into a waiting car and we were driven to the town, naturally in a state of anxiety about the delay. If we failed to make the plane from Athens to Istanbul the day after tomorrow, we would have no way at all of finding Enver and Emine, who were to come to Istanbul to meet us but who had somehow neglected to give us an address in Istanbul at which they could be reached!

By way of narrow streets with poor houses we reached the center of the town, which was crowded with peasants who had come to sell their produce and to buy supplies. Farm wagons and horses everywhere, women in the dress of the East, and a look of poverty. This was Muslim Serbia.

The driver deposited us with our luggage at the town's modern government hotel. As we stood waiting at the desk, a tall thin man with a moustache strode forward and took charge of us saying, "*Assalamu alaik.*" At once we felt at ease. He added in English, with a wistful smile, "Are you Muslims? Excuse me for asking?"

"*Wa alaikum salaam.* Yes, we are Muslims and we are very happy to meet you," Selim responded, extending his hand to this new brother-in-faith who had in an instant made us feel at home. The man picked up our luggage, despite our protests, and carried it to our upstairs room as we followed. Although he had done the service of a porter, it was impossible to think of paying him, as he was a respectable man and a fellow-Muslim, and when we thanked him, he smiled and put his hand over his heart, a touchingly eloquent gesture common among Muslims which can mean either "You're welcome," "No, thank you," or at times is used as a gesture of greeting or respect, depending on the circumstances.

Since we were involuntarily detained here, we would have an
opportunity to see a little of at least one Muslim community,
although probably there would now be no time to see Skopje.
After talking briefly with our new acquaintance who was curious
to know about us, we had lunch in the hotel's restaurant and
afterwards set out to see the town.

Near the hotel stood a mosqueless minaret, an old *hamam* and
an aged, weather-beaten mosque. Crowds of peasants and townspeople, a mixed population of Muslims and non-Muslims as
denoted by their different dress, filled the streets.

We went first to see the old mosque. A sign on its door
said that it had been built by Soofi Sinan in early Ottoman times;
although it was still used for prayers, it was also a museum to
which admission was charged. Afterwards we walked in the
opposite direction through the main street of the town. The
commercial section, consisting mostly of shops stocking supplies
essential to farmers, was crowded with wagons and peasants clad
in Muslim dress. We strolled along the sidewalk in that throng,
conspicuously foreign with the camera and our different clothes.

For Selim and me this atmosphere was neither new nor
unexpected, and it had great appeal for us despite its poverty because it was a part of the Muslim world. For the children,
however, it was all very new and strange; they walked along in
absolute silence, unable either to comprehend or to find anything
appealing in this suddenly completely Eastern environment.
Nine-year-old Maryam was particularly disdainful and upset by the
poor and primitive conditions which she was seeing for the very first
time. As we walked along together hand-in-hand, I told her that
she must learn to accept it, for Turkey would no doubt be
very similar.

This was too much; her eyes filled and her lips trembled.
"You said Turkey would be nice, not like *this!*" she exclaimed,
fighting back the tears, "How will we ever be able to live
there then?"

"Ankara is a big city," I reminded her, "It won't be like this,
of course, but I'm sure that little towns and villages in

Turkey aren't much different. You feel this way now because it's all so new and strange, but after a while when it becomes familiar you'll feel very differently, I know."

"No, I won't; I never will!" she cried. For many days she had been in this sort of distress, increasing as we neared our destination; anxiously she reverted to the same questions almost daily. How would she and Jamal and Nura manage in Turkey, at school? Who would love them now that our good friends at home were not there? How would she cope with it all?

This was the same child who had looked forward so eagerly to our travels, now coming face-to-face with a concrete situation in which there were, at closer range, a vast and frightening number of unknowns. I tried to reassure her that we were going to others who love us dearly—Enver and Emine, whom she did not remember clearly, Cemile, a Turkish girl with whom I had enjoyed a warm friendship through correspondence, and others whom we would surely meet—and I pointed out that one must adapt to changing conditions and live life as it comes. Jamal and Nura showed no sign of this sort of anxiety and seemed confident that they could handle whatever came along, even if they did not like it. I knew that Maryam would also be able to do so, but she continued to feel fearfully certain that she never could. Once she had made this adjustment, I thought, she would never again be subject to such fears, for she would have learned that she was adequate to deal with new situations and changing conditions as they arose, *insha'Allah*. And although I sympathized wholeheartedly with what she was feeling, nonetheless this was, unfortunately, the reality of the Muslim world today; here, as in so many other places, Muslims were obviously at the bottom level of the population economically. I could only hope that she and the other two children would come to love and identify with the Muslim world regardless of its economic conditions, and would learn to judge it not by its standard of living but by the qualities which I hoped we would find in its people, qualities which reflected their Islamic faith and identity.

Thus we walked along the main street of that little town, so crowded with peasants that it was difficult to find space to walk, Selim with Jamal and Nura, and I with Maryam and the camera.

We went to look at two or three other mosques on side-streets, one down a narrow, muddy lane in which villagers were saddling up to go back to their farms, townspeople mingling among them, but the mosques were evidently always kept locked except during a brief time for each of the five daily prayers. Then we returned to the hotel to eat, pray and rest.

Toward evening we went for another walk. The town was half-empty now, for the peasants had loaded up their wagons and gone home. At this time the townspeople, including the non-Muslim segment of the population, became more noticeable, and from the differences in dress, I was confirmed in my opinion that the young people we had seen promenading in Peć the previous evening had undoubtedly been non-Muslims.

All during our travels in Yugoslavia I had been interested in observing the state of religion in the country. I had seen a number of reasonably well-maintained churches at various places, although they were considerably fewer in number than in any other European country we had visited. Here, instead of wayside shrines, one saw in every shop, office and public place the portrait of Tito, the symbol of progress and modernization rather than of traditional values, and modernistic sculptures of vast dimensions and questionable aesthetic value were erected as monuments in various places. My impression was that while Muslims or Christians might observe their forms of worship without hindrance, religion in any form was de-emphasized. It might not be openly prohibited, but there was such a markedly secular atmosphere in Yugoslavia that one could easily grasp the fact that religion had little or no place among the values officially endorsed by the Yugoslav state.*

We passed by a large, well-cared-for Orthodox church, but as it was now sunset, the time of *Maghrib* prayer,** we did not go inside but returned to the little museum-mosque of Soofi Sinan which was nearby to pray. The mosque was very plain, but very beautiful to me in its aged, venerable simplicity, with the fading light of the sun upon its buff, centuries-old walls. The interior,

---

*See for example *Yugoslavia,* by Phillis Auty, Walker and Co., New York, 1965, pp.15-16.
** See Glossary for names and times of the five daily prayers.

although electrified, was illuminated now only by candles due to a power failure. Selim and Jamal went to the front to join the tiny congregation of men, and an attendant gave me a lighted candle, showing me the steps leading up to the women's gallery. It was an incredibly narrow and steep stone spiral staircase, illuminated only by the flickering light of our one candle as the girls and I groped our way very slowly to the top. We were the only female worshipers present.

From the gallery, a kind of interior balcony along the back of the mosque, we looked down on the few male worshipers and the *imam* who would lead the prayer. The floors, both downstairs and in the women's section, were covered with carpets, and in front of us lay several *tesbihs*—strings of beads used for counting as one recites *dhikr*, the glorification of God—left for the use of women worshipers.

We prayed the three *rak'ats* of *Maghrib* prayer, the girls and I standing in a row shoulder to shoulder following the *imam*, who recited in very good Arabic, bowing to the floor before the Beneficient God Who had fulfilled our dream and longing to be among Muslims, with a deep sense of joy and peace; my eye caught the glint of tears of emotion on Nura's cheeks. After the prayer was finished, the electricity was restored and we descended the staircase. I found the others outside, Selim talking to the *imam* in hesitant Arabic, answering his questions about our family. We returned to the hotel, happy and refreshed by our first congregational prayer among our fellow Muslims on this journey.

We had dinner in the hotel's restaurant, sitting in darkness illuminated only by a few candles because of the power failure. As we ate, performers belonging to a small rock band appeared and began to warm up; soon they were thumping and blowing away so loudly that I felt my head would burst. The incongruity of this with the at least partially-traditional community around us was indeed most startling and unpalatable, and as soon as we had finished eating, I took the children upstairs to bed after that long, eventful day, while Selim sat a little longer surveying the scene, his tolerance of noise much greater than my own.

August 31: For the first time this morning I heard the
adhan—the call to prayer—coming from a mosque in the dawn,
a very moving experience which to me will never become old or
to be taken for granted, as an invitation and a prelude to the
morning prayer. We began the day early in the hope that the car
might somehow be finished early, and to our great relief shortly
after breakfast the garage telephoned Selim to say that it was now
ready; we put our luggage hastily together and waited on the
steps of the hotel for a taxi. Our Muslim friend of the previous
day passed by just then, and we said goodbye to him; as
before he showed the same grave, smiling courtesy, the gesture
of the hand on the heart when we expressed our thanks to him.
He asked one of his acquaintances who had a car to take us to the
garage *in lieu* of a taxi, which did not come, and shaking
Selim's hand cordially, wished us a good journey and
"*Assalamu alaik.*"

At the garage there were endless delays, but at last the
baggage was stowed securely in place and we started out. We
passed through more villages; at one place we missed the road and
drove back and forth, asking various people along the way,
"Skopje?" with a meaningful inflection and getting different and
contradictory directions from each one. However, when we reached
Skopje, a big city, because we were so pressed for time due to our
long delay in Prizren, it was impossible to take time for anything
except a glimpse of a few Ottoman minarets in passing. After eating
lunch in a big restaurant, we resumed our journey, reaching the
Greek border early in the afternoon, and continued driving until
night, the trip completely uneventful. We passed the night at a
deserted, lonely hotel far from any town, where I had all sorts of
uneasy visions of what might happen to unwary tourists in such
an isolated place—but, thank God, nothing did!

September 1: Today—Turkey: Istanbul and Enver-Emine. Journey's
end! And to God is the end of all our journeys; may He guide
us to all that is good.

Since we were still about two hundred miles from Athens, and
the flight to Istanbul left at 2:30 p.m., we continued our journey
at daybreak after *Fajr* prayer, stopping only for breakfast at a

poor roadhouse. We reached Athens at half-past ten, winding our way hurriedly through the heavy traffic of the vast modern metropolis with the help of a map and signs. When we reached the airport there was a very long worrisome delay involving the rented car, but at last, with the help of a friendly official, the matter was concluded satisfactorily and just in time.

The flight was, after all, late, and as we sat silently waiting in the crowded boarding area, for the first time since we had left home I became conscious of being very nervous. We were coming to the end of the journey, and all the hopes and expectations I had built up during these past months would soon be held up to the light of reality. I must now put aside my desires and dreams and, like Maryam, come squarely face-to-face with existing conditions.

How would it be? Would we feel a sense of coming home among our fellow-Muslims, or would we find that the western-ization which had swept over Turkey had all but destroyed its Islam? Although we were surely prepared to find a great many traces of such influences, yet we were indeed not without a strong hope that we would also find signs of an Islamic renaissance and that we would eventually number many sincere Muslims among our friends. And of course, we would be with Enver and Emine again, the friends to whom we felt so close, who had, more than anything else, aroused our deep interest in Turkey.

At last, up into the sky again. After an hour's flight we came down over Istanbul. I strained to catch a glimpse of the city from the porthole of the jet, but on my side there was nothing but a vast blue sea, over which we came down to land.

CHAPTER 3

ISTANBUL

Yeşilköy Airport, Istanbul. An unimpressive low wooden building with a platform on top, crowded with people. As our feet touched Turkish soil for the first time, walking toward the terminal building, we looked up at them. Yes, they looked just as I had thought Turks would: men with moustaches and the vizored caps of peasants or laborers, women in scarves and light coats, as well as some women and men in the latest-style Western fashions. We had arrived. But where in all this would we find Enver and Emine?

Suddenly a familiar figure in a yellow dress detached itself out of the crowd on the roof and came running toward the railing, followed by a tall blonde young man with a moustache. It was Emine, calling, "Marian Abla! Selim Ağabey!" and beaming at us with a radiant smile such as I had seen on her face many times at home but could never, in all sober reality, have hoped or expected to have seen looking down at me from the roof of the Istanbul airport, Enver, laughing with joy, one step behind her. Yes, it was they at last, thank God!

"Marian Abla!" Emine crowded so close to the railing that she seemed almost ready to climb over it and jump down among us.

"Emine!" I called, "It's really you! Oh, come down, please—the right way!"

"We will!" she replied, and both figures disappeared from the roof. Five minutes later, as we stood in the queue of incoming passengers waiting to clear formalities, they were at our side. Such a hugging and kissing and crying and looking at each other among us women and girls, such a shaking of hands and fervent repeated embraces among the men-folk! The same dear, lovely girl we had known, respectfully greeting Selim, crying on my shoulder with emotion, hugging the children warmly to her, while Enver beamed on us all, saying heartfelt words of welcome, exclaiming how much the children had grown since he had last seen them, and asking after our healths and our trip.

But this crowded area was not a place to talk or to be together. After completing the formalities, we went into a large adjoining hall to retrieve our baggage. It was so full of people that there was hardly room to move, and the whole place was extremely shabby and tumble-down, with holes in the rough wooden floor and stray cats sitting about here and there. Was *this* Istanbul? I asked myself with a sudden sense of dismay.*

As soon as our baggage was collected, Enver hailed a taxi. Since the airport was many miles outside Istanbul, there was little of interest along the way until we reached the outskirts of the city. Then many small mosques with the typical tall, pointed Turkish minarets came into view, and the children were entranced, saying with each one, "There's a mosque, there's a mosque!" My first impression was of a crowded, sprawling metropolis with quite heavy traffic, the high minarets of mosques which punctuated the skyline at intervals denoting its Muslim identity.

The taxi stopped at a small hotel on a quiet side street in a heavily-populated area where Enver had reserved rooms for us. For a few moments we just stood in one of the rooms looking

---

* The old air terminal is being replaced with a new building at a cost of 850 million Turkish *liras*.

at each other, embracing and kissing and shaking hands all over again, Emine and Enver beaming with joy. Then we all sat down to talk, catching up on major items of news, none of us really able to believe, even now, that this was actually happening and that we would really be together for the next several months.

Although some years had passed since we had last seen them, these friends were just the same; nothing had changed. Enver, an architect, was a tall, lean man who radiated a quiet sincerity, deeply religious, kind, thoughtful, and at the same time full of dynamism and inner fire, qualities which had focused our interest on Turkey initially. He was also exceedingly well-informed and articulate, knowledgeable about the problems facing his country and its history, the Muslim world, and many other matters. Slender, graceful Emine, with her beautiful big dark eyes, suited him in every respect. She had a university degree in literature and now worked in a library in Ankara. Highly intelligent, quick to understand and to learn, the years she had spent in America had in themselves been an education for her, deepening her personality and broadening her mind. She was a loving, thoughtful girl, ever considerate of the welfare of others, warm and sincere, and, I truly believe, incapable of ever doing anything mean or unkind. Like almost all upper class Turkish women, she wore Western dress. She and Enver were a lovely, appealing young couple. Yet, although they had been married several years, the blessing of a child which they so much desired had not been granted to them so far.

Both of them, we found, had forgotten a certain amount of their English, having almost no occasion to use it in Turkey. However, when they questioned us about how much Turkish we had been able to learn, we shamefacedly had to admit that although we had acquired books and had made a start, the time and atmosphere for sustained study had been lacking and we had learned almost nothing so far.

"I wrote to you that it is very necessary to learn a little Turkish before coming," Enver admonished. "You will really be in difficulties here without it."

"Oh," I replied, not really too concerned, "surly there will be many people who know English. At least *you* do, and Cemile (my pen friend, about whom I had written to Emine), and we'll work very hard to learn now that we're here."

He shook his head in disappointment. "I wish you had learned something before coming," he said. "It is so important for you."

When they had been in the United States, they had been in our territory, somewhat in the position of our guests. Now all of us, a family of five people, with all our necessities of getting settled and adapting to life here, would be *their* guests and *their* responsibility to a certain extent, and they would introduce us to their homeland. They had warned us in their letters not to expect too much of contemporary Turkey, but we also knew from innumerable earlier discussions with them and with other Turks that in some areas we would find many things of great worth.

If we liked the idea, Enver said, we would stay in Istanbul for the next five or six days and see something of its historic places before going to Ankara, where his mother who lived with them was waiting eagerly for our arrival. We would stay with them as long as possible—throughout our entire stay in Turkey if we thought it good, or at the very least until we were able to settle into our own place at our leisure. "You know that our house is yours and that you are just like our own family," Enver said warmly. What was there to say to such loving and totally sincere hospitality? We promised to stay with them until we could find a place to our liking, knowing that any other arrangement was out of the question in a relationship such as ours.

We asked many questions about life in Turkey and talked the hours away, while the children stood out on the balcony watching the life in the street. We drank tea in tiny glasses which were sent for from below, and then performed our prayers in the hotel room, Selim leading. In the evening Enver procured a taxi and we went for a long drive through a portion of the city. As it was dark, and moreover everything was completely new and strange, I was able to take in very little, forming no real impressions, carrying away no concrete memory but simply absorbed in looking and trying to orient myself to this totally new environment, while Nura and Maryam clung to me in silence.

Afterwards Enver took us for an excellent dinner of Turkish food in a pleasant restaurant. All around us now we were hearing Turkish spoken, and indeed, our friends were in effect our only link with the world as it became clear that English and other European languages were really very little known here. I began to realize how correct Enver and our other Turkish friends had been in their insistence that we should learn at least a little Turkish before coming and to wish that we had made a more serious effort at it. Now it sounded in my ears, such a strange, confused melding-together of unfamiliar sounds that I could not make out any individual words but heard everything as one undifferentiated block of sound.

After dinner our friends brought us back to the hotel, and then they returned to the home of Enver's aunt with whom they were staying. We said our prayers and slept, thanking the Merciful God with all our hearts for the joyful and promising realization of our long-cherished dream and desire.

September 2: On this first morning in Istanbul, the *adhan* for the *Fajr* prayer—the first of the daily prayers which is observed between dawn and sunrise—came to us like a wonderful chorus of voices reaching out from every side, raised to call Muslims to the remembrance of God Most High as the first act of the new day. This is the only time when all these voices are clearly audible here, for the noise of traffic during the day and evening makes hearing them at the other four times of prayer very difficult unless one is quite close to a mosque. There is no one instant when all the *adhans* begin, but a period of perhaps fifteen or twenty minutes when, as the sky grows light, a single thread of distant recitation begins the call, followed by another and another, so that presently there may be five or eight different strains at once, each unique and distinct yet all resembling each other, intertwining into a pure wave of melodious sound coming from the distance like an echo. No effort is or could be made to blend these distinct threads into a harmony, but the harmony is always there, its effect wonderfully solemn, deeply impressive, moving. Will I ever forget this first morning's *adhan* in Istanbul? I wonder if the Holy Prophet, peace be on him, when he instituted the call anticipated what it would become when there were many mosques scattered throughout a vast city, and how it would stir the heart. I think he must have.

Enver and Emine met us at mid-morning in the hotel's little restaurant where we were having breakfast of very strong tea in small glass *bardaks,* black olives, Turkish bread and white cheese, which none of us particularly liked at first. They greeted us joyfully, Enver gave some instructions to the hotel management on our behalf, and then he said that by way of introduction to historic Istanbul we would spend the major part of the day at Topkapı Saray, the palace of the Ottoman sultans, which I knew by reputation as a museum.

On the way our taxi passed through an old section of the city near Sultan Ahmet's Mosque (the Blue Mosque) and Aya Sofya (Hagia Sophia), which are situated quite close to each other. The Blue Mosque, an edifice of grey stone with domes piled on one another to form an unbelievable architectural monument, was strikingly impressive, and we were eager for an opportunity to see its interior. Aya Sofia was a somewhat ponderous structure in the style of a Byzantine basilica. It had been a church in Byzantine times, and after the conquest of Istanbul by Fatih Sultan Mehmet (Mehmet II) in 1453 it had been transformed into a mosque; after Atatürk's time it had been made into a museum, and no prayers were now observed there.

Topkapı Museum was quite close to these two great mosques. We entered the vast compound of what had been the residence of many rulers of the Ottoman dynasty through a red stone portal ornamented with an Arabic inscription, via a ticket window. Inside were long colonnaded halls, a mosque, minarets, towers, turrets, kiosks and gardens. The palace was built on a projection of land surrounded by water on two sides, and from it we could see the minarets and domes of Aya Sofya and the Blue Mosque, pale in the haze of the city.

Before we began our tour of the Museum, Enver said, we should have lunch. One of the old structures within the palace had been made into a charming restaurant, with tables both inside and on an outdoor terrace. We naturally chose to sit outside in the shade of the ancient walls, enjoying the company, the setting and the meal to the utmost.

Afterwards we walked among the old buildings whose very stones reverberated with the tread of history—a not always noble history, unfortunately; I was busy with my camera, thinking of those who had lived out their lives in this place in times past. The children, for whom everything was very, very new, exclaimed in admiration over many of the beautiful ornamental details, Enver explaining what we saw with his deep knowledge of Ottoman history, Selim in his quiet philosophical way observing and taking it all in, and Emine and I hand-in-hand, talking quietly together.

We marveled at the delicate ornamentation of a kiosk decorated with brilliant tiles and colored glass windows, which, Enver explained, was for the *Sünnet* (circumcision) of boys born in the palace. Beside it stood a small mosque, its weathered grey walls revealing its age, within which, in the manner of a museum, are displayed relics of the Holy Prophet, peace be on him: his standard and mantle, which Turks call his *emanet* (trust), which had been the symbols of the power and sovereignty of the Ottoman Empire, enshrined in a heavy gold casket in a small ornate chamber, together with his sword and other relics. There were also the swords of the first four Caliphs, Abu Bakr, 'Umar, 'Uthman and 'Ali, may God be pleased with them, the beloved companions of the Prophet and his successors as heads of the Muslim community and state; there was the Qur'an which the venerable 'Uthman had been reading when he was murdered, its ancient pages stained with his blood, and other relics of the Prophet's companions.

Tourists came and went, looking at these things quite without feeling, naturally, but for me it was a very moving experience to see what had once belonged to the greatest of Muslims, those who were so near and dear to the Holy Prophet, peace be on him, and who are examples for all Muslims to follow. It is as if one were reaching back fourteen hundred years to touch for an instant the lives of these saintly men as one looks upon the sword which 'Ali used in the defense of Islam, and at the very Qur'an, with its faded, square script, from which 'Uthman was reading at the time he was killed, that sacred book whose Divine message had inspired the aged Caliph to bear martyrdom in the path of God. It saddened me to think that these things were kept in a museum, to be stared at, commented on and even misunderstood by non-Muslim tourists, and I hoped that after seeing them some might be led to wonder and enquire about Islam, after all. But then, I reminded myself, Islam is not a religion of relics, and they have no place in it except possibly as tangible reminders to Muslims of their Prophet, peace be on him, and his eminent followers.

In a vast colonnaded hall scores of fantastically opulent treasures, which had belonged to the Ottoman royal treasury, were displayed in glass cases, a reminder of the very rich cultural heritage of Muslims, articles of incomparable splendor and artistry, many of them gifts to the rulers of the Muslim empire from other monarchs. In another building were housed displays of wonderful Arabic calligraphy: illuminated Qur'ans and other books, with the most exquisite, minutely-detailed ornamentation, and framed Arabic inscriptions on the walls. The children were boundless in their admiration. We could not take in everything, of course, but I marveled at these beautiful and rare works inspired by faith in God. In another wing old costumes, including a robe and headdress of each of the sultan-caliphs, were displayed. There was yet much, much more to see and at the same time a unique atmosphere to be felt and experienced, but the museum was closing and reluctantly we left. How quickly the afternoon had passed!

Enver now took us to nearby Sultan Ahmet's Mosque, called the Blue Mosque. As we approached, I was surprised and shocked to observe that the grounds outside the mosque, which should have been beautiful gardens, were only bare earth without a blade of grass or a flower. Evidently neither the government nor the Muslim community took the responsibility of maintaining the beauty of this magnificent house of worship and its environs.

This mosque, like many of the larger Ottoman mosques, included a vast complex of out-buildings, among them what had been a *madrasah* and a library in former times. I studied the great grey stone structure with its six graceful minarets and dome rising upon dome before us like a range of mountains, an awe-inspiring sight. As Emine and I entered the inner courtyard together, a man selling prints with Qur'anic inscriptions approached me, offering them for sale. Emine explained to him that I was an American Muslim, not a tourist, and then, in one of those heart-warming gestures of friendship which one meets with so often in the Muslim world, he presented one of the ornamented sheets to me as a gift. I accepted it gratefully, asking Emine to express my thanks to him, feeling the sudden, unexpected kindness of his action.

Inside the mosque, we stood looking about us, marveling at its architectural grandeur and beautiful decoration: stained-glass windows at the front, blue-tinged ornamentation over the upper parts of the walls, and massive, fluted columns having the same bluish tint. Great lamps, hoops of metal holding glass vials which had for centuries held oil, depended from the immensely high domes on slender chains, forming the spider-web-like effect I had imagined. We had now neither sufficient time nor understanding to take in the immense complexity and beauty of the mosque's architecture and planned to visit it again before leaving Istanbul. At the same time, I noted with dismay that the floor of this incomparable house of worship was bumpy and uneven, and that the worn old carpets which covered it gave off the unmistakable odor of perspiration and humidity, a sad evidence of official indifference to the preservation of its stately and irreplaceable beauty. We prayed our *Dhuhr* and *'Asr* prayers and then left.

Emine now suggested that we should see one of the most interesting places in Istanbul, the famous covered bazaar known as Kapalı Çarşı. Going by taxi to a dingy area surrounded by fruit stalls near which stood an old mosque blackened with years of city grime, we entered the bazaar and at once found ourselves in a wonderfully interesting, appealing miniature world, the vast 'shopping center' of Old Istanbul,* a labyrinth of little narrow, covered streets

---

* The oldest section of the bazaar was built in 1461 by order of Fatih Sultan Mehmet; the rest was erected in the sixteenth century by Sultan Süleyman. It was destroyed by fire several times and rebuilt in its present form in 1898. The bazaar has many gates and a great number of individual streets many streets having shops selling only one type of merchandise.

appearing to go on for several miles. Here were hundreds of shops selling varied merchandise: cloth, antiques, handicrafts, rugs and carpets, housewares, shoes, slippers, jewelry, and so on. The bazaar bustled with shoppers, a fascinating scene; even Selim, who ordinarily dislikes shopping, savored its atmosphere and enjoyed our walk through it.

We window-shopped until closing time, when the children were quite worn out and very hungry. Enver and Emine now took us to a nearby restaurant on the upper floor of a building where they again, despite our protests that we could not thus continue to be their guests permanently, were our hosts for a very pleasant dinner. As we were leaving, we heard the sound of Turkish music somewhere below, and Emine said with a smile that it must be a *Sünnet* (circumcision) party. Here was something else new; we went downstairs in the direction of the music.

On one of the lower floors a big room, rented out for such celebrations, was arranged with tables and chairs; balloons hung from the ceiling and the atmosphere was that of a party. A gathering had begun to assemble; women (mostly fashionably dressed in Western styles but the elderly or more humble ones wearing kerchiefs), men, young people and children sat at the tables or walked about. A band played a dance tune, and a few couples on the floor were dancing sedately in the Western manner. Near the door, in a bed with an ornate white satin quilt and a beruffled satin-covered pillow, reclined a sweet-faced boy of perhaps ten years who had that day been circumcised; it was clear that this event of which he was the chief dignitary was the greatest occasion of his young life. His white-bearded grandfather, and his grandmother, clad in a black scarf and dress and looking older than she evidently was, sat smiling nearby. As guests entered, they kissed and touched to their foreheads the hand of the grandfather and shook hands with his son, the boy's father, congratulating them on the occasion.

Up to that time we had been standing unnoticed in the doorway, observing all that was taking place. Now Enver, perhaps explaining that we were visiting Muslims, requested the grandfather's permission to enter, with appropriate words of congratulations on the occasion, and we seated ourselves at a table near the door. As I wanted very much to photograph the scene, Enver asked permission of the grandfather, who willingly consented. We sat for a little while longer and then left.

Out in the street, Selim and I plied our friends with questions. How was it possible, we asked in astonishment, that the Islamic prescription of circumcision, which was supposed to be done in a private manner in an appropriate Islamic atmosphere, could be celebrated in this frivolous manner, particularly with the accompaniment of dancing, as we had observed, and even drinking, something evidently quite common in Turkey? Moreover, I could not help feeling that to wait until a boy was eight or ten years old to perform his circumcision was very unsound from a psychological point of view. I also asked about the socio-economic status of the family we had just seen, and Emine said that they were lower middle class people. The expenses of a *Sünnet* celebration, she told us, would consume the savings of an average family; however, the gifts which the boy would receive, including gold medallions and fabric for suits which are generally worn by both men and boys in Turkish cities, would often repay some of the expenditure involved.

It was late now, and Enver hailed a taxi and brought us back to the hotel. As usual during our travels, we prayed *Maghrib* and *'Isha* prayers together in the shortened form permitted to travelers, and thanked God from our hearts for this wonderful, interesting day.

September 3: Enver and Emine arrived early in a taxi which had been hired for the whole morning to take us sight-seeing; the driver, an acquaintance of their aunt's husband, seemed to be a very polite, gentlemanly person. Our first stop was to be Eyyub Sultan Camii, the special mosque of Istanbul where people go to pray for blessings on important occasions such as examinations or the *Sünnet* or opening of school of their children.

Our friends took us first to an old cemetery adjacent to the mosque, where stood a cluster of beautiful and somehow touching Ottoman tombstones similar to those we had seen at the little mosque in Peć. As Emine explained, the graves of men were marked by vertical headstones with stone turbans carved at the top and those of women with stone rosettes. In the courtyard of this famous mosque was a sort of small kiosk with a roof like a hat, having faucets for making *wudu*—the ablution for prayers—but it was dirty and the stones on which water had fallen for centuries were green with algae (the condition of the ablution facilities at all the mosques we were to see in Istanbul). The courtyard was full of boys in the typical white *Sünnet* suits and spangled caps (of whom there seemed to be an unusual number just now because of the approaching commencement of the school year), school children in dark uniforms, and men and women who looked simple and pious. Pigeons in great numbers fluttered and walked about among them, to Maryam and Nura's delight; vendors sold bird seed, white muslin scarves for prayers printed with mementoes of Eyyub Sultan Camii, *tesbihs* for reciting *dhikr,* rose oil and other small articles.

We now passed into an adjoining building which housed the tomb of Abu Ayub Ansari, may God be pleased with him, for whom the mosque was named. Abu Ayub was one of the eminent companions of the Holy Prophet, peace be on him, in whose house the Prophet had first stayed when he migrated to Medinah. Abu Ayub had come to Istanbul (then Byzantium, the capital of the Eastern Roman Empire) with the Muslim army several years after the death of the Prophet. He had died there in about 51 After *Hijrah,* and the tomb and mosque had been erected in later years, presumably at the place where he was buried.

The tomb was inside a very richly-ornamented chamber behind a grill in a corner of a small room whose walls were covered with glowing ornamental tiles. People crowded into the room. Some of them, like ourselves, lifted their hands and recited *al-Fateha,* the opening verses of the Holy Qu'ran, for the soul of the Prophet's companion who was buried here; others, overcome with deep emotion, wept and showed their feelings openly.

It is hard to describe what I felt as I stood for the first time at the grave of one who had walked and talked with and intimately knew the Holy Prophet, God's peace and blessings be on him; it was an incoherent, unnamed emotion which brought a tightness to my throat and the sting of tears as I stood looking on. Yet while it was a unique and very meaningful experience to me to be in this place and I felt its impact, praying for God's blessings and peace on this companion of His Messenger who had been so close to him, there could not be more than that. Islam is not a religion centering around the memory or glorification of any human individual, not even its Prophet, peace be on him; the praise, the worship, the adoration, the supplication are only for God, Who had sent His servant, Abu Ayub, into the world to spread His blessed light. Thus, presently, together with other visitors, we passed out of the burial chamber and into the bright, sunlit courtyard of the mosque.

It was now a little past noon, and we soon heard the *adhan* for the *Dhuhr* prayer, happy that we would be able to perform our *salat* here. We entered the mosque, which at once struck me as light and beautiful, the men and Jamal joining the large congregation of men on the main floor, and Emine, the girls and I going to the women's gallery upstairs. It was very crowded with women and girls, many in school uniforms; the entire mosque, in fact, was full.

I looked about me before the prayer began. The mosque was small and lovely, having been recently restored. There were windows with ornamented designs at the front, very beautiful painted ornamentation on the dome and around the sides, and a clean, pale green carpet covering the floor. The prayer was performed as it is everywhere in the Muslim world, with additional recitations from the Qu'ran afterwards. When everyone had left the women's gallery, I made photographs of the interior of the mosque, rejoicing in its simple, light, serene beauty.

Up to this point I had just been observing, gathering impressions, asking questions. The feeling which predominated in my mind at present was a sense of confusion and contradiction. I was seeing a city in which past and present were inextricably blended—

a past whose life and spirit had been governed by faith in God and the living expression of that faith in a society—but which was now (as we had been warned to expect) dominated and overruled by the atmosphere of westernization and the lack of Islamic identity. At the same time, although the society as a whole was turned away from Islam and many of its people had adopted Western habits to the extent that they were indistinguishable in dress and appearance from Europeans, the *adhan* is called five times a day, the presence of mosques and worshippers denotes a Muslim country, and it is also clear that Islam is alive and cannot die in the hearts of the common people. How does one understand and reconcile these two opposite and incompatible aspects of the same society? And then the further, far more vital question: *Is Islam merely this—prayers and pious observances—or is it really what I have come to understand, that is, a total frame of reference and way of life to guide individuals and societies, no part of life being outside of its domain?*

Now after the prayer in Eyyub Sultan, which had been attended by a host of men and women whose hearts obviously held a great love and devotion for Islam despite the westernization rampant in the society, I experienced a moment of triumphant clarity, and my questions gave way to a comprehension of truth. The mosques and *adhans,* prayers and devotions, I realized, are one aspect and element of Islam—a vital and basic one, an expression of consciousness of God and an essential part of the way He has prescribed for mankind—but this is not the whole of Islam; it is merely one aspect of it, and in what I was seeing around me, the total system of Islam was absent. Here was, indeed, the observance of prayers, the love, the deep reverence, the sincere piety of heart and outward expression which I was observing among these simple Turks, but all this existed largely in an ideological and social vacuum, since Turkish society as a whole—at least in the big cities—was so clearly very far from Islam. Thus it was obvious and only natural that the one aspect, although it is among the most important and basic ones, which is still observed remains largely sterile and without influence.

The courtyard, the countless pigeons, the kiosk for *wudu,* the vendors and the *Sünnet* boys, the tomb and the mosque—all these made Eyyub Sultan an unforgettable and moving place. Presently we rejoined our taxi driver, who had been waiting all this time, and Enver directed him to our next stop.

We drove through an old section of the city, through ancient streets where stood quaint old weathered wooden houses, to a quiet hilltop overlooking a muddy waterway, the city spread out in the distant haze. Here stood an aged little wooden house where the Frenchman Pierre Loti, who had loved Istanbul so much that he had settled here, had lived. His house is now a teashop where antique Turkish handicrafts are exhibited and sold; it is situated at what must have been in his day a very lovely spot, overlooking Haliç, the Golden Horn, which once—not so very long ago—was a beautiful and very historic waterway. The Golden Horn is now anything but golden, its bank fringed with railroad tracks, dingy warehouses and other ugly installations, but still, with a little imagination, it was not difficult to visualize its former beauty.

We had glasses of tea in the teahouse and admired the charming old-style Turkish interior of the ex-Frenchman's house. Low benches covered with bright rugs stood against the walls, carpets were hung above them, and all-in-all there was an air of warmth, modest comfort and great charm. I could understand how Pierre Loti must have felt, for now that the strangeness was beginning to wear off a little—the sudden impact of a vast foreign metropolis coupled with the obvious cultural and linguistic differences—a liking for this city had begun to dawn in me, despite all the elements I had observed which I could not comprehend nor reconcile. The mementoes of its Islamic past, neglected though they were, were enough to inspire such a feeling despite all else.

Enver's *teyze*—maternal aunt—with whom he and Emine were staying, had invited us for lunch, and accordingly the driver now took us in the direction of her house. On the way we stopped while Enver did an errand, the rest of us waiting in the taxi. One of the countless boys who do a small vending business in the streets of Istanbul passed by, bearing on his head a wooden tray full of the sesame-seed-covered rings which Turks call *simits*. A *simit* fell down from the tray onto the pavement; the boy stooped down in such a way that the remaining rings would not fall and retrieved it, kissing it and touching it to his forehead in the traditional Turkish gesture of respect, and put it back on the tray with the rest of the *simits*. This incident made a considerable impression on me, reminding me of the profound respect for God's precious gift of food I had seen among Muslims, including Enver and Emine. They did not let crumbs fall on the floor to be trampled on but picked them up carefully, always hesitated to throw away left-over food, no matter how little, and if food fell down, picked it up and sometimes kissed it in the same manner as this boy had done to demonstrate their respect for God's bounty. I thought of the immense amount of food wasted daily in the homes and eating establishments of America, and pondered over the contrast in attitude and behavior.

The pleasant taxi driver, who now seemed more like a friend than a paid chauffeur, although we could not communicate at all, dropped us all on a street of apartment houses, where we entered the door of an elderly building. Enver's *teyze* lived three flights up. She answered our ring of the bell with smiles and greetings of great warmth and cordiality, a sweet, warm little bird-like woman, happy to see us and loving us at once, taking the children especially to her heart. She made us welcome in her pleasant apartment; there were carpets on the floor in every room, simple, adequate furniture, and spotless cleanliness. Emine helped her to lay out a big dinner, with many dishes, before us, and we ate heartily, enjoyed being together, and felt profoundly happy and at home. Although the *teyze* did not know a single word of English and we ourselves knew only the most rudimentary Turkish words of greeting and thanks, repeated over and over, here, marvellously, lack of words was no barrier to warmth and love. Sign language helped, and talking in one's own language, even though the other did not understand it, conveyed the friendly feeling and tone of sincerity, and no vocabulary was needed to comprehend the loving spirit behind the incomprehensible sounds.

The rest of the afternoon was spent in making other visits with Enver and Emine. As it was not convenient to take all the children, Jamal and Nura stayed behind with *Teyze,* who had eagerly offered to keep them with her, while Maryam, uneasy at the idea of being separated from us, went along with us on our rounds. It was evening when we returned to *Teyze's* house. She and the children had gone out, but her husband was at home, a big man who exactly matched his wife's cordial manner and made us welcome with great friendliness. We sat together in the formal drawing room drinking tea, and to our surprise (and I am sure to his), even without the interpretation of Enver and Emine, we managed some sort of elementary communication, although neither he nor we knew anything of each other's languages.

Presently *Teyze* returned with Nura and Jamal; they had gone to a mosque for *Maghrib* prayer and then for a long walk. The children had enjoyed themselves in spite of the language handicap, and it was evident that *Teyze* had also enjoyed their company. It was impossible not to love this affectionate little woman; we parted from her and her husband warmly with whatever words of thanks we knew, hoping to see them again, and returned to the hotel to pray and sleep after this pleasant, happy day.

September 4: Today we were invited for more sightseeing by a couple who are good friends of Enver and Emine's; together they all picked us up in a taxi from the hotel soon after breakfast. Ibrahim Bey spoke English, but his wife Sevil Hanım did not. Their two children, three- and five-year-old boys, completed the party.

We went first to see Sülemaniye Camii, one of the masterpieces of the architect Sinan and the loveliest in the galaxy of Istanbul's Ottoman mosques. Sülemaniye's greatness lies not only in its splendid external architecture but also in its interior, which is simple, direct and uncluttered, reaching the heart with its deep peace; the painted ornamentation on the dome and walls, its beautiful windows and lighting, all speak of serenity and inner depth.

We stayed in the mosque for a long time, my camera busy, and some of us praying *nafil salat.* Afterwards we visited the adjacent cemetery with its rows of beautiful Ottoman tombstones, which I always found somehow gravely touching. Here stood the tomb of Süleyman the Magnificent for whom the mosque is named, called by Turks 'Kanuni Süleyman' because of the greatness of his legislation; we recited *al-Fateha* here, observing the relative simplicity of the final resting place of one of the greatest sultans in Ottoman history.

The highlight of the day was to be a boat trip up the Bosphorus, which leads into the Black Sea. We went by taxi to the ferry docks, a dirty, smoky corner of the city from where ferries depart to sections of Istanbul lying on the Asian side, to the nearby islands, and to other parts of the shore of the Bosphorus; we were all to be Ibrahim Bey's guests, despite our protests.

We would journey up the Bosphorus nearly to the end of the ferry's route, have a picnic lunch (provided in various baskets and bags), and return to Istanbul by evening. The Turkish water transport system seemed quite efficient and, in a city surrounded by water on all sides, a very vital and indispensible part of its life; a great deal of daily traffic from the various parts of Istanbul and along the Bosphorus was efficiently handled by this means.

In the interval before our boat left, we said our *Dhuhr* and *'Asr* prayers, shortened and combined in the manner of travelers, at an old mosque across a very busy thoroughfare, whose exterior was black with the smoky grime of many years. Then we boarded the ferry. It had several decks and was spacious and pleasant. We sat together on the hard wooden benches of the main deck, chatting pleasantly as we sipped tea and ate *börek,* squares of very thin pastry filled with parsley and white cheese or ground beef; Ibrahim Bey talked with Enver and Selim, and the three of us women chatted together, Emine translating between Sevil Hanım and me.

All the children were somewhere outside, and I was in mortal fear the whole time that one of the little ones might fall overboard. When Ibrahim Bey's younger son was not heard of for some time, Emine shared my worry and went in search of him. She soon came back happily, after having found the boy, with a message to us from the captain. He had learned of our presence through her enquiry about a boy who belonged to the party of the "American Muslims," and had invited the self-same American Muslims and their friends to make use of his cabin for the remainder of the trip. We were naturally delighted with this unexpected kindness. All of us clambered up the steep stairs to the top of the ship, with words of appreciation to the captain, and took our places in one of the cabins. For the next two hours or so we enjoyed a magnificent view of the beautiful shores of the Bosphorus from this vantage-point, changing to the other cabin as the smartly-uniformed officer and his mate changed sides from time to time.

The ferry kept close to the right shore, which was dotted with villages and small towns, venerable *konaks* (the mansions of old Turkey) by the water's edge, minarets of mosques glimpsed in the distance, and the ancient Rumeli Hisarı, a castle whose walls are said to be built in the shape of the Arabic letters 'm-h-m-d' in remembrance of the Holy Prophet, peace be on him. Although the ferry stopped from time to time to take on or discharge passengers, we moved through the water at a good speed. The men and children stood outside by the railing in the fresh breeze, the children as happy as only young ones can be who have no immediate cares and are delighting in a new experience, language no barrier between them, while we women sat in the cabin chatting, Emine translating, Sevil Hanım's fingers flying at her knitting. The whole experience passed so quickly that later I could retain only a few sketchy memories.

At last the ferry stopped near the end of its route before returning to Istanbul; we were nearly at the Black Sea by now. We got off with our bundles for the picnic and entered a small fishing village by the water's edge. At a crude restaurant, the best the place afforded, Ibrahim Bey asked if we might sit at the tables outside to eat our food, ordering bottled drinks and *ayran,* a very popular beverage of yogurt and water. Our hosts spread out the food, simple and delicious, and we ate it with relish. Afterwards the children wandered about by the water's edge while we sat talking together in a relaxed, contented mood.

Toward dark we gathered up our belongings, ready for the ferry when it appeared on its way back to Istanbul. There was no captain's cabin this time, and we sat on one of the lower decks, the children outside pressed against the railing watching the dark waves and the lights twinkling along the shore. Thus the return trip passed uneventfully and we reached the city in the night, full of gratitude for the generous hospitality shown to us by Ibrahim Bey and his wife, who had not permitted Selim to spend so much as one *kuruş* during this outing. We parted from them with warm and sincere thanks, hoping to have an opportunity to meet again.

September 5: This morning, as Enver and Emine had some business to attend to and could not be with us until afternoon, they sent the pleasant taxi driver of the other day to fetch us from the hotel for a tour of some other places of interest.

After visits to various mosques, we decided that we would return to the Blue Mosque, which we had visited the first day, and we reached it just in time for the *Dhuhr* prayer. Selim and Jamal joined the congregation of men at the front of the mosque, while the girls and I went to the women's gallery at the rear; it was so crowded with women worshipers that it was hard to find space to stand.

From their dress it was obvious that almost all the women there were simple and uneducated, or elderly. I was very conscious of our foreign appearance, and it was no surprise to me when some of the women came up to us after the prayer and began to ask questions. I could understand almost no word but was able to tell them only, "American Muslim."

"*Maşallah!*" some of them responded heartily, crowding around the girls and me, patting our shoulders and praising God for our being Muslim. Their sincerity and warmth touched me deeply, and I reached out my hand to embrace some of them. Among these simple women, most of whom wore the light, knee-length coats and head scarves of the conservative city-dwelling Turk, I felt a sense of being at home, of belonging, which cut across all other differences to bring us together. This was indeed what I had come to Turkey to experience.

During the prayer I had been vaguely aware of a large group of foreign tourists standing in one corner of the mosque, the flashbulbs of their cameras going off occasionally even while the prayer was being performed. I did not, *could* not, belong to that world, even though I had been born in it, grown up in it, lived in it, understood it, spoke its language and observed many of its outward conventions; it was to *this* world I belonged, and I left the mosque with a feeling of great joy. Yet I pondered over the obvious fact that almost all the women who had prayed with me here were simple and uneducated, many perhaps illiterate. Outside in the street were modern Turkish women, educated and worldly, dressed in the latest European styles, while here in the mosque were the simple, the unlettered, the humble, in their conservative dress and with their devotion to Islam.

Why is this? I asked myself. Why are the uneducated and humble Turks full of love for Islam, while most of the educated and affluent try to pretend that they and their country are part of Europe rather than of the Muslim world, imitating Western ways and caring little or nothing for Islam? Islam had not been sent just for the simple and uneducated; it was for all people of every level and status. Indeed, it had been sent to expel ignorance and credulity, appealing profoundly to man's reason as well as to his feelings, and providing a faith and way of life which would improve the condition of mankind and raise it up, not debase it nor leave it where it was. Why, then, was there this great gap between the simple 'religious' people and the educated, secular, Westernized people in Turkey, and how could this gap be closed? There was as yet no way for me even to approach the answers to these questions, and I continued to observe what lay about me, my mind full of questions taking shape, being reviewed and rethought as I groped for understanding.

A little later, after a brief visit to Aya Sofya, Enver and Emine met us by pre-arrangement at the outside gate of nearby Topkapı Museum. Emine's eyes opened in astonishment as I recited to them the names of the days of the week in Turkish: *"Pazar, Pazartesi, Salı, Çarşamba, Perşembe, Cuma, Cumartesi . . ."*

"Very good, Marian Abla," said Enver approvingly. "Where did you learn that?"

"From the signboard there which gives the days and hours of the Museum," I told him. "I memorized them while we were waiting for you."

Emine laughed and put her hand through my arm affectionately. "Marian Abla, if you continue like this, you'll be talking Turkish within a month!"

"How I hope so!" I rejoined warmly, feeling the need for some elementary grasp of the language more with each passing hour.

Later we went to visit old acquaintances who lived in a distant section of the city, traveling by bus and taxi; only then did I grasp how vast and spread-out a city Istanbul actually is. The newer areas totally lacked the historical interest and elements of Islamic atmosphere which characterized the older sections. Apart from occasional newer mosques, they looked just like parts of any Central or Eastern European city, and most of their girls and women were very westernized indeed in dress, makeup and hair styles, in no way distinguishable from European women. Taken as a whole, present-day Istanbul appeared a rather nondescript city belonging neither to the East nor the West. Only its mosques and the *adhan* five times a day, scarcely audible above the roar of endless and confused streams of heavy traffic, some other structures of historical interest, and the dress of the minority of conservative women, could enable an observer to know that it had any connection whatsoever with the world of Islam. And yet at the same time, I sensed that to those who lived in it and loved it for its venerable history, who knew it inside and out, it must offer so many unique and lovely nooks and corners, replete with religious or historical significance or natural beauty, that despite its general nondescriptness few cities of the world would be able to compare with it.

September 6: The end of the journey was at hand; tomorrow we were to set out for Ankara. Today, then, was to be devoted to shopping, for without question Istanbul had far more to offer in this respect than Ankara.

We had thought about the things we would need to set up our household. After visiting in various homes, we realized that certain items were essential for proper Turkish hospitality, which is very formal. Cologne was always sprinkled on the hands of guests at the beginning of a visit, candy was passed in attractive dishes, Turkish coffee was offered in tiny cups with matching saucers, and tea served in small glasses with little saucers and miniature spoons for stirring. These were among the first things we would buy.

Late in the morning we reached the famous covered bazaar, Kapalı Çarşı, enjoying the unique flavor of this favorite shopping place of the whole of Turkey. The beautiful ornamental objects, especially those with Islamic motifs such as pottery, tiles, plates and other articles, appealed to me greatly, and we bought a few such things for our future home in Ankara.

After lunch, as the children were quite tired, Selim and Enver returned with them to the hotel, while Emine and I went back to the bazaar to finish our shopping. We wandered hand-in-hand down lane after lane of shops, looking into windows intrigued by the vast array of interesting merchandise, enquiring about prices and making an occasional purchase. With Emine's help I bought a number of articles not strictly necessary but appealing and beautiful, which I knew I would treasure. She asked about prices and bargained on my behalf, always telling shopkeepers earnestly that as I was not a tourist but an American Muslim, they should not charge me tourist prices. Some of the shopkeepers were totally indifferent, but others expressed interest and modified their prices accordingly, and in one particular shop selling small rugs, this information attracted considerable attention.

When Emine told the proprietor that I was an American Muslim, another man who happened to be in the shop began talking to me in fluent English.

"Are you really Muslim?" he asked. When I replied that I was, he said, "*Maşallah!* Do you know how to pray?"

"Yes, of course," I answered, feeling quite embarrassed. For a Muslim, praying is a common obligation, not a matter to be talked or boasted about. At the same time, however, I wanted this man to realize that it is not beyond the capacity of anyone who embraces Islam to pray regularly and to fulfill all other religious obligations as well as any 'born' Muslim.

"Bravo! It is very good," he told me approvingly, and exchanged some words in Turkish with the shopkeeper; I am sure my face was very red from being the object of such pointed enquiry and attention. Emine bargained with the shopkeeper for four small beautiful handmade rugs I had liked, and then, to my surprise, he offered me such a low price that I could hardly believe it, about half (he said) his usual price. "It is because you are Muslim," the English-speaking man said. I conferred with Emine, hesitating. I did not want to give him, just because of being an 'American Muslim,' so much less than his usual price. She pressed me to accept his offer, and then, concluding the purchase, we marched away joyfully with these treasures. I did not like Emine's mentioning my being Muslim because it seemed to me to be trading on my religion, but at the same time I also did not like being charged more than was proper because I appeared to be a foreigner. Thus I left Emine to manage things in her own way, which she would have done in any case; I was entirely dependent on her for every word which was spoken, as English was so little known here.

We returned to the hotel, bringing food from a restaurant for dinner for all of us. A little later Ibrahim Bey, his wife and children came to visit, and thus we sat talking until quite late. It was about midnight when I finished my prayers, hastily gathered together our belongings, and closed the valises for the last time, for we would leave quite early in the morning for Ankara.

Insha'Allah, tomorrow journey's end. O our Lord, we ask You for good in what lies ahead and we take refuge with You from all that is harmful, and we pray to You to guide us to true faith and submission to You in all we do . . .

CHAPTER 4

ANKARA

September 7: We had eaten a hasty breakfast in the hotel's little restaurant and were ready to leave when Enver and Emine arrived in a taxi, which took us to a bus terminal where we boarded a very modern and comfortable waiting bus. Besides the driver, the bus had a steward whose sole occupation was to look after the comfort of the passengers; from time to time he passed out candies and bottled spring water (served in all better Turkish restaurants and perhaps the favorite drink of the Turks) and sprinkled the hands of the travelers with lemon-scented cologne for freshening up.

Since the traffic was heavy, it took over an hour to get out of Istanbul. Our bus, together with many other vehicles, stood in line waiting to board a ferry to cross the Bosphorus to the Anatolian (Asian) side. Once on the ferry, we all got out of the bus to look at the scenery. Emine and I stood together among the cars and trucks at the railing of the boat, the dark waves lapping at the sides, gazing at the receding silhouette of Istanbul—the unbelievably grand mosques, Topkapı Saray and all the rest of that historic ancient-modern city. Ours had been but a very brief glimpse and impression, and I longed to return over and over to know it better. How long, I wondered, before I would see it again, hardly doubting that it would be possible to come and go at least once or twice more before leaving Turkey.

By now I had begun to take considerable notice of individuals, and I asked Emine many questions about various well-dressed people who caught my attention. I saw many heavily made-up, modish women, and I asked her over and over, Would this be a Muslim, or was it a member of one of the non-Turkish minorities? Each time she told me, judging only by the woman's appearance or speech, No, this was, despite the incongruity, a Turk and a Muslim. Most of the uneducated city women I had seen wore light Western-style coats which came just below the knee and scarves which often covered part of the forehead so that no hair could be seen. Now I had to learn to accept the fact that these women, with their dress which passed for conservative and Islamic, and the modern, well-dressed Westernized women with beauty-shop hairdoes and manicures, were part of the same grouping and supposedly held to the same beliefs and values. There was much to understand!

I remember little of what we saw on the way apart from noting that the villages and towns along the way seemed relatively prosperous, with none of the extreme poverty which we had seen in the hinterland of Yugoslavia. Emine and I sat together most of the way, exchanging thoughts. I also plied her with innumerable questions about Turkey and about what we were to expect in Ankara, but although she had all the essential information, still it was difficult to visualize the concrete situation until we should see it for ourselves.

The way was long and the bus traveled rather slowly. The highway was good enough, but as it had only two lanes and as almost all the traffic consisted of buses and trucks which passed each other continually, I was very thankful that we had a careful driver. We saw two or three quite serious accidents involving buses and trucks, which Emine said were very common in Turkey.

We stopped at mid-morning for tea at a pleasant restaurant, later for lunch at a very modern rest stop, and once more for tea later in the day. In the late afternoon we came into a barren terrain of lava rocks, a veritable desert. It was in this setting that we found Ankara on a bright, hot, late summer day—a vast, spread-out city lying in a valley between bleak, dark lava hills. What a site for the capital of a country, I thought. Far away in the distance I saw two cliffs separated by a valley, on one side of which I made out something which seemed to be a citadel with a flag flying. Emine said that this was the castle at Ulus, and although it looked somewhat forbidding as we came nearer, I noted with pleasure that there seemed to be at least *something* here which promised to be interesting.

The bus drove through the streets of what could have been a modern city in Italy or various other European countries, with no obvious distinguishing features of either architecture or population to indicate that it belonged in Turkey. As we got down with our luggage at the bus company's terminal, I wondered with dismay, "What is this place we have come to?" A taxi took us past clean, spacious angular government buildings and row upon row of modern apartment houses amid the swirl of heavy traffic. From the point of view of living standards, it seemed good enough, certainly; but was this colorless modern city, without personality, without a single mosque visible, part of the Turkey upon which I had placed so many hopes and dreams, and which I had been so fully prepared to love? Was it for this we had come? The route to Enver's house, where his mother was expecting us, lined with more government buildings and apartment houses, confirmed my first impression that Ankara was indeed a cold, spiritless place, with no history, tradition and above all, no Islamic identity. I wondered how I would ever be able to like this place and what it would be like to live here. Well, we should soon see . . .

(Actually, my initial impression of Ankara was entirely correct in relation to the major part of the city, that is, its newer areas. However, a city known as Angora or Ancyra had stood in what is now Ulus the old section of Ankara, since pre-Roman times, and in antiquity various battles had been fought on the dry, dusty plains on which the city now stands. Roman ruins, including a temple of Augustus, the Ulus castle which it is said was originally built in Roman times, picturesque old houses, aged mosques and simple people who were recognizable as Muslims were to be found in the old part of the city. In time to come, I was to return to this area again and again to catch a glimpse of the real Turkey, the Anadolu which we had come to visit, in the midst of a sea of personality-less modernity, and each time when I turned my face back to the new Ankara, it was to be with a feeling of disgust bordering on despair.*)

* See Notes (2) and (3).

All of us were tense with anticipation during that taxi ride: we had reached the end of our journey. We would stay with Emine, Enver and his mother for the present until we could establish ourselves in our own home, and now that our career as tourists was over, we must settle down as soon as possible and begin our life here in earnest. The taxi stopped before a large apartment house, fairly modern but showing premature signs of age; Enver was out in a moment and had run inside to bring his mother. We stood for a minute on the sidewalk with our mountain of luggage piled about us, looking around, Emine at our side. Everywhere there were apartment houses, a good deal of motor traffic, and the streets were full of pedestrians, mostly in modern Western dress.

Enver came running back, followed by his mother, a short, middle-aged woman clad in a housedress, with a warm, kind face. She embraced the children and me heartily and shook Selim's hand, speaking heartfelt words of welcome in Turkish: *"Hoş geldiniz, efendim, hoş geldiniz!"* We could only try by our smiles and manner, and by the few words of Turkish now at our command, to return her warmth.

Our friends led us into the house with more words of welcome. The apartment was up two flights of stairs, pleasant, spotlessly clean and nicely-furnished. It was bulging with furniture which, I realized from what Emine had said, must in part be meant for us, for she had somehow managed to procure for us a set of dining and drawing room furniture. With all this extra furniture in the apartment, we were also five extra people to stay until we could get settled—but this only seemed to be taken as a matter of course and of great pleasure by the entire family.

We were all very tired after the long bus trip. As soon as we had washed, dinner was on the table and we were seated around it, now part of a Turkish family. We had been traveling for the past twenty-four days and it seemed wonderful to be in a home again. Thank God, the end of the road had been safely reached.

Food **was piled** onto our plates, and Aynur Abla (as we were to call Enver's mother) waited on us solicitously, despite our protests. She had been **a wid**ow for many years, and, as in many Turkish homes, lived permanently with her son. She was so sincere and spontaneous in her expressions of affection and welcome that I felt completely dismayed and lost at being unable to communicate my own feelings to her except through the interpretation of Enver or Emine, or through a smile or handclasp.

Up to this point, all Turkish speech was an unintelligible jumble to me, out of which I could distinguish no single words or even sounds as yet. However, Selim, being familiar with classical Arabic and Persian, was trying out words from both languages and finding to his encouragement that they were usually Turkish too (although both pronunciation and meaning were somewhat different in many cases), since Turkish had many centuries ago incorporated a vast number of Arabic and Persian words into its basic vocabulary. Thus, while he had begun to communicate from the very beginning, the children and I had no such advantage, and I felt very much chagrined at finding nothing at all in the collection of various European languages of which I knew a smattering which could be useful here.

After all the fatigues of the day, the emotional impact of having reached the end of the journey and having seen at last the place in which we would be living for the next few months, and all the strangeness and newness of being part of a Turkish family with all its subtle interrelationships, part of a household speaking a language of which I could understand no word, I found that I could hardly eat, and the children too were so used up and as yet unaccustomed to the food that they ate scarcely anything, despite the solicitude of all the family. After we had prayed, the entire house was re-arranged to accommodate us comfortably; the best of everything was given to us, and we slept at once, thanking God for all His countless blessings.

The next morning Aynur Abla and Emine served us a cheerful breakfast of boiled eggs, Turkish bread, butter, honey, preserves, black olives, white cheese and tea, refusing all my efforts to be of help. We must now think and talk about what had to be done, having had time by now to consider these matters. We were weary of being without a home and only wanted to be settled in our own place as soon as possible. Emine, who had made all sorts of enquiries for us, gave us essential information about the dates on which schools would open (the following Monday), what schools might be good for the children (the choice now narrowed down to two or three), possible apartments, and other vital matters. We sat together to consider the order of priorities with the help of our friends.

It was now Tuesday, and schools would open in six days, although the Middle East Technical University where Selim would be studying would not open until mid-October; we had reached here at this time only in order that the children might be able to start school from the beginning of the term, and it was essential to find a proper one for them immediately. We must procure Turkish *liras* in exchange for dollars sufficient for our needs, find a suitable apartment, acquire all the essentials for housekeeping and move in, and it must all be done in a short space of time, for we could be nomads no longer.

During the days which followed, we managed these major necessities one by one. On the first morning we took care of our financial needs, and later in the day went with Emine to investigate schools for the children, going about by taxi when necessary and by *dolmuş** whenever possible. All schools, both public and private (apart from a few private ones primarily for the children of foreign diplomatic or military personnel), were Turkish-medium. Since it was obvious that the children would get more individual attention at a private school, we went to see a few institutions where we talked to the principals, explaining that we did not really expect the children to keep up with studies at their own level but mainly hoped that they might learn Turkish during the first few months. The following day we decided to enroll them in an institution whose principal had impressed me favorably; a great amount of paper work, with signatures and tax stamps, a vast outlay of money for fees, and time and patience were required for completing this arrangement. I waited in a state of anxiety for the coming Monday when, for the first time, I would bring the children to a school where no English was spoken and leave them to manage on their own resources.

How would they do it? The questions which had been troubling Maryam during these latter days now loomed very large. She had

A collective taxi shared by several passengers going to various destinations along the same route.

been reassured by the kind, loving friends among whom we had begun our life in Ankara and by finding that its living standard was quite adequate, and now only the question of school remained in the minds of all three children, and of each of the adults as well. Enver and Emine, concerned and loving, were very conscious of the difficulties they were facing, and they and Aynur Abla did their best to make them feel happy and at ease.

After these matters were taken care of, Selim and I began to look for a place to live. The housing in Ankara consisted almost entirely of apartment buildings, and thus we went about, in the beginning with Enver or Emine and later with Aynur Abla since they had to return to work, searching for 'Kiralık Daire' (Apartment for Rent) signs in apartment buildings. After going with our friends a few times, we were soon able to go alone, following up sign after sign, asking for the 'kapıcı' (caretaker-janitor) of the building, armed only with politeness and a few essential words of Turkish sufficient for pursuing our enquiries.

We looked at a number of apartments which were all undesirable for one reason or another: either dark and dingy, up several flights of stairs, having a gas smell always lingering in the corridor or on the steps, too expensive or too small—and in one instance too big. After four or five days of this, Selim and Enver came back from the city one afternoon talking animatedly. They had happened upon an apartment which they thought might possibly be suitable; I was to return with them to see it the next afternoon.

When we went to see the apartment the following day, taking Emine and the children, the kapıcı of the building, a tall, very thin man, let us in. The apartment was cheerful and light and bright, although somewhat small, and the location pleasant and convenient. Thus, having seemingly exhausted most other possibilities and ourselves as well, we decided at once to take it. Alhamdulillah, the end of the search, the end of the road. We had found a home.

The apartment, as it happened, was situated not too far from a big old mosque, one of the very, very few in modern Ankara, which we had passed several times on our errands. By now we had been to the center of the city, called Kızılay, with Enver or Emine a few times, and I had been quite depressed by what I had seen and felt:

a cold, stark, somewhat nondescript commercial district with elegant shops in which all types of expensive merchandise, particularly women's fashions, were sold, crowds of Turkish-speaking shoppers strolling about — and I in the midst of them, unable to communicate with anyone and feeling terribly cut off and alone. Thus, after a few days in this westernized Ankara, the possibility of being near a mosque — a house of worship of God, which somehow seemed to be such a very rare thing in this capital of a supposedly Muslim country — in whose vicinity I had seen some real Turks, a few simple people in modest dress, the sight of whom gave me new heart after the slightly-comic imitation Westerners who form the majority of Ankara's inhabitants, made me very happy. It happened that the *adhan* for 'Asr prayer was called while we were looking at the apartment. It was quite faint because of the distance of the mosque and the noise in the street, but it was enough to assure me that it was nonetheless audible from where we would live, and I thanked God for it. That *adhan* would be my best and most treasured companion in the months which lay ahead, I thought.

The apartment contained two fair-sized bedrooms which would be for ourselves and the girls, a very small room which would be Jamal's, a drawing room *('salon')*, a dining area just big enough for the massive table and chairs which Emine had procured for us, and a kitchen with a sink and cupboards. There were two bathrooms, a large one with Western-style fixtures and a smaller Eastern-style one. A gas hot water heater, which subsequently proved to be very inefficient, was attached to the kitchen wall, and the building was centrally heated. It was a pleasant place, but as it required some repairs and a very thorough cleaning, it would take time and effort to turn it into a home.

As in all Ankara apartment buildings, our building had some apartments below ground level and several floors above, with four or five units on each floor. The *kapıcı* and his family lived in the basement, that is, in the second level below the ground floor. I hoped that we might find some congenial families living in the building; there seemed to be several small girls the ages of our daughters, and already we had a budding acquaintance with a helpful woman in a neighboring house who spoke a very little English. In the meantime, I had written a note to Cemile, my pen-friend of long standing who lived in Isparta, to tell here that we had arrived; I knew that when she returned to her university in Ankara at the beginning of her school term in October I should be seeing her, as she had expressed great eagerness to meet us.

Monday, the first day of the children's school, arrived soon enough. Aynur Abla and I (the others being otherwise occupied and Emine at home sick) took them to school by *dolmuş*. The halls were full of parents with their children, none of whom seemed to know what to do or where to go; at length all assembled on the playground, each class forming a line. Aynur Abla saw to it that the children were put into the respective lines for their grades; although they said nothing, they were certainly very apprehensive, and I am sure I was equally so. Nura looked blank and dull, an expression which I saw on her face only when she was anxious or uncertain, Maryam very unsure of herself, and Jamal morose and unhappy as they stood silently waiting among all those strange children with whom they could not exchange a single word. I felt so much for them in this situation, but there was nothing which anyone could do except to give encouragement and moral support; they had to see it through on their own, with the help of Allah and the many good qualities which they possessed, for this school situation, although hardly ideal, had seemed the best solution which we could manage under the circumstances.

There was no possibility of talking to the teachers at that time, and in any case none of them could speak English. The school's first-day opening exercises, with speeches by the principal and other dignitaries, the singing of the national anthem, etc., were held, and then the lines of students trooped inside. I had to turn and walk away so that no one would see the tears which *would* come, but Aynur Abla saw and tried to comfort me. Although I could as yet understand no more than a very, very few words of Turkish, the patient lady, in close contact with foreigners for the first time in her life, talked to me slowly and slowly, groping for words which I might possibly recognize and never giving up due to my apparent denseness. I was by now able to pick up a single word here and there in conversation, although Turkish was still one solid block of strange sounds, with many frequent repetitions of -k, -z, and -sz and other elements which were very unfamiliar, and I could only hope, very fervently, that the

day would somehow come when I would be able to understand and
to express my ideas; in the meantime, I was obliged to convey a
whole phrase or sentence of varying degrees of complexity with a
single word or a gesture.

Aynur Abla now took me to each of the children's classrooms
where I stood, helplessly silent, smiling at the teacher and hoping
that she might be king to the child who was so precious to me, my
good companion speaking a few words to the teacher about them. I
was most concerned about Maryam, but when we went to her classroom, I found her with two children who knew a little English; so
far so good. Still I wondered how the children would manage,
especially this middle child who had been so heart-broken about
leaving her home, her friends, her school and everything else which
was familiar, and so apprehensive day after day during these past
weeks about her ability to handle the situation.

Now Aynur Abla, acting on my behalf, filled out some more forms
for the children, paid more fees, and then looked enquiringly at me
to see what I wanted to do next. Tired and sad at heart, I said un-
grammatically, "Ev get, ev get" (Go home, go home), unable to
think of anything else after this.

Emine felt much better by afternoon, and she and I returned to
the school at closing time to pick up the children. To our surprise
and delight, they were all very happy with the first day and each of
them had found friends; it was much more than any of us could realistically have hoped for. We did some errands at Kızılay, the center of downtown Ankara, including the purchase of school uniforms
for the children. Turkish youngsters in public schools wore cotton
smocks with collars, but at private schools it was hardly that simple.
At the children's school the girls' uniform consisted of a woolen jum-
per and a blouse, and woolen trousers with a jacket bearing the
school's emblem for boys. After we had paid the staggering sum of
540 T.L. ($36)* for these three outfits readymade, I began to get an
inkling of how and where money went here. The stipend Selim was
receiving monthly was quite high for Turkey, but at this rate of expenditure it would hardly be sufficient!

* At that time the exchange rate was approximately 15 T.L. = 1 U.S. dollar; 100
kuruş = 1 T.L.

The next days were spent in a round of errands which had to be done one after the other in a logical sequence, with much running about here and there. We made numerous trips to acquire household necessities, for apart from the furniture and few kitchen utensils which Emine and Aynur Abla insisted on lending us, we had nothing. I went with Emine when she was at home, or with Aynur Abla, Selim or even alone, always taking a bus or *dolmuş* to Kızılay or to Ulus, where the shops were not as elegant and the prices were a little lower. Since the geography between Enver's house and these points was quite simple, there was no problem in getting about; *dolmuşes* and buses went straight there and back from the stops in our vicinity. The first time we had gone to Kızılay, Enver had pointed out to us the Gima Building, a tall modern structure having about twenty floors, and this became our reference point for downtown Ankara until we could become familiar with it.

When we went shopping alone, we talked to shopkeepers in gestures and the primitive rudimentary Turkish which we now knew, encouraged by the fact that we were always treated courteously and fairly. Bargaining was of course out of the question at this point, and in any case I considered it as a rule as undignified and unbecoming — *if* necessary. All-in-all we managed our shopping with dispatch with the help of Enver's family, and before long their apartment held a number of our purchases essential for housekeeping. We had given an order at a shop to have mattresses and pillows made, and when these were ready we would be able to move to our own place.

Curtains to cover the bare windows were also among our first necessities as soon as they could be made, but up to now I had not been able to find any inexpensive material which I liked and I was searching for a place which sold bright, colorful fabrics made in Gaziantep, a length of which I had bought in Istanbul. Emine recalled that she had seen a shop which sold this material up the hill at Ulus and accordingly we decided to go there to buy it.

We went to Ulus by *dolmuş*, getting down at the usual place near a large shopping plaza beside which stood an equestrian statue of Atatürk flanked by other figures. At the end of one of the main streets of the area which abounds in numerous jewelry shops, each having a glittering display of gold ornaments in windows illuminated by light bulbs, rises a very steep hill, the summit of which is crowned by the castle which I had seen from the bus when we arrived in Ankara. We walked very slowly up the extremely steep, narrow street, which was lined with shops and crowded with people, looking at merchandise, asking prices and making occasional small purchases, while I savored with great enjoyment the flavor of this pleasant old bazaar.

At length we reached the top of the hill. The narrow street grew even narrower here, a loosely-suspended canvas slung overhead between the shops on the two sides of the street as a protection from the sun. The bazaar was thronged with the poor, uneducated city dwellers who in appearance resemble villagers, and the shops sold merchandise for this class of people, displaying their wares outside. Here were none of the sophisticated elegancies of Kızılay but such goods as were largely basic and essential: fabrics, shoes, housewares, hardware, furniture, inexpensive rugs and carpets, and so on, each in its own small shop.

At last we found the shop for which Emine was looking; its windows held a fascinating display of small articles: hand-crocheted strings of tiny colored flowers used as edging on kerchiefs, cummerbunds, shawls, prayer scarves, antique embroideries and other items. Here too was the colorful Gaziantep fabric we wanted, and we bought ten meters for curtains. At the top of a narrow flight of stairs, the mezzanine of this little old shop held hundreds of antique embroideries and women's dresses from another era: long gowns made of richly-embroidered velvet or a lighter fabric with stripes and bright, lovely patterns, opening in front with slits on the sides, to be worn with a *şalvar* and a head covering. These irreplaceable treasures were mostly brought here, no doubt, by villagers who had fallen upon hard times and needed money more than the relics of their ancestors. After browsing here with great interest for a while, we took our purchases and left. I was greatly refreshed by contact with the Muslim Turks of this area who say *"Esselâmün aleyküm"* instead of *"Merhaba,"* the usual greeting, or the artificial *"Gün aydın"* used by westernized Turks. Here was my real, honest, Turkey, the precious Turkey I had come to see and to know, hidden away in the oldest corner of Ankara, after all!

Emine and I returned to the street at dusk. From a mosque a few doors away, very small and hardly visible in its secluded niche between shops, came the sound of the *adhan* for *Maghrib* prayer, and we decided to go there to pray. It was a plain, simple little mosque, with an upstairs gallery for women. Our worship there filled me with a deep sense of joy and peace. As we descended the steep Çikrikçilar Hill, walking among the crowd of colorfully-dressed traditional Turks, holding each other's hands and chatting, I was for the moment totally and utterly happy.

After a relaxed, peaceful Sunday, the next day there is again school for the children. They are managing to hold their own; each of them has found either a child or the teacher herself in his or her classroom who speaks fragmentary English, and they are beginning to learn their first words of Turkish. In class they copy whatever the teacher writes on the blackboard without understanding anything. There are also some unexpected complaints: many of the children behave very badly, they say, and the teachers are surprisingly harsh, hitting, shaming and shouting at their pupils, apparently having a great deal of freedom in how they treat them and unable to maintain discipline in any other way. I had certainly anticipated problems, but not ones of this nature. Every day except Sunday (Saturday is a half-day) they leave the house at 8 a.m. and return home, quite tired, at 3:30 in the afternoon.

During these days I continue my shopping for household necessities, taking *dolmuşes* and rushing around Kızılay or Ulus, many times alone when the others are all occupied. I manage somehow with the few words of Turkish I have learned, and although I am still frighteningly cut off from what is going on around me, I now feel that I am adequate to handle the situation and don't hesitate to go by myself, knowing that I will manage somehow. The following day we are to move into our apartment, after spending many days in Enver's house.

Aynur Abla has cooked, cleaned and labored for us indefatigably, and each night the family has turned the house upside-down to accommodate us all comfortably. Aynur Abla seems to accept all this as perfectly natural and part of her obligation to us as their guests, perhaps in the hope (far-fetched though it seems to me now) that we may one day be able to communicate with one another, for clearly she likes us very much. I don't even know the proper words to thank her for all she is doing, or even if it is *proper* to thank her, in a country where words of thanks are met with the traditional Muslim expression, *"Estağfurullah,"** and I cannot admire enough the patience, hard work and self-sacrifice of this woman for us—people who are after all foreign to her—simply because we are Muslims like herself and because we are dear to her children.

Now a feeling of identification and love, born of my experience on Ulus hill and the neighborhood of the mosque, among the simple and decent ordinary Turks, begins to grow up in me. I try to communicate it to the children, but they are still able to think only in terms of America; their minds are as yet almost closed against everything here as they continue to talk about what they have left behind. I suppose that this is only natural and hope that it will change in time. We have now met some of Enver and Emine's friends, and as Turkey becomes for us and for the children no longer an abstraction, I am sure that warm relationships with old and new friends will also play their part in helping them to begin to feel at home here.

Our moving takes place, with a truck hired to transport the heavy furniture from Enver's house to ours. We have paid the *kapıcı* and his wife 40 T.L. for a thorough cleaning of the place; they have worked very hard and it is spotless. Enver has wired in the light fixtures which we have bought for the living room; the mattresses and pillows are now finished and we have acquired bedding; kitchen utensils, Turkish-made and of good quality, have been bought, together with the essential glasses and tiny spoons for tea and the little cups and saucers for serving Turkish coffee; curtains are in the process of being made for the windows; and we have purchased essential items of furniture which, together with what the Envers have provided, are quite enough for our needs. We sleep in our new house for the first time. It will take quite a lot more effort to turn it into a real home, but I have already put some decorative touches here and there which make it feel a little homelike already.

The following morning Jamal wakes up with a quite heavy cough.

* Literally, May God forgive me (from accepting or wanting thanks).

That day, Sunday, is to be holiday for us all; we have invited Enver's family to a restaurant for dinner. We sit out at a table under grape vines, savoring the mild late-summer weather, eating dishes which are new to us and enjoying ourselves royally, for the moment completely at peace. Afterwards we go to Gazi Osman Paşa district together to drink tea in a pretty tea garden called Cennet Bahçesi—Paradise Garden — where tables are set out on terraces in leafy bowers. The place is crowded with people drinking glass after glass of tea, playing cards and chatting, and the children go exploring while we sit sipping our strong, hot tea. I had been marveling at the lovely weather of these days, one day of cloudless blue sky and mild temperature following another until I had thought that it would always be like this, but today is a bit cloudy, with a chilly breeze.

As soon as we return to our new apartment, Jamal begins to cough — a hard, dry hacking cough which does not improve with cough syrup or lozenges from my medicine chest. For the first time in many days, Maryam and I have a long talk, which is good for us both. As I had anticipated, the child who seemed so anxious, so vulnerable, is beginning to find herself, to learn that she can cope with whatever comes, that she will have friends and good experiences wherever she goes. In the late evening a big load of coal is dumped onto the pavement under the window of our bedroom, and men work shoveling it into the cellar until very late in the night; the next morning it all starts over again very early. Upstairs above us someone evidently owns a television, for we can hear it through the ceiling until quite late.

By now I have given much thought to my early impressions of Turkey and of Ankara, of the people we have met, and of the situation in general. The predominant theme in all my feelings so far is confusion and contradiction, a simultaneous attraction and repulsion which, until I understand much more, I cannot even begin to resolve. As far as Ankara itself goes, there is really not much for me to like or to identify with in what we have seen thus far; it appears to have no history, very little of the kind of culture I had hoped to find, nothing particularly Turkish except for my dear Ulus and its hill, and there is also a lack of beauty and a coldness about the city itself which inspires negative feelings. But perhaps more than any of these aspects, there is the uneasy feeling of being cut off and virtually incommunicado. Selim is far ahead of me, with his knowledge of Arabic and Persian words common to Turkish, while I have not yet even begun to grasp any of the basic elements of the grammar and have only succeeded in picking up a few scattered words so far. The children too have learned almost no Turkish and are not getting much help from their teachers, who seem rather indifferent and overworked.

The next day is quite chilly, for the balmy weather has finally broken and the sky is completely overcast. As yet the gas has not been turned on in the apartment, and I go to my neighbor in the next building, Güneş Hanım, who is able to understand me with her slight knowledge of English and who goes to telephone the Havagaz Ofisi on our behalf. Jamal and Nura are both at home sick, and Jamal's cough sounds quite bad. Emine takes him to consult a Turkish pediatrician, who says he has bronchitis and prescribes penicillin; it is very difficult for him to get to sleep at night with his continuous dry cough.

The next morning I am awakened very early by Jamal's coughing. Again today it is cloudy and the apartment, with its tile-covered cement floor and brick walls, is very cold; the 'kalorifer'—the building's furnace stoked by the kapıcı—has not yet been turned on for the winter. And there is still no gas in the apartment. I go to my neighbor again, who brings over a steaming embrocation for Jamal and puts in an emphatic telephone call to the gas office; the gas men come at last, apologizing for some mistake which kept them from finding our house the day before. We now have hot water, and can cook and wash, a suddenly uncommon and delightful luxury. We have purchased a four-burner gas stove with an oven as well as a small refrigerator, Turkish-made and quite comparable to American-made products. Hence in terms of conveniences, we are quite well off, apart from not having a washing machine, which is within our means but is something we feel we can manage without for these few months. These appliances each cost what is roughly one month's salary for a fairly well-paid middle-class Turk, and hence substantial numbers of city-dwellers are able to afford them.

Jamal's dry hacking cough gets worse and worse. We try using steam, but there is no improvement. I am so sorry for his plight and, as Selim is at home, I go in search of the American library, which I finally locate in a distant section of the city, bringing him books to read; this at least helps to distract his mind from his illness. We move his bed into the kitchen, keep a kettle steaming over low heat all night, and he sleeps through most of it.

I am very anxious about the boy. Clearly the penicillin has not helped, for he has fever and is obviously acutely ill. I talk to Enver the next morning. He finds a specialist and brings him to the house; he is a pleasant, conscientious doctor who speaks fluent English. He examines Jamal very attentively, listens to his chest for a long time and asks many questions, spending more than an hour with us. He says that the penicillin is ineffective for this problem and prescribes another antibiotic and cough medicines, asking us to contact him again if things do not improve. We pay his fee very gratefully, thankful for his interest and kindness, and are happy to have some reliable advice about our son's condition.

September 30: I have a great deal of housework—the ordinary, daily chores—and besides that, getting the house into shape to be lived in. Jamal is still in bed and coughing a good deal. The *kalorifer* is turned on just when I feel I will perish with the cold, for this brick building is extremely chilly in the grey fall weather. I make an arrangement through Emine to have the *kapıcı's* wife come once a week to clean, and am so thankful that I will have some help, for cleaning, washing, cooking, etc., are taking all my time. I am also learning a little Turkish, word by word. We see the Envers very often, exchanging visits, and they are constantly alert to help us in any way necessary.

October 1: We have now settled into something of a daily routine, although Jamal is still home from school and is still coughing. I hope *insha'Allah* he will be able to return to school at the beginning of next week.

Day follows day, uneventfully. Each morning I awaken for *Fajr* prayer with the beautiful *adhan* coming faintly from the distance;

then I make breakfast, get the children off to school, and spend the rest of the morning doing housework. Lunch is generally finished by two o'clock and then there is somewhere to go, some matter which needs attention, or I am so tired that I must sleep for a while. And I ask myself: Is this a life, is this what I have come here for? Is it a mere unrealizable dream that people should have enough leisure time to pursue meaningful objectives apart from daily work in a society which also possesses standards and values other than materialistic ones? And then I ask myself all over again: *Does Turkey possess such values and standards, or is it basically—at least among the upper middle class people among whom we live—a poor copy of the West, belonging neither here nor there, having discarded what was good and valuable together with whatever may have been in need of change?* And yet, although upper class Turks on the whole may be turned away from Islam, still the majority of them profess Islam as their religion and claim to be Muslims! There is such a marked element of contradiction in everything I see around me that I am totally bewildered by all the opposing trends, so profound and obvious is this pull in opposing directions. It seems to me that this nation is the victim of a strange schizophrenia in its collective personality, a split down the center of its very being, producing this extreme sense of conflict and confusion whose cause and origin I am not yet able to understand at all.

It is quite clear that Islam is alive and valued here among a great many of the common people, but what can they do alone? And while it **is true** that the majority of upper class, educated Turks seem to have turned their backs on Islam and are trying to run away from it and from their history, obviously there are still some among this class who have deep faith and commitment, Islamic knowledge, and who are in a position to instruct others. *How can communication be built between these two Islam-loving elements of the population, something which seems absolutely essential for the future of Islam in Turkey . . .?*

The news is that Jamal Abdel Nasser, that so-called spokesman for the Arab cause who imprisoned and tortured countless devoted Muslims whose lives were like a light in this world, and even executed some of the greatest among them, for no other cause than that they called people back to Islam, is dead; now he will have to give an accounting before his God for all he has done—a man who held so much power in his hands that few imagined he would die so soon, just like any other human being. On another front there is terrible trouble and devastation in Jordan as a result of the conflict between government forces and the guerillas who want to take power, and talk about a U.S.-Soviet confrontation over the issue. As always, U.S. foreign policy is inept and reflects the mentality of a leadership which thinks first and last only of national self-interest, acting as if the entire world should devote itself to bolstering up U.S. security and well-being. The newspaper contains open admissions of U.S. duplicity and underhandedness in dealing with the situation in order that other nations may be brought to act solely in its interest, evidently in the usual blissful conviction that the American outlook and way of life are *the only* outlook and way of life. How little Americans, with their general lack of understanding of other cultures, know or care about the values and ways of life of peoples living under other systems in other parts of the world that they feel so justified in playing God over them! And yet (going round and round in circles and always coming back to the same point), *What is here? Is Islam here, are Muslims striving hard in God's cause, that I should feel such a tie with this land . . .?*

October 4: Two days ago a meeting for mothers was held at the children's school. I went, accompanied by Aynur Abla, and we talked briefly to Nura's and Jamal's teachers, explaining to the latter about his illness. When I say "We talked," I mean of course that Aynur Abla talked while I stood there smiling helplessly, trying to convey the impression of an interested mother; later Emine told me that Aynur Abla had reported that the teachers like the children and speak well of them.

When we went to Maryam's room, however, we found the teacher absent and the whole class in a terrific uproar. All the children were doing whatever they liked, and the confusion and noise as twenty or thirty children shouted and pranced about was such that we could not hear ourselves speak. We waited in vain for the teacher to return and finally left for the meeting, as the turmoil in the classroom continued without any control. I must say that I conceived a very poor opinion of the discipline of the school from

·this incident, confirmed by what I hear from our children. Many of the teachers are quite young, with much make-up and mini-dresses, and are apparently incapable of maintaining discipline without the use of beating, slapping across the face, shouting, scolding and shaming, and our children are understandably uneasy in this situation, especially as they never know when they may be subjected to such treatment themselves.

The meeting, as it turned out, was to discuss various school matters with the mothers. I could understand almost nothing that was said, but at the same time I found to my astonishment that I was able to communicate with and to understand a few things which Aynur Abla said to me for the first time; I grasped that the first breakthrough and dawning of light in my comprehension of Turkish had occurred, and thanked God.

Jamal had been much improved, almost like himself during the past days and my mind was easy about him at last, but two evenings ago he again began to cough. The next morning he was still coughing hard, and became worse as the day progressed. Very much concerned, in the evening Selim went to Enver's house, and he and Emine immediately went to bring Cahid Bey, the specialist. Jamal was asleep when he arrived, totally exhausted after a long day of continuous coughing, and the doctor examined him carefully without waking him. Then followed a very long conference without any definite diagnosis being arrived at, and presently Cahid Bey left, saying that he would return the following day to examine the boy thoroughly and try to come to a decision about his illness.

While we were conferring with the doctor, visitors arrived whom Emine received at the door on our behalf: Aynur Abla accompanied by friends of theirs, a young couple who had been planning to visit us for some days, and at the same time our helpful neighbor, Güneş Hanım, and her husband, who had heard about Jamal's new illness and decided to pay a formal visit of condolence. Although there was nothing common between the two groups of visitors and in spite of our language handicap, nonetheless somehow some sort of communication was possible with everyone, through the mediation of our translators, and altogether it was a very pleasant and memorable visit, the first real company we had had in our house so far.

Now Turkish hospitality is rather formal and standardized, and there are several steps involved. When a visitor comes, he is welcomed at the door with appropriate words; hands are shaken, among more traditional Turks, younger people kiss the hand of older ones and touch it to their forehead, and women embrace and kiss one another. The visitor is given a pair of slippers to put on, for it is generally considered improper to come into a Turkish house wearing shoes, bringing the considerable dust and dirt of the street into the always-immaculate home and especially onto the carpet, and most families keep several pairs of slippers near the front door for the use of guests and family members, who also interchange shoes and slippers whenever they come in or go out. The visitor is then ushered into the *salon,* made to sit on the most comfortable chair, and then cologne, candy and cigarettes are offered. If it is a formal visit, coffee—thick black Turkish coffee—is served in tiny cups, to be followed after an interval by tea and refreshments; however, if the visitor is a friend rather than a formal visitor, tea and refreshments are served without the preliminary coffee. Turkish tea is made in a double-boiler kettle, the upper part of which contains very strong, concentrated tea which is diluted in each glass with plain hot water from the lower one, according to individual taste.

Thus passed our first evening of visitors, a bitter-sweet occasion because of our worry about Jamal. The next morning his cough began as soon as he awoke, but it was not as severe as yesterday and he was able to sleep much of the morning. The *kapıcı's* wife, Gül Hanım, whom I had liked very much because of her pleasant face, came to clean. However, I could not help being irritated by her handling things which were lying about and by her jabbering at me in very rapid Turkish of which I could not understand a single word, sometimes talking very loudly to make me understand better and again coming very close and dropping her voice to a whisper to see if this would not improve my comprehension. Childishly I felt glad that Jamal was there so that she could hear me talking to him and would realize that I am not absolutely deaf, dumb or stupid and am able to speak in *some* language, even though it is not Turkish.

Selim went to the University for the first time today and will go regularly after this to begin his program, although classes will not start for several days yet. This evening the doctor, Cahid Bey, returned. He asked numerous questions about Jamal's earlier history, again examined him very thoroughly, and talked to Selim and me at great length, concluding that he has bronchitis complicated by asthma. He stayed for over an hour-and-a-half, prescribed several medicines and left, saying that he treated Jamal as if he were his own son, and that we should consider him not as a doctor but as a friend. We were indeed grateful to him for his help in this very difficult situation; may God reward him for his kindness.

By the next day Jamal had made good progress with the new medications and by evening was hardly coughing at all, *Alhamdulillah*. In the afternoon I went to the city to find a small present for him, as he had been having such a miserable time of it. By now shopping there has become very interesting and enjoyable for me. Each time I explore some new area or reconnoiter the old ones again, and I have found many very nice shopping places in the *pasajs* (arcade-type shops) around Kızılay. This time I went to a *pasaj* housing jewelry and antique shops and bought some inexpensive antique coins—Roman, Seljuk, Byzantine and Ottoman—for Jamal. He was highly delighted with this notable addition to his small collection, and later in the evening Enver's family came to have dinner with us, a happy evening.

As the following day was pleasant and Jamal was much improved, we decided that we would go on a much-needed family outing. At one side of Ankara is an area called Atatürk Orman Çiftliği—Atatürk's farm estate—part of which has been made into a small, pleasant zoo. Here we spent a couple of happy hours, wandering about looking at the animals and also at the people on that mild fall afternoon; perhaps there would not be another such beautiful day for a long time, as the weather was becoming quite chilly now. In the late afternoon we went to Enver's and at their insistence stayed for dinner. It had been a lovely, pleasant day. I could only thank God with all my heart that Jamal was so much better and that the weight of his illness had been lifted from my heart, and I gave money to a beggar as a token of my gratitude for His mercy to us all.

CHAPTER 5

DISCOVERY

October 10: It has been several days since I have had a chance to write, as earlier I was busy with housework, taking Jamal to the doctor, shopping, visiting Emine and Aynur Abla, and was also very tired as well. But there is so much to write about.

How can I explain this new movement within my soul, this response to the environment which is so surely present in spite of all the contradictions and problems of which I am so much aware? Despite the fact that I am in the house and leading a rather routine life, broken only by trips to town and occasional visits, I am not bored nor lonely, rather only frustrated at being unable to communicate properly with people around me. I am finding something—I don't yet know what—for which I searched in vain at home. Day after I am thinking, thinking, thinking . . .

I am alone in the house until mid-afternoon now, as Selim is at the University most of the day and Jamal has gone back to school. There is more time to relax, to do some reading on essential subjects, and for my writing. During the day and evening, in the midst of my activities, I often hear the soft sounds of the *adhan* coming from our mosque; sometimes I step out into the balcony to hear it better, repeating its moving phrases, and slowly its distinctive style is becoming fixed in my mind. We have been to the mosque a few times for *Maghrib* prayer as a family, and twice I also went alone, but as I was the only woman present, I felt rather awkward and decided not to go by myself again. If Selim is at home on Friday, he goes there for *Jum'a* prayer; otherwise, as he is at the University most of the time now, he prays in the room set aside for prayers on the campus.

Cahid Bey had asked that Jamal have tuberculin and various other tests at a hospital, to be done early in the morning. In pursuit of this matter, I had a rather comical experience with illustrates very well the endless inefficiency which one encounters here in any situation involving paper work and documents, for in Turkey the most routine matter—even withdrawing money from one's bank account or getting medical tests done—becomes a legal formality involving tax stamps and official signatures.

On two consecutive days I took Jamal to the hospital breakfastless as he was not permitted to eat before the test. On the second day one test was done, but another procedure, for which I had already paid, could not be performed for some reason. Accordingly, I was sent back to the cashier's office (where I had paid for both tests the previous day, and had been given a receipt with tax stamps and signatures) to get a refund of 30 T.L., leaving Jamal to wait for me in another wing.

Now behold the scene: I go to the cashier, a man who sits in a glassed-in cubicle taking money and writing receipts, and show him the receipt on which the doctor has written that the test has not been done and that the 30 T.L. should be refunded. This cashier speaks no English, but conveys to me that I must go to the *Müdür* (director). Both the *Müdür* and his associate across the hall are out, so I sit down to wait for them. One of the shabby white-clad men who are empoyed for menial tasks and errands comes to me, wanting to be helpful; he looks at the receipt and carries it off somewhere. Meanwhile, the cashier, being disengaged for a moment, looks around to see how I am faring; when he motions me to go to the *Müdür's* office, I reply in gestures that he is out. The cashier comes around to see about it, saying something to the errand man who has the receipt. I am then taken into the cashier's inner office, where I try to explain the situation in Turkish to another official, who returns the receipt to me and again tells me to wait for the *Müdür*. I go back and sit down.

Now another errand man—an old fellow—takes the receipt, and he and two or three others of the same profession discuss the situation and walk about in several different directions trying to do something about it. I have found that in most cases humble people like these are much more sympathetic and helpful than those who have some pride in their office and power in their hands. One of these men takes the receipt into what seems to be a laboratory and talks to someone, and at length he comes back, telling me, *"Hocam geliyor"* (My teacher—or superior—is coming). I sit, thinking of Jamal waiting breakfastless in another wing, very late for school for the second consecutive day. I think about the fact that 30 T.L. is only two dollars, and that the best thing to do would be just to leave and forget about it, but I realize that no Turk in his right mind could or would leave 30 T.L. which is his, and that I will lose face tremendously and be considered a rich, wasteful foreigner who would rather lose his money than time if I do this. Finally I go to the errand man, who is standing there with my receipt, saying that I will come back Friday morning, when I am supposed to return with Jamal. No, no, he says, *"Şimdi hocam geliyor"* (The teacher is coming *now)*, and he does come, from a nearby room—a tall distinguished-looking man with a moustache, wearing a white laboratory coat and having an air of being someone important there. He takes me to the *Müdür's* office (perhaps *he* himself is the *Müdür?)* and says crisply in English, "Yes, please?"

I show the receipt and explain that my son has not had the test indicated and that I am supposed to get a refund of my money. He studies the receipt carefully and at length says reproachfully, "Why did you do this? It is now a big formality to get the money back!" I explain how it happened, and he scribbles something on the back of the receipt. Again I am ushered into the office of the second cashier, where the same man makes a note of my address, and then the first cashier gives me the 30 T.L. without any more difficulties. I thank him and leave, highly amused by all these pompous and cumbersome formalities, and at the same time chagrined at time wasted in this manner without rhyme or reason. I guessed from what I saw that the inefficiency extended to all other areas. I thought of how this sort of artificial generation of busy-work and complications saps one's energies and wears one out, besides preventing any real accomplishment. However, I also felt that in Turkey these sorts of things do not necessarily occur because officials are determined to harrass people, but rather because there are so many rules written into the books that officials and clerks are tied hand and foot by endless regulations, often very arbitrarily applied. In any case, I returned to my patiently-waiting son, gave him his breakfast and medication, and took him to school by taxi.

That afternoon the door bell rang. I peeped out the tiny lens built into the door and saw an unknown girl with a scarf on her head. When I opened the door, she said, "Marian Abla?" in an enquiring tone, and then I knew at once; it was Cemile, the warm-hearted girl with whom I had been corresponding. In the beginning she had obtained my address from a mutual acquaintance and had written to me, her letter beginning, "My dear Muslim sister. . ." Our interest in Turkey had already begun to develop at that time and, impressed by her way of writing and her Islamic feeling, I replied in a long letter. From that time we had exchanged letters, the friendship between us deepening as time passed, and when we prepared to go to Turkey, I had always thought, "Well, we have at least two friends there who are very dear to us, Enver-Emine and Cemile!" After we had rented our apartment I had written her our address and had been expecting her for some time.

I folded her in my arms and brought her inside. In no time at all we were at home with each other, spending the next three hours or so talking like the old friends we already were, exchanging news and ideas and coming to realize that we had indeed not been mistaken in our impressions of each other from our letters.

Cemile was a pleasant-faced girl from Isparta, a town quite far to the south of Ankara, who was doing graduate study and research at a university here. She had originally learned English in high school where, she said, she had had a very outstanding teacher, and she had continued her studies at the university, and read and practiced it at every possible opportunity. She gave me some idea about her study program and her university, her family and her interests, and in turn showed a very real interest in our various Islamic activities at home, our recent travels, and all that had happened to us since our arrival in Turkey. As I knew from her letters, she was a strong, knowledgeable Muslim with deep understanding and commitment, which were clearly expressed in her speech and behavior.

When the children came home from school, she greeted them like dear younger brother and sisters, playing with the girls and talking to Jamal about his interests. Selim, who returned a little while later, was also well impressed with her. When she left with a promise to return soon, I was happy; it is the beginning, I hope— or rather the continuation of—a good friendship.

October 13: It was very essential that I find a way to pursue a regular, formal study of Turkish if I were to progress beyond my hopelessly limited stage. I had talked this over with Emine and she had mentioned a well-qualified teacher about whom she had heard; accordingly I enrolled myself with her for lessons. I have attended three sessions so far, and from the standpoint of learning Turkish it is very satisfactory. The teacher, Zeynep Hanım, a very elegant, attractive matron in early middle age, is very skillful and extremely patient; yet in spite of her excellence as a teacher, I cannot like her as a person.

This lady is so westernized in speech and manner that when she speaks Turkish I have to remind myself that she is, after all, a Turk. She is of that group of Turks who would like to westernize, or rather to de-Arabic-ize Turkish. For example, in the dialogue of the first lesson, we had:

"Nasılsınız?" (How are you?)

"Iyiyim, mersi. Siz nasılsınız?" (I'm fine, thank you. How are you?)

The students took turns repeating this dialogue, and when my turn came, I substituted *"Teşekkür ederim,"* the classical Turkish "Thank you," for *"Mersi,"* which is an expression I despise, borrowed, like many others current in today's Turkish, from French and used by westernized Turks.

"Please," says Zeynep Hanim to me, "say *'Mersi,'* not *'Teşekkür ederim!'* " Again, she teaches us to say *"Bir şey değil,"* an empty expression which literally means, "It's nothing," substituted for the beautiful, meaningful *"Estağfurullah,"* and other of her comments—although she moves along so fast that there fortunately isn't time for too many of them—indicate the same attitude throughout, to be passed along to the foreigners who come to her to learn her country's language and at the same time something of its culture.

Recently Selim and I decided that we should try to see something of Turkey before winter makes traveling impossible. Accordingly, he rented a car and brought it home early Saturday afternoon. Emine had given us some travel folders, and we set off in the direction of Kayseri, our destination being Göreme, where there are interesting rock formations in which Christian hermits had lived many centuries ago.

After leaving Ankara, we traveled in a very bleak area where there was almost no population and very little cultivation; everywhere low mountains, an exposed terrain and an extreme bleakness of landscape. Later some trees and more population appeared, the villages scattered near the road or on hillsides, all cultivable land within sight tilled. The villages in this part of central Anatolia are extremely poor, their crude houses built of mud bricks. Women, especially older ones, wear ample head coverings, the lower part of their faces often hidden, and the colorful dresses of the region. Herds of fine woolly sheep and goats, accompanied by shepherds and an occasional big dog, graze here and there; men ride donkeys, heavily laden. Every little town and village has its mosque, a small, minaretless building in the poorer ones, and in the more prosperous ones a solid structure with a minaret.

The car we had rented did not make very good mileage; the roads were narrow, much-patched and rough, and trucks and buses were almost the only vehicles. We were not able to reach Kayseri by evening as planned and instead stopped at a town called Kirşehir, where we had our dinner in a *lokanta* and, without any difficulty, found accommodations for the night, feeling quite triumphant that, after only a few weeks in Turkey, we were able to manage well enough language-wise, thank God, to be able to travel alone.

In the morning we were ready to set out quite early after the usual breakfast of olives, white cheese, bread and tea. There was nothing of special interest until we reached a small town called Gülşehir, where we encountered a strange topography. Numerous sand-colored spires and pinnacles of rock, most of which had windows and small notches cut into the sides, dotted the landscape. The town stood against a rocky hillside, some of its houses built directly onto or into the rock cliff. We named the strange pointed rock formations, called in Turkish *'peri bacası'* (fairy chimneys), 'galumpoes' for want of a better word.

On through Nevşehir, a bigger town full of people—poor peasants, women with half-covered faces, old-looking young boys with very short-cropped hair and square-shaped heads—and from here down a road past an elegant, very modern hotel, approaching a veritable forest of rock chimneys. Here was a small town built on a hillside, with narrow, stone-paved streets, picturesque, asymmetrical houses, and colorful but very poor people; down the hill (16% grade) were more chimneys in which people evidently live to this day. This was ancient Cappadocia,* and a scene straight out of the remote past, of another time and place; modernization had touched this area with an extremely light hand so far. There was a grace and beauty in the women, with their Anatolian peasant dresses and faces wrapped on top and bottom with a kerchief so that only the eyes and middle portion of the face showed. On our way back through this same little town, we passed a young woman who had lost her head covering; her hair was braided into numerous long, thin plaits, and I wondered how often she would take these all out and braid them back up again.

After the descent from this town, it was a very little way to Göreme; the intervening distance was dotted with rock spires and turrets, some of which had been hollowed out, decorated and used as churches. At Göreme itself, there were veritable ranges of these rock towers stretching out to a great distance. We left the car beside a curio stall and started at once to explore this interesting geological scene; only a few visitors, a number of Turks among them, were present on this balmy, pleasant day. The masses of rock spires which had in times past been inhabited by recluses devoting their lives to God formed a strange, almost unreal panorama around us.

---

* Site of Jewish settlements in the days of the Macabees. According to the New Testament, Jews from Cappadocia were present at Pentecost (Acts 2:9), and the letter of 1 Peter was addressed to the Christians there who were mostly Jewish converts.

There were rock chimneys of all sizes and shapes, with windows and doors cut into their faces; some of these had evidently been inhabited recently, for unsavory traces of modern human beings had been left behind in them, perhaps by hippie squatters. The early Christian monks who had lived here had labored hard to create an atmosphere of piety in the interiors of their cells, and truly they had succeeded well. Tiny chambers and chapels had been hollowed out of the rock towers, some in the shape of a cross, with an arch for each side and a dome in the middle; a few had stone columns or more complicated arches. The simpler ornamentation consisted of plain geometric patterns and crosses painted in red, but there were also very colorful Byzantine-style frescoes depicting the life of Jesus, peace be on him, whom Islam considers a prophet of God, and his apostles, executed in painstaking detail, although in places badly scratched and marred, even with initials carved into them.

The complicated work of forming and decorating all these chambers must have taken many, many years. Apart from admiring the ingenuity and artistry of these efforts, I was also very much moved to think of the devotion and love of God which had impelled men to leave the world to live as a community in that strange, barren place; for although there is neither asceticism nor priesthood in Islam, God Himself has testified to the devotion of many Christian monks and priests in the Holy Qur'an.*

The main part of the rock complex extended for miles and miles and must have numbered many hundreds, even thousands, of individual rock spires, although obviously all of them had not been inhabited; similar formations were to be found in other areas nearby and even in other parts of Turkey. We wandered about from chimney to chimney, exploring chambers in upper and lower stories which communicated with other rooms by means of low tunnels, trying to take in the details, making photographs, and thinking of those who had lived there in centuries past.

* Holy Qur'an, *al-Maida* 5:85-88.

It was late in the morning before we paused to consider the time. It would take about six hours to reach Ankara from here, and it was possible to return either by way of Kayseri, or to visit an ancient underground city about which we had heard near Nevşehir and then return through Hacıbektaş, a small town we had passed on our way where stood the tomb and *tekke*—a gathering place for adherents of a Sufi order—of the Turkish saint Hacı Bektaş Veli. We decided on the latter course of action, retracing our route to Nevşehir and out the other side of town. When we reached the next little town, we followed signs for the buried city, and leaving our car in a dingy parking area, paid admission and passed through a door in a low outcropping of rock.

A strange, unbelievable world lay here under the ground: a labyrinthine set of chambers, without any light whatsoever from outside (but now illuminated electrically); low, narrow tunnels in which one had to bend almost double to stand or walk; and a series of levels or floors, one below the other, to what depth below ground level we could not determine, for one bare rock chamber led to another just like it and each appeared indistinguishable from the other. There was no way even to guess how these chambers and tunnels had been constructed nor how people had managed to sustain life in them.

It was not a place to stay in nor to explore extensively, for there was nothing to see except unadorned chambers and tunnels cut out of rock, apparently without an end. And after we had been there for a while, each of us began to feel very much boxed-in, not only by the crowd of visitors in those narrow passages, but also by the place itself; the thought of an electricity failure (a common enough occurrence in Turkey) did not leave my mind. I think all of us shared the same strong desire to get out into the open again, but when we looked for the way out, we only found ourselves in the same place in which we had been previously, without any sign of exit.

After more wandering, we presently found the entrance and breathed the clear, crisp air outside with a sigh of relief. It was a place well worth seeing, but also a place from which one wanted to escape very soon! The travel brochure gave no information concerning the ancient inhabitants of the underground city, but I heard it said that a colony of Christians had lived there in early times in order to escape persecution. Their situation must have been grave indeed, I thought, to live in such extreme and unbelievably difficult circumstances.

Back to the road again, with a stop for lunch, as we retraced our route of the preceding day to the little town of Hacıbektaş; we left the car opposite the *tekke* of Hacı Bektaş Veli, the founder of the Bektaşi order of dervishes, which is now a museum. Several buildings stood within the *tekke* compound—a mosque, the communal quarters of the dervishes, and the building housing the tomb of its fourteenth century founder who, it is said, was a very learned and saintly Muslim, although unfortunately many of the followers of the order he established had somehow degenerated very markedly during the course of the centuries. We at once encountered a group of moustachioed men who started talking to Selim, and when they learned that we were Muslims, they became our friends and guides.

In the communal building there was a small chamber where, our companions explained in Turkish, the dervishes had gathered for their devotional practices. In the vast kitchen, a collection of cooking utensils, including two enormous copper vessels, each having four handles for lifting, were exhibited. There was also a beautiful old-style Turkish dining chamber, with carpets on the floor, cushions along the wall, and a low, round table on which stood a large covered vessel, with a spoon provided for each diner.

We now went toward the building housing the tomb of the founder, passing through a portal where, unexpectedly and—we thought—very inappropriately, stood a bust of Kemal Atatürk; for although the place was now a museum administered by a branch of the Turkish government, it seemed to us rather too much that an image of this questionable leader should appear in this place which had been devoted solely to the glory and worship of God. By now we had seen Atatürk's pictures, statues and busts in a great many places. This was nothing unusual, as pictures and statues of national heroes are displayed in many countries, but in a Muslim country like Turkey it was yet another incongruous element because Islam very strongly discourages such depictions; moreover, in Turkey there seemed to be altogether too many of these, in too many places, and almost all of them were strikingly ugly and repulsive. In each of the children's classrooms at school I had seen an Atatürk head plus a large statue in the corridor. Now the Turks who were with us made derogatory remarks about the bust, pointing to it and making pushing gestures with their hands to show that this 'idol' should be thrown down.

In the building housing the tomb of Hacı Bektaş Veli, which was very clean, beautiful and well-maintained, a number of objects were displayed, museum-style, and there were several tombs covered with green embroidered cloth. The tomb of the founder was in a small separate chamber; we recited *al-Fateha* beside it and at each group of other tombs, accompanied by the men who explained what we were seeing to Selim. As we were coming out of the building, the *adhan* for the *Dhuhr* prayer was called from the *tekke's* mosque and we went to pray; there was an upstairs gallery for women in which the girls and I were the only worshippers. Prayers in Turkish mosques generally have Qur'anic recitations before and after the *salat* itself, with the customary *du'as* and *dhikr* with the use of *tesbihs*. Larger mosques have a government-appointed *imam* who leads the prayer and another functionary who recites from the Qur'an, generally with very good intonation and pronunciation. Turkish *imams* wear black robes and a red *fez* wound around with a white turban during prayers, but they are prohibited by law from wearing this dress outside the mosque.

When the prayer was over, we were quite concerned about the time, for it was now past three o'clock and we must reach Ankara by evening. Night driving had proved to be very hazardous the previous night since the lights of our car were very dim; several times we had almost run into horse-drawn carts, unable to see them until we were almost upon them. Our companions pressed us very warmly to drink tea with them, but when Selim explained that we must reach Ankara before dark, they did not insist further and walked to the car with us, wishing us a safe trip as we resumed our journey, very happy to have met with them.

The rest of the trip was totally uneventful, as we retraced the route of the previous day. Nightfall found us still some distance from Ankara, and we had to take cover behind the lights of another car in order to manage with our weak illumination. We reached the city, had dinner at a restaurant at Kızılay, and returned home. It had been a very enjoyable and interesting trip, but since its cost had been an exhorbitant 1400 T.L., a month's salary for many middle class Turks, we decided that in the future we must do our traveling by bus.

It is early morning. Asleep again after *Fajr* prayer, I am jolted awake by the loud ringing of the door bell. It is the *kapıcı* with his basket containing loaves of Turkish bread, which he takes around to every apartment in the building in the morning and again late in the afternoon; Jamal jumps out of bed and answers the door, telling him that we do not need bread this time. A little later the bell rings again; this time it is the boy who sells eggs, which we buy daily, and yogurt. A box containing change is kept on the dining table near the door, and it usually contains enough coins and bills to take care of these transactions and the grocery shopping as well.

There is another regular tradesman, and this is the *sucu*—the water seller. In Ankara as in many other places in Turkey, many people do not drink the tap water because it contains large amounts of minerals and is said to be harmful; hence water from springs, carried in huge glass bottles, is brought from house to house by truck or horse and wagon. We usually buy this water twice a week, the *sucu* coming with one of his enormous sealed bottles on his shoulder; his partner is a boy, perhaps his son, of ordinary stature, who seems to find no difficulty in lifting or carrying these huge, heavy bottles all day long. They always take off their shoes at the door and enter in their stocking feet in order not to soil the floor with dirt from the street, pouring the water into our big plastic storage vessel which has a faucet for withdrawing water. Many times, without this reserve supply, we would be in real difficulty, for the water is often cut off unexpectedly, occasionally for long periods, and we sometimes have to use our spring water for making *wudu* and other necessities besides drinking and cooking.

This morning the *kapıcı's* wife, Gül Hanım, is cleaning. As always she tries to talk to me; by now I can make out a very little of what she says in her eastern dialect with the help of the dictionary, and I can also converse with her a little, although she constantly asks me why I don't learn Turkish. She tells me that she is going to visit her mother in her village near Diyarbakır for a few days, and I am happy for her because she and her husband work extremely hard day after day without any time off. She seems to like me because I am a Muslim and because I pray regularly, and always asks me questions, which usually end with her referring to America as a country of *'gâvurs'*—heathens—and it is clear that she thinks it a very unhealthy place for a Muslim to live.

It is noontime, and I am alone in the apartment busy with my reading. Going downstairs to look for the mail, I see Güneş Hanım, my helpful neighbor, passing in the street. We manage to converse a little with her fragmentary English and my fragmentary Turkish, and nothing will do but that I should join her for lunch. I bring the food I have warmed from last night's dinner to share with her, happy for her hospitality. Her apartment is, as always, spotlessly clean, the work of a dedicated Turkish housewife who, like most of her contemporaries, spends most of her day in doing heavy housework and cooking.

She tells me that one of her neighbors is giving a tea and invites me to go with her; I accept with pleasure. Later I learn that many women hold open house for their female friends on a particular day of each month; this is the occasion for this gathering. Presently we go to one of the upstairs apartments in her building together, appropriately dressed for the occasion. A pleasant-looking older woman is the hostess, and there are six or seven ladies present, most of them with their knitting or sewing. As I am a stranger to all of them, Güneş Hanım tells them something about me; I can understand enough to realize that she is telling them that I am a Muslim who observes prayers, undoubtedly quite an unusual phenomenon among this class of half-traditional, half-westernized Turks. However, there is a minimum of curious looks and questions, and I feel at home among them. There is the usual low-keyed, bland chatter which invariably goes on at such women's gatherings, and tea and pastries are served. I have my little dictionary with me and keep looking up words which catch my attention as they come up in the women's conversation. For now Turkish is no longer simply an undifferentiated block of unidentifiable sounds to me; I am able to pick up single words and express simple concepts with the few verbs I know in present and past tense, so excellent and fast-moving has my Turkish instruction been. Thus, Selim with his knowledge of Arabic and Persian, has the vocabulary, and I now have the beginning of the grammar, and together our ability to communicate grows apace.

In the early evening Selim and I go out to buy groceries from nearby shops. At a greengrocer's the shopkeeper is very courteous and pleasant and begins a conversation with Selim. As a rule, wherever we go we are treated not as foreigners or strangers but more like guests or fellow Turks, and this is indeed heartwarming; it has come to feel like home now. By now I have begun to pick up some of that softness of speech which I have noted in Emine and others, and people usually respond to it. After supper there are also visitors, and I am happy with my full, busy day.

October 15: The Turkish lessons move along rapidly, with difficult assignments, but the benefits are great and my ability to communicate is improving daily. In the second lesson we learned the conjugation of the present tense, which is completely regular, and this one single element of grammar opened up to me in one sweep, as it were, the whole door of communication, which previously had not only been shut but had also been an absolutely impenetrable mystery. With a few verbs, some nouns and a slight knowledge of other very basic grammatical principles, I was suddenly, to Aynur Abla's great astonishment, able to speak, and I now began to grasp the nature of some of the sounds I had heard repeated over and over but whose elements and relationships I had not been able to comprehend at all.

Turkish is a language of great complexity due to the fact that grammatical forms are constructed largely by adding suffixes, one on top of the other, so that even if one knows nouns and verbs it is nevertheless impossible to read even elementary Turkish until one has mastered the complex elements of construction-formation through suffixing. Arabic and Persian words, which have been a part of Turkish for centuries and which still form a very large percentage of its total vocabulary, are now regarded as 'foreign' and 'backward,' and many have been gradually replaced with newly-invented, synthetically-fabricated words, with the effect of creating a great gap in communication between the older and younger generations, and of making Turkish, which was a very rich language, an impoverished one, as one newly-coined word is used to express several meanings and to replace several words of different shades of meaning. As for the basic language and grammar, they have their origins in Central Asia, where to this day Turkish and its dialects are spoken by the millions of Turkic peoples of the Soviet Union and China, as well as by Turks living in Yugoslavia, Iraq, Iran, Afghanistan and other countries of the Muslim world. Of course, what I am speaking at this point has very little resemblance to proper Turkish, but it is enough for me just now, and a heady excitement and exhilaration fill me at the thought that I can now communicate at least on an elementary level and at the rapid progress I am making.

Yesterday afternoon I picked up the children at school and we went shopping at Kızılay. We were still there at *Maghrib* time, and as I did not want to miss the prayer at its proper time, I decided that we would go to pray in a place which is used as a mosque in one of the *pasajs* in the vicinity, for there is not a single real mosque in the central part of this city of more than one million.

The mosque was in the basement of a building housing many shops, at the bottom of a flight of steps; the wall beside the stairs was lined with racks for shoes from top to bottom. I supposed that we would remove our shoes at the bottom of the steps rather than at the top, which would mean walking down the stairs in our stocking feet. However, as we started down in our shoes, a man called out to me, saying sharply in English, "Madam! This is a mosque. It is not an arcade market."

My hands were full of bundles, and it was easy to see why he might have thought we were tourists, especially as women and children very seldom pray in Ankara mosques. Nonetheless I was very hurt and humiliated, and replied, "I know that! We are going to pray!" He then grasped the fact that we were Muslims, and said more gently that we should take off our shoes and put them on a rack at the top of the stairs. The mosque was a big carpeted basement hall intersected with square pillars, but without any separate place for women. I was relieved when a man put a *seccade* for us behind a pillar, as I felt very conspicuous; perhaps seldom had any Muslim women or children prayed there before.

As we went out after the prayer, several men gathered around us, one of them asking in English who we were. When I said that we were Americans, he was very much surprised and told the others, who exclaimed in astonishment. He asked for our address and gave me his in return, saying that his adult son who speaks fluent English would come to visit us the next evening. We waited for him the next evening and after that, but he never came, perhaps unable to find our house because of the peculiar numbering of streets in our area, and I was left with a haunting feeling that the man to whom I had talked might go to his grave under the conviction that I had given him a false name and address, for any reason he might choose to believe . . .

Jamal and the girls are very unhappy in school. They say that many of the children are mean and unruly, and complain bitterly about the viciousness of their teachers, who even hit children across the face, such methods apparently being the only effective way they know of keeping discipline. The school is very expensive and continually requires all sorts of extra fees for special clothes or this or that activity. As the children are receiving no special attention which would enable them to learn Turkish and continue their lessons with understanding, we are thinking of changing them to another school where they can be happier. The girls have made a few acquaintances in our neighborhood and often play outside with them now, and Jamal stays busy with reading and his own projects.

October 16: This is a country steeped in contradictions, so much engrained in the social structure and way of thinking that most people are unaware of them and cannot even begin to explain them.

Here, on the one hand, there is a law that one cannot say anything which is considered offensive against Kemal Atatürk, the 'Father of Turks;' his picture or bust is displayed in every office, public place and school room, in many shops and restaurants, and even in many homes; his statues are scattered here and there in prominent places in every Turkish city and town; and one gets a strange feeling that civil liberties such as freedom of speech, press and religion are not guaranteed to any Turkish citizen if they run counter to what appears to be the First Commandment of Turkey: Speak no evil, hear no evil, think no evil of Him. And the Second Commandment is like unto it: Thou shalt have no other gods before Him; for if He was wrong, thou shalt say that He was right, and if His words and decrees run counter to the word and decree of God, thou shalt do according to Him and not according to God, and shalt say that God's law is old-fashioned, reactionary and backward. Yet at the same time, we see the spirit of Islam very much alive among the people, Islamic religious occasions celebrated with fervor, and the very character and soul of the people founded upon Islamic ways of thinking and living.

These reflections were prompted by the fact that today Selim went to *Jum'a* prayer at Kocatepe Camii, a vast mosque in the Ottoman style being constructed near the center of Ankara. Today is *Berat Kandili,* one of the holy nights of the Islamic year, and Selim estimated that about three thousand men prayed *Jum'a* prayer at Kocatepe Mosque today. On this occasion there are observances in the mosques, readings of the Holy Qur'an and *Mevlûd,* * and exchanges of special sweet dishes and greetings among traditional-minded or religious people.

What can one say? Only that there are two spirits and two forces claiming Turkey and animating its people. This is a land over which successive waves of peoples and cultures have passed; only

---

* Arabic *Milad.* The Turkish *Mevlûd* is a lengthy poem narrating the life of Prophet Muhammad, peace be on him; it is recited on the *Kandils,* to commemorate the birthday of the Holy Prophet, to celebrate a baby's birth, forty days after a death, etc. It is a purely traditional observance, not from Islam. The Turkish *Mevlûd* was written during the fifteenth century by Süleyman Çelebi.

time will tell whether Islam was merely one more wave, to be covered over in our day by secularism and materialism, or whether it was a vital, living reality which can never die out of the life of its people and which, if suppressed, springs to new life with a clear, conscious commitment instead of the traditional acceptance of the religion of one's ancestors without thought or understanding . . .

October 22: Life goes on. Jamal still has a cough and once in a while, especially at night, a more serious problem with difficulty in breathing if the cough is really severe. We have taken the children out of the useless, expensive private school in which they were so miserable and enrolled them in a public school within walking distance, and they are happier there; school is only half-a-day instead of a full day and they are home by lunch time.

It happened by chance that some time ago we met a young couple with a little daughter, the Dogans, whom we have now visited a few times; they had lived in England, and we found that we had many things in common. Bahadir Bey, a government official, is a kind, wise man and a true Muslim, and his wife, Deniz Hanım, a school teacher, is a very warm, sincere and hospitable lady. Some weeks ago Deniz Hanım's elderly, ailing mother, who had lived with them, died. Yesterday was the fortieth day after her death, and in the evening the traditional Turkish observance of *Mevlûd*, which we were invited to attend, was held in her memory.

A large group of relatives and friends had gathered, sitting and talking quitely among themselves, men on one side of the *salon* and women on the other. Presently a tape of the five-centuries-old chanted *Mevlûd* poem narrating the life of the Holy Prohpet, peace be on him, was played. It is in the old classical Turkish which has so many Arabic words and constructions, recited in slow, reverent cadences whose effect is very moving. At first I felt awkward and shy in this gathering, as I was a stranger to everyone present except the hosts, but soon I was just another one of the company which had gathered to recall the life of the Holy Prophet, God's peace and blessings be on him, in memory of the dead woman. Everyone sat listening very quietly, some of the people weeping, and no word was spoken.

After the *Mevlûd*, tea and other refreshments were served, and then a tape of *ilâhis*—Turkish hymns of praise of God or remembrance of His Prophet or other saintly men—was played. This music combined instruments and voices, with a male singer or group of singers; it had a quality of great power, vitality, spiritual depth and inwardness, which I felt to be the product of the deep faith in God of its originators.

As I sat listening, I reflected on the Islamic conception of God. I who have come to Islam by the way of Christianity have now, by the grace of God, refined my conception to such a degree that there is no room in it for anything except the realization of the transcendence, sublimity and greatness of God, Who is far removed from anything which man knows or can conceive of. What thoughtful person is there who, in this age of space travel and ever-increasing knowledge of the vastness and complexity of the universe, can confine his conception of God to that of a super-human being or a bearded dignitary sitting upstairs, unless he has chosen to close his eyes completely to the realities of God's creation? Such anthropomorphic notions are entirely contrary and opposed to the Islamic conception of God. Over and over the Holy Qur'an denies the validity of such ideas, stressing that God, the Creator and Sustainer of all that exists, is exalted far above and not to be compared to any of His creatures, whose characteristics as limited and finite beings are not applicable to Him: "Say, God is One, God is the Self-Sustaining; He begets not nor is He begotten, and there is none like Him;" "God—there is no deity but He, the Living, the Eternal . . ."*

With this purity and sublimity of conception, the possibility of attempting to bring God down to the level of His creatures has never existed among Muslims, as it has among people of almost every other religion; in Islam there is nothing like the notion of God's having any similarity or kinship to human beings, even to the very best of men, His prophets, may His peace and blessings be on them all. Unfortunately, however, today many Muslims have adulterated their Islam by all sorts of attitudes and practices which are totally at variance with the concept of God's absolute sovereignty and authority over man, the true meaning of *"La ilaha illa Allah"*—There is no deity except God. Among these are the exaggerated respect, reverence and even unquestioned obedience which many Muslims give to religious leaders or to *pirs, walis* and *shaykhs* living or dead, which even goes so far as to make supplica-

* Holy Qur'an, *al-Ikhlas*, 112:1-4 and *al-Baqara* 2:255.

tions to them or to venerate their tombs—this although even the Holy Prophet, peace be on him, the best of mankind, whom Muslims love and respect above any other human being, advised his companions, "Do not exaggerate in praising me; rather say, 'He was God's servant,' " rightly fearing the consequences of such exaggeration. We further see many who call themselves Muslims giving too much deference and honor to those in authority among them, even though their personal lives (and in the case of rulers and government, their rule) may be totally at variance with the laws and standards of Almighty God; we see social status and wealth becoming the ultimate *desideratum* and goal for many so-called Muslims, replacing God as the object of love and worship; and we see that many of those who call themselves Muslims (that is, those who submit to God) are all too often the slaves of their own whims, desires or physical wants rather than of their true Master, God Most High, or again, that they are enslaved by some man-made ideology, system or -ism, although Islam came to liberate man utterly from servitude to anything or anyone other than his Creator and Sustainer. The Muslim, therefore, must not merely be satisfied that he has not contaminated the purity of his belief in *tawheed*—the absolute Oneness of God—but must also stand with utmost vigilance at the door of his own soul and at the gates of society to see that no association with God's power, sovereignty and authority be permitted access ...

It is a little past nine in the morning and there is so much work to do, but still I must say a few more words before I put away the typewriter. At the gathering last night, although we were strangers to everyone present except the hosts, we were accepted and treated as one of the group without question, and I felt completely at home and at ease in the gathering. There was none of that inquisitiveness (or alternately, indifference) with which foreigners are so often treated at home, but rather great friendliness and warmth on the part of a number of people. I don't know if this was because we are friends of Bahadir Bey and Deniz Hanım or because we are Muslim or for some other reason, but it was wonderful to me, especially when I reflect on the fact that we can hardly communicate even the most simple ideas in Turkish as yet. This is true goodness and sincerity among human beings, this is what Islam is. No legislation, no amount of speech-making, peace demonstrations, "What-this-world-needs-is-love" slogans, not the United Nations nor any other 'peace-loving' organization in this world can ever hope to produce its like!

CHAPTER 6

QUEST FOR UNDERSTANDING

October 28: Today is the beginning of the *Cumhuriyet Bayramı*—the Republic Festival—marking the establishment of the Turkish Republic in 1923. When I went to Ulus this afternoon, all buildings were hung with red-and-white Turkish flags, big and small. Huge heads of Atatürk printed on cloth hung from many buildings, extraordinary-looking depictions reminding me of the "Big-brother-is-watching-you" slogan in Orwell's book, *1984*. These portraits (or occasional full figures) of Atatürk are ten to fifty times life-size, done in very lurid colors with the most unpleasant expressions of countenance; on one building you see an immense scowling head with a green complexion against a red background, on another a yellow face against green, and so on. On this occasion statues of Atatürk are also decorated with wreaths and elegant floral displays like offerings placed before an idol.

I have been reading to get some background about this Mustafa Kemal—or, as he called himself, Kemal Atatürk, preferring to drop the 'Mustafa,' it is said, because it is another name for the Holy Prophet, peace be on him—who figures so prominently, although he has been dead these more than thirty years, in modern Turkish life. You cannot move from your house without encountering his image—either a picture or head or statue—and his words and ideas perhaps many times over. Strangely enough, it is a very conspicuous feature of the Turkish representations of their hero that they almost invariably depict him as somber, frowning and frightening-looking; evidently, judging from all I have seen and read, this was his habitual expression.

After centuries of rule of sultan-caliphs of the Ottoman dynasty, of varying characters and abilities, a movement toward westernization began in Turkey during the eighteenth century, gradually gaining momentum as the economically, militarily and industrially undeveloped Ottoman Empire suffered increasingly in the world of the European power struggle. Although once incomparably superior to Europe militarily and in its genius for science, learning and other expressions of culture, the Muslim world had become stagnant and rigidified and had lost its dynamism, and hence could be more or less easily dominated by superior physical forces; for at the same time as it lost the dynamism which Islam imparted to it, the quality of its material, intellectual and cultural life also declined, rendering it an easy prey to the more powerful European nations and to. ideologies imported from Europe which were not only believed to be inseparably connected with its material superiority but also considered to be essential for its attainment by the Muslim world. *

The early twentieth century witnessed the disintegration of the Ottoman Empire. During World War I, it joined Germany in an attempt to defeat Britain and France; however, when Germany was defeated, its Ottoman ally naturally shared its fate, and a peace was declared which proposed to put Thrace (now the European part of Turkey) and most of Anatolia (its very much larger Asian wing) under joint European mandate. It was at this time that Mustafa Kemal, a young officer in the *Sultan's* army, emerged as a dynamic leader who was able to form and take command of nationalist and religious forces within Anatolia. Within a short time this movement had gained much popular support and control, and as it gained momentum Kemal and his forces, although vastly inferior in numbers and strength, succeeded in setting up the first Turkish National Assembly, in compelling the Allied powers to guarantee the territorial integrity of what is now known as Turkey, and in forcing the occupying Greek armies off Turkish soil.

From this beginning, important though it was for ensuring the freedom of Turkey from foreign domination, it was only a matter of time before virtually all power rested in the hands of this new leader and his chosen confederates. After abolishing successively the offices of *sultan* and *khalifa,* he declared Turkey a republic, with

---

* See Note (1).

power vested in a parliament, cabinet and president. At least in theory power was to be shared among these three branches, but in reality Kemal emerged as the dictator of Turkey, while repeatedly claiming that sovereignty rested with the people.

Kemal instituted sweeping 'reforms' for modernizing Turkey and bringing it into the family of 'civilized' nations, which in his conception meant the nations of Europe. Because of his deeply-engrained antipathy toward Islam, his profound sense of humiliation at the backwardness of the Muslim world, and his feeling of awe at the great material achievements of the West, this, to his mind, could only be accomplished by abruptly breaking, once and for all, the hold of Islam over the hearts and lives of the Turkish people. Thus, instead of trying to rectify the abuses of Islam where they existed and attempting to bring about a true understanding and practice of the religion, his reforms aimed at trying to cut the Turks off completely from their sense of Islamic identity, from the social system of Islam, and from the ties with their Islamic past and the rest of the Muslim world.

His method of attaining these ends was completely dictatorial and arbitrary, over-riding and suppressing all opposition, entirely without reference to what the majority of Turks wanted, or indeed what they urgently needed, despite his continuous reiteration of the principle of popular sovereignty.* It included such measures as prohibiting the wearing of the traditional *fez* and the *kalpak,* and ordering instead the wearing of Western-style hats and caps; replacing the Islamic calendar with the Gregorian and changing the day of rest from Friday, on which the weekly obligatory congregational prayer is observed throughout the Muslim world, to Sunday;** replacing the civil and family laws based on the Islamic system with other codes copied from various countries of Europe; changing the script from Arabic to Latin and expurgating Arabic and Persian words from the Turkish language, replacing them with unknown 'old Turkish,' as well as newly-coined 'pure Turkish,' words in an attempt to break with the Islamic (although not with the *pre*-Islamic) past and to isolate Muslim Turkey from the remainder of the Muslim world; encouraging Turkish women to copy their highly-'emancipated' European counterparts in dress, free

---

*   Notes (24-25)
** For 'Hat Reform' see Notes (4-6); change of calendar and rest day, Note (7).

association with men, and Western-style social and occupational activities; promulgating secularism as the basic principle of the Turkish state; and making various religious reforms and suppressing religious education.* Most ironically, at the same time as Kemal so vigorously promoted westernization, insisting that Turks must and should, whether they liked it or not, turn themselves into Europeans (the very Europeans against whose political and military domination he had struggled so valiantly to preserve his homeland!), he also eagerly promoted the notion of Turkish nationalism, reminding Turks of their supposed pre-Islamic roots in Central Asia. The centuries of Islamic civilization which lay between Turkey's ancient pre-Islamic past and the future Europeanization which he envisioned had no real significance or importance in his mind—the culture, the achievements, the very life of the past eight hundred years of the nation simply canceled out of the history of his people by one man's whim!

Although Kemal was exceedingly able, power corrupted him totally. In his personal life he was sexually promiscuous and a chronic alcoholic;*** his death was attributed to cirrhosis of the liver secondary to alcoholism. From his youth he had had great doubts and reservations about Islam, and in later years is said to have been a convinced atheist.**** After his death, Ismet Inönü, one of his top generals, carried on the work of reform and the purging of Islam. During his regime there was a period during which, in many places in Turkey, it was forbidden to teach the Holy Qur'an and to read it in Arabic; some mosques were turned into storage depots and even used as stables, and Islam was treated as a dead, useless encumbrance upon a so-called progressive, modernizing Turkey, pointing only to backwardness and fanaticism.

However, once the Peoples' Party *(Halk Partisi)* of Atatürk and Inönü was removed from power, Inönü's successors did much to

* For change of legal code, see Note (8); alphabet and language reforms, Notes (9-11); emancipation of women, Notes (12-14); secularism, Notes (15-16); religious reforms and religious education, Notes (18-20).
** See Notes (21-22).
*** See Note (26).
**** See Note (23).

rectify this intolerable situation, imposed by dictatorship and in no way corresponding to the thinking or wish of the majority of Turks. Islam, which had been so much crushed as to have been almost destroyed in the life of the people, began to re-emerge,* and thus today, as the result of all these factors, Turkey is in a palpable state of ideological crisis. The struggle—politically, economically, socially, morally—between the various anti-Islamic, secular-materialistic elements and those who are turned toward God and Islam continues, as we are seeing. Firm in the hearts of the common people and of a small number of the educated and well-placed, Islam and its spiritual and moral values are officially in disrepute with those who would have Turkey be a part of Europe rather than of the Muslim world, where, geographically, linguistically, culturally, religiously and ethnically, it obviously belongs. Little wonder, then, at the sense of conflict and division which pervades this society, the sense of unresolved ideological dilemma and confusion!

October 29: The celebration of the holiday continues. On the way to Ulus yesterday afternoon I saw a group of students on parade from one of Ankara's leading private high schools, the girls dressed in very short grey band uniforms, with white gloves and claret red caps. I continued to speculate on what the next generation of well-to-do, educated, city-bred Turks will be like, and what this carbon-copy imitation of the West in external aspects will eventually do to this society, may God help it!

This imitation and loss of religious and national identity is most obvious in the appearance of many city girls and women. Turks are very nationalistic, but this national pride is totally lost when it comes to accepting European ways as the prototype of all that is admirable. Thus, at Kızılay and other places, westernized girls and women delight in exhibiting the very latest European styles—the wide bell-bottom pants, mini-, midi-, and maxi-dresses and coats—and every newstand sells European fashion magazines featuring the latest designs and patterns, which are also used by dressmakers for fabricating the most up-to-date Western fashions for their clientele. I have begun to realize how much it costs a Turkish

* See Notes (28-29).

woman to dress so stylishly, for the prices of the elegant ready-made clothes one sees in the shop windows of Kızılay and Ulus, or alternatively the more customary cost of fabric and tailoring, are extremely high, as are all prices. These well-dressed, ultra-modern girls attract much attention, each appearing to try to outdo the other in her wardrobe, so that Kızılay at times appears to be a fashion parade route. The numerous *kuaför* shops do a thriving business, and beauty-shop hairdos and manicures, often created by the hands of male *kuaförs,* are extremely common among upper class women. However this sort of fashion-madness, thank God, goes on as yet only among very modern and westernized women, while others are very moderate and reasonable in their habits.

It is almost *Ramadan.** We have now been in Turkey for fifty-nine days. All is familiar now, although each day when I go outside our apartment or hear Turks talking in the street, I still pull myself together with a little shake, realizing all over again that this is the language in which I must now communicate with everyone around me, which, although I am no longer cut off as I was before, still requires a real effort. Now I think the time has come when the strangeness and the frustration have worn off somewhat when the worry I felt from time to time about handling things has passed, when I am able to some extent to communicate, to survey our situation here more realistically and with less wishful thinking or anxiety entering into my judgment.

It is all, to speak honestly, a very indistinguishable mixture of good and bad. I have not talked about Selim's research and study program before, for his classes began only a short time ago and it took him a while to evaluate the situation. All-in-all, his program is well-organized, his professors helpful, his courses useful. However, the situation as a whole at the Middle East Technical University (known as M.E.T.U.) where he is studying is disturbing.

---

* The Islamic month of special devotional activity, during which fasting between dawn and sunset by abstaining from food, drink, smoking and sexual relations is obligatory on all Muslim adults. As the Islamic *(Hijrah)* calendar is lunar rather than solar, the dates of *Ramadan* and all Islamic observances and dates travel backward in relation to the solar calendar approximately twelve days each year. (Continued on next page.)

M.E.T.U. has long been the breeding ground of the student communist movement in Turkey, from where it has spread to other universities in Ankara and other cities, and it appears to be gaining momentum already very early in the semester this year. I have visited the University, which lies off one of the main roads out of Ankara, some seven or eight kilometers from the city and at some distance from the nearest populated area. It has a large, adequate, modern campus with starkly modernistic buildings constructed of grey cement, having an air of incompleteness. There, as at Hacettepe University and other institutions, the walls of buildings are decorated with scrawled political slogans and political posters. The appearance of many of the M.E.T.U. students is also noteworthy. They do not look like other Turks, but have closed-up, unsmiling faces, many with long hair and the long, drooping moustache which is the hallmark of the Turkish communist, in contrast to the clear, open face and short, trim hair and moustache of the average Turk. The students appear to run the University and apparently have more to say about its affairs than the administration and faculty, and the leftist trend among students is so strong that people who hold other views are either a tiny vocal minority or are silent *en masse*.

This is Selim's world at present, apart from home and friends. My experiences, quite naturally, are altogether different and more positive. The Turkish lessons, my friendship with Emine and Cemile, who has proved to be a very dear, loving and truly Islamic girl, doing errands or shopping, my reading and writing, apart from the family and household, all make my life now pleasant, in-

---

In practice, the observance of fasting is commonly as follows: generally a meal (*suhoor*) is eaten very early in the morning, ending before the first light of dawn appears; this is followed by *Fajr* prayer at dawn. The fast is broken at sunset with food and drink (*iftar*), followed by *Maghrib* prayer. Besides the usual daily prayers, additional prayers, called *tarawih*, are observed either collectively or individually throughout the month. *Ramadan* is not simply a period for refraining from satisfying otherwise-lawful bodily needs; it is also a month of especially intensive religious activity, and fasting moreover means controlling the tongue and temper as well as the appetites. Unlike the fasting of other religions, the fasting of *Ramadan* does not carry the implication of penance for sins; rather it is prescribed as a means of learning self-control and self-discipline and increased devotion to God.

teresting and full of good experiences.

Yet it is such a strange land in so many ways. The greatest need among all Muslims—nations, groups and individuals—throughout the world today is unity. We have realized that there are a number of Islamic groups and organizations in Turkey, most of them composed largely of educated people. Each has a different approach and emphasis, each is working for Islam, and each is presumably sincere; however, there is no cooperation, no working together among them, and one gets the impressions that each is convinced that there is only one acceptable approach, that all others are wrong, and that it has a monopoly on being right and truly Islamic. This goes so far that even among sincere Muslims, numerous rumors are circulated about the various groups and their leaders, many of which we have heard by now, always adding to the mistrust and lack of unity. It is thus very difficult to evaluate any of these groups objectively, since Muslims from one group often disagree with, mistrust and try to discredit all others, and it often appears that Turkey is run by rumor and suspicion.

I mention this here to show that there clearly *are* many Islamic groups in Turkey. In total these certainly include quite a large number of educated Turks, but under these circumstances each group goes its own separate way alone, and thus no concerted effort is ever made for the cause of Islam. There is a very urgent necessity for a mass-scale movement of committed Muslims working and cooperating together, forgetting their minor differences; but in the meantime, as they do not come together to formulate a joint plan of action, Turkey as a whole drifts further and further away from Islam, divided by small and petty differences, in the grip of its enemies both within and without. And yet, as the very soul of this land has been almost completely destroyed by the shattering break with its past and its Islamic identity and traditions, it is perhaps rather a source of wonder that such movements and groups of God-loving, God-fearing people exist at all. I pray for the time when all Turkish Muslims will come together under the banner of Islam to cooperate with one another with sincerity and brotherliness.

November 5, 5 *Ramadan: Ramadan* began here without any notice-able change, except that each evening at *iftar* time there is a spe-cial radio program with the reading of the Qur'an and *ney* music. *Tarawih* prayers are observed in all the mosques each evening and the minarets are illuminated with lights.

I have not been well, and Nura and Jamal have also been sick, Nura with a bad nighttime cough and Jamal troubled with asthma-tic symptoms, especially at night. One afternoon he went out to play with boys who were having a *futbol* game in the street, and presently came in wheezing badly, almost unable to breathe and later coughing very hard because he had been running. Thus it has become, for the present, a chronic problem; the poor fellow cannot do any physical exercise or participate in the normal activi-ties of his age without its triggering off an asthmatic attack, al-though prior to our coming to Ankara he had never had any problems of this sort and the contributing factors are not known. He spends all his free time reading or working on his own projects, which he certainly enjoys, but he feels at the same time, I know very well, an acute sense of dejection about his problem. I have spent much time with him, especially during his earlier illness, trying to keep up his courage, letting him know that no one goes through the world without trials and difficulties, and that as a Muslim he should be patient and not lose courage. We have also talked for long periods at a stretch about political affairs, econo-mics, religion and many other aspects of life, and his understanding has broadened immensely as the result of his travels and new exper-iences, even in this short time and with these problems, thank God.

November 20: Lately there have been various functions and gather-ings, meeting some new friends, invitations to *iftars* and so on. I had a very pleasant and surprising experience one evening when we were invited to *iftar* at a home in which men and women were separated and dined in different rooms. The hostess (whom I was meeting for the first time) and I were the only women. Hence for me it was sink or swim; either I would manage with the Turkish I knew or we would sit silent. And I managed it, *masha'Allah*, I managed it! We talked steadily during the whole mealtime, with great goodwill and consideration (and no doubt a considerable stretch of the imagination) on her part; I somehow found the words for whatever I wanted to say, and it was an enjoyable and quite triumphant evening for me, thank God.

The last few days, however, have been quite difficult. Jamal's asthma flared up into a very nasty attack, despite some new medications; we then took him to a new set of doctors, who gave much helpful advice and a different kind of medication, on which he is now doing much better, *Alhamdulillah*.

One basic fact has become clear to us by now, namely, that Ankara is different from the rest of Turkey; other areas of the country are not like this, from all accounts, even Istanbul with its westernized and un-Islamic elements. We are impatient to go to Konya, Bursa, the Black Sea, the Mediterranean coast and other places, if possible, to get a glimpse of the real Turkey. *Insha'Allah* we will be able to do it in the spring. As February is a vacation month at M.E.T.U. between the two semesters, we are planning to travel to Pakistan to visit our relatives around the beginning of that month, and thus we must conserve our resources of money and energy for this major trip; moreover, winter is not a time for traveling in Turkey, since the weather is bad in many areas. Ankara is now cold, invariably cloudy, often muddy from rain, and its air unbelievably polluted with soft-coal smoke from all the stoves and furnaces of the city, all of which is highly conducive to prolonged respiratory infections and makes getting about difficult. The problem of getting around in Ankara is, however, a subject all by itself.

The traffic in Ankara is terrible, a driver's nightmare. There are three forms of public transport here—bus, *dolmuş* and taxi—which make up the bulk of the traffic, besides private cars, which, as they are enormously expensive to buy and quite costly to maintain and operate, are few. All taxis and *dolmuşes* are huge American cars (station wagons are used as *dolmuşes* as much as possible), some of immense antiquity, kept running somehow year after year.

While there is on paper a book full of traffic regulations, it is difficult to see much evidence of any law or system in the traffic patterns of this city. Lanes are unmarked and everyone drives essentially how he pleases, passing in crowded streets, making wild left turns from side streets into oncoming traffic, using the horn at random even if there is nothing in the way, and disregarding pedestrians, who in turn disregard traffic and even signal lights in the city. At times I get the impression of a city of maniacs driving! Thus, while Ankara is certainly in the twentieth (or even the twenty-first) century in terms of the vast numbers of vehicles on its crowded streets, Turks who do the driving often appear to belong to another period in their lack of comprehension of the potentially lethal qualities of motor vehicles. If one goes outside the city, numerous accidents are to be seen, most of them involving buses, for people travel from city to city mainly by bus, and on the highways trucks and buses play grim games with each other, trying to pass on the two-lane highways.

One wonders about the real meaning behind this disorderly, mad traffic when one observes the gentle and kindly spirit of the average Turk; but then, taxi or *dolmuş* drivers are not as a rule gentle, kindly average Turks but more often those who have parted company with the more wholesome ways of the society. These drivers seem in general to be a rather rough lot, that spoiled and corrupted element which is to be found everywhere in the East and which is a very harmful influence on the society. Although I have driven with several pleasant, courteous older chauffeurs, enjoying an exchange of remarks with them, they are unfortunately hardly typical of the majority of their profession.

Then there is the problem of buses. There are far too few of them and they are often so crowded at rush-hour that it is impossible to accommodate all the persons who are waiting. I have seen people push themselves in when the bus was too full to hold one single person more as the back door closed shut on them, and once I saw an elderly man knocked down (and set on his feet again) by the pushing passengers, so thick is the crush. As one enters by the rear door and exits by the front, when someone who is near the back wants to get out, he has to squeeze his way out by main force, a distressing situation indeed, especially for women.

The *dolmuşes* are just as bad. At evening rush hour there are enormously long lines of people waiting to go home from the city by *dolmuş*. As on buses, since there is no separation of men and women, a woman may be sandwiched between man (and *vice-versa)*, their bodies touching, and I have heard of very unpleasant incidents occurring under these conditions. It is indeed disgraceful for a country with a Muslim majority not to have public transportation systems which are more considerate of the dignity of Muslim women.

Ankara is a modern city by Middle Eastern standards, with its neon lights, many modern-design buildings, shops displaying the latest fashions, very numerous banks, night clubs, the national opera, ballet, theater, and so on, exactly resembling a European city and not having the redeeming features of Istanbul by which it can be recognized as Muslim. One can only observe, listen and try to understand how a society afflicted by such a far-reaching split in its collective personality can continue to function, for it is necessary to be blind, deaf, and dumb not to perceive the other, the *real* Turkey, under the veneer of westernization even in this, the country's most westernized city. When I talk with some common Turk—a shopkeeper or even a menial worker—with his rough dignity and innate courtesy, I am struck all over again by the realization that I did not know what real manners, real politeness, real civilized behavior were until I came here. These are the beautiful distinguishing characteristics of the traditional Turk, which come entirely from his Islamic heritage and which today are rapidly being lost among all those who have turned away from its humanizing traditions.

November 30, the last day of *Ramadan*. On *Lailat al-Qadr** we went with Enver's family to Hacı Bayram Camii, a very old and much-revered mosque in Ulus—the special mosque of Ankara—for *tarawih* prayers. As soon as we reached the compound of the mosque we encountered beggars, sitting or standing in humble attitudes. It was a bitterly cold, windy night, and I felt so much for those who sat on the freezing pavement, showing their crippled or deformed limbs—several men, two women (one with a baby), and a

---

* The Night of Power, commemorating the first revelation of the Holy Qur'an to Prophet Muhammad, peace be on him, about fourteen hundred years ago. It is observed on the night preceding the 27th day of *Ramadan*.

mentally-defective youth who kept laughing. Fortunately we had some coins with us, but I wished that we had many, many more. All during this month we have seen beggars wherever we have gone, and many have come to our door as well.

The men and Jamal went in the main entrance of the old mosque, while Emine, Aynur Abla, the girls and I went around to the side entrance for women. Here we encountered such a number of women coming down the stairway of the women's gallery that we could only with difficulty reach the top. However, the gallery itself was so crowded that we could not find any space for ourselves, and thus there was no alternative except to leave—without praying *tarawih* in congregation on this very sacred occasion, and without even catching a glimpse of the mosque, which we had not seen so far. And this in a city where women ordinarily never pray in mosques! Enver was looking for us below when we went down, and we left amidst the wretched host of the miserable and defective in the frosty darkness and bitter wind, thanking God for His abundant blessings to us.

Although *Ramadan* in Ankara has been quite inconspicuous, nonetheless its collective devotional aspect has been evident here despite the unobtrusiveness of its observance, and despite the fact that in Turkey, unlike most other Muslim countries, no alteration is made in office and work hours to compensate for the difference in living habits during this month. This spirit is seen mainly among the devoted Muslims who frequent the mosques and observe the discipline of *Ramadan* faithfully. For them it is not simply a month of abstaining from the gratification of physical needs by day, but also a period of increased and concentrated devotional activity: reading the Qur'an, if possible in entirety, observing *tarawih* prayers in the mosque or at home, giving charity to the extent they can afford, restraining the tongue and temper—in short, a month for worshipping and serving God with increased piety, zeal and devotion, and there is no doubt that even among those who are merely marginally religious or even only semi-traditional, there is a vestige of 'religious' feeling during this month.

As always, of course, there are the usual contradictions. If one is out at *iftar* time, he can observe shopkeepers in their shops breaking their fasts and praying *Maghrib* prayer right behind their counters. But imagine a typical *bakkal*—a grocer's shop—where all foodstuffs besides meat, fruits and vegetables are sold, one wall of which is covered with shelves holding bottles of wine, whiskey, etc., in which pious Muslim shopkeeper who has fasted all day prays *Maghrib* prayer one minute and sells a bottle of *şarap* the next! For in Turkey, as in many other 'Muslim' countries today, beer, wine and liquor, which are absolutely prohibited by Islam, are available without license at all liquor shops and many *bakkals,* and it is nothing unusual for the *bakkal's* proprietor to be a Muslim who prays regularly and who decorates the walls of his shop with framed Qur'anic inscriptions; nevertheless, these people apparently see no contradiction between their religious obligations and earning a large proportion of their income with this prohibited trade. If this is pointed out to one of them, he will merely tell you, "Well, the *bakkal* across the street, the two on the next street and the one on the corner all sell alcoholic beverages. If I don't I'll go out of business, and God knows that one has to live. Besides," he may add virtuously, "I only sell it. I don't drink myself."

Turks are certainly not unaware of the Qur'anic prohibition against alcohol; they simply choose to ignore it as unimportant, and as a rule only the staunch practicing Muslims—those who are considered backward and fanatical by many—do not drink. The government itself owns manufactures for producing alcoholic beverages, and many of its officials drink, perhaps under the impression that drinking and intoxication represent a step up the ladder of 'civilization' because they are common in the 'advanced' countries of the West!

Thus our *Ramadan* in Turkey has come and gone, and tomorrow is *'Eid al-Fitr.* * This month we have been more troubled with

* *'Eid al-Fitr,* the Festival of Fast-Breaking, comes at the completion of the month of *Ramadan.* It is a time of great rejoicing and celebration throughout the Muslim world.

collective health problems—Jamal's, Nura's, mine—than at any other period. Because of a prolonged bout of gastritis, I myself have been able to fast for only four days during the entire month, but *insha-'Allah* I will be able to make it up later when I am well.*

This evening, everything being finished and ready for 'Eid, we had the last *iftar* with Enver's family. Later in the evening Selim and I went to Ulus, crowded on the eve of the festival with more people in the streets than I had ever seen in any American city, even before Christmas, to look for some persons to whom we might give our *zakat al-fitr*,** for we had searched in vain for a beggar in our part of town. We finally found three beggars on the same street and Selim gave them the money.

During this month, when there have been beggars coming to the door as well as many times the usual number in the streets, I have given to all I saw whenever I had money and was thankful for the opportunity to do anything good. Earlier in *Ramadan,* a woman in the dress of a villager, her face partly covered, stopped me in the street near our house as I was on my way to a Turkish lesson, silently holding out a prescription to ask for money to buy medicine. I gave her whatever little bit of change I had in my purse and went my way, but when I had gone a little distance I began to feel very badly that I had not given her more, thinking of what her needs might be. I looked back; she was sitting on the curb near our house. Returning hurriedly, I told her, *"Bir dakika"* (Just a minute), and went into the apartment while she waited outside the door. I took the smallest bill available, which happened to be a 50 T.L. note, from the money box on the table and gave it to her, explaining as well as I could with my limited Turkish that as I was sick and unable to fast, I was giving her this to her in lieu of

---

* Persons who are ill, travelers, and women during menstruation, post-partum bleeding, pregnancy and lactation have permission not to fast for the duration of these conditions, but all missed fasts must be made up before the beginning of the next *Ramadan* if possible. However, if one has a chronic or permanent illness making fasting hazardous or impossible, he is obliged instead to give in charity the equivalent of one full meal for each day of fasting which he has missed.

** *Zakat al-fitr* is a special charity for 'Eid al-Fitr. It consists of the price of a standard meal to be paid on behalf of each member of the family, regardless of age, to some needy person before the 'Eid prayer. Unless this obligation has been met, the prayer of 'Eid al-Fitr is not accepted by God, according to a sound *Hadith*.

fasting (since I was not sure whether I would be able to make up my missed fasts later or not). She thanked me, wished me *"Geçmiş olsun"* (Get well), and we both went our separate ways.

Yesterday this same woman came to the door, remembering me and asking for anything I might have to give her, especially old clothes; I gave her 5 T.L. and one of the neighbors gave her a loaf of bread. She then asked if I had any work she could do. As I would have been glad to have some steady help with the housework, the *kapıcı's* wife not coming regularly now, and as I liked her appearance very much, I asked her to go to Enver's house this morning to talk to one of the family, knowing that it would be extremely unwise, with my scanty knowledge of Turks and Turkish, to admit into my home a complete stranger unless someone whose judgment was reliable had found her suitable.

Everyone was at home today preparing for *'Eid.* In the morning, just as I was leaving for Kızılay to do some shopping, the woman returned, bringing a note from Enver, who wrote that he had talked to her (Emine and Aynur Abla were out at the time) and in his opinion she was reliable. When she expressed her willingness to go to work immediately, I gave her cleaning materials and told her what needed to be done. She was wearing a *şalvar* and vest, and her head was covered with a kerchief draped over the lower part of her face; she uncovered it in talking to me, and I saw that she was wholesome, good-looking and kindly. On seeing Selim, she put the kerchief back over her face, modest behavior which impressed me favorably.

As soon as she began her work, I went on to the city to do my errands. I was gone for a couple of hours, and when I returned Maryam came running to tell me enthusiastically what a good worker the woman was. I was really very pleased with her work and asked if she would come again, as I would be happy to have some steady, reliable help, especially with the laundry; she promised to return to work four days later. I gave her some candy for her three children and, remembering the prescription, asked her who had been sick. Her mother, I understood, had been quite ill, and with the money I had given, medications had been bought and she was now improved. Her husband was in the army, she said, which meant that as an ordinary soldier he was earning nothing. This pleasant-looking, open-faced woman, then, was no common beggar but a decent, respectable woman who had fallen upon hard times, honest and willing to. work. I had liked her very much at the first sight of her face when she uncovered it before me—a good-humored, pleasant face—and that afternoon when I prayed the *Dhuhr* prayer, I thanked God that I had been able to help her and that she would in turn help me by her work. So far I had had almost no contact with a woman of this class, those simple honest souls who make up the bulk of the Turkish population, and I looked forward to a good association with her, hoping that it might even be possible to visit her home one day. Now to finish everything for tomorrow, *'Eid.*

December 3, the third day of *'Eid: 'Eid al-Fitr (Ramazan Bayramı* or *Şeker Bayramı* in Turkish), the joyous celebration of completing the month of fasting prescribed by God, has come and gone, our first and last *'Eid* in Turkey.

Shortly after the sun had risen on *'Eid* morning, Selim and Jamal set out for the mosque for the *'Eid* prayer. The girls and I watched them go wistfully, wanting to attend the prayer too, for at home we had never missed an *'Eid* prayer and I could not understand why in Turkey (or at least in Ankara) women do not go to *'Eid* or to *Jum'a* prayers, although there is a sound *Hadith* (saying) of the Holy Prophet, peace be on him, which makes it clear that all women are supposed to attend the *'Eid* prayers. I thought of all our friends and dear ones scattered around the world—Muslim friends whom we loved very dearly in various parts of the United States, relatives in India and Pakistan, a Muslim brother in Eastern Europe, a sister in Saudi Arabia, another brother who had shared our Muslim community's life now in Iraq, and many others—and was suddenly lonely and at the point of tears, remembering.

Jamal came back from the prayer half-frozen; there had been so many worshippers that people had been praying far out into the street on this very cold morning, each bringing his own *seccade* to pray and sit on. We gave the children their gifts—handmade dolls in Ottoman dresses, books and jewelry for the girls, books and a Turkish-motif sweater for Jamal. While we were having breakfast, various people came to the door to exchange *Bayram* greetings with us—the water man, the egg-and-yogurt man and the garbage collectors—and we gave them each a small gift of money. When the garbage men asked for *"Sigara,"* I gave a pack to each of them; when I mentioned this later at Enver's they laughed at my generosity, saying that they had expected only one or two cigarettes each.

In Turkey as in most of the Muslim world, the *'Eids* are occasions for visiting. Immediately after breakfast we went to pay our respects to Enver's family. We women embraced and greeted each other warmly: *"Hoş geldiniz, canım. Hayırle Bayramlar!"* (Welcome, dear. Happy *'Eid!)*
"Hoş bulduk. Size de, size de!" (Well-met. To you too, to you too!).

A little later when we returned home, the streets were full of well-dressed people going visiting, the women in new clothes of the very latest Western styles (a strange irony, I thought, for Muslims celebrating their principal religious festival), children shooting off fire-crackers and rockets, and a couple of street musicians drawing a crowd of youngsters. It was in sharp contrast to Christmas at home, when there is very little traffic and almost no people in the streets; here every place was full of life, and the human element was the most conspicuous feature of the occasion. Apart from the second *'Eid, 'Eid al-Adha (Kurban Bayramı* in Turkish), which would be two-and-a-half months later when we would *insha'Allah* be in Pakistan, it was the greatest holiday of the year. However, even today some shops such as grocers' were still open, for life must go on; those who needed supplies must be able to obtain them and those who sold them must continue to earn a livelihood.

The first visitors came to us soon after we reached home. First came the *kapıcı* and his wife, going to each apartment in the building to exchange *Bayram* greetings, shaking hands all around and sitting for a while. We had dolls for their older daughters, small toys for their younger ones, a pretty scarf for Gül Hanım and a gift of money for her husband. Today he was resplendent in a suit and his wife wore an ample pleated skirt with heavy stockings instead of her usual *şalvar,* as many village women do on special occasions. After them came friends to whom we served Turkish coffee and the traditional Pakistani dessert which I had made the previous day; later the Doğans came, and, as they were leaving, a neighbor woman whom I had never visited but who always called out a cheery greeting to me and the children whenever she saw us. After supper Enver, Emine and Aynur Abla came and spent two pleasant hours with us.

The second day of *Bayram* passed in much the same way in visiting and receiving visits. In the evening Enver and Emine came with their mother; the young couple had other visits to make, but Aynur Abla was tired and so would stay behind with us. And wonder of wonders, to the amazement of all of us, throughout her stay of an hour-and-a-half, we kept up an uninterrupted conversation with her on various topics in Turkish! I knew then, with a sense of great thankfulness and triumph, that her hope that we would at last come close to each other had not been in vain; we could now, although still in a very elementary and imperfect fashion, communicate, and this hope, which I had so fervently shared, had become a reality. Later Emine told me how surprised and pleased Aynur Abla had been, for as she or Enver were always on hand to translate on other occasions, his mother had hardly recognized the extent of our progress in Turkish previously.

The visiting continued today. We went to our neighbors, Güneş Hanım's family, who had been so helpful to us in the beginning, and then to visit a family who lived upstairs, the Erbuluts, who had also been quite friendly. They had recently acquired a television set, costing about 5000 T.L., and ever since had had a constant succession of visitors on television nights (a usual practice, since television is not very common yet in Turkey). Handan Hanım spent her time working extremely hard in the house from morning to night, particularly on days when she cooked for the TV fans, taking up her knitting in spare moments or passing time with her friends. I now sent Maryam upstairs to ask if we could pay a call, and as they were free we went.

Their drawing room was elegant, with fine modern furniture, a handsome carpet, beautiful curtains—and of course the television set, enthroned upon a stand. They brought Turkish coffee for us, and then, as I declined it, a tiny glass of liqueur, which they pressed first on me and then on Selim. Handan Hanım told me without any discernible embarrassment, just as if it were something quite natural, that her husband enjoys drinking very much, but that during *Ramadan* (when his wife and children had been fasting) he gives it up until the month is over. Although they know that we are practicing Muslims, it was clear that they saw nothing offensive or even incongruous about pressing us to drink, and perhaps were even surprised at our declining it, so common and accepted is drinking in Turkey among all except serious Muslims. We left them struck once again by another extraordinary manifestation of the strange, commonly-accepted and unquestioned split in Turkish life and thought.

The rest of the day was spent in a round of brief visits with Enver's family to various friends of theirs, many of whom we knew by now. The usual practice is to visit older relatives and friends on the first day of *Bayram,* and on the second and third days other friends; each person visited is supposed to repay the visit at some time during the three days. On this *Bayram,* candy—especially sugar-coated almonds—is offered together with Turkish coffee; as a rule visitors stay only for a very short time, but if they remain longer, tea and other refreshments are served as well. Today, going about with Enver, we literally stayed at most houses for only a matter of minutes, just paying respects and drinking coffee or tea, having many stops to make in order to include all to whom a visit must be made. Although this produced a rather hectic round of rushing about, these three days were extremely enjoyable. And thus our *'Eid* passed . . .

I come now to an incident which has disturbed me very much. On the first day of *'Eid* I looked in the top drawer of Jamal's dresser, where I keep my jewelry, for the four gold bangles which had been a gift of Selim's sister Sharifa, but was unable to find them. Thinking I might have misplaced them, I searched elsewhere but still did not find them. Later in the day I mentioned this casually to Aynur Abla and Emine, who immediately asked whether they could have been taken by the woman who had cleaned for me the previous day, or even by the *kapıcı's* wife, who had also cleaned from time to time. I had anticipated that they would say this, but as my own mind was perfectly clear of any suspicion against either of them, I vehemently denied such a possibility, saying that I would answer for the honesty of both women as I would for my own. To suspect Gül Hanım, who certainly had the trust of every family in the building, was unthinkable, and the decent manner and lively, kind, good-humored face of the other woman, Hatice (Khadijah), had impressed me so well that I could not begin to suspect her.

We searched again for the bracelets in various drawers in the house without finding them, and I temporarily dismissed the matter from my mind, still unwilling to suspect Hatice. This was Monday, and she had agreed to come to work again on Thursday morning. When Thursday morning came, I waited for her anxiously and with a fast-beating heart. Nine o'clock came and went, nine-thirty, ten— and no Hatice! By then I was extremely upset and was forced to come to some exceedingly unpleasant tentative conclusions, conclusions to which Emine and her family had come long before.

I went over in my mind the whole sequence of events of our first meeting and her later coming to our house, her manner and appearance and speech—every detail of my contact with her—and there was absolutely nothing which I could construe as suspicious or which I could, by any stretch of the imagination, bring to bear on the possibility of her having stolen my jewelry.

When she had approached me in the street to ask for money to fill the prescription, and later when she had come here begging, she could not have known beforehand that I would admit her to my house or that there would be portable valuables to which she would have easy access. This could not be the work of someone stealing once in her life or on sudden impulse, I reasoned, for in that case how could she have faced me so openly, or told me how my money had helped her sick mother, or spoken so frankly and pleasantly? The only possibility, then, was that she was a highly-skilled professional thief and a consummate actress, possibly operating through a gang, as Enver asserted might be the case. She had left her name and address with him, giving as her place of residence a section at the back of the *'Gecekondu'* area of Ulus.* Perhaps the name and address were false; they *must* be if she were a professional thief. I clung to the hope that she would yet turn up; perhaps her mother, one of her children or even she herself was sick. Yet there is now not much hope left in me.

I know that she had tidied the top of Jamal's dresser, in one drawer of which—unlocked—were the bangles and other jewelry. Although Selim and the children were all at home, no one had been in Jamal's room when she was cleaning it, and it is clear that she had enough time alone there to rearrange Jamal's books and other possessions on the top of the dresser.

Time will tell the answer. Perhaps the bangles are misplaced after all, and when we quit this apartment we will find them, *insha'Allah.* What is so disturbing about the whole matter is that I had liked the woman so much and had found her face and manner so pleasing and open and honest. My main joy in finding my jewelry would be in knowing that my judgment had not been mistaken and that I had not placed confidence and liking in one who was flagrantly dishonest and criminal—and also, quite naturally, that the valuable gift (four *tolas* of 22 karat gold) given to me by the sister-in-law I dearly love would be in my possession rather than in the hands of a thief!

December 4: During the *'Eid* holiday we had a refreshing break from all problems and everyone was well, thank God. Now I am prepared for more health problems as this cold, bleak, polluted Ankara weather takes its toll in the form of respiratory ailments. Day after day the sky is a monotonous leaden color, with occasional rain; once in a while the sun comes out for some hours or for a day or two, but it doesn't last long at this time of year. Everything is

---

* Literally, 'thrown-up overnight,' i.e., houses built and completed within one night. Such houses are protected by Turkish law from being demolished except by means of protracted legal proceedings, even if erected illegally on public or private land.

grey or mud-colored, and there is no hint of beauty or cheerfulness anywhere.

We are enveloped, by day and by night, in an ocean of thick grey smog, as the thousands of chimneys of Ankara pour forth clouds of soft-coal smoke, which makes Ankara one of the most polluted cities of the world. In Kızılay and other areas which, like ours, are in the bottom of the bowl-shaped depression around which the city radiates, the pollution is so bad that all winter long a very heavy grey pall hangs over everything until late morning or noon, and these low-lying areas of the city can hardly be seen on an ordinary day from any of the hills of Ankara. Jamal must cover his nose and mouth whenever he goes out in order not to have trouble.

Now we will go back to our usual daily routine: after *Fajr* prayer, prying awake three very tired and cross children, Jamal the most tired of all because his normal sleep pattern has been disturbed by his illness; listening to Nura's frequent complaints (sometimes Maryam's too) of stomachache and her very real fear that her teacher will yell at her or beat her, or that boys will tease her; making breakfast and sending them out into the cold, damp, smoke-filled air; trying to pull myself together to get a lot of work done, but being discouraged by the heap of dirty laundry which must be washed and then hung to dry in layers on the radiators all over the apartment, meals to be cooked, dishes to be washed, and by my own weariness and inertia. I am fighting with a terrible-sounding cough and praying that it won't turn into something serious.

And yet, while conditions of life are not so easy and there are many things which are annoying and very unIslamic as well, nevertheless I am happy here. At home, we can enjoy efficiency and easy living—but to what purpose, when the profound difference between our values and the prevailing ones makes it impossible for us to identify with the society and to find inner peace? May Allah help us to find the right way.

Later in the day: This morning Jamal suddenly realized that the woman Hatice must have opened his dresser drawers, for he recalled that his pyjamas had been lying on his bed and that he had found them inside his drawer on the evening of the day she had worked. There was now no need for any further questions about what had happened to the bangles.

When Jamal and I came back from an errand at Kızılay in the middle of the afternoon, Maryam said that Selim and Enver had been looking for me; they were going to the police concerning the woman. I was quite disturbed by this news. Although all circumstances pointed to her guilt, we nevertheless had no *positive* proof against her, and it might still be that I had somehow misplaced the bangles so that they could not be found; her good name and reputation could be forever ruined by bringing an accusation against her if she were innocent. However, I trusted to their consciences and good judgment and was certain that they would do nothing in the matter which was not completely right.

They returned a short while later. They had gone to the police supervising the area where the woman had said she lives; Enver had her full name and the address she had given him. The locality was a very bad one, notorious for harboring criminals, including murderers, and policemen had even been killed there. A uniformed policeman and a plainclothesman had been assigned to go with them. The detective went to the address she had given, asking for Hatice Piliç. He was told that no such person lived there, but that a woman of that name lived next door. Bringing Enver and Selim to identify her, the detective asked for her at the next house. They were amazed to find that the person claiming that name was a very bedraggled but handsome fifteen-year-old girl, and of course both Enver and Selim attested that this was not the person. The police questioned her, asking if she had any enemies who could have given her name and address to harm her, but nothing could be gotten out of her. There was nothing further to be done except leave, especially as the car was now surrounded by angrily-muttering residents of the area. The police confirmed Enver's statement that numbers of gangs operate in this manner, that giving the name and address of someone the criminal dislikes is not uncommon, and said that they could do nothing further about the case.

Thus it is clear and certain: the good-looking, decent woman in financial distress, with her three children, her husband in the army, the sick mother whom my money, given *in lieu* of fasting as a religious obligation, had helped, who had talked so nicely and had done such good work, about whose domestic help and acquaintanceship I had been so happy and thankful to God, was a vicious, extremely cunning thief who had no compunction about robbing one who had befriended her. Looking again through the drawer where the jewelry had been, I found that other pieces were missing which I had not noticed earlier, all gifts of relatives, and wondered unpleasantly whether I might not one day find my missing valuables displayed in a jewelry shop window somewhere in the city. On the positive side, however, I was not only thankful that she had not taken everything, for there were other things of some value, but also that I had not yet bought the jewelry I intend to take to Pakistan as gifts for our relatives.

Enver, that good and sincere man, was very much distressed and blamed himself over and over again for having recommended her, and Aynur Abla repeatedly said that if *she* had been at home to talk to *that* woman, she would have understood everything at a glance. However, I told them with complete sincerity that I myself had found her good and wholesome in every respect, that her face and eyes had been honest and open, and that no one could have discovered her evil secret. Nevertheless, I was privately thankful that it was not only my own judgment about her which had been so much in error but also that of a Turk highly skilled in judging people, one who knew his fellow-countrymen inside and out. And still I cannot recall anything about her which would have betrayed her, for to me she had seemed in appearance, speech and manner such a decent person that the whole thing is almost incredible.

After this, I am much more careful. I always look out the peephole in the door to see who is there before opening it and insist that the children must do the same if anyone comes while I am out, and I do not encourage beggars who come to the door or anyone collecting for a charitable cause, thinking that they may be colleagues of Hatice's. The Turkish friends to whom I have related this incident have, without exception, been extremely distressed and shocked that such a thing could have happened in their country, blaming themselves for not having warned us that such elements exist, or asking in horror what Turkey is coming to, feeling that such an occurrence is a blot on the honor of their land. It was suggested, too, that I was very careless to leave my valuables in an open drawer when there were strangers in the house. Still others said that the woman's approach from the first was quite typical of the style of these thieves, and that one does not give 50 T.L. to a beggar whom one doesn't know. I now began—rather too late—to keep the jewelry drawer locked and to hide the key; somewhat fruitlessly to be sure, for we had as many keys as we had drawers, kept where they could easily be found, and each of the keys was identical!

CHAPTER 7

INTIMATIONS OF TROUBLE

December 11: Sometimes, as if in a clearly-written book, one catches a glimpse of the unfolding of history and the destinies of men and nations. At this moment it seems to me that I can see with surprising clarity this unfolding of Turkey's history and the moving of trends within it toward what, if there is no change, will be their inevitable culmination.

Over this nation successive waves of civilization have passed, left their mark, and faded away. One sees the imprint of them on the faces of Turks, which are the faces of Central Asia, the faces of the Middle East, and the faces of southeastern Europe, all blended into one people. Turkey is full of the reminders of these civilizations—the Hittite relics, the crumbling ruins of ancient Rome and the Byzantine Empire, the pious structures of the Seljuks, and the devout, monumental works of the Ottoman period, and finally in our time, the marks of that secular materialism which is leading Turkey into dark and troubled ways.

Of this latter movement there are hundreds of signs and indications, but they are twisted and unclear to read, as there is not one trend at work but many. One sees them embodied in such things as Western styles of dress, Western household furnishings, Western tastes in arts and entertainments, words from Western languages incorporated into Turkish and now regarded as part of it, Western habits and social patterns gradually finding a foothold in the society, and above all, Western values and standards coming to be accepted and taken as the norm. At the same time, there appears to be a contrary and opposing trend in the importation of leftist ideals and methods, which are proliferating very rapidly and dangerously among the student population and others. The primary aim of the leftists seems to be to disrupt and produce chaos in the society, and to tread underfoot the Islamic values and all who propagate and exemplify them; for they are shrewd enough to realize that their strongest enemy and opponent is Islam, and at the same time far too ignorant and biased to grasp the fact that Islam is itself the greatest revolutionizing force for social justice and political freedom the world has ever known, operating as it does first to change the hearts and lives of individuals and then to transform the society into one in which justice, freedom, morality and righteousness alone prevail.

Thus we observe two apparently opposing trends in today's Turkey, westernization and communism. However, if one analyzes the matter dispassionately and looks into it a little more deeply, he gradually begins to realize that Western-style materialism and communism are both parts of the same secular materialistic frame of reference, points marked along the same line, with somewhat different approaches and methodologies, to reach essentially the same ends. Although Western-style materialism, unlike communism, may give lip-service to the idea of God, nevertheless, like communism, it gives Him no significant place in its scheme of things, and thus, like communism, it acts basically as if He does not exist or does not matter. Thus in practice both systems are nearly equal in their denial of moral absolutism, visualizing morality, if it exists at all, as a system evolved by man in response to whatever is necessary or expedient for a specific time, place and set of circumstances, rather than as a permanent, Divinely-ordained law binding on men of all times, places and circumstances.

This, then, is the point of departure. From this common starting point the roads divide to reach destinations which, although somewhat different in emphasis and practice, are nevertheless basically similar, parts of one ideological continuum. While Western-style secular materialism aims at maximum material satisfaction for the individual, its communist-style counterpart aims at maximum economic development of the society, into which individuals are subordinated. While one emphasizes the individual at the expense of the society as a whole, the other emphasizes the society at the expense of the individual. Nevertheless, both are unanimous in their emphasis on material values, means and ends; in the belief that man and his affairs are all-important, that sovereignty over human affairs rests with man alone, and in a continual glorification of man's achievements and potentialities; and in the non-recognition of the sovereignty of God as the Ruler and Legislator of the universe and mankind, and of the absolute, transcendental laws and values which come from Him. And in both the orientation of life around purely materialistic values, or humanistic values at best, has come about, in the simplest possible terms, because of a great emphasis on material development accompanied by a lack or decline—or even a systematic official suppression—of spiritual values to counterbalance it. I now realize that a similar cause is operating in the case of Turkey in driving its people into the arms of secular materialistic ideologies, whether they have their origin in the West or in the communist world.

In the case of Turkey, as a study of its history and the trends currently at work within it show, this cause has been in the making for the past two hundred years or even longer, having its genesis in the Ottoman intellectuals' conviction of the backwardness of the Muslim world, cowed as they were before the material development of the West and becoming ever more and more stagnant and uncreative due to the gradual loss of the dynamism which Islam had infused into them when it was a complete way of life for their nation. In an attempt to change the situation, Atatürk made no attempt to distinguish between what was basic and essential, of supreme value and importance to the society, and what needed change; to him, everything having its roots in Islam or in tradition was equally bad. Thus, centuries of deep faith in the transcendent God and His law, and the translation of that faith into a concrete society, were forcibly swept away, to be replaced by what one man considered to be the highest values of human civilization, namely, westernization and material progress.

It may be true that Kemal Atatürk helped save Turkey from being dismembered and gobbled up physically by Europe, but at the same time—evidently without even grasping the contradiction, which manifests itself everywhere so glaringly in Turkish life today

—he gave over his country, body and soul, to forcible conquest by the values and ideologies of the very Europeans whose mastery of his homeland he had resisted so strongly. Indeed, he would not be ruled by them nor allow his people to be ruled by them, *but instead he himself imposed the rule of their value-system on his people.* He was, in short, the most mentally-defeated, culturally-subordinated of all the leaders of the Muslim world, choosing to turn himself and his people into an imitation of those whose ways were utterly alien to the accepted values of the society, although he had lately risked his life many times over in order to avoid their domination of his homeland.

At the same time, in utter contradiction and opposition to this philosophy, Atatürk invented a brand-new, freshly-coined and previously non-existent notion of 'Turkishness,' unearthing the shadowy ancient background and obscure accomplishments of pre-Islamic tribal peoples as the matrix of historical greatness for his people to fall back upon. They were taught to believe that they were Turks before they were Muslims and that their true identity was Turk, not Muslim. Thus the universality and brotherhood of Islam was replaced by the petty local self-interest and self-absorption of nationalism, and relics of Hittite paganism became more precious to many Turks than the God-centered monuments of Islam.

In introducing and promoting such notions, Atatürk and his like-minded associates indeed betrayed and deceived their people, for indeed, it was Islam which had uplifted them and infused life into their society, which had raised them to the pinnacle of spiritual and cultural vitality, and which had ennobled them by the beauty of the system of life it brought to them. Thus, when they were Muslim, truly believing and truly practicing, they achieved a measure of greatness and their way of life and many of their institutions were universally respected and admired. Today, without Islam, they are nothing—not Muslim, not European, and barely even retaining the characteristics of Turkishness, whatever they may be; culturally, ideologically, politically, even materially, bankrupt and near to disaster.

What wonder is it, then, that in this state of ideological vacuity Turks turn to other systems and philosophies to give meaning to their lives, to replace the system which belongs to them but which they have never, apart from some individual committed Muslims, understood nor tried to apply in recent times? Emptiness must be filled in some way, and if one has nothing (or is convinced that he has nothing, which is the same thing in relation to practical matters), he will grasp at straws; and indeed, compared with Islam, the complex of secular materialism, whether it leans toward the East or toward the West, is less than a straw in the shallowness and emptiness of its conceptions and its obvious inability to direct the life of man toward goals of real meaning and lasting value.

At the same time, crumbs of religion are thrown out to placate those who still have any interest in it, while applying to the utmost limits the Western principle of separation of religion and politics, although this has no meaning within the framework of Islam, in which, since every part of man's personal and collective life is governed by and lived for God, there can never be a division of it into compartments labelled 'religious' and 'secular,' 'God's' and 'Caesar's.' Thus the rulers of Turkey, in order to break the hold of Islam on the society as a whole, to permit it only as a purely personal matter between a man and his God (if he persists in believing in Him) but not as a force to shape the society, has attempted to reduce Islam to mere formal observances, to the *Bayrams,* to the occasion of a death, or for observing the worship aspects at the very most—but surely *not* for application to every aspect of life, for the regulation of relationships between man and man, between men and women, between nation and nation, or for the governing of social, political and economic affairs. The Turkish government has attempted to sequester Islam inside the mosque and confine it there so that it will be cordoned off from involvement in the political and social life of the people—if, like a necessary evil which must be tolerated to appease the common people, it has to have any place in the society at all. It was surely not for the purpose of serving Islam that Atatürk provided for a religious works department in the government of Turkey; its establishment was a clever, coldly-calculated aimed at keeping Islam firmly under the hand of the government lest it get out of control and in order to manipulate the people by its means.*

* See Note (17).

Thus, from the principle of separation of religion and the state, it is a very easy step to that domination of religion *by* the state which we observe not only in Turkey but in many other parts of the Muslim world; and when the state is dominant over religion, the state with its man-made laws and regulations becomes the ruler, authority and criterion, the object and focus of loyalty and devotion, rather than God, the true Ruler of man and his institutions.

In a society whose basic orientation and guide was Islam, which once recognized Who is the Sovereign of the universe and the true Lord of men, which submitted both the ordinary affairs of its individuals and the more weighty matters of rule over them to His sovereignty through obedience to the *Shari'ah*,* and in which there was no law above this law of God, even though human lords might sometimes try to rise above it or skirt around it in their drive toward the fulfillment of some base ambition or in their grasping for power—in such a society the notion that religion is a private, part-time matter between an individual and God, having nothing to say about politics, government, economics, social issues, morals and every other aspect of the society, has no place. This notion was conveniently imported, by men having no faith themselves, from Europe, where it had gained currency with the increasing loss of faith in Christianity and the consequent secularism which has been rampant in the West for the past two hundred years and more, to do its work of dividing and weakening the life of Muslims in like manner.

In this analysis of the trends at work in today's Turkey, we observe one trend comng to the fore at this time which makes me fear for the future of this country. This is the communist movement, spearheaded by university students, notably from M.E.T.U. At various universities in Turkey today, there are frequent boycotts of classes by students, student marches and demonstrations, and news of students being killed and wounded, largely engineered by leftists and often countered by rightist (nationalist) factions who also use guerilla-type tactics. At M.E.T.U. itself, incidents and problems in-

---

* The legal system derived from the Qur'an and the *Sunnah* of the Prophet, which includes all aspects of international law, judicial and legislative matters, criminal, civil and personal law.

volving the communist faction crop up with unfailing regularity.

Although there is no mosque on the M.E.T.U. campus, a room in the basement of a dormitory has been used for prayers. This has now, through the permission or instigation of the *Rektör*, Dr. Erdal Inönü (son of Ismet Inönü, the inspired successor to Kemal Atatürk in 'reforming' Turkey and purging Islam), been demolished and closed. Dr. Inönü, who from his actions appears to be a leftist sympathizer, declared that the existence of a mosque on the campus violated the principle of 'secularism,' that inviolable and sacrosanct pillar of the Turkish constitution placed there by Atatürk himself; at this, some leftist students, either acting on their own or at his implicit or explicit suggestion, went there to smash up the *minbar,* wreck the premises, and manhandle a few Muslims who had come there to pray. It is reported that the leftist students at M.E.T.U. have warned the practicing Muslim students, of whom there are after all a number living on campus and observing prayers, that they can pray by themselves if they want to but must not pray in congregation.

It is well-known that stores of bombs, guns and other weapons and ammunition are cacheted in the M.E.T.U. dormitories, in preparation for the time when they will be needed. How do these come there, and how are they made or supplied? It is known that many of them are made with ingredients from University supplies, either secreted away bit by bit or perhaps taken even more openly with the connivance and approval of leftist-oriented faculty and administration. When, how and for what will they be used? No one knows; it is anyone's guess. It is rumored that most likely they will be used to spread chaos and terror among the population at large in order to quieten and subdue it, or again, that the communists' attempting a *coup* against the government is not an impossibility.

All this is an open secret. However, as the universities of Turkey are autonomous and no police may enter the campus without the consent of the *rektör,* the situation smoulders on at an increasing tempo without anything being done to deal with it before it explodes.

The communist terrorists are armed, organized, dedicated and daring, and obviously have resources at their disposal. At this point it is not clear from where their income and supplies of munitions and explosives, other than locally-manufactured ones, is coming, but it is obvious that there is strong financial backing behind them. There are also the militant rightist groups which are primarily nationalistic in their orientation; they too are organized, retaliating against violence done to their own members. And of course there are the westernized, the Kemalists and other anti-Islamic elements who are doing their very best to keep Muslims from ever achieving any power and influence in the society with as much fervor and intensity as if Muslims were the deadly enemies of Turkey and its people.

On the other side are the Muslims, without military, political or even much economic or social power. I have now come to realize that an expression in the Qur'an which used to puzzle me—"the party of God"*—represents an actuality in the world of men. I have come to realize that there are only two possible groups, God's group or the opposing group; there are only two possible goals, toward God or away from Him; there are only two possible ways of life, God's way or some other way.

I used to believe that people were in the main decent and harmless, and that no one would want to bother Muslims because people were basically good. Perhaps this is largely true for Muslims in America and other parts of the Western world, both because their number is too small to constitute a real threat and also because there is, at least at the present time, a very great degree of freedom of conscience and practice, amounting almost to an anarchy of beliefs and values; but in much of the rest of the world the situation is very different. Other elements (often ones who themselves were born into Muslim families and who bear Muslim names) will *not* permit Muslims to establish an Islamic society and live according to the blessed light of God. Those who oppose Islam—who oppose the freedom of man from obedience to lords other than the One God, the Sovereign of the universe, who oppose justice, purity and righteousness—will, as they have done ever since the time of the Qur-

* *Al-Maida 5:59* and *al-Mujadila* 58:22.

aish* of Mekkah, try to stand in its way, and ultimately there can be no half-measures. Either the forces of God—those who uphold His sovereignty over mankind and strive to establish His rule in the world—will, by His help, prevail, or the forces of evil and oppression, which are ever-organized and ever-ready to seize any opportunity they can find to take command over the lives of men. I know it as a truth: *either Muslims (and all those who desire to serve God alone throughout the world) must stand up and struggle and live and if necessary die for God's cause, or others will stand up and destroy them and all whosesome values for causes other than God's cause, for as God says in the Holy Qur'an:*

"...To those against whom war is made, permission is given (to fight) because they are wronged; and verily, God is Most Powerful for their aid. (They are) those who have been expelled from their homes in defiance of right, (for no cause) except that they say, 'Our Lord is God.' Did not God check one set of people by means of another, there would surely have been pulled down monasteries, churches, synagogues and mosques, in which the name of God is commemorated in abundant measure. God will certainly aid those who aid His (cause), for verily, God is Full of Strength, Dominant."**

This struggle, the struggle between those who submit to and serve God alone and those who want to compel people to submit to and serve something other than God, must be fought on all fronts and levels—through education, through preaching, through private and public exposition and discussion, through the mass media, and through every other means of influence which Muslims can muster —if possible without resort to force. Yet when all other measures fail, at some point it may be necessary for Muslims to use physical means to deal with oppression and tyranny in order to preserve their society and their freedom. At times the Muslim may be in a situation in which he is obliged to make a choice between the security and enjoyment of this brief life and the other, permanent Life-to-Come, in which he must decide to set aside all personal needs and desires in exchange for this most vital of all the needs of a *human* being: the right to be free from enslavement to the arbitrary demands and requirements of men in order to serve and obey Almighty God alone.

---

* Pagan compatriots of Prophet Muhammad who opposed his message and fought against him and his followers with unrelenting harshness.

** *Al-Hajj 22:39-40.*

There are some sincere people in the West who oppose the use of force on principle and to whom any individual or group advocating it is necessarily wrong. To them this statement of the necessity of being willing to fight and die, even for one's own freedom and dignity and that of one's society, will be very repugnant, for they honestly believe that war and fighting should be avoided at all costs, even if it results in every sort of degradation, oppression and injustice to the victims of this state of 'peace.'

This is an attitude which can be held only by those who believe that death is the greatest tragedy, the ultimate evil, the final termination of man's brief existence, and that life must be preserved as long as possible at any cost, regardless of its quality; it can never be held by those who believe in God and the Hereafter and take it as their goal. It is also a very idealistic attitude, surely, one which does not adequately take into consideration the nature of human beings, a great many of whom are very willing to use violence and to kill others for vicious, evil causes. Let them come to Turkey today, or to any other country where the struggle between freedom and totalitarianism is being waged between a peaceful, passive people and a dictator or power bloc having unity, organization, armed strength, resources, dedication to the death, and an utter absence of moral scruples concerning the tactics and methods it uses—without indeed acknowledging the existence of any morality—and see how effectively they can be dealt with by peaceful means! In fact, Turks have been dealing with all their enemies and the enemies of Islam without any real resistance, and the end result is that today they are enmeshed more firmly than ever in the coils of these adversaries, who become more and more daring and certain of their power and slowly close in to squeeze the last drops of Islam—of honor, purity, decency and every wholesome tradition—out of the lives and hearts of the Turkish people *because there is no effective resistance.*

Those who use force can only be effectively opposed by force if they accept no other method of reasoning or persuasion, and let us beware—for God's sake let us take note!—lest we realize too late what we should have realized from the beginning in dealing with these enemies of human freedom. God has told Muslims in the Holy Qur'an that it is their duty to

"... Fight them on until there is no more tumult or oppression, and there prevail justice and faith in God altogether and everywhere. . . ,"*

laying down their lives in the struggle if necessary. In recent times there have been very few instances of Muslims rising up against their oppressors on a large scale, even after every method of dealing with them has been tried, *although Muslims are not permitted to compromise with injustice and tyranny.* I am convinced that the Muslim world would not be in its present degraded condition if there had been such resistance to the death, and I am also convinced that its condition will never improve unless and until Muslims are prepared, first, to unite in the cause of Islam regardless of minor differences, and second, to lay down their lives if need be in order to preserve their values, as God has commanded them to do. For freedom and dignity do not come automatically, and at times they can only be preserved by some members of the society striving for them no matter what the cost; but life without them is meaningless, and tyranny ever waits for a chance to conquer passive or fearful men.

December 15: The elections for forming a constitutional assembly in Pakistan were held a few days ago. It seems rather certain from early reports that Mujib-ur-Rahman, with his leaning toward Bengali autonomy, has carried East Pakistan, and the possibility of Zulfiqar 'Ali Bhutto's Peoples' Party having taken the West wing seems rather likely, to our very great dismay, after what we had heard from many Pakistanis about the Jamaat-i-Islami's** steady gains and the Islamic fervor of the people.

Yes, here and there, and even in the 'free world,' it is essentially the same problem. People do not realize that spiritual and moral values have to be carefully nurtured, cherished and fought and even died for, if necessary, and when they reach the state of letting them slip through their fingers, other and even opposite values will be sought by some of the people (often by the young among them, for youth is restless for new things, very adept at recognizing when something is wrong, and usually quite poor in coming up with more promising solutions due to its lack of knowledge and experience) to

* *Al-Anfal* 8:39.

** The major Islamic movement and Islamic political party in Pakistan, which was very active in the December 1970 elections.

take the place of what preceding generations valued and nurtured so tenderly. Think of the beginning of Pakistan, that tempestuous and terrible time during which millions died in the birth-pangs of a new nation in which, supposedly, the Muslims of the Indian subcontinent would live under an Islamic government. Although many Pakistanis who lived through it and are still alive today remember, many others have forgotten the lesson of history and have gone to seek other ways. It will be the death of the most valuable and important thing they possessed, which the majority did not cherish sufficiently to fight for by word and deed, I am afraid; but perhaps the election results will yet prove to be otherwise after all, *insha'Allah*.

Last weekend we were invited to dinner at the Doğans'. I know the loneliness and heartbreak which Deniz Hanım says she experienced during her stay in England, arriving there without knowing any English or how to cope with the life, and she in turn has great sympathy with our attempts to adjust to life here. She is a warm, sweet woman, always doing for others, and her hospitality is boundless. Over dinner I talked about buying gifts for relatives in Pakistan, and she eagerly offered to take me shopping in Ulus—even to take me, just for the interest of it, to the areas far up the hill and to the castle itself which I have not yet seen, as she knows these places well—and we finally agreed upon yesterday afternoon, when she would be free, for our outing.

It was a dull, chilly, drizzly afternoon. We went to Ulus by *dolmuş*, walking arm-in-arm under her umbrella from the *dolmuş* stop up the street of brightly-illuminated jewelry shops, where she helped me in buying some handsome jewelry to take to Pakistan from shops where ornaments bearing Arabic inscriptions of '*Masha 'Allah*' are displayed side-by-side with gold medallions depicting the profile of Atatürk, which, incongruously, are often given as gifts for marriages and *Sünnets*. From here we continued up the steep hill through my beloved Çikrikçilar Yokuşu. I had been there a few times since my first memorable expedition with Emine, and it had never become dull or stale for me; I was always eager for a chance to go there again and delighted in its special atmosphere.

After several stops along the way, we came out the other side of the hilltop bazaar and trudged slowly toward the summit through very steep, narrow streets, wet with rain and mud, where there were many small shops and the full flavor of the real Anatolia, with an entirely different breed of people from the majority of the inhabitants of the newer parts of Ankara. When we reached the top of the hill, we suddenly stood before the ancient castle which crowned its summit, said originally to have been built in Roman times; it had a clock tower and I noted some odd stones bearing Greek inscriptions scattered here and there in its grey stone walls. Before it at stalls where mounds of nuts, raisins and other foodstuffs were sold, a couple of *şalvar*-clad women with shawls over their shoulders stood deliberating over their small purchases.

We passed through the castle gate; inside, old houses, narrow lanes, steep slopes, an aged mosque or two—a different world, picturesque and engaging. It was a place to which I would never have dared to come alone, but now, here with one who was familiar with it, I tried to take in the unique flavor of this corner of old Ankara, imagining what scenes these aged stones had witnessed during the course of centuries.

Dusk came early on this cloudy, cold winter's day, as Deniz Hanım and I made our way, chatting, over the rough streets of the castle-town. One of her very close friends lived here, and she asked if I would like to call on her. Knowing that Selim would be at home with the children by now and that he would not expect me until late, I gladly agreed.

We knocked at the door of an old house, simple and plain and immaculately clean as are virtually all Turkish houses. Her friend was a pleasant woman wearing a long dress and a kerchief, surrounded by a number of children; her husband, a heavy-set man slightly past middle age, was observing a fast that day.* They were happy to see Deniz Hanım, for she had not visited them for a long time, and made us welcome with warm words. We sat together chatting in a small sitting room heated by a stove. When it was time for supper, nothing would do but that we must share their meal.

* Fasting outside *Ramadan* is optional and follows the same pattern as during *Ramadan*, with *iftar* at sunset and generally a morning meal *(suhoor)* before dawn.

We took our places at a table in the simple dining room, heated by another stove. Dinner consisted of a stew with meat followed by a dish of potatoes, lettuce, green onions, yogurt and bread, with which we sopped up the gravy of the stew. As they talked together I tried to follow the conversation without much success and to show my appreciation of their hospitality. They made no distinction with me because I was a foreigner; for them I was just another woman, a Muslim like themselves and the friend of their close friend who was cordially welcome among them.

As soon as the supper was finished we had to take our leave, for it was getting late and was quite dark by now. We looked down over Ankara, whose lights twinkled and shone like thousands of stars in the near and far distance. This castle with its homes and mosques had stood for centuries and, barring some catastrophe, would stand for many hundreds of years more, *insha'Allah,* a symbol of the stability of the common people of Turkey, rooted in Islam and as solid as the very soil of this land.

Deniz Hanım took my hand and we edged our way down a slippery, muddy slope, holding onto one another; then we retraced our route down the hill arm-in-arm, chatting happily as only two women can who are congenial friends, satisfied and refreshed by our outing. Once again on the street of brightly-lighted jewelry shops, a few more small purchases, and then back to the muddy Ulus *dolmuş* stop—back again to the old everyday world from which we had had a few hours' respite during this pleasant afternoon together. I hoped that I would have more opportunities to visit the homes of solid, plain people such as I had seen today, with their wholesome way of life grounded on Islamic traditions of family solidarity, kindliness and hospitality.

Thus I returned, as if from a long distance, to our muddy neighborhood, where the chimneys gave forth their endless heavy grey smoke into the night air; but nothing could dispel the glow of warmth from the day's good experiences . . .

December 25: My Turkish lessons are now in their third month, and they are going wonderfully well for me. A certain sweeping feeling of triumph and power comes to me at times when, by the grace of God, I have mastered some new element of Turkish grammar. To be talking in a language which four months ago was totally unknown and baffling is one of the most interesting and marvellous things which has ever happened to me. Sometimes, of course, it happens that I make a glaring error and express myself so incorrectly that I get a blank look from a Turk, and then I become more realistic and humble in my appraisal of my budding new skill—temporarily!

It has been something of a relief to be away from the usual Christmas rush and commercialism in America; the only Christmassy things here are the decorations in the windows of apartments of foreigners and in foreign official buildings. It is now the worst part of winter, very cold, and now instead of raining it snows on and off, sometimes for several days at a stretch, the cold creeping and blowing in through all the cracks around the doors and windows of the apartment. The *kapıcı* has to work extremely hard stoking the furnace, beginning at 5 a.m. and ending at 11:30 or even later at night. A terrible, hard life, without enough sleep or rest with all the other work he has to do; his wife cleans for various families in the building five or six days a week and has no time to look after her children, who wander about outside in all weathers without sufficient clothing, despite which they seem much more robust than any of our children, notwithstanding their permanently runny noses.

Currents of great unrest are in the air. Süleyman Demirel, the Prime Minister, has been sharply criticized on various counts, and there are many voices clamoring for his resignation. There is some fear that the leftists may try to engineer a *coup,* or alternatively that the military may effect a military *coup* in line with the traditions of past years, as Demirel seems powerless or unwilling to cope with the communist radicals. We wonder what will happen and can only pray that Turkey's worst days are behind her, not to come, *insha' Allah.*

January 5, 1971: We have passed four months in Turkey now, and during this period many new impressions have come and gone:

during the first weeks, my interest and enthusiasm weakened by a sense of frustration and a feeling of being cut off because of my inability to communicate, by the confusion of what I observed and my inability to bring all these impressions together and make any sense out of them; the problems and anxieties of the days and nights when Jamal coughed incessantly, when the girls also seemed to be ailing often, when I was so tired myself, and when I yet clung stubbornly to the web of dreams and hopes I had had woven in my mind about Turkey before our coming here—my dream of an Islamic society. Then the partial fading of that ,dream, the shattering of my ideal, as it became clear that all the contradictions and confusions actually represented almost a movement *away* from Islam, fed by the disregard and even contempt for religion among the majority of the educated and affluent, the absence of Islamic knowledge and understanding among the pious masses, the lack of unity and communication between various Islam-loving elements in the society, and all the political and social problems of Turkey today. With all this, a real love growing up within me for the traditional Turk, with his deep self-respect and dignity, his innate decency, his kindliness and sincerity, and his God-fearing way of life—Islamic qualities which are very real and very much alive among the people of this land—and a terrible pity and sadness for the destruction of this noble heritage, little by little, by the forces of modern *jahiliyyah,** so devoid of respect and decency, coming as they do from the West, from the communist world, and from within Turkey itself.

Last week was a terrible week of incidents perpetrated by communist militants. A student was shot and killed at one of the Anara universities; two policemen on guard duty in front of the U.S. Embassy here were wounded, the guard booth riddled with bullets by passing terrorists shooting from a car; the home of a British family in which there was a Christmas tree was bombed: incidents came almost daily. Demirel did nothing, fearful, it seemed, of exceeding the constitutional limits of his powers and meeting a fate similar to that of Adnan Menderes.** In Ankara's English

---

* Arabic for 'ignorance'; in a specific sense, ignorant of God's guidance.
** Prime Minister of Turkey during the period 1950-1960. He was overthrown by a military *coup,* tried and hanged. One of the charges brought against him was that he had exceeded the constitutional limits of his power by his suppression of student uprisings.

newspaper, "The Daily News," which gives the impression of being an organ of the U.S. government, as well as in Turkish newspapers, the talk about his resignation continued.

On top of this came the sickening holiday called *Yılbaşı*—New Year—an artificially-manufactured occasion taken notice of by the upper classes. I saw great crowds of shoppers in Kızılay and Ulus buying gifts *á la* Christmas at home, and Christmas-like decorations (including the same artificial metallic Christmas trees we have in America) in many shops; I saw Turkish-made New Year cards bearing Christmas tree motifs and learned with great surprise that even many well-educated Turks are unaware that Christmas and New Year are two separate and entirely unrelated occasions in the West. Who could have expected such things here? *Yılbaşı* eve Selim sat watching television with Enver, Emine and Aynur Abla in the lobby of a big hotel. As he told me later, it was a completely empty program of one trashy popular song after another, a bill of 70 T.L. for two rounds of tea and the television, drunks dancing out of the hotel as they were leaving, and a lot of noise of cars honking in the streets, fire-crackers exploding, etc.

This is 1971 in Turkey. Those who think and feel and care look around them with horror because of what is happening to their country, and a few of these try to make some effort to improve the situation. The rest of the population, like dumb animals, eat, enjoy their endless glasses of tea or their beer, go to their work daily or clean house and cook from morning to night, go visiting, play cards or watch television, and do not concern themselves with all these things. Meanwhile, the enemies of Turks—who are Turks themselves—who are also the enemies of Islam and of Muslims, plan their plans, wait for them to ripen, arm themselves, spread chaos in whatever way is possible under the given circumstances of the moment by terrorizing all who oppose them in ideology or actuality into silence, depending on the majority's continuing to remain busy and stupefied with material preoccupations, and bide their time until the right moment, with help and support from like-minded groups outside Turkey. "And they [the unbelievers] planned, and God planned, and God is the best of planners."* Who can say,

* *Ale Imran* 3:54.

then, what plan God in His wisdom has for these Turkish people, who have been oppressed and who have oppressed themselves as well, until little remains of God's religion among those who are supposed to have knowledge and to lead, leaving Islam largely the domain of the simple and uneducated, who, although they may be pious, lack deep Islamic knowledge and also knowledge of the world and of the tactics of the enemies of Islam, and who have no influence whatsoever except through sheer force of numbers, which is often no force at all?

What then is there for educated Turkish Muslims to do? As I see it, the greatest hope at present lies in acquiring as much education and training as possible, by means of which they can obtain positions of responsibility and leadership through which they can influence others; in uniting for this cause with other Muslims and working as one solid unit toward this end, forgetting all minor differences for the sake of the greater goal to which God Himself calls them; and in making a very earnest and far-reaching effort to communicate with, to educate and to activate the masses of simple Turks who love Islam, always seeking help from God Most High, and not giving up hope and patience. " 'When will God's help come?' Ah, indeed, the help of God is always near"—but at the same time, "Man shall have nothing but what he strives for."*

There may be some among Turkish Muslims who feel that they have done their best. They have obtained a higher education and a good position and should now be in a situation to be influential if they ever will be, but their mouths are closed because of fear for their positions or even, in some instances, for fear of life itself. Some of these may decide that the only solution is to migrate to some other place where they will be secure from oppression and free to work for Islam. And yet, unless freedom is so severely limited that there is no possibility at all to practice and to propagate Islam, to stay and continue the struggle, to fight on somehow, is better, for if all the sincere Muslims leave the Muslim world, who will be left to carry on the effort for Islam? Better, too, to struggle and if necessary to die in a land where there are Muslims to struggle and die for than to live out one's life in security in a place where one comes in perpetual daily and hourly conflict with the values of the society and its ways of life.

*Al-Baqarah 2:214; al-Najm 53:39.

Others, although remaining in Turkey, will compromise because this compromise is almost forced on them by the social pressure of being considered backward, reactionary, fanatical, old-fashioned and ridiculous, hoping for the time when their country will have moved far enough in the opposite direction that they can bring their true ideas and true identity out of hiding, as it were, and express them openly in word and deed. I am sure that a great many Turks today fall into this category. Still others will compromise for the present because they feel that if they work indirectly they will be able to accomplish something for Islam, while if they come out and speak openly in the name of Islam they will be immediately shut up and unable to achieve anything at all. At present this is a method which has attracted a number of sincere Muslims, for due to the indirectness of their approach such people have succeeded in being able to continue to work, while others who are more direct and outspoken have been silenced or inactivated. However, at the same time, the impact of such Muslim individuals and groups on the society does not appear to be very great and is also likely to be painfully slow, so that it is possible that by the time they begin to have a real impact, the society may be altogether lost to Islam. I also wonder if there is not a danger for these sincere Muslims who compromise or function indirectly that, although they may keep their jobs and their reputations as modern, sensible people, they may ultimately miss playing a real part in the Islamic revival in Turkey which must, I believe, be accomplished by a mass movement at all levels of society; and besides this, they may in the end come to accept the prevailing norms as right and proper so completely that they cease to differentiate between what Islam requires and what they themselves are doing temporarily, solely because of the necessity of survival or in order not to expose their position when they are so powerless.

And there is yet another group: those who are prepared to risk their all for the sake of Islam, not exposing themselves unnecessarily or being foolhardy, but assuming, when circumstances require it, the problems and dangers inherent in standing firmly on the side of Islam and accepting this as a requirement of the situation because they cannot bear to live with themselves and do otherwise.

For this Turkey which I love, this ancient land over which century after century has passed, first with a slow, quiet spreading of Islam largely through the work of Sufis, those saintly Muslims who, through preaching and example, brought others to the light which was kindled within their own souls, and then in waves of conversions of crude tribal nomads, Christians and others, all drawn to the light of brotherhood and human dignity through faith in the One God—this Turkey is now in the throes of a mortal struggle, a struggle which is being echoed today throughout the Muslim world, now flaring up in this corner, now in that—in Syria, Lebanon, Palestine, Egypt, Sudan, Ethiopia, Iraq, Pakistan, India, Indonesia—to keep this brightest of all lights from dying out of the life of mankind . . .

One of the fronts upon which the attack against Islam is most prominent and vicious is in the sphere of morals. One sees how, slowly, perhaps even deliberately, the morals of Turkish society are subverted through the mass media and pornographic literature (tabloid newspapers and sex magazines with nude women on the covers flooding the market, openly displayed and available, as I have seen, even at some stationery shops where young children go to buy school supplies); explicit movies both Western and Turkish; the importation of completely unIslamic Western fashions for women; imported tastes and practices in the relationship between boys and girls slowly gaining currency in the society; and, coming down from governmental levels, an insidious propaganda which stigmatizes Islam and all that it requires in the way of high moral standards and pure behavior as backward and fit only for an earlier period when people were not really 'civilized.' Anyone having even a little foresight can easily visualize the effect which all this will have on the society within a relatively short time, as today the process of imitation of Western modes of behavior is well underway.

It is easy to understand the manner in which this deterioration is coming about. Boys and girls growing up in the morally-polluted atmosphere of the westernized sections of large Turkish cities, where there is a breakdown in traditional values and patterns of behavior, without knowledge of religion or any moral values, without having the slightest conception of what Islam is or what it teaches, without even knowing how to pray, slip gradually further and further into the new westernized patterns of behavior which are so rapidly gaining currency. Today many city boys and girls move together in groups or couples, spending time at movies, discothéques, dances or at the beach, and progress from these to much more harmful activities, without even being aware that what they are doing is destructive to themselves and a great sin in the sight of God. Even if such youngsters yearn for something better and more meaningful to fill their lives, there is no source from which they can learn it and no guide to show them the way, since their parents often have no knowledge of Islam and little idea of how to guide their children, and since effective Islamic education does not exist in Turkish schools. Before long, this sinned-against and sinning new generation of Turks will have grown up and will be in control of the society, bringing up the next generation, and the next and the next, with even less conception of its religious identity—its morals vitiated, its traditions despised, its religion forgotten and spurned more and more with each passing year. It does not require extrasensory perception to grasp the fact that such a society, with its present glaring moral, social and spiritual weaknesses, cannot realistically hope to hold such evils as communism at bay without the help of Islam, nor can it hope, without Islam, to accomplish anything of real value for itself or for the world community.

Let me try, after this, to give an idea of conditions at M.E.T.U. during this period. I have already commented on the unwholesome, un-Turkish appearance and the arrogant demeanor of the communist students, the posters plastered on buildings (red or brown silhouettes of marching workers brandishing their tools, featuring slogans against *Amerikan emperyalizm* and many others), and the anti-Western slogans scrawled on the walls of buildings ('*Kahrolsun*'—wrath—to whomever one wants to denounce, mainly Americans, etc.). I was on the campus recently and in the lobby of the second floor of M.E.T.U.'s student center saw several types of leftist, anti-Western displays related to causes dear to the left; there was also a long table of books for sale which includes works by all the well-known leaders of revolutionary movements of the past, as well as by leading contemporary communists and revolutionary figures from every corner of the globe.

As I have related, arms such as Molotov cocktails and others are being manufactured on the campus, evidently with University supplies and with the knowledge and connivance of some of the faculty and administration, and are stored in the dormitories; the posters are also being printed on campus. In recent days, the car of an American professor bearing a U.S. license plate had all its windows smashed, and two Turkish professors were manhandled by leftist students because they refused to contribute to some fund espoused by the leftists.

At any sort of an issue, a general meeting of students is called, and the result is always a boycott of classes. Each Friday for the past four successive Fridays there has been a student boycott over some issue (canceling the Friday sessions of two twice-weekly classes Selim is taking, so that in four weeks he has attended only four sessions of each!), usually to protest the killing or wounding by rightists of some communist student on some campus in Turkey, and a boycott also followed the decision of the government to place a police post on the campus to keep down the student unrest. This unrest has spread from university to university throughout Turkey, following the leader M.E.T.U., and during this week almost all the universities and *fakültes*—colleges which are branches of a university—in Ankara have been closed temporarily due to student unrest.

It may be asked whether the majority of students or faculty at M.E.T.U. are communist and if not, why they accept all this in silence. The number of dedicated, hard-core communists at M.E.T.U. is estimated at approximately three hundred, out of a total student body of about six thousand; yet this number is able to terrorize and intimidate dissenters into silence by open or implied threats of violence or even death. For faculty or graduate assistants, the price of open disagreement is simply too high: the loss of one's position (for which, in Turkey, one has generally labored and struggled extremely hard) and extreme difficulty in finding other work, the loss of one's prestige, and the invariable threat of physical violence. These are the factors which force into silence those who dissent all over Turkey today, and the government continues to do nothing. Yes, in Turkey civil liberties are guaranteed by the Constitution—but to whom? Under these chaotic conditions, certainly to communists, but never to Muslims!

Another prime example of this situation in miniature is Gazi Eğitim Institüsü, a school in Ankara where a Muslim boy whom we know, a nephew of Deniz Hanım's, is a student. This high school teacher's training institute has, in fact, been known since the 1920's as a communist-oriented institution where standards of morals are very lax. It is a kind of junior M.E.T.U., where youngsters of less than twenty years of age, fresh from high school or teacher training school, whose heads are often empty of other ideas and values, easily fall prey to the initiated leftists in higher classes, swallow their propaganda, and become in turn the initiators of others; these are some of the future high school teachers of Turkey, who will also be assigned to teaching Islamic studies in many cases, together with other subjects. There are others, to be sure, who do not go along with the communists, as well as some who value Islam, but they are silent, intimidated, not wanting to be noticed. I once went to this school and observed that its atmosphere was very unwholesome: the same arrogant, un-Turkish faces as at M.E.T.U., boys and girls pairing off and lingering about together (something which, despite all the westernization in Turkey today, is not socially acceptable, and which marks those who do it not only as *ahlâksız* but also as *terbiyesiz*—both immoral and mannerless). If such people are to have the training of the coming generations of Turks in their hands, what can one realistically hope for their future?

The Turkish class moves along more slowly now, with infinitesimal progress from one lesson to the next as the grammar becomes more and more complex and difficult. But since the beginning, I have been both interested in and disturbed by the many conflicting elements I have observed in the behavior and speech of the teacher, Zeynep Hanım. Sitting in her class for the past many weeks, I have studied her from all possible sides. At last I have realized that in the contradictory, conflicting things she says—not having any idea that they are contradictory, as she is a reasonable woman in other respects—I am seeing the confusion, the dilemma, the split of the Turkish mind in miniature.

I will not go into the ambiguities which I have observed in her personality and behavior; apart from these, her speech and attitudes represent manifold contradictions. At times she teaches us words which are rapidly being incorporated into Turkish from European languages, particularly French; at other times, she lashes out against these, against the artificially-manufactured 'new Turkish' words, or against obsolete words from the ancestral Turkish of Central Asia. Most of all, however, she has many times expressed a great anti-pathy and hatred for Turkish words of Arabic origin. Lately I have had to hear over and over, "This is an Arabic word, not Turk-ish"—*"Not Turkish,"* when it has been part of Turkish for the past many hundreds of years, and when probably at least one-fourth, or perhaps even much more, of all words in contemporary Turkish (and a much larger proportion in the Turkish of earlier times) are "Arabic," in continuous daily use by millions of Turks of all ideo-logies (including Zeynep Hanım herself), particularly in legal and commercial spheres! But to add to the confusion, this same lady fre-quently uses Islamic expressions such as *"Maşallah," "İnşallah"* and others (although sometimes perhaps a little sarcastically) in her ordinary conversation in the class, although there is no need at all for her to do so.

Here it is, then, the split and contradiction of the modern Turk, tied with his heart more or less unconsciously and involuntarily to that God-conscious attitude which once pervaded all the Muslim world, including that part which today is called Turkey, and which is an inseparable part of the language, but with his mind set against the past, against Islam, against Arabic and even Arabs. In the be-ginning, as she used these Islamic expressions frequently and be-cause of the pure Islamic name she bears, I naively assumed that this meant that she was at least nominally a Muslim, but at last I have realized from all her attitudes, behavior and even her open admission that this is simply not so, and wondered why, in that case, she continues to use them. Habit, unconscious adherence to the form of a language which cannot so easily be purged of its very life and soul, nothing more—certainly not anything related to reli-gious conviction. If she is indeed illustrative, as I suppose her to be, of the split in the soul of Turkey, may God help it!

Otherwise our life goes on in the same manner. We do not go out as often now because of the bad weather, but there are frequent exchanges of visits with Envers. Our other frequent visitor is Ce-

mile. Her visits to us and her love for us are one of the greatest
joys of our life here. Her feeling for us has become so strong that
she shares in our every interest and experience, and we have returned her feelings with the same warmth. Her understanding of
Islam is deep, true and mature, her thinking in most matters very
like our own, and her devotion and desire to serve God and to
help her people intense and unwavering.

As for the children, they now no longer think in terms of America but have come to feel that this is home, at least for the present,
and they have made a good adjustment and are happy here. Their
school continues to go along from day to day without their learning
much, although considerable progress in their Turkish is noticeable
now. The teachers certainly seem harsher than their American
counterparts, scolding a good deal and sometimes beating, but still
it is better than the private school, particularly as there is only half-
a-day of it.

Overlooking the playground of their school, as probably at most
other schools of Turkey, stands a scowling black bust of Atatürk on
a pedestal, indeed a proper figure to be an inspiration to children.
Maryam and Nura tell us that sometimes other children come and
surround them, saying, *"Selâm Atatürk, selâm Atatürk!"* and demand that they make a bowing gesture toward that statue, showing
to what an extent some of the children of Turkey, like their elders,
are already infected and seriously ill with the disease of idol- and
man-worship . . .

CHAPTER 8

HARD DAYS

January 8: Two afternoons ago Enver took us to Ulus Castle, which had appealed to me so much that I wanted to take the rest of the family to see it. Inside its walls we met a youth who volunteered to guide us up to the ramparts, taking us through a narrow passage which we would never have found or dared to enter by ourselves. From the ramparts we overlooked all of Ankara, spreading out before us in every direction, the pale, purple-grey volcanic mountains in the distance. Below the castle walls lay the picturesque cluster of the old city's red tile roofs, the minarets of its small mosques interspersed among its houses and shops; beyond, the scattered squalid hillside tenements around Ulus; and in the far distance the modern buildings of New Ankara with the tall structures of Kızılay and adjacent areas, the further parts of the city sprawling out and over the hillsides in all directions. What was it like, I wondered, to live within the walls of this castle, amid its ancient stones and time-worn houses, one of the procession of souls which came and went as century followed century? How many upheavals had this aged citadel witnessed, and how many more were yet to come while it still stood . . . ?

As I have written, the anarchy on university campuses had reached such a pitch that it was impossible that things should continue in this way. A meeting of all the *rektörs* of the universities of Ankara was held and a resolution, to be proposed to Parliament, was passed, specifying that armaments are to be confiscated, an armed police post is to be put on each campus, posters are not to be put up without permission of the *rektör* and the existing ones are to be removed, and the leaders of boycotts are to be expelled.

After this, there was the question of what would happen next at M.E.T.U., in the vanguard of all the leftist student unrest in Turkey. It was felt that the *Rektör,* Dr. Inönü, although himself not a communist, was a leftist sympathizer who would not go along with the strongest measures of the proposal but would find ways to circumvent them. Today some classes were interrupted by communist students who demanded that the instructors and students go to a general forum, at which it was apparently decided not to accept any of the proposed legislation, the result of which would obviously be the closing of the University. At these assemblies, facts and statistics are presented in such a way that, unless one is clearly aware of their distortion and untruth and of the lying, deceitful tactics of the communists, he would be easily taken in by them. The public has also been presented with totally false and misleading information to keep it from being aware that the student and faculty bodies have themselves refused to accept the proposed legislation.

Thus there is in Turkey an ever-increasing educated elite of communists trained in and resorting to every sort of deceit, trickery, smear tactics, threat and intimidation to accomplish its evil aims— those who will be members of Parliament, the holders of high positions in judicial, administrative, military, economic, educational, communications and social planning spheres, wielding power and influence in all vital areas of the society in succeeding generations. It breaks the heart to see all this happening, and God only knows how it will end. In the meantime, the common people of Turkey are oblivious to the menace, living in their small, stable world of work and family, and incapable of even imagining what may lie ahead for their country.

The other day when I was in a shop in Ulus, the proprietor and others began talking to me. When they learned that I am an American Muslim, there was the usual '*Maşallah*-ing' and then one of them asked what I thought about Islam in Turkey, apparently expecting to hear something very favorable. I replied, with my limited Turkish, that it seemed to me it was in serious trouble and very much weakened. Why? they asked. As I did not have sufficient command of the language to go into all the reasons—these complex matters which have been occupying my mind for the past months—in very brief fashion, I satisfied myself with remarking on the communist threat. I was very taken aback by the reply I received. "The communists? Oh, we can deal with them very easily. In three days we will sweep Turkey clean of them!" If this is typical of the thinking of the average man-in-the street, how ignorant and deluded they are not to realize that it is much more likely that Turkey will be swept clean of naive people like themselves by those who know both how to sweep physically by means of terrorism and how to sweep such simple minds with their shameless, lying propaganda!

How is it that youth fresh from high school enter universities or other higher educational institutions and within a short time are indoctrinated, committed and begin to propagate their new religion? I recall a statement which Deniz Hanım, who is a school teacher, made recently, which struck me very strongly. She said, "Turkish children are brought up and finish high school very innocent." Innocent! If it be 'innocence' not to know right from wrong, what parent has a right to keep his child innocent up to the age of sixteen or eighteen in a time and place in which every sort of harmful ideology is competing for the allegiance of that child's mind! To leave him thus 'innocent' means to leave him not only incapable of distinguishing good from evil and truth from falsehood, but also by-and-large 'innocent' of any sort of positive values as well. The one hour a week—optional after the eighth grade—of Islamic studies offered in Turkish public schools, often taught by teachers of other subjects who may have no knowledge of Islam or who may be atheists or communists, does not go very far toward training the child in a system of life which is hardly practiced anywhere around him; and if he later becomes a Muslim in the true sense, it is often *in spite of, not because of,* what he has been taught about Islam at school. Thus the mind of the youngster, having learned no positive values in any sphere, remains like a blank page, to be written upon by the devious propaganda of the leftists, who have no scruples about using any methods which will serve their ends, or alternatively by the empty materialistic appeal of the Kemalists.

The simple fact is that the past few generations of Turks have possessed no system of beliefs or values which will resist such encroachments, have not been trained in analyzing or in distinguishing right from wrong, and have no idea of the treacherous means to which unGodly people will resort to gain their ends. When the hold of that most excellent of value systems, Islam, was broken on their lives, it was replaced by nothing more vital to the human spirit than nationalistic and materialistic ideologies as a value system, and by a drive toward modernization, technological advancement and greater material satisfactions as a concrete goal. Moreover, the self-respect and pride of Turks through their identification with the Ottoman—that is, with the Muslim—community had been lost, and they were now not only not great but, indeed, very, very small, with no real voice in world politics and no noteworthy status in the community of nations. Thus, their egos hurt by lack of identification with something which could give them status and self-respect as a nation, their individual and collective minds empty of real values and incapable of distinguishing among the clamor of various conflicting ideological claims, when they are turned loose in the world, many among the young generation of Turks are lost, even without a struggle, to the vicious forces which are competing for their allegiance; and with each loss of a young person to the side of wrong, Turkey advances that much further along the path of everything which tends toward the disintegration of the society and its individuals.

It seems quite probable to me that even if a way is now found to halt the spread of communism and to destroy its hold upon its most ardent devotees in Turkey, some other system, perhaps equally destructive to true human and spiritual values, may arise to take over Turkish hearts which have been lost to Islam, unless the trend away from Islam can be stopped by concrete and effective action. *For no man can live "by bread alone." The human heart must have something to give itself to, some cause or* raison d'etre, *and if men have turned away from the best of ways, replacing obedience and submission to the Lord of men with obedience to men or the desires and whims of men themselves, they may easily turn, in their need for something to live for and to cherish, toward the worst ones.* This is, after all, the basic message and meaning of Islam: to serve, obey and be devoted to no one except God Most High. For every human being who does not serve and obey God alone knowingly or unknowingly obeys and serves something or someone else, something infinitely lesser, something created like himself, and hence—like any man-made system or ideology—as subject to error and the obvious limitations of human understanding and knowledge as the least of mankind.

I have tried to express in a poem the state of mind of the materialist entrapped in the philosophical rationale for disbelief, closed up toward the natural promptings of his heart to believe and to open itself toward God. Perhaps the individual carrying on this dialogue with himself is a present-day Turk . . .

A Muslim's voice said, "TAUBA ESTAĞFURULLAH." [God forgive me.]
Within, another voice replied:
"What have I done that I should always say this?
Have I committed some crime, that I should
always abase and accuse myself before God?"

The Muslim said, "SUBHANALLAH."
The other voice within replied: [Glory be to God.]
"Why should I praise God all the time?
Is He then so badly in need
of my commendations, to feel His own greatness?
I for one cannot believe in such a petty God!"

The Muslim's voice said, "ALHAMDULILLAH."   [Thanks be to God.]
Within, the other voice replied:
"But why should I give thanks to God,
when I neither asked to be born nor was consulted,
and if He chose to give me life,
He owes me my provision—
so why give thanks?"

The Muslim said, "ALLAHU AKBAR."
From within the voice replied: [God is the Most Great.]
"Man has done such great, great things;
why credit God Who only gave the power to do them,
while man by his own efforts has done all the rest?
Then why should we go on praising God's greatness?"

The Muslim said, *"LA ILAHA ILLA ALLAH."*　　　　[There is no deity
Then within, all was silenced;　　　　　　　　　　　　except God.]
the voice spoke no more.
But the sound of weeping came,
came from the one who knew at last
of so many *ilâhs* [deities, objects of worship] set up on the altar or the heart,
who wept for the confusion, wept for the cynicism,
wept for the inability to be thankful,
to acknowledge the mercies of God Most High,
to praise and glorify Him,
to ask for His forgiveness:
who wept for what man has lost in losing all this;
and at last in deep earnestness the voice within cried out,
"TAUBA, TAUBA ESTAĞFURULLAH!"

Think, Turks! Think, people of the land I have learned to love, what you are permitting to happen, while you lazily keep your minds from thought, stupefied by indifference, going about your daily lives without concern for your religion, your country, yourselves, your children, your children's children and all the generations to come!

January 10: We still do not know what is going to happen at M.E.T.U., but the worst can be expected. All these months—even years, it may be—of preparation and build-up have not been for nothing, that is certain.

That all this is being financed and directed from outside Turkey is now unquestionable; truckloads of smuggled bullets and other armaments have been stopped at the borders and it is asserted that the money for all the communists' various activities is being funneled in from outside. One guess is that with so many willing workers for communism inside Turkey, the Soviet Union is attempting to balkanize this country and turn it into another satellite like the nations of Eastern Europe, in fulfillment of a long-cherished desire to bring Turkey under Soviet domination. At the same time another communist thrust is believed to be coming from neighboring Syria, where Turkish leftist youth are said to be training in the camps of communist guerilla groups who have taken advantage of the Palestine problem to tutor communists from every country of the Middle East in terrorist tactics, while they themselves cooperate with Israeli communists; and it is possible that China may have a hand in all this too somehow. Although the number of revolutionary communist students in Turkey is not very large at present, today many confirmed communists also hold high positions in government, law, commerce, communications, and are known to be present in the lower ranks of the armed forces; and thus, if nothing is done to stop all this, despite all the Islamic elements, despite the goodness and sincerity of the common people, the possibility of a full-scale revolution which may bring Turkey under total communist domination, God forbid, is not unimaginable in the near or distant future.

The M.E.T.U. communists have warned some of the practicing Muslim students on campus that if the police stage a raid to destroy the printing presses and confiscate armaments, they will be used as hostages to the police, and if they try to move out of the dormitories before this threat materializes, they will be barred by the terrorists from attending classes. Apart from such serious threats, there is also continual harrassment in a more subtle fashion of practicing Muslim students in communist-dominated schools, with the infliction of regular and very deliberate insults to their religious feelings. These religious students—and other committed Muslims in exposed positions in Turkey today—live in an atmosphere of perpetual tension, the expectation of trouble, the sense of having no place where they can feel at ease or at home, in many cases putting up a brave resistance yet being gradually worn down by all these problems.

And yet, in spite of everything, in spite of the fact that life here is becoming increasingly difficult for us and for every serious Muslim just now, I would nonetheless be glad to remain here for the rest of my life. Turkey is a land where enough remains of Islam to make me prefer to live, struggle and die here rather than to live in ease and comfort in a land where many of the society's basic values conflict so sharply with my own and where I must continually compromise even in many of the small matters of daily life. For in America, although we do not have to face serious problems like these, although there is freedom and tolerance for our beliefs and activities, with each passing year I feel increasingly that I do not belong, that I cannot possibly fit in, and that I completely reject the basic premises of the society and its way of life.

For years, it has been made clear to me by everything I heard and read, coming from the indisputably authoritative source of the American behavioral expert—the psychologists, psychiatrists, sociologists and other learned people—that anyone like myself who is unable to fit in is maladjusted, abnormal, and hence in error. Later Islam gave me a standard, a criterion and an authority for a way with which I could identify, in which I felt comfortable and at peace with myself. However, it was not until we came to Turkey, until I began to examine and try to understand the elements of a true Islamic society (both those which I found present and those which were lacking), that I began to re-evaluate this maladjustment to the contemporary society of the United States.

Many of my reactions of earlier times, I realize today, were correct and true. For if we define 'normal' as whatever is current and common in a given society and 'adjustment' as fitting in with prevailing social patterns, then by definition we are obliged to accept as 'normal' the deterioration of the social fabric and loss of stable values which has increasingly come to characterize American life, and 'adjustment' as being able to be comfortable and to fit into a society which is marked by such disturbing phenomena as the breakdown of close, warm family ties and the insecurity engendered by it; the proliferation of unhappy marriages, broken homes, divorces and the disturbed children produced by them; the sex-oriented atmosphere, shamelessness and lack of concern for integrity and purity, the increasing prevalence of illicit sexual relations and also of homosexuality; the high rate of crime and juvenile delinquency; the steadily-increasing numbers of the emotionally disturbed, mentally ill and suicides; the spiraling rate of alcoholism and drug addiction; the current generation gap and marked rebellion of youth; the problems of hippieism and dropping out from society; the degraded, jungle-like atmosphere of large cities; the pollution of the environment; the wastage of natural resources; and the standardization, vulgarization, commercialism and depersonalization which prevail in America and other parts of the Western world at the present time.

When, as in America today, the definition of 'normal' comes to be equated with 'common' or 'average,' abnormalcy gradually comes to be taken as the norm. Thus the average American is subtly pushed by societal pressures to lower his standards and modify his behavior by a succession of minute, imperceptible stages without even being aware that he does so, to a level which he would never have chosen voluntarily and which would have been totally unthinkable to him only a few years earlier. To defend this state of affairs, the argument is put forward that as conditions change, values and behavior must also change, and thus the definitions of normal and abnormal too are subject to major revision. By an extension of this sort of logic, if the day ever comes—as it is not impossible it may—when crime and depravity of every sort become customary and accepted, normalcy will still be defined as adjusting to and living by the prevailing standards, and the person who feels out of place, who is unable to accept and adjust to such a society, will still be considered odd or abnormal.

But is there not a broader, deeper adjustment than mere adaptation to the prevailing norms of a particular society and in no way dependent on them, namely, an adjustment to the laws and standards of the Creator of men and of the human spirit? If this is one's criterion rather than mere conformity to the practices or requirements of a local culture, regardless of how degraded they may be, then one arrives at an absolute rather than a relative standard of what is 'normal,' and thus adjustment to a debased society rather becomes a measure of abnormality, an indication of maladjustment to being a creature of God, a member of the human family which has a basic human dignity to uphold, and spiritual and moral needs and values which are a fundamental part of its nature, not merely the physical and material drives which are the lowest common denominator among men and beasts.

Thus for me and for all Muslims—indeed, for all those who are truly religious of any faith—normalcy and adjustment are defined as accepting and living according to the norms of God, no matter how much human norms may differ from them. Rather than to give up one iota of my adjustment to the standards prescribed by the All-Wise God, I have voluntarily accepted to be 'abnormal' and 'maladjusted' in relation to most basic aspects of the society in which I happen to live. My true home is *dar al-Islam*—the abode of Islam— that is, that country which is ruled by the law of God (the *Shari'ah*) and where Muslims live according to the precepts of Islam in entirety, something which does not exist anywhere in the entire world today; for while there are, to be sure, many countries whose people are predominantly Muslim in name and by profession, and communities of committed Muslims here and there who *live* Islam, at the present time, to our great shame, no state exists which can be considered to have a genuine Islamic government and where the teachings of Islam are applied in totality. And so, for me and for all Muslims, there is no real home in this world, no single place where the true criteria of what is normal for a *human* being are universally accepted and lived. We are passing by, on a journey which is soon over, going from God to God, and seeking with what He has given us "the Home of the Hereafter."* To God is our returning, and we are on our way to Him . . .

January 15: A few nights ago, police entered the M.E.T.U. campus, ostensibly in search of a car carrying youths who had robbed an Ankara bank of a large amount of money (bank robberies having become 'normal' these days), suspecting that they were on campus. The arrival of the police at night tipped off the students that a raid or search was imminent, and they had time to secrete away their stores of arms, which they buried or concealed somehow. The next morning when Selim went to the campus, he found that it had been cordoned off and that the *Rektör,* after calling a hurried faculty meeting, had decided to close the University, for as Turkish universities are autonomous, the *rektör* has the option of shutting down his institution if police wish to enter without his requesting it. Thus a very uncertain situation was, for the time being, brought to a head.

The students were expelled from the campus and left, many walking, carrying their baggage, which was searched and apparently some weapons were found. Some buried arms and munitions, plus a great number of copies of the "Maoist Manifesto," were discovered, but the great bulk of armaments was not. The University was then closed for the next five days.

Examinations for the fall semester, scheduled for next week, may have to be postponed because of these events, possibly result-

*Al-Qasas 28:83 and al-'Ankabut 29:64.

ing in the shortening of the month-long vacation in February during which we were to have visited Pakistan. Due to this situation, our travel program is now completely uncertain and there is no way to know whether our plans will be able to materialize or not.

It is not clear whether the search for the robbers' car was merely a pretext for searching the campus; apparently the police did not enter the classroom buildings but only the dormitories and were on the whole not very serious in their search. Although the University is still closed, the police have left, access to the campus is free, and there is no sign of any activity. The latest incident is the placing of a bomb in front of the house of the *Rektör,* Dr. Erdal Inönü, which apparently broke in the windows and doors. The reason for this unkind act, when he has been so helpful in allowing and abetting communist militancy on his campus? Communist students apparently want the expulsion from the University of all rightist—that is, nationalist—students, and want to be entirely free to make the University not a center of learning but solely of revolutionary activity.

In this disturbed situation, it is as impossible to predict our own immediate future as that of this troubled land. It seems possible that under these conditions M.E.T.U. may be shut down indefinitely. In that case, although Selim is on a year's leave from his work and the holder of a fellowship grant for study here, we will have little choice but to simply pack up and go home to take up the thread of our life in America—without Selim's completing the studies for which he came and without our having had sufficient time and opportunity to really see and understand Turkey.

Turks who have lived through all the problems of the past fifty years and have seen almost all Islamic activities come to a halt in their country, the prohibition against reading the Qu'ran in Arabic or teaching it, the dwindling of Islamic education to a mere meaningless token which is calculated not to affect youth at all (or perhaps even to turn them against Islam), and the complete change in the tone and orientation of their society, should not be at a loss to understand that today's revolutionary leftist Turkish youth, with their arrogant demeanor and insolent bearing, are the fruit of that tree of ignorance and denial of God. Yet I look beyond all this and see the Turkey which was, which might have been, and which to some extent still is among the true Muslims of this land, and I find here something which I can deeply love and identify with. Leaving all this will be, God knows, very difficult for me, the more difficult if we have to leave before the time we had intended, perhaps without seeing much more of the country than this blighted Ankara. But Allah knows what is best for us. I can only be thankful with all my heart for all the good He has given us—and how could I feel otherwise, even if all this good were not my portion in this world, if He sees fit to send anything to me?

This has been my frame of mind for several days, fed by the total state of unrest and bleak future of this suffering Turkey, and my own small personal dilemma of not finding a home for my heart in this world. Under the impact of these thoughts and feelings, I wrote my first—and perhaps last—poem in Turkish in an effort to express them more meaningfully, with help from Cemile.

Misafirim bu dünyada,	A visitor am I in this world,
Misafir ve yabancıyım.	A visitor and a stranger.
Asil yurdum burada değil,	My permanent home is not here;
Hakiki yurdum Allah'la,	My true home is with Allah.
Ahirette, Allah'la,	In the Hereafter, with Allah,
Allah Allah Allah Allah.	Allah Allah Allah Allah.
Bu dünyada müskuller	The difficulties of this world
Allah'tan gelen imtihan.	Are a test from Allah.
Burada uğraşmak vazifemiz,	Here striving is our duty;
Mükafat orada, Allah'tan.	The reward is there, from Allah.
Ahirette, Allah'tan,	In the Hereafter, from Allah
Allah Allah Allah Allah.	Allah Allah Allah Allah.
Müteessir olma, ya canım,	Be not sad, O my soul;
Derd ve zahmet tecrubedir,	Pain and trouble are a trial.
Uğras, uğras yurdunna dogru,	Strive, strive toward your home,
Hakiki yurdum Allah'la.	Your real home with Allah.
Ahirette, Allah'la,	In the Hereafter, with Allah,
Allah Allah Allah Allah.	Allah Allah Allah Allah.

January 20: Recently all of us except Selim were sick, and we made two trips to the doctor within one week. Jamal had a troublesome

cough complicated by asthma, and again the old burden on my mind, not knowing what to do to help him or what would follow. Thank God he is better now.

The children are living here under conditions which in America would have seemed to them unbearably difficult and dull, are doing well under them, and their sense of perspective and imagination are deepening. Jamal is thoughtful and concerned about various problems in the world to which he has just recently awakened, and Maryam says that she likes it here and doesn't want to go home— good news to our beloved Turkish friends who feel very sad and apologetic about what their country has been able to offer us under these difficult circumstances. And while Nura is quite young, nevertheless this experience is proving to be very meaningful to her as well, although I hardly expected as much. All three are making good progress with their Turkish, and the girls have playmates in the building and nearby.

Restlessness and a feeling of being unsettled pervades our life at present. We had planned to leave for Pakistan in another week or ten days, in which case we would now be joyfully planning for the trip. As it is, we don't know when we will be able to go, although most matters pertaining to our journey are complete. Everything is uncertain. May Allah guide us.

January 21: Yesterday was the most difficult of the days we have spent here. The two days preceding it, when M.E.T.U. reopened after its five-day closure, were peaceful and quiet on campus—a bad sign. Selim was preparing to go to the University late in the morning when Güneş Hanım came hurrying over with the information that a major disturbance had taken place on the campus. Selim tried to telephone, but there was no reply from the University's switchboard. Under these conditions we both felt that it was better if he did not go to campus that day, although he had work to do. Later we were able to get clear information about what had taken place.

The preceding night there had again been a police action on campus against the bank robbers who were hiding there and who had sought asylum with the *Rektör*. Their identity had now been established without any question: they were members of the Dev-Genç, a revolutionary communist group composed largely of students; some were M.E.T.U. students, and they had known that they would be relatively safe on the campus. All night firing had taken place on campus as a resistance measure against the police, and it continued into the morning: dynamite, bombs, pistols and the dormitories reported to be armed with machine guns on every floor. The University was then closed, this time indefinitely.

Perhaps it is a weakness in me that at a time like this I should have thought first of our own personal situation and second of the situation at large, over which, in any case, I have not the least control, but I could not help it. Selim had come here to take some courses in relation to his field of work and hopefully to collect technical data for a research project on which he was working at home. The fall semester had now been completed (although in a very disturbed and inadequate fashion due to all these problems, including the frequent cancellation of classes due to boycotts and student forums, which had naturally affected all serious students adversely) except for the final examinations which were to have been held very shortly. We had expected to leave immediately after the exams for our month-long trip to Pakistan, reaching there in time to spend 'Eid al-Adha with Selim's brother in Peshawar. The fate of the final examinations and, indeed, of the remainder of the academic year, is now completely uncertain, and of course it is essential that Selim be in Ankara when the final examinations are given. Thus, leaving entirely out of consideration what may happen to the remaining portion of the academic year, it is very possible that the trip to Pakistan may have to be very much shortened or even postponed for several months in the face of these changed circumstances.

With these latest disturbing incidents, despite our very strong personal inclination and desire to stay on, both of us have come to feel that there is no justification for remaining here and no alternative to returning home soon if the situation continues to be so troubled (or if the University remains closed, one or the other of which seems highly probable), for Selim's studies under these circumstances have been extremely frustrating and inadequate; complicating the matter of course is the fact that we want to leave for Pakistan very soon if possible. Thus there seem to be three alternatives before us now: to go to Pakistan, return to Turkey and leave for home as soon as possible if the situation has not improved meanwhile; to go to Pakistan, return to Turkey and stick it out here for better or worse until summer, hoping that these problems may somehow be resolved; or to wind up all our affairs here at once, go to Pakistan and return to America from there. And if we stay, there is the continual anxiety about Selim's safety on campus, for those known to be committed Muslims are not safe, although it is clear that the terrorists are not seeking to kill or to harm foreigners and are not even much interested in harming individuals, but rather in creating chaos, in forcing the present *Rektör* out, and probably in toppling Demirel's government.

While matters were at this pass, Cemile, who has become so close to us, arrived, very much shocked to hear this latest in a series of bad news, understanding and sympathizing deeply with our personal dilemma. I love her, Emine and all our friends so dearly and cannot bear the idea of parting with them so soon! Later in the day Selim and I went to talk to Enver and Emine and then with Bahadir Bey, consulting with them about the probable course of events and asking their opinions about what it would be best for us to do under these very uncertain conditions; however, as it was completely impossible to predict what would happen, they were unable to give any answers to our questions which would help us to arrive at a decision. We returned home, thinking deeply, and at length decided what we had wanted to decide from the beginning— that we would stay on; we were just not emotionally prepared to leave now. Nonetheless, I was not convinced of the rightness of this decision in a situation where the courses dictated by wisdom and by the heart are so much at variance, and have continued to waver and to go around and around in circles concerning what we ought to do ever since.

This morning Selim has gone to talk to his department chairman, after which he should be much more clear about the situation, *insha'Allah;* I am writing this during his absence at the University. Before he left, I urged him to take whatever action seemed best to him, depending on circumstances, and thus, from all indications, I am almost sure what the outcome will be, namely, that he will decide to leave. Yet truly, after all these weeks of tension and anxiety, I am almost beyond caring; if conditions are this bad, it is both fruitless and unwise to stay on. It is with the deepest regret that I am forced to come to this conclusion, but there is now no other way, and I am fully prepared for his returning with the decision that we return home as soon as we can make suitable arrangements, via Pakistan.

January 22: Yesterday afternoon Selim did not come home from the University when I expected him, and I became a bit worried. Cemile had come around noon, aware that a decision was about to be made. Her face reflected the sadness she felt at the dilemma which the behavior of her countrymen had forced upon us and at the possibility of our stay being terminated so abruptly. *"Ablacığım,"* she said, putting her arm around me, "I know Turkey very well. When you first wrote to me that you were coming here, I was afraid that you would have some very serious disappointments with the state of things here, but I did not imagine anything like *this!"*

At three o'clock, by which time I had become quite concerned about Selim's prolonged absence, he walked in, smiling broadly, and said quite offhandedly, "We are going to Pakistan the day after tomorrow!" I was thunderstruck by this sudden announcement and, grasping the fact that we were to stay on, so happy and relieved that I could find no words. Selim told us that he had talked to his advisor, who had been extremely kind and considerate, urging him to leave for Pakistan at once, for the final examinations would not take place until the University reopens, presumably after a month or six weeks, by which time we would have returned. Thus all the problems seem to be solved, temporarily at least; the matter of what events may follow upon the reopening of the University we have put aside for the time-being, trusting that during this interval an intensive effort will be made to find a workable solution to these problems.

No leaving Turkey now, and we are free to go to Pakistan immediately! I could have danced and sung for joy, so thankful and happy was I. How good God has been to us!

When I came down from my cloud of gratitude and delight over the way events had fallen out, I began to close with the very real problems of getting everything finalized in the one day which remained before our leaving—and guests were coming for dinner tonight! However, we were essentially ready, and only a few last-minute matters yet remained to be taken care of.

Selim and the children went to Enver's to tell them the good news, and I did not refuse when Cemile insisted on staying to help me in any way possible. The visitors stayed for a long time, and after they had gone Cemile and I washed the dishes, finished the remaining packing, and talked until very late, for we would not meet again until our return from Pakistan. We were up for *Fajr* at six, and Cemile returned to her university a little later, with countless warm good wishes for our trip.

The travel plans had initially been to fly directly to Peshawar without any stops on the way in order to be there in time for the coming *'Eid;* now, however, as we have more time than we had anticipated and want to spend some of it in traveling, they have been considerably altered. As the first leg of the journey, we are to fly to Erzurum in eastern Turkey with an Irani acquaintance of Selim's, Firoz Shahidi, who is employed as a translator here; he lives in Qazvin in northwestern Iran and has extended to us a warm invitation to visit his home as this city is on our way. Firoz, a smart-looking, very self-assured young man who I guessed was from a quite modern home, visited us the other evening. I did not especially like him on first acquaintance but the invitation to his home had been warmly tendered, and we were grateful to him for making it possible, due to his familiarity with the best mode of travel from Turkey through Iran, to see something of his country. He assured us that it would be quite easy to get a bus from Erzurum to Qazvin and on to Tehran, from where we will continue the journey to Peshawar by whatever means of transportation and route seems best.

I had begun my plans and preparations for this trip as soon as we were settled in Ankara, getting things organized little by little. Now everything was complete, and it only remained to get the apartment ready for our absence. Today Aynur Abla also went to the children's school on our behalf to have their names withdrawn from the rolls. We had had this in mind for some time, for they have not been happy in school and have learned virtually nothing in the way of subject matter due to their insufficient Turkish. As we had sent all the books for their respective classes from America, it will be more fruitful if they work in these at home after our return.

It is hard to believe that all the years, the last few months, of waiting to revisit Pakistan are really coming to an end. I can hardly express my anticipation and delight, for now *insha'Allah* will come a whole host of new and very interesting and happy experiences for us all. I must get de-Turkeyized and become Pakistanized for the next month or so; there is no way to express how much I have become attuned to the Turkish 'frequency' by now, after my early struggles with the language and everything else.

Now new adventures will come, new adjustments will be made, and I can only pray to Allah our Sustainer for good health, safety and protection, through His mercy, from everything harmful on this journey. How interesting, how supremely enjoyable, to travel from place to place and see a new part of the Muslim world. How it revives and stimulates my mind, bored and wearied by all the problems of recent weeks and by the bleak monotony of this dreary Anakara winter!

Section Two

JOURNEY TO THE EAST

CHAPTER 9

IRAN

March 4, 1971, 7:30 a.m., in the air somewhere west of Karachi: We settled ourselves in the jet airliner for the long flight from Karachi to Beirut, Beirut to Istanbul, from where we would go on to Ankara—the whole of the Middle East, with all its complex life and culture, crossed over in a matter of hours. In the beginning of the flight, a jovial pilot had talked to the passengers at intervals via the public address system, and presently a good hot substantial breakfast was served, after which the stewardesses retired and were seen no more. During the remainder of the flight, most of the passengers, whiling away the time, had no choice except to sleep.

Maryam and Jamal sat with Selim, keeping themselves occupied somehow, and Nura was beside me, quietly entertaining herself in various ways. My mind, tired from the abrupt changes of the past few days and numb with a weary sadness, wandered back and forth over the events of the past thirty-five days of travel. . .

★ ★ ★

I recalled that first day of the trip, when I had awakened very early in the morning with the fresh, joyous realization that today was the day, the day for which we had waited so long. Strangely enough, though, I did not feel as much about it as I had expected; perhaps, I thought, the initial travel and change of environment had affected me so much that another, lesser change could have only limited impact.

★ ★ ★

That morning, by the time everyone was up and ready, I had completed all my work in the house. A short while later we were on the way to Enver's, for with their usual thoughtfulness, they had insisted that we must come to them for breakfast, even though we had had dinner with them the evening before. A little later, as we left their apartment together for the airport, to my great astonishment, Emine, standing at the head of the stairs, threw a panful of water after me in such a way that it flowed down the steps without wetting me. I turned around, looking at her in amazement. She and Enver laughed at the expression on my face and Emine said, "Marian Abla, it's an old Turkish custom to send travelers off in this way, with the meaning, 'May your way be as smooth as flowing water.'" With that, she put away her pan, locked the door and linked her arm in mine, sensing all that was passing through my mind as I took a silent leave of their house and street until our return. I would miss them everywhere I went, I knew, and remember them, especially dear Emine, innumerable times.

As our family with Enver, Emine, Aynur Abla and the Irani boy, Firoz Shahidi, settled ourselves on the Turkish Airlines' bus going from the downtown terminal to the airport, threading its way through the heavy traffic of the city, a deep sense of delight and thankfulness to God for the days which were ahead took possession of me, for I hoped for wonderful and interesting experiences on this trip. The cares of the past months, the tensions of the last few weeks, were all forgotten and fell off my shoulders, as it were, in anticipation of the new scenes and adventures which lay ahead during our travels, the period of reunion with our near relatives, and the opportunity to acquire a deeper understanding of the Muslim world, and now I was as excited and happy as a child who is traveling for the first time. The children chattered animatedly in the seat behind Selim and me; looking around at them, I smiled with contentment and received their answering smiles and the girls' warm hugs around my neck. At last I was feeling what I should about this great adventure!

Esenboga Airport, not large but adequate and modern, although usually quite empty, was very crowded today; everywhere groups of intending pilgrims to Mekkah sat about on the floor on their luggage, which consisted mostly of cloth-bound bundles, waiting for their flights. Almost all of them were poor villagers, using the savings of a lifetime in order to make their pilgrimage to God's house, one of the religious obligations of a Muslim and the greatest experience of his life. This year all *Hajj* traffic from Turkey was by air, for the border with Syria was closed, ostensibly due to an unusual outbreak of cholera in Turkey, and also, it was said, because of the traffic between Turkish and Syrian communists, among whom the Turkish revolutionaries were being trained and from whom they might also be getting material assistance.

When our flight proved to be very late and its departure time indefinite, we insisted that Enver and his family must not stay waiting to see us off. As Firoz was a very intelligent boy whose Turkish was extremely fluent and who was completely at home in Turkey, we were perfectly confident of his ability to manage anything which we ourselves could not, and reluctantly Enver and Emine agreed to return to the city. Bidding us the warmest of farewells and good wishes, with hearty embraces and handshakes, they left us, and I caught the sudden glint of tears in Emine's soft eyes.

The flight to Erzurum was announced while we were having lunch in the airport's restaurant—two hours late. With a sense of great relief and joy, we hurriedly finished our meal, walked down the steps and entered the waiting jet. Now our adventure was actually about to begin! The children were overwhelmed with excitement, and I think each of us felt the same sense of eager delight as we began our journey. I prayed to God for a safe trip, good health, and His blessings in whatever lay ahead.

We flew over barren brown hills in endless series and later over high, snow-covered mountains, an intense whiteness on the ground everywhere below. After about an hour we landed in Erzurum; there was snow on the ground and it was extremely cold. The airport was very crowded, a place where, without Firoz, we would undoubtedly have encountered considerable difficulty in managing matters. In this part of Turkey, the Turkish which is spoken is similar to Azeri (or Azerbayjani), a dialect also spoken in northwestern Iran which is influenced by both Turkish and Persian, and since Azeri rather than Persian was Firoz' mother-tongue, he naturally had no problem here. He moved in and out of the crowd collecting the baggage in the crisp, penetrating cold.

A bus took us to the city, which at a casual glance seemed poor and unimpressive, with low buildings and the impression of only two colors everywhere—the gray-brown of the buildings and the white of endless snow. Everyone got out at the Turkish Airlines' city terminal. While the children and I waited there, Firoz, who had been in Erzurum many times, took Selim and some other passengers to enquire about buses bound for Iran; they returned after quite a long time with news of a bus to leave early the next morning. The buses for Iran left, it seemed, when enough people had gathered to make a trip worthwhile, and passengers simply waited in Erzurum for as long as necessary to collect a sufficient number. Our party consisted of six persons, and this was enough, with others already waiting, to start a bus the next day.

Firoz now took us by taxi to a plain, clean, centrally-heated hotel, where we thawed out gradually from our brief encounter with the intense cold. In the evening we went to an eating place near the hotel for supper together; it was colder than ever and the streets were icy. We sat chatting through dinner in the dingy *lokanta* where groups of men ate at crude wooden tables. I groped for some sort of understanding of our companion's character, which, apart from his obvious intelligence and vitality, was still an enigma, and was by now much interested in visiting his home and seeing something of the environment which had shaped his development. Certainly, although it was apparent from some things he had said that he was not entirely without knowledge of Islam, he did not speak as a convinced Muslim (indeed, it seemed probable that he had little conviction about most things), and there was no way to guess what the religious climate around him might be.

We returned to the hotel in the bitter cold through the snowy streets and slept early, full of thankfulness to God for His limitless blessings to us and joyous anticipation of what lay ahead.

The next morning our bus sped out of Erzurum in the pale freezing dawn, the temperature around zero degrees Fahrenheit. We were in all thirty passengers: besides ourselves, two Pakistanis, three Indians, several hippies probably bound for India, and a number of Turks and Iranis, including an old peasant in a turban, the only person other than ourselves whom I ever recollect seeing praying on a bus or plane during our travels in the Muslim world.

As we left the city, the white of snow glimmered under the lightening sky. The modern, comfortable bus was extremely cold, and although the heat was turned on full, even with all the warm clothing we possessed we were not able to be comfortable until much later in the day. As we rushed through the bleak wintry countryside, very sparsely populated and with snow-covered mountains everywhere in the background, I was very conscious that while we were now still in the Turkish *milieu* we were hurrying away from Turkey and its culture into another atmosphere, another linguistic zone, although I could not yet know how different or similar it would be.

We stopped at mid-morning for a poor lunch at a primitive *lokanta* and then continued on our way, passing small, very miserable snow-bound villages, evidently without any sort of amenities. Later, in the extreme northeastern corner of Turkey, we came upon two high snowy peaks, obviously extinct volcanoes, which dominated the white, empty landscape; on the other side of them lay the Turkish-Soviet border. One of the peaks, Firoz informed us, was Mount Ararat, commonly supposed to be the Jebel Judi mentioned in the Qur'an, upon which the ark of the Prophet Noah (Nuh), peace be on him, came to rest. I photographed it through the frost-striped windows of the bus.

Early in the afternoon we passed into Iran. For the rest of the day we continued to drive through endless vistas of empty, snow-bound countryside, the white mountains always in the background. In the early evening there was a brief stop for food at a poor restaurant where there was now an Irani flavor; two turbaned villagers sat gazing at us while we ate as they stolidly puffed on water pipes. We now took counsel with Firoz. Qazvin was another two-hundred-and-forty miles distant, and if we continued our journey now we would reach there very late in the night. Because of the severe cold which penetrated into the bus despite its heater and in consideration of the children, it was decided to break journey in Tabriz in northwestern Iran.

Accordingly, we left the bus in Tabriz with our companion at an unheated hotel; the outside temperature was reported to be minus fifteen degrees Fahrenheit. Firoz procured a taxi and took us to a more modern, centrally-heated hotel. Now all about us we were hearing Azeri and snatches of Persian spoken; Turkey was behind us and we had indeed entered a different cultural atmosphere. After supper and tea, we said our prayers and slept at once, very tired from the long day's travel. Firoz had checked into the schedule of departing buses, and we were to leave the next morning at ten o'clock for Qazvin and his home.

In the morning, after a quick breakfast in the hotel, we went by taxi to a frigid bus station where we boarded a waiting bus. Tabriz, which was even colder than Erzurum had been, appeared to be a spread-out city with low buildings — no tall apartment houses and street after street of shops and individual homes which were walled on all sides for privacy. We saw few mosques and quickly realized that they were either away from the street front or hard to recognize because of their rather inconspicuous architecture and the absence of high minarets. Everywhere snow, ice, people heavily wrapped up, and now for the first time I saw women wearing *chaddors*. The Irani *chaddor* consists of an enveloping cloth, rounded at the bottom, which covers the head and falls to the feet, held together inside the front with one hand; it is made of a soft, light fabric with a small, delicate print. The face is generally uncovered, although it can also be worn covering the face if desired. Underneath the *chaddor* most city women wear Western dress, while others wear the typical dresses of their region or ethnic group, often without a *chaddor*.

The way out of the city lay among beautiful snow-covered mountains, the road very snowy in spots but the driver intent on passing every other vehicle in spite of it. The population was very sparse, with occasional small, miserable hamlets of mud huts breaking into the white of the endless vistas of snow.

At noon we stopped for lunch at a poor roadhouse, where we were served heaps of greasy *pilau* with bits of lamb. Later we passed some small villages and one or two impoverished, dismal-looking little towns. The villages were incredibly poor: mud huts, with no electricity and no visible sign of a water supply, no trees, no shelter from the blinding summer sun nor protection from the bitter cold of the harsh winters of north-western Iran except mud walls, hopefully enclosing some sort of a crude heater.

Later in the day the snow and high mountains thinned out and cultivated hills appeared, and we passed through two or three better-looking small towns. We reached Qazvin by mid-afternoon. Firoz had sent a telegram to his father, and he was at the bus station waiting to meet his son and guests — a heavy-set, smiling, prosperous-looking businessman, together with various other male relatives and close friends who came forward to greet us. Selim, who knew workable Persian, was now in his element.

We were all put into taxis with our luggage and presently stopped before a large, handsome walled house set away from the street. A big family welcomed Firoz and ourselves — his mother, an attractive, modern, stylish matron in early middle age, and a number of brothers and sisters, boys of various ages and teen-age girls in miniskirts. The house appeared to be new, spacious, well-furnished and as modern as any house in Qazvin could be (although without central heating, every room having an individual heater instead), clearly a costly and luxurious establishment.

Our belongings were put into two comfortable bedrooms warmed by oil heaters and having fat quilts on the beds, and then we were seated in a pleasant drawing room, where tea, pastries and pistachio nuts were put before us. Two women servants, one appearing to be middle-aged and the other much younger, but so small, lean, pinched-looking and humble that it was hard to accurately estimate their ages, went in and out performing various services from time to time. They wore *chaddors* but not as they were worn outdoors; instead they were draped in such a way that they covered their heads, were crossed over their breasts and tied in a knot behind their necks.

Although all the family of course knew Persian, at home they spoke Azeri like all Azerbayjanis, whether in Turkey, Iran or Russia. This dialect can largely be understood by a Turk, and similarly Azeri-speaking people can partially understand Turkish. While we were able to recognize Turkish or Persian words, there were many sounds which seemed very curious to me. For example, the Turkish *'çok güzel'* (a very common expression pronounced *'choke güzel'* which means 'very pretty' or 'very nice') in the Azeri dialect becomes *'chokkh joozel,'* and similarly many other familiar Turkish expressions were disguised and rendered almost unrecognizable to us by this interesting inflection. I could only savor with the deep delight of a traveler very much involved with all that I observed the linguistic, cultural, ethnic and other new flavors which I was experiencing for the first time.

We sat talking by means of Selim's Persian or through the English translation of Firoz. It was easy to see that this high-spirited, clever youth was the favorite of his family, and there were many indications that he had had his own way almost since the moment of his birth. In the evening a huge meal was put on the table, everything done in very good style; the platters were heaped so high with food that it almost rolled off, and each person's plate was piled with a great mound of *pilau* and chicken, as if for the meal of a giant, despite our protests that it was much too much. I complimented Firoz' mother on the food in Turkish, smiling my thanks, and tried to be a good guest in spite of the problem of communication.

After supper we chatted for a while, as more tea and beautiful big pistachio nuts were put before us, and then retired, thanking the Merciful God for this very enjoyable and interesting day.

The next day, on which we had looked forward eagerly to seeing something of Qazvin, an old and historic city, was a very blank one, partly due to the severe cold. From the time we had breakfast until we retired at night, visitors came and went, tea and food were served, and while others were occuped in various ways, we could do nothing but sit. Each time Selim or I suggested that we would like to get a glimpse of the town, Firoz replied, "Yes, we are going in a little while." Thus, as we could not decently leave them all and go by ourselves, we had no choice. We continued to sit, one of the household but communicating little with anyone, and feeling, although we were being entertained very lavishly in **terms of food** and drink, very much out of place.

In the morning a middle-aged family friend had **come, together** with other visitors who dropped in and out; we were **quite surprised** when Firoz said that this plain, ordinary-looking **old man was in** reality a very wealthy businessman with millions of *toumans** **in the** bank. His father and the old man sat down to play **backgammon,** and afterwards Firoz too played with him and won a **new shirt.**

At last after a heavy lunch, the blankness of the **day was broken** by a short visit to the outside world. Since it was **bitterly cold, it** was hardly possible to walk much without far **more adequate** clothing than we possessed. Men were wrapped up **in coats and** mufflers, and everywhere there were women in *chaddors.* **During** our short walk I had an impression of a rather provin**cial and drab** town with low buildings. Firoz insisted that there was **not much to** see, but even if there had been, we could not have gone **far on foot** in that biting cold. He took us to an old bazaar, so**mething no** longer new to us, where there was little variety and **considerable** standardization in the goods available. We returned to **the house** quite soon, Firoz declaring — as people all over the wor**ld are fond** of doing — that the weather was very unusual and severe.

We spent the remainder of the day in more sitting, ta**lking to a** couple of the visitors who spoke English, drinking tea, **and feeling** restless and out of place; I entertained myself for a **while by** looking at a big stack of albums featuring family ph**otographs** which were offered for my amusement. Presently the p**laying of** backgammon recommenced. The old man wanted back **the shirt** Firoz had won in the morning and they played aga**in, Firoz** acquiring another shirt and a pair of trousers, a substantial **winning.** Now all the family was assembled, visitors came and we**nt in a** steady stream, and the eating and drinking started aga**in, while** several of the men, including Firoz' father, sat in ano**ther room** playing poker and drinking whiskey. The record pla**yer in the**

* At that time, 76 Irani *riyals* = 1 U.S. dollar, 10 *riyals* = 1 *touman.* **The Irani** currency is generally expressed in terms of *toumans* rather than *riyals.*

dining room blared forth continuous loud, vulgar Irani music, adding to the din.

My study of and conversation with Firoz had by now yielded the unavoidable conclusion that, as he was the logical product of the atmosphere in which he had grown up, everything good in him which might have come to life under other circumstances was dead or dying under such influences. To be sure, he had been extremely helpful and hospitable to us, he spoke idealistically about serving his people and about the need to help his country, but apart from this, it was hard to discern either in him or in his parents any sign of values or concerns apart from materialistic ones. He would marry, as we knew, a worldly girl from a well-to-do family, he and his wife would establish a household on much the same pattern as that of his parents, and they would raise another generation of worldly, spoiled children. The sense of distaste which had been growing up in me all day for the crass materialism of this family now overcame my appreciation of their hospitality; we did not belong among and could have no real relationship to people whose way of life was so totally at variance to the standards of Islam by which we lived. I finally retired to the bedroom, where the children had been reading or drawing most of the day, as a refuge from the weary effort of just sitting and from the noise, confusion and distasteful atmosphere.

There was another huge dinner, the table very crowded with all the guests. Afterwards Selim and I sat in the drawing room with Firoz and one or two others who wanted to talk to us, the men closeted in another room playing poker and drinking, the record player behind us forming a very noisy background for conversation as one of the boys of the house came every little while to put on another record. Presently, unable to stand any more of the unending loud music, the continuous eating and drinking, the boisterousness and the general atmosphere of the drawing room, I went to bed. Tomorrow we would leave for Tehran by a morning bus.

The next morning we prepared ourselves hurriedly for the continuation of our journey, feeling more than happy to be leaving this household where we had felt almost like prisoners although its hospitality had been so lavish in terms of physical comforts. During our travels, we were to have the opportunity to visit one single Irani home, and as God willed it it was this one (although certainly it was quite untypical of the area, which is known to be conservative and religious). It was obvious that the main — perhaps the only — goal of these people was their own material advancement. While they called themselves Muslims and had even been for *Hajj*, the remainder of their obligations had been cast aside and trampled on as the drink flowed under their roof, their men and boys gambled, they ate and drank with insatiable appetite, enjoyed every luxury, and apparently gave no thought to any other aspect of existence. But what had affected me most was the contrast between this empty, decadent family and their humble dependents, the house servants, with their simple, decent looks and restrained behavior. Firoz' mother, as I had seen, worked hard with them, preparing food which was cooked in another part of the house and bringing it to the living area for serving and eating, and there were other, part-time servants to help as needed. I had asked what the wages of the two women were and was told 50 *toumans* a month apiece—that is, a little more than six dollars — plus food and lodging, I supposed, and perhaps clothes. The previous night in Tabriz we had learned what this sum of money represented in the economy of Iran when we spent 90 *toumans* for two moderately good hotel rooms without a private bath for only one night!

Now as we were getting ready to leave, the thought of those two kindly-faced, humble women did not leave my mind. I sought them out in the kitchen at least to say goodbye, wanting to embrace them, to thank them for laboring so hard on our behalf during our stay, and to do any small thing I could for them if there were some appropriate way, but they were not to be found. And the strange feeling came to me that the only people in that household with whom I could feel any sense of kinship were those two lowly serving women, my sisters in Islam. Overwhelmed by the atmosphere of triviality, materialism and lack of meaningful purpose in that family, I felt that all the wealth in the world could not hide the lack of true civilization so apparent in the behavior of its members, no matter how hospitable they might be to their guests.

We ate breakfast with Firoz and his parents, and then, muffling ourselves in our sweaters and coats, prepared to leave the house for the bus station. I now saw the two slight, lean servant women pick up our heavy suitcases and, evidently clad in nothing warmer than their ordinary clothing covered by their tied-up *chaddors*, lift them to their shoulders and carry them up the alley to the street in the bitter early morning cold. There was no time even to shake hands or to say a word of thanks to them, only to call out goodbye in Persian as they passed us in returning to the house. Well, visitors came and went continually in that household; what were we to them except other guests who had stayed for a moment and then passed on, when they were used to serving guests day in and day out? How could they remotely imagine all that I was feeling about them? Nevertheless, I earnestly hoped that if they should ever remember us at all, it would be as people who had spoken gently and treated them as fellow-Muslims.

The family took us to the bus station by taxi. We expressed our thanks and appreciation for their hospitality, and they bade us a very cordial farewell, standing by the side of the bus in the early morning cold until it departed.

As we rode through the streets of Qazvin, I think each of us felt a keen sense of relief and joy in being out of the stifling, uncongenial atmosphere of that house, as well as in being on our own as a family for the first time during this journey. The sense of deep joy and interest leaped up in me as it had done at the beginning of the trip, not dampened in the least by the unwholesome and oppressive experiences of the previous day.

As we continued our journey across the Irani countryside, I read my first words of Persian, written in essentially the same script as Arabic with a few additional letters, on a wall where a sign advertised 'Koka-kola.' From that time on throughout our travels in Iran, I tried to read wherever possible. It was a very exciting, fascinating experience to me to come from Turkey where after such a struggle I had at length learned a few elements of the language, through the transition zone of the Azeri dialect into Persian-speaking Iran; there was a clear, obvious continuity in this slow transition of the language, Turkish and Persian first blending into the composite Azeri dialect before it changed into pure Persian. I realized for the first time how very many words Turkish has in common with Persian, either Persian words which are found in Turkish or Arabic words common to both Turkish and Persian. Later I was to get a glimpse of how this continuity progressed in Persian-speaking Afghanistan, blending into Pushto in the border areas of Afghanistan and Pakistan and then into the Urdu of West Pakistan, which also has great numbers of both Persian and Arabic words. And next door to us lay Arabic-speaking areas of the Middle East, whose language was the common source of innumerable Persian, Turkish and Urdu words.

With all this, I could only marvel that the vast region which we call the Muslim world has not been able to put aside its cultural and political differences in order to become the solid, powerful unit it has the potential of being. This part of the world holds an immense reservoir of resources, a huge amount of natural wealth, which rightfully belongs to all its inhabitants through the beneficence of God. With proper planning and development, these resources could be developed and utilized to benefit all its people, a large proportion of whom are now so appallingly poor. But instead of this, they either lie largely untapped and undeveloped due to lack of means, poor planning and inefficiency, while others, notably in the form of the immense wealth of oil, are being drained off very rapidly and their benefits going either into the hands of foreign companies or into the pockets of a few whose immense wealth is in disgraceful contrast to the poverty of the majority. These irreplaceable resources, which the bounty of God has given freely for the benefit of all, are such as could give vast economic power and leverage to the Muslim world if there were unity of purpose and action, exercise of intelligence and foresight, and commitment to utilizing them in the best interests of all the people among the governments and leaders of individual nations. The unfortunate continuation of foreign intervention in the affairs of Muslim countries, although the age of imperialism is supposedly past, the insincerity, selfishness and lack of wisdom among many of the leaders of the Muslim world, and the disunity and indifference of the people due to their lack of understanding of and dedication to the Islamic principles of brotherhood and mutual cooperation, have indeed made of this Muslim

world, to which God has given so much, an abject and miserable
spectacle in our time . . .

Early in the afternoon we reached Tehran, a vast, spread-out
metropolis with a population of about three million, fringed by a
wide industrial zone, and a taxi driver immediately took possession
of us. The traffic was heavy but nevertheless much more orderly
and well-behaved than that of Istanbul or Ankara, with small European cars instead of the endless American giants of Turkey. The
city as a whole seemed comparable to Istanbul, with some very
wealthy and modern sections.

After getting settled in a hotel, we sallied forth on foot. We
spent the afternoon seeing whatever we could of the city and
making travel arrangements for the next leg of the journey, namely,
from Tehran to Kabul. We had wanted if possible to go by bus
since there was much of interest to see *en route,* our appetite for
land travel now having been thoroughly whetted, but since no definite information about buses past the Iran-Afghanistan border was
available, we concluded that it would be best to fly. As this
arrangement left us with a little extra time for traveling, we decided
to spend it in seeing Isfahan, some five hundred kilometers south of
Tehran, which was reputed to be one of the most beautiful cities in
the Muslim world, leaving by bus the next morning; we would
return to Tehran three days later to continue our journey to
Pakistan.

Modern Tehran, especially its wealthy and elegant sections,
formed an extremely sharp contrast to the other parts of Iran we
had seen. Here, instead of the innumerable streets of apartment
houses which characterize Istanbul and Ankara, there were individual houses, set behind the street or walled for privacy. The
streets were full of women, mostly clad in *chaddors* but with a
substantial number of *chaddor*-less women in fashionable Western
dress also to be seen.

From the high viewpoint of the multi-storied Plasco Building
where we had our lunch, we had searched the city, which lay
spread out before us on three sides, for mosques but could see only

a few having domes or minarets; later we realized that the majority of Tehran's mosques are constructed in a domeless, inconspicuous style without minarets which makes them relatively hard to recognize. A little later we went by a taxi to visit a large mosque which we had seen in our part of the city, the Masjid-e-Shah. This Mosque of the Shah was set into the middle of a bazaar so crowded with pedestrians and traffic that one could hardly cross from one side of the street to the other; I saw women wrapped in *chaddors*, bearded Shi'ah *'ulema* wearing white turbans and dark brown or black flowing robes, Kurds, Pathans, Mongols and other peoples in their varied dresses. It was a very colorful, interesting scene — much more interesting than the mosque, which, being of mid-nineteenth century vintage, was architecturally rather disappointing. I longed to take pictures in the bazaar among the people, but being a foreign tourist and a woman really did not dare, and thus had to satisfy myself with pictures of the mosque.

Early the next morning we were on a bus bound for Isfahan, leaving most of our luggage at the hotel to be called for on our return. On the south side of the city there was some industry, long chains of slum housing, then plains and fields and many broken remains of large buildings with arches and domes, some of which were still inhabited, which were evidently *karvanserais* — accommodations for travelers built in earlier times. Mountains lay on every side and there were scattered villages, many of whose mud houses had domed or arched roofs. At mid-morning there was a brief halt for food, and then we continued on a road winding among canyons and volcanic hills.

The city of Qum, a religious center, lay approximately midway between Tehran and Isfahan; its streets were full of Shi'ah *'ulema* in their turbans and dark robes. Just off the road we caught a glimpse of the blue and gold domes of a vast mosque or tomb. The children exclaimed over it in wonder, catching only a brief look in passing and as I looked I thought, *"Is this really I, Marian Kazi, sitting in a bus traveling across ancient Iran and seeing all this?"* At times the journey had a curious flavor of unreality, of a dream too improbably and too good to be true! How thankful I was to God for it all!

At noon the driver turned on the radio, and the *adhan* for the *Jum'a* prayer was heard. We were naturally very much interested in observing the state of Islam and Muslims in Iran as well as we could in such a very brief time. Because Iran, unlike Turkey, has retained some of the obvious outward aspects of the Islamic system such as greeting with *"Assalamu alaikum,"* the privacy of walled houses and the dress of the majority of women, it was possible to get the impression that Islam in Iran was in quite a good position, especially after coming from Turkey where so many of the outward elements have been changed. But was this really the case?

We had heard many reliable reports of the under-cover suppression, imprisonment, torture and even murder of Muslims in Iran, from which it was clear that the government of the Shah is active in suppressing those Muslims who want to bring back a living and dynamic Islam into all aspects of the society, or who dare to speak out against the autocracy of one man who rules not by the law of God but by his own personal whims. The Shah is known to have an effective and active secret police, a strong military which keeps him in power, and many of the tools of repression and oppression which are common to dictators of all types, and which make him — despite the grandiose publicity he has received in the American press as an 'enlightened' and forward-looking monarch and friend of the West, who is intimately concerned about bettering the condition of his people — one of the most oppressive rulers in the world today.

With such a policy and the power to execute it, the Shah does not need to openly attack the Islamic traditions surviving in Iran which are common to Muslims throughout the world; these do not threaten his rule, while those elements which pose a threat are summarily dealt with. At the same time, Islam and its traditions, which should be reinforced from the top levels of the society, are continually being torn down and derided by implication by this immensely rich, luxury- and power-loving king and his wife who is displayed so conspicuously in public, as well as by the wealthy westernized top layer of the society, an example of whom we had seen so much to our dismay in Qazvin. The Shah's great egotism, his lavishing upon himself and his display of power such immense sums of money, his styling himself by such outrageous appellations as *'Khodaigon Shahinshah Aryamehr'* (meaning 'God, the King of Kings, the Sun of the Aryans', which in the Islamic frame of reference are the clearest and most blatant *shirk*, that is, attributing divinity, supreme authority or sustainership to someone or something other than God), his imitation and revival of the 'greatness' of pagan pre-Islamic Persia,* all have served only his own cause against Islam, and clearly prove any profession he may make of devotion to Islam to be the most absolute deceit and hypocrisy.

As we approached Isfahan the grey mountains still loomed in the background. Although the snow we had encountered at high elevations along the road had disappeared, all was bleak and bare in the grip of winter.

A helpful taxi driver took us to a pleasant, modern hotel, and a short time later we set out with him for a look at the city. It was late afternoon when we returned to the hotel after a long, interesting tour of various places he had suggested. We had, however, so far seen none of the mosques for which Isfahan is so famous. As we had driven through the center of the city center we had glimpsed the lovely turquoise dome of one of these mosques. We now set out on foot to see it at close range.

The main street of Isfahan is very beautiful. A wide median, planted with trees and greenery for the use of cyclists and pedestrians, separates the traffic, and both sides of the street are lined with interesting antique and handicraft shops, for Isfahan is the center of Iran's handicraft industry as well as a tourist center. From here we caught a breath-taking glimpse of an exquisite sky-blue dome on top of a plain buff wall, a part of the very famous mosque of the Madrasah-e-Chahar-Bagh.** A magnificently-

---

* It is hardly necessary to comment on the Shah's reportedly having spent 300 million dollars of his people's wealth on the recent 2500th anniversary celebration of the pagan Persian Empire in this connection, the more shocking in view of the poverty, illiteracy, disease, filth and lack of basic amenities which afflict such a great proportion of the people of Iran.

** The Mosque of the *Madrasah* of the Four Gardens, built in the early eighteenth century.

ornamented gate covered with mosaic arabesques and calligraphy led into its courtyard from the main street.

Selim and the children went in together, while I stayed behind taking photographs and entered the gate alone, lingering inside the inner portal to admire the rich yellow-and-turquoise mosaics which covered its arches, niches and walls. Then, very slowly and deliberately, I turned toward the stone-paved courtyard of the mosque.

Slender trees covered with white bark, now leafless, grew in the courtyard, a rectangle enclosed by a structure having double-storied white painted arches, all part of the *madrasah*, and a small channel bisected it. At the left was an area which is now used for prayers, where two men stood praying. But it was the little mosque at the right to which my eye and heart turned in wonder, my breath almost taken away by its extraordinary beauty: a marvelously-balanced egg-shaped dome covered with brilliant sky-blue mosaics decorated with arabesques, a richly-ornamented portal topped by two small minarets with ornate balconies, and the whole structure flanked on both sides by the facade of the *madrasah* with its white arches.

For a few moments I stood trying to take it all in, lost to the world, marveling at the unbelievable beauty of line and color of that exquisite, delicate dome and its supporting structures. Never had I seen a building so utterly lovely, so bright and joyous. I could hardly believe that it was really I who had come from America on the other side of the globe who was standing there looking at it with this pair of eyes. Each of us wandered around the compound, studying it from various vantage points, experiencing it in his or her characteristic fashion, the children amazed and moved by its breath-taking beauty. I took numerous photographs, wanting to preserve this memory and retain it as long as I lived. As I thought of the deep faith and love of God Most High which had moved Muslims to build such a house for His worship, the tears rolled unheeded down my cheeks.

And I thought of the Istanbul mosques, whose grandeur and solemnity had also moved me so much. I could only feel sorry when I recalled the miserable, neglected condition of their bare grounds, the black grime with which many of them were encrusted, the dirtiness of their ablution areas, and the carpets of Sultan Ahmet's Mosque which smelled of must and perspiration; but I would not be untrue to the memory of them as I stood here, where obviously care and concern had restored the original brilliance of this mosque to its present condition. They were, in a completely different style, equally glorious and moving monuments of man's desire to erect a living expression of his faith which would draw the heart toward God and be used for the most sublime of all purposes, for His worship. The Istanbul mosques were deep, sober, awe-inspiring, the little mosque of Isfahan light, delicate and airy; there one found a great solemnity and inwardness and peace, here an exuberant, tender joy and gladness. The five of us prayed two *rak'ats* of *nafil salat* and then we left.

* * *

Beside me now on the plane, Nura, totally unaware of where my mind had been all this time, drew pictures on a tiny tablet and chattered to herself and to me. I hardly heard her many questions, answering them mechanically, remembering the bright, never-to-be-forgotten glory of that winter day in Isfahan. This child too had loved that mosque and often recalled it, mentioning it like a dearly-loved friend. During these travels the children had been observing, taking in all that was new; yet perhaps only Jamal was really old enough to grasp and retain the deeper significance of what we were seeing: the Islamic connections, the cultural context, some trace of historical forces. Nevertheless, I knew that *insha'Allah* the memory of it all, supported by discussion and my photography, would remain in their hearts and minds in time to come, and that, in the years ahead, they would be increasingly able to relate their understanding of and identification with the Muslim world to what they had seen on this trip when they were children.

* * *

The next morning was spent in going about with our taxi driver. Isfahan was indeed a beautiful city, with many places of great interest and stately loveliness: the Minar-e-Jumban, a structure with shaking minarets; the Zoroastrian fire temple at the top of a steep hill; a beautiful old Armenian church; the Chehel Sotun, an ornamental pavilion; the beautiful square of Naqsh-e-Jehan, with an interesting covered bazaar, the most 'oriental' of all the bazaars we had seen, and the handicraft shops lining three sides of the vast square; the Ali Qapu Palace in the middle of one side of this square and the Sheikh Lutfullah Mosque opposite, and on the fourth side the glorious Masjid-e-Shah (in this case the seventeenth century Shah Abbas the Great), a glowing structure of predominantly turquoise mosaics which was unquestionably one of the grandest architectural works of the Muslim world; the Jum'a Masjid, insignificant-looking at the first glimpse one gets of its exterior, fruit stalls clustered around it up to its very walls, but with its many sections dating from various periods — the oldest, a series of pillars, arches and domes in buff brick, each sequence different in detail from all the others, from Seljuk times — its striking blue-and-buff mosaic ornamentation and many other wonderful details, it is indeed a most beautiful and venerable mosque; a visit to a carpet manufactury, where girls and women sat on raised beams before warps stretched over wooden frames and, with fingers flying so fast that I could hardly make out what they were doing, cut and tied, cut and tied, following an intricate pattern marked out on squared paper; the Khaju Bridge, the handsomest of the three old bridges of Isfahan, again dating from the time of Shah Abbas the Great, with its very durable and aesthetic engineering which includes an exquisitely-ornamented little pavilion in its center; and finally, glimpses of various localities of the city: the humble mud-colored dwellings at its outskirts and center, and stately mansions glimpsed behind walls surrounded by gardens. All-in-all Isfahan was a city of rare charm,· even in bleak mid-winter, almost justifying the old adage, *Isfahan nisf-e-jehan''* — Isfahan is half the world.

During the cloudy and very chilly afternoon, we returned to do some shopping in the covered bazaar and in the shops flanking the great square. The most cherished of the small things I bought, perhaps, were the tiles I obtained from a tile manufactury — ornamental ones for each of the children, Emine and myself, and two plain glazed tiles of a melting sky blue color recalling the incredible turquoises of Isfahan which were for Emine and me. As we were coming out of a shop, Selim stooped down, picked up something from the ground and put it into my hand; it was a fragment of a turquoise tile, perhaps a very old one, its color dark, deep and rich. I knew that I would always treasure its battered, broken form as a memento of this beautiful city where thousands of Muslims had labored to build a concrete expression of their faith in God and to make Islam the dominant feature of their culture and way of life.

As we returned to the hotel, Selim remarked that although our travels were very enjoyable and interesting, they were nonetheless quite barren of human contacts. He had with him the address and telephone number of a young Isfahani Muslim named Hossein who had been a friend of Bahadir Bey's in England, and decided on the spur of the moment to telephone his home. Hossein himself answered, and when Selim introduced himself he seemed both surprised and pleased, and said that he would be at our hotel in ten minutes' time.

He met us in the lobby, an appealing, curly-haired young man who spoke fluent English. When we asked him to join us for dinner, he said that he had already eaten but would take tea with us. He then took us to a pleasant restaurant nearby, making some suggestions about foods he thought we might enjoy and apologizing very earnestly that we who were fellow Muslims, his friend's friends and visitors in his country, should be reduced to dining in a restaurant instead of being welcome guests in his home; unfortunately, however, his mother was seriously ill and matters were completely upset at home, as everyone was involved in her care. We were very sorry about this news and realized that he had perhaps made a considerable sacrifice in leaving her; however, when we urged him not to take time away from her, he assured us that as all the rest of the family were at her side, there was no problem in his being away for a little while.

He asked many questions about Bahadir Bey and his family, about Turkey and about our travels, and seemed altogether very intelligent and keen. Presently, when an understanding had grown up between us, he began to talk about conditions in his country, so rich in oil and other natural resources, but the common people, as we had seen, so miserably poor and neglected.

"From what we've seen so far," Selim commented frankly, "it appears that Iran consists primarily of just one big city and all the rest hardly counts."

"Yes, that is perfectly true," Hossein replied with great earnestness. "Many Iranis are very concerned about all these problems, but there is no easy solution to them."

Then, with an openness which surprised us, he went on to talk about conditions in his country, verifying what we had heard many times over. He said that foreign exploitation in the form of oil interests is draining Iran's wealth. No one, however, can criticize the Shah. A very strong military and police organization is maintained to ensure his power, and a huge proportion of the country's budget is alloted to it. He said that if anyone opened a business without displaying a picture of the Shah, he was likely to be arrested, and any public speech about any matter whatsoever must include some mention of the ruler.

Although he spoke so openly with us, he said that today in Iran one did not dare to talk freely even to one's own brother, for the secret police is extremely active, confirming the reports about the extreme harshness of governmental repression which were already quite familiar to us. While there is no difficulty in practicing the worship aspects of Islam, Hossein said, no suggestion by Muslims that the affairs of the country — social, political, economic — be regulated by the injunctions of the faith which all profess is tolerated. Meetings and gatherings to discuss these aspects of Islam are completely prohibited. Irani prisons hold many thousands of Muslims who are jailed for calling for Islam or for criticizing or working against the existing regime, and the hair-raising, barbarous tortures and even murders of these prisoners, among whom are a number of religious scholars, continue to increase.

The meal now long since finished, the children sat at one corner of the table amusing themselves during this conversation with some quiet games, while Selim and I silently pondered over what Hossein had said, full of grief at the terrible situation of our Irani brothers. Although this had been known to us since a long time, to hear it in such a poignant and telling way from an Irani who might at any time be directly or indirectly affected by such far-reaching oppression, and in his own country, naturally moved us deeply. A veil of indescribable horror and ugliness seemed to lie over the whole country which lay in the grip of such a monstrous violation of all human freedom and dignity. "May God help you, brother," Selim said warmly, "and show the way to deal with these terrible problems."

"It is a very difficult situation," Hossein replied with a tired smile. "The anti-government movements in Iran are now completely underground. One movement is a communist one and the other is Islamic. If the communist movement becomes dominant, it will simply bring the country under another sort of tyranny or lead it to complete chaos, and God knows we do not merely want to exchange one kind of oppression for another. The people are ready to support the Islamic movement, which is led by dedicated Muslims who are prepared to fight against oppression to the death. But under existing conditions there is no way Muslims can communicate effectively with each other, for there is no possibility of having open meetings. Yet we are doing our best, and today in spite of all the repression, the main trend among Irani students and intellectuals is a movement toward Islam."

We sat quiet, thoughtful, aware that Hossein had opened his heart to us as if we were old, trusted friends. Our minds turned over and over these grave problems of our Irani brothers-in-faith, knowing that there was no easily-available solution to their almost desperate plight. All over the Muslim world, although much of their lands were so rich in natural resources, Muslims were almost at the bottom of the heap of humanity, oppressed and suppressed, mere pawns in the hands of their own hostile, anti-Islamic government or of external powers, and often blindly unaware of their precious Islamic heritage and ready to follow other systems out of sheer ignorance of Islam. What would they still have to suffer and endure before their right to human dignity and freedom could be restored? And yet, as we knew, this restoration could only come, with the help of God, through their own striving; no one else could do the job for them, and until they were prepared to do it for themselves nothing would change, for as God says in the Qur'an, "Verily, man shall have nothing but what he strives for."*

All of us realized that our visit together must now come to an end, for Hossein must not stay away any longer from his mother. We bade him a warm farewell, with prayers and good wishes for his mother's health, and, more quietly, for the health of his country. As I watched his lean, wiry figure striding rapidly down the street and out of sight, one of the many souls whose life had touched ours for an instant in the journey through this world and was gone, I prayed

Al-Najm 53:39.

that out of such dynamic and committed Muslims as this, the Islamic renaissance of Iran and of all the Muslim world might presently be born . . .

I had now found to my surprise and joy that I could understand a very little Persian, with the help of the Turkish and Urdu I knew, and was able to pick up words and phrases with surprising rapidity. The experience of linguistic and cultural transition from one part of the Muslim world to another, each professing the same faith and its culture being formed by it, and each at the same time bringing its unique cultural, ethnic and linguistic contribution to form a local Muslim culture, absorbed me completely. I pondered over the deep meaning and truth of the verse of the Holy Qur'an which says,

"And among Our signs is the creation of the heavens and the earth, and the variations in your languages and your colors; verily in this are signs for those who know."*

as we continued our journey across the Middle East.

My mind completely taken up with the present, I had thought very little about Ankara since we had been gone. Now, setting apart a warm and tender corner full of love for the good friends who had shared these months with us, I recalled what we had left behind—the dreary mid-winter scene and all the old problems—and could only feel depressed as I pushed the recollection out of my mind for the time-being. I had come to love Turkey and to identify with what was good in it, with its sufferings and struggles, but the loathing I felt for westernized Ankara, the center of all that is bad in the land which Islam had once shaped, had somehow crystallized within me during our absence.

Now, too, I looked ahead to this journey's end, God willing, in three more days. Several years had elapsed since we had been in Pakistan, and it was but natural that there should be many questions in my mind about what I could expect there. After the difficulties of my earlier experience, when everything had been totally new and strange to me, I now preferred to expect the worst rather than hope for the best; yet now I and everyone else, and the country itself, were several years older and hopefully wiser and more mature, and now my standard for judging everything was only Islam. How would it all be . . .?

** All Room 30:22

The next morning when the taxi took us to the bus station, we asked the driver to stop at the gate of the *Madrasah* mosque for five minutes. It had snowed in the night, and this time the little mosque was surrounded by snowy trees, with snow like a white fur speckling its dome, surely the most lovely and moving house of God's worship in the world. Thus, a last prayer and a photograph, and we left it, *insha'Allah* to return one day . . .

The journey back to Tehran was uneventful. We returned to our previous hotel, taking very minimal accommodations, for the night would be very short indeed. Our flight to Kabul left at 5:30 a.m., and instructions were left with the desk to awaken us at 3 o'clock.

I had been observing the dress and behavior of Irani women wherever we had gone. Although some sections of Tehran were very westernized, with women in the latest styles and heavily made-up and coiffured as in Ankara, the majority wore *chaddors;* indeed, in some localities it was unusual to see a woman without one, and although some women wore their *chaddors* in careless fashion, the conservative women were very particular about them. This covering struck me as graceful and appealing but also as somewhat impractical, for it must be held together from inside, leaving only one hand free, and requires repeated adjustment to keep it covering the hair and from trailing on the ground. It is also so light and fine that it does not conceal completely, and it was thus easy to recognize mini-skirts underneath many times. However, one very good feature is that, as most women wear *chaddors* of essentially the same type of fabric, it minimizes the difference in social class; yet I had also seen *chaddors* of an obviously much more expensive black lacy fabric calculated to reveal the affluence of the wearer, which was also more transparent than the rest.

As our bus from Isfahan had crossed the city, we passed a girls' high school just as the students were coming out; all of them wore very short dresses except one *chaddor*-clad girl who stood out very conspicuously among her companions, and I could not help wondering how she fitted in and what her life might be like among them. I thought of the future of Irani women and the westernizing trends coming down from the top levels of the population. Although on the whole the women of Iran were more Islamic in their dress than Turkish women because of their *chaddors,* still it seemed only a matter of time before most city women discarded them and the female population of urban Iran joined their sisters in other 'Muslim' countries in the endless, depressing uniform westernization of dress, discarding Islamic standards of modesty so that they can be considered 'advanced' and 'modern,' unless something dramatic happens to reverse this trend; after all, under a great many of the *chaddors* a Western dress, often a mini, is already visible. Of course the village women and those belonging to the various diverse ethnic groups all across Iran will still retain their traditional dresses, but they cannot influence anyone and are certain, in time and with increasing contact with city life, to be gradually influenced themselves, as I had observed in Turkey.

What I was seeing was just one more reflection of that appalling defeatist mentality among Muslims which insists that what is Western—what is foreign, imported, having no logical development or connection with the native society and its values—must necessarily be better than what is indigenous and at the same time Islamic. However, I reflected, perhaps this is only natural in view of the fact that Irani women always have before them the very prominent example of an ultra-westernized Queen who is constantly before the public eye.

From the time we had set foot in Iran we had been much struck by the conspicuous display of the picture of the Shah in every restaurant and business establishment; there seemed to be even more of these in Iran than pictures of Atatürk in Turkey. Nowhere in the Western world, I reflected, is it deemed necessary to emphasize and underscore the almost superhuman importance and authority of a head of state in such a fashion. Here the portrait of the ruler was often accompanied by those of his wife and sometimes his children. The Queen was always shown bareheaded, bejeweled and wearing the latest Parisian fashions in what was the clearest, most obvious affront and disregard of Islamic conceptions of modesty, setting the tone for other Irani women who want to imitate the dress and behavior of the women of the West.

And yet, I considered, perhaps this was simply the logical outcome of the use of pictures and statues depicting public figures by Muslims. The Holy Prophet, peace be on him, expressed strong disapproval of graphic representations of human beings and animals, and for the most part Muslims adhered faithfully to this prohibition. For this reason the splendid Islamic art and architecture grew up around ornamentation utilizing calligraphy and floral and geometric motifs rather than pictures or statues of the Prophet, his companions or any other persons. Nevertheless, depictions of people and animals found their way into the art of Muslims with the production of book illustrations portraying the life of the Holy Prophet, peace be on him, various epics and stories, and portraits and miniatures, paving the way for the pictures and statues of rulers and other 'great men' which today have become one of the indispensable tools of maintaining the rule of vested interests through reiteration of their ideas and power over others.

The more I have thought about the deep significance of this prohibition, the more its basic wisdom has become clear to me. It is obvious that the public depiction of a human being, whether by a statue or picture, carries with it a marked implication of reverence and respect—first of all in the mere fact that this individual has been considered important enough to depict, and secondly in placing the picture or statue of that important personage where people will see and be 'inspired' by it or admire it (indeed, it is not unknown for people to give more attention and respect to a picture or statue than its original received or merited when he lived among them). Such depiction, therefore, carries with it an implication of being above the ordinary run of human beings whose pictures are *not* made and hung in a public place for everyone to look at and for whose benefit such pictures *are* hung, and of exaggerated 'greatness' or even a kind of immortality.

Muslims are not permitted to bow or to show special deference to any human being, no matter how high his position or how great his authority or respectability (and by extension, so much the more before any *representation* of a human being), for all men are inherently equal before Almighty God, and homage and reverence are due to Him alone. It is largely due to this prohibition that they have not drifted into the error of other religious communities and lowered themselves to the level of kneeling to and worshipping, or at least giving exaggerated respect and reverence to, an image of a person who, when he lived, was nothing but a finite and limited mortal like anyone else; indeed, adherence to this prohibition has helped very greatly to preserve the pure character of Islamic monotheism. And although today the prevalence of pictures and statues of rulers and other persons of 'importance' has not led to the greatest sin of associating them with God's divinity or worshipping them in the most obvious form, nonetheless it has served to set them above other men as objects of undue respect, admiration, emulation and obedience, and has become a vital instrument for maintaining the rule of human authority and domination over the minds and lives of men. We can be very certain of the truth of this statement by observing the severe punishment meted out to those who attempt to deface or destroy images of national heroes in some Muslim countries, among which Iran is a very notable example.* Muslims must make every possible effort to rid themselves of these and other similar, very harmful means of perpetrating the domination of one human being over others, for only then can men's hearts be released from enslavement to other men and their ideas into undivided devotion and service to the true Lord of men.

We slept early, for the night would be very short. In fact, it proved to be even shorter than we had anticipated. The hotel desk, having instructions to awaken us at 3 a.m., for some reason over-zealously carried out its responsibility a full hour too early, following its first call with another at 2:30 (just as we had all fallen asleep again) informing Selim that a taxi was now waiting downstairs to take us to the airport. After this there was no possibility of sleeping again, so we got up and were ready ten minutes later, reaching the airport by 3:30. There we waited in a state of utter exhaustion to catch the flight for Kabul, which did not leave, after all, until half past six. Pakistan was now *insha'Allah,* unbelievably, only one day away!

---

* Hossein had mentioned during our discussion in Isfahan that anyone who defaces or destroys a picture or statue of the ruler is sure to be arrested and imprisoned, and possibly even sentenced to be hanged.

CHAPTER 10

INTRODUCTION TO PAKISTAN

Early the following afternoon, after several hours of traveling, the ancient, rattly silver-painted bus on which we were traveling from Kabul to Peshawar struggled up the narrow, winding Khyber Pass road, which made me think of Kipling and the struggle of Pathan tribesmen against the British *Raj*. The bus was filled with Pakistanis and a few Afghans; we shared the back seats with two other passengers.

We had arrived in Kabul early the previous morning after a two-hour flight over endless chains of rugged, snow-covered mountains. As a taxi took us from the airport to the city, I looked about for a capital city-like atmosphere but saw only low, unimpressive buildings and people with a great look of poverty muffled up against the cold; snow covered the higher elevations all about the city, which seemed to be set in a great valley surrounded by mountains on all sides. We took rooms in a huge old hotel run on the British colonial style with much pomposity and comfort; although ordinary by American standards, for Afghanistan it was obviously luxurious.

Our immediate concern was to make arrangements to get from here to Peshawar, now only a few hours' drive distant. After enquiring at the hotel, we went to the sole existing Pakistani bus line in the city to make reservations for our trip. At the tiny bus depot in the window of which "Luxury Coaches" to Peshawar were advertised, sat a pleasant-faced Pakistani ticket agent with smiling eyes; I felt a great sense of relief and a feeling that I was coming home when he and Selim began to talk in Urdu, Selim's mother tongue. Travel in countries unknown to me, with different languages, had been wonderfully interesting and enjoyable, but they had not been like home. My Urdu was rather limited (indeed, I found that I could not speak as much as a single sentence and could not even recall individual words after my systematic study of Turkish, although my comprehension had not been affected), having been picked up very haphazardly during the course of many years, but it was nevertheless familiar and homelike to me, and the ticket agent exuded friendliness and security. We reserved the last four remaining seats on the bus for the following day just as two hippies (these seemed to be very much in evidence in Kabul, undoubtedly because of the absence of restrictions on drug traffic in Afghanistan) with unusually wild manes came in to make their reservations.

Later in the day we went for a taxi drive around the city. I tried to take in as much as I could, but the contrast with Turkish and Irani cities was so marked that I succeeded in carrying away only a few general impressions. We had observed hard living conditions and poverty all along our route, but here they were coupled and augmented by the very harsh winter-time climate and rugged topography which made Kabul look very poor and bleak, although it is reported to be a pleasant place in summer.

We passed bazaars with open stalls selling various merchandise, extremely crude and primitive; I saw very little in the way of real shops, although these must exist somewhere in Kabul, for the upper class here, though few in number, was completely westernized in dress. Men were wrapped in shawls, blankets or coats against the cold, their faces often reflecting the bitter poverty in which they lived. Very few women were in the streets and almost all those I saw wore the *chadiri,* an all-enveloping garment covering the entire body including the face, with lattice-like openings over the eyes so the wearer can see out without being seen, similar to the 'shuttlecock' *burqa* which many poorer women wear in Pakistan.

From the point of ethnic variety, Kabul was the most interesting place I had ever seen. There were Pathans with sharp, regular features in their typical dress and turbans, many carrying rifles, a number of diverse ethnic strains reflecting a Mongol heritage, with as many varied types of dress, and many other different peoples. The city was immensely spread out, with high hills rising here and there in the middle of it, the city flowing around them on all sides and continuing until the next hill and going on around it; it was impossible to grasp its size or anything concerning its geography in that brief time. Here there was no question of apartments versus private dwellings; the majority of the homes we saw were very crude, and only members of the middle and upper classes, very few in number, had proper houses, although for the most part these were also very modest, surrounded by walls for privacy.*

We slept early that night. Tomorrow, I thought, God willing, journey's end. I was thankful for Kabul which, with its extreme conditions, had prepared us for Pakistan, and infinitely grateful to God that we had all been healthy so far, for the possibility of some serious illness on the way had never been absent from my mind.

We were ready for our journey early the next morning. At the bus depot several Pakistanis waited, and again I felt the same surge of reassurance at the thought of going 'home' among them. Pakistan had been familiar and accustomed to me, a known quantity, ever since we had lived there years ago. I was happy that I should feel so even after so many years' absence and only hoped that the children, who had taken quite a while to adjust to the relatively eastern atmosphere of Turkey, would not find it hard to adapt to or feel at home in the much more oriental culture of Pakistan.

The road to Peshawar led through a winding canyon and into a very spectacular gorge, descending steeply from the high altitude of Kabul, where it had snowed during the night, into a plateau where it was much warmer. Presently the bus stopped abruptly by

---

* At the time of this trip, Zahir Shah was the ruler of Afghanistan. In 1973 he was deposed in a *coup* and his brother-in-law, Daud Khan, became head of state. His rule has been an absolute dictatorship. At the time this book goes to press, the Islamic movement in Afghanistan—the major challenge to tyranny and oppression—is being ruthlessly crushed, its leaders in exile, prison and some even having been executed by this tyrannical, communist-oriented ruler.

the side of the road and the ticket agent with smiling eyes, who was traveling with us, got up and announced in Urdu that we would now take a break to relieve ourselves. But where? For there was nothing here except a thick grove of orange trees covered with ripe fruit. The passengers scattered among them, the women, some of them clad in *burqas*, going a little further among them than the men for privacy.

This was a new experience to us. Thus far in our travels in Turkey and Iran there had always been some sort of toilet facilities, although often very crude, and I had learned not to be very demanding on this score. Now I was to learn that even the seemingly basic necessities of four walls and water for cleaning oneself could be done without and that the only thing which was truly essential was a modicum of privacy. I also grasped more clearly how in hot countries this lack of sanitary facilities leads to diseases such as dysentery, cholera and typhoid, the flies which are everywhere present during the hot season acting as the carrier of bacteria from contaminated feces to fruits, vegetables and other foodstuffs which are invariably displayed and sold in open stalls due to lack of better facilities, or even to produce still in the fields or fruits on the trees.

We resumed the journey, the old bus rattling on at a good pace, although the driver was very careful, through flat country with mountains, mostly of volcanic origin, in the distance. At one place I caught a sudden, startling glimpse of huge, headless figures of Buddhas carved into the buff face of cliffs away from the road. The countryside became increasingly warm and pleasant, with rivers and tropical vegetation; there was village after village now, trees and tropical plants surrounding them, but conditions were exceedingly poor and primitive. I caught glimpses of mud huts near the drainage basin of a river; poor villagers moved about in groups on this balmy day, the women wearing dingy *shalwaars* with tattered veils on their heads. The warm climate took away that sort of misery produced by harsh winters such as we had seen in Kabul, but substituted another sort, as well as the health problems of a tropical climate, for it during the burning summers.

I pondered over the primitive and backward conditions of life I had observed among Muslims during this journey. We Muslims are proud to say that there are seven hundred million of our co-religionists in the world today, I reflected; but of what benefit is this number when so many live in such stark poverty that they know nothing other than the grinding struggle for daily existence, when they have hardly any voice in the destiny of the lands they inhabit, ruled by leaders or governments which often do little or nothing to better their conditions of life or even actively work against the welfare of the people, and when so many understand virtually nothing of Islam? How many of these could be counted if the count were of those who truly understand and *live* Islam rather than being 'Muslim' merely in name or profession? Islam had come to lift people out of their degradation, physical and spiritual; such conditions existed among Muslims today because they or their forebearers had failed to apply Islam. Then how could we, to whom Allah had given the responsibility of reconstruction, go about the immense task of rebuilding and reviving the Muslim world? How large these questions loomed in my mind now, after the miserable and degraded living conditions and the profound social and political problems which we had observed among our brother Muslims during the past days.

Around noon we stopped for lunch at Jalalabad, a good-sized town; a great many rough men milled about the crowded, primitive bazaar on the main street beside which the bus stopped, its floor by now littered with orange peels and shreds of chewed-up sugar cane. The ticket agent showed Selim one among the many crude restaurants along the street which may have been better than the rest; we climbed up an incredibly dirty staircase and took our places in a room with tables, chairs and a sink for washing hands, where Qur'anic inscriptions with very colorful ornamentation decorated the walls. Selim ordered spinach and *pilau,* together with *kababs* which were being broiled on skewers over a charcoal fire next to the dusty street. At this point I was really beyond worrying much about conditions or food; this was how it was and we would make the best of it—and the meal was delicious.

An hour or so later (after another brief halt at another grove of trees), we had crossed the border; a steady stream of porters and camel caravans laden with goods flowed past into Afghanistan. At last we were in Pakistan and would soon be with our relatives! I shivered with excitement and anticipation as the bus, which had changed from right-hand to left-hand driving from the border, rumbled and quivered slowly up the tortuous road amidst the forbidding, rocky mountains, with startling glimpses of deep, rugged chasms below. Then, after a small primitive town called Torkham, the mountains were behind us and we entered the plains of the Frontier Province, stretched out before us in a dull pall of haze.

I think I shall never in my life forget the scenes and mood of our coming to Pakistan that day: everywhere the muted greenery of a semi-tropical landscape overhung with dusty haze, a half-overcast sky overhead; the villages much more prosperous and solid than those we had seen in Afghanistan, western Iran or eastern Turkey; in every village, even the smallest, white mosques with the typical facade of tiny white domes which one sees all over West Pakistan; big white square dwellings with high walls and square turrets, resembling forts, standing amid the green of the countryside. After the primitive and extreme conditions and climate we had seen throughout our earlier travels, it looked beautiful to me, indeed.

As we neared Peshawar, there were scattered houses, cattle along the road, fruit stalls, and many pedestrians and *tongas,* the two-wheeled horse-drawn taxis of West Pakistan. Each of us was now silent with anticipation and suppressed excitement as we neared the end of the journey. Selim had sent a telegram to his brother Abdur-Rahman from Kabul giving the time of our arrival, and we hoped that he would be at the bus station to meet us.

My impressions blurred until the bus stopped at the depot. There beside it stood a group of beloved familiar faces beaming up at us: Abdur-Rhaman Bhai and his wife Haleema Bhabi,* and

---

* *Bhai*=older brother; *bhabi*=older brother's wife in Urdu (also used as titles of respect and affection for older persons who are not related, like the Turkish *ağabey* and *abla*). Older relatives are always addressed by their titles in Pakistan, a custom common in many parts of the Muslim world, while younger ones are called by name.

Shakeel and Aziza Bhatti, old friends whom we had known in America. I was rather shaky, I must admit, as I helped to collect our belongings and climbed out of the bus. Loving hands reached out to us and hearty words of welcome were spoken; the uncle and aunt gathered up the children with great love and tenderness, and there was great embracing among us women and among the men. We had come at last.

The passengers and luggage were divided between Bhai's and Shakeel Sahib's small European cars, and we drove up to a big elderly red brick house in the city, surrounded by a pleasant lawn, large trees and shrubbery. How lovely it looked to us after the wintry deserts of our travels and the dull bleakness of Ankara! Bhai's three children, Ashraf, Fawzia and Shireen, aged fourteen, eight and five who had not come to the bus because of shortness of space in the two little cars, now came out on the verandah to greet us, very, very shyly. Our luggage was brought into the house and we sat down to tea, very much in need of it.

The children and their cousins approached each other with initial caution, but after a short time they were quite at home with each other; it would take a little longer until they felt free and comfortable with me. Fawzia and Shireen took the girls out to play on the lawn in the pleasant warmth and beautiful greenery, and the two young *sahibs,* Ashraf and Jamal, talking animatedly, went for a walk around the neighborhood. As for the rest of us, we spent the afternoon and evening talking with great enjoyment. Toward evening it became quite chilly and the night was downright cold; we all put on sweaters and coats, and in every room electric or kerosene heaters helped to take the edge off the chill, for here despite the cold few people had real stoves.

We were installed in two bedrooms with the best of everything in the house, and very tired, went to bed soon after dinner. For myself, the fact of being in Pakistan and with our relatives at last after such a long time was hard to grasp and had a sense of strange unreality about it. From my heart I thanked the Beneficent God for bringing us here safely and for our wonderful and interesting travels. There was great peace within me that night; I felt as contented and happy as if I had come to my own home.

Abdur-Rahman Bhai was the chief research officer in a government installation, a civil servant, and Haleema Bhabi was the principal of a public school. Their son Ashraf, a pleasant, well-mannered, intelligent boy, who soon found that despite their different backgrounds he and Jamal had much in common, was a student in a private high school, and the girls in an elementary school where English was taught from the first grade. Thus, apart from little Shireen, who already knew some words of English and who had her sister always on hand to translate between herself and her cousins, there was no problem of communication. Fawzia and Shireen soon lost their shyness toward me; they were delightful, warm, loving little girls. After a day or two, Shireen began to come to me for hugs and a spare lap to sit on occasionally, and the two of us were soon able to communicate with each other very nicely without needing help from anyone.

The house was on one of the quiet streets at the perimeter of the city. Although elderly and showing signs of its long use, it was spacious and more than adequate, and its garden and big trees were very pleasant. It was constructed of brick with terrazzo floors, and, like all Pakistani houses, was designed for hot weather with high ceilings, ventilators and hook-ups for ceiling fans in every room. There were four good-sized bedrooms, two baths, a dining room, drawing room, kitchen with a storeroom, detached servants' quarters, and verandahs in front and back; the whole compound was surrounded by a red brick wall with a gate. The domestic staff consisted of Ramzan, a part-time servant boy from the nearby tribal area who helped Haleema Bhabi with the preparation of food and cooking and who washed the dishes, a sweeper boy (a Christian, as all members of this profession are in West Pakistan) who came once a day to sweep the floors and wash them with water, to clean the bathrooms and courtyard, and a gardener who came when needed.

On the first morning there was a trip to see the city, both Bhai and Bhabi taking leave from work. My first impressions of Peshawar were of big old trees, including palms, roads which all looked alike all having red brick houses surrounded by walls and trees, a vast military cantonment, bicycles, *tongas,* some private cars, and many people on foot, including women in *burqas*. The shops of the main bazaar, Sadar, struck me as relatively crude, and I was quite surprised that a major city of Pakistan the size of Peshawar did not have anything better to offer in the way of shopping establishments, which all sold a rather limited variety of merchandise. All-in-all, Peshawar seemed a pleasant, green, quiet town with a slow-paced life and peaceful atmosphere.

At, this point, tired from our travels, we had more appetite for talking than anything else. For my benefit most of the conversation at present was in English, which everyone spoke almost as fluently as Urdu. Actually, English was so widely known in Pakistan that not speaking Urdu did not constitute much of a problem except in talking to servants or tradespeople, but nonetheless it piqued me that I could not now speak even the most simple sentences. When I tried I would pull a Turkish word out of my mental reservoir instead, or a mixture of Turkish and Urdu, for the systematic study and daily usage of Turkish had completely emptied my mind of any other fragments of languages I had known previously. Of course both of us enjoyed talking about our own recent experiences and exchanging views with Bhai and Bhabi; otherwise talk about the situation of Pakistan, especially about political matters, predominated. These were the days just after the hijacking of an Indian Airlines plane by two pro-Pakistan Kashmiri youths; the plane was sitting at Lahore Airport with the boys inside it, and no one knew what might happen.

By now I was helping Haleema Bhabi with light work in the kitchen. Even with the domestic help she had, there was still a considerable amount of housework for her to do. Without such help in Pakistan, the most simple household tasks were so cumbersome that a servantless woman would have no time for anything except housework from morning to night. For example, in America or Turkey I was used to cleaning the floor with a vacuum cleaner, broom or mop when it was dirty. Here, however, this was not done. This was considered dirty and demeaning menial work unsuitable for a respectable *begum sahiba,* both because of the dirty nature of the work itself and because of the way it was performed, for the *jamidar* who cleaned would sweep squatting with a short stick broom and then go over the floor, squatting, with a wet rag. Washing dishes was also regarded as menial work unsuitable for a respectable woman even if there was a sink in the kitchen; where there was no sink or the servant preferred not to use it, the dirty dishes were washed at a faucet in the back courtyard or a detached kitchen. The complicated way in which food must be prepared, the lack of a hot water supply, efficient cooking stoves (for gas was not yet available in many places) and other simplified methods of housework, plus a rather artificial standard of 'respectability,' made housekeeping in Pakistan and many other less-developed parts of the Muslim world very difficult and created an unnatural dependence on servants among the middle and upper classes, especially on the despised *jamidarnis* who did the most menial tasks, in contrast to Turkey where housework was, by comparison, much more simplified, easy and was also considered perfectly dignified. Thus it happened that many times when Pakistani or Indian women came to the West, they struggled with cleaning, dishwashing and other household work for the very first time in their lives, and as a result felt totally overwhelmed by such unfamiliar tasks.

The second of the two 'Eids, 'Eid al-Adha—the Feast of Sacrifice—was to be on February 6. This holy day commemorates the Prophet Abraham's willingness to sacrifice the life of his son Ishmael,* peace be on them both, at God's command. The Holy Qur'an relates the story thus:

> "[Abraham prayed:] 'O my Lord, grant me a righteous son.' So We gave him the good news of a boy ready to suffer and forbear. Then, when (the son) had reached (the age of serious) work with him, he [Abraham] said, 'O my son, I see in a vision that I offer thee in

---

* According to the Old Testament, it was Abraham's son Isaac who was to be sacrificed. This error in the Biblical account is made clear by the fact that it mentions the object of sacrifice as Abraham's *only son*, who at that time was Ishmael, yet gives his name as Isaac (Genesis 22:2). According to the Qur'an, the two sons of Abraham (Ibrahim), Isaac (Ishaq) and Ishmael (Isma'il), were both prophets, as was their father; Isaac was the progenitor of the Jews (Banu Isra'il) and Ishmael of a branch of the Arab peoples (Banu Isma'il).

sacrifice; now see what is thy view.' (The son) said, 'O my father, do as thou art commanded; thou wilt find me, if God wills, one practicing patience and constancy.' So when they had both submitted their wills (to God), and he laid him prostrate on his forehead (for sacrifice), We called out to him, 'O Abraham, thou hast already fulfilled the vision!' Thus indeed do We reward those who do right; for this was obviously a trial, and We ransomed him with a momentous sacrifice [i.e., the substitution of a ram in place of Ishmael]."*

Muslims of all times and places since the beginning of Islam have commemorated this event, which reminds them that Islam demands from them such complete trust in God and submission to Him that they must be willing to give whatever they love most, even their own lives, when necessary, in His cause. This *'Eid* takes place at the time of the *Hajj,* the annual pilgrimage to Mekkah, and the sacrificing of animals in remembrance of Prophet Abraham's submission to God and his sacrifice of the ram is a part of the *Hajj* rites; the meat of the animals is of course to be used for food. At the same time, Muslims all the world over who are able to afford it sacrifice animals at their own homes; the flesh of these animals is divided into three parts, one-third for the use of one's own family, the second for distribution among relatives, friends and neighbors, and the third to be given to the poor. Three goats were being kept in an empty room in the compound of Bhai's house for slaughter on *'Eid* day. Sharifa, Bhai's and Selim's younger sister, would be driving up from Lahore for the festival with her family.

The day before *'Eid* we had finished our lunch and were sitting on the front verandah where, during this cool season, we found the warmest sun. Sharifa and her family were expected to arrive late in the day. It was still early spring, and flies and mosquitoes had not yet made their appearance. The red brick wall separated us from the road, where pedestrians, bicycles, *tongas* and occasional cars passed by at a leisurely pace; the tall trees threw patches of shade mottled with sunlight onto the garden. Aziza and Shakeel Sahib were having tea with us, and we sat talking about the possibility of going to the Old City to make some purchases for *'Eid.*

---

* *Al-Saffat* 37:100-113.

In the middle of our conversation, a red Morris with luggage on its carrier drove up, and we all rose in astonishment and pleasure as Sharifa, her husband Nizamuddin and their children Rafiq and Asma got out; they had reached Peshawar much earlier in the day than we could have expected. Sharifa, clad in a dark blue *sari,* beamed with joy and clasped us all in a warm embrace. For her it had not been so long since we had met, as she had visited us in the United States a few years earlier, but the joy of our all being together again in Pakistan was unforgettable and infinitely sweet for every one of us.

Rafiq, who had been a little child when we had last seen him, was now a young man, grown up and taller than his father; Asma, his younger sister, was a slender girl of thirteen. The eight cousins now had the opportunity of a lifetime to be together, and as all of them except Shireen spoke fluent English, they were fast friends from the very beginning. However, Rafiq, being too old to join in Ashraf and Jamal's play for the most part, preferred to be with the adults and take part in our conversation.

As we sat together on the verandah, we now made the details of our recent situation in Turkey—how remote it all seemed!— known to Nizam and Sharifa, who, in a state of unbounded delight at being reunited with us all, searched our faces again and again with a look of love. None of us would forget this joyful day, indeed!

Later the conversation came back to the preparations for tomorrow, *'Eid.* A few items were needed from town, and Aziza and Shakeel Sahib volunteered to go with Selim and me to bring them. I especially wanted to buy Peshawari slippers for the girls and myself to wear on *'Eid,* for we had no footwear with us except the travel-worn shoes on our feet. The place for slippers, Aziza said, was the old city; I was delighted with the prospect of getting a glimpse of the old section of Peshawar, and we drove off in Shakeel Sahib's little Austin.

Somewhere in the middle of the town we made a turn or two and entered the labyrinth of the old quarter, the like of which I had never seen before: street after street of primitive wooden shops, more like stalls, on the top floors of which were flats with latticed windows for privacy, Pathans in every sort of wrap and dress, many types of native merchandise which caught my eyes, and such dense throngs that it was difficult to get through with the car. We left it at a corner where there were several shops, one beside the other, specializing in beautiful, ornate Peshawari slippers and sandals of many types and styles. We went to the largest of these, where each piece of footwear seemed to me like a work of art, with its lovely embroidery, and selected our purchases: flower-decorated slippers for each of the five girls, and for me, a gold-embroidered black velvet pair which I knew I would treasure for years to come.

After this there were other purchases to be made, and we trudged through the maze-like, narrow streets looking for the right shops. The crowds were so thick that it was difficult to walk; the acrid smell of smoke mingled with various other scents filled the bazaar. There were relatively few women about, and the majority of these were completely covered in *burqas,* for most Peshawari women observe *purdah*—that is, they do not mix with men unless they are relatives or very close family friends, and when they go out they wear *burqas,* usually with their faces veiled.

Our errands completed, we returned home to dinner, in which Aziza and Shakeel Sahib joined. Now the talk was almost entirely in Urdu, which, although I still could not speak, I could follow if the subject matter was relatively simple; however, if the conversation became more complicated, I would often lose the thread. But unlike my previous experience in Pakistan when I had felt baffled and frustrated by my inability to understand and speak Urdu, it now did not trouble me. I felt completely at home, knowing that I had a secure place in the family's regard and not requiring that everyone should speak English for my benefit or that I must know everything that was said; I knew that if anything concerned me which I could not follow it would be translated. I sat in front of the electric heater in the drawing room, sniffing with a developing cold and watching as Asma painstakingly applied *henna* to one of Maryam's hands in a flower-and-leaf design for 'Eid. Thank God, there had been no adjustment problems of any sort for any of us; Selim, the children and I were happy, Jamal's asthma seemed to have disappeared, at least temporarily, and all was well.

The children, indeed, had responded to Pakistan and to their relatives with such enthusiasm that they now declared unqualifiedly that they liked Pakistan much better than Turkey. I took this with a grain of salt. It was one thing to be a beloved, welcome, visiting family member without responsibilities of any kind, but an entirely different matter to be settled in a place and have to cope with its daily routines and problems of living. Just now, however, the memory of bleak, polluted Ankara, with its even greater burden of ideological pollution, was uppermost in all our minds rather than the feeling of identification and affection which we had come to feel for Turkey as a whole. I realized now how tired I had been with the problems which had absorbed us there and rejoiced in the chance to be away from them, to see new scenes and to be with those whom I loved dearly for this brief time. I gave all my attention to the experience at hand, becoming involved with and trying to understand Pakistan better.

On 'Eid morning the men and boys went to a nearby mosque for prayers; here too women did not as a rule go to 'Eid prayers, and I watched them go with a wistful sense of missing the best part of the festival. During their absence, the five girl cousins dressed in the identical outfits Sharifa had bought for each of them for the occasion—beautiful lavender-colored *ghararas*—suits consisting of a wide, gathered, split skirt with matching tunic and *dupatta*—and when they were further embellished with jewelry for the occasion they looked altogether very lovely. We then went for brief visits to exchange 'Eid greetings with two of Haleema Bhabi's neighbors and returned home.

I went out on the back courtyard just as Selim was slaughtering the second of the goats, slitting its throat with merciful swiftness with a very sharp knife. This was a new experience for me, for I had never seen an animal killed before, and indeed, it left me with much to think about; but not just then, for there was much work to do.

After the carcasses had been inflated and hung, the servant Ramzan and the butcher who was making the rounds of houses that day to help with processing the meat, removed the skins and began to strip the meat off the bones. We women changed into old clothes and returned to cut the meat into small pieces. It was divided into three equal parts—one for ourselves, one for neighbors and friends, and one to be given away in charity. During the morning, gifts of meat were brought to our house by the servants or children of neighbors, and in return Haleema Bhabi sent them back portions of our meat. The skins and heads of the goats had already gone for some charitable purpose, and all day long, as a succession of the poor came to the door, portions of meat were given to each one; when the meat was exhausted, small amounts of money were given in its place. On this occasion it was the right of the poor to ask and the duty of those who had slaughtered animals to give to them. Meat was very expensive here, as in Turkey, and this 'Eid would be one of the few times during the year when the poor would have meat to eat.

Aziza and Shakeel Sahib now arrived, and we women exchanged embraces and hearty " 'Eid mubaraks." These friends had been with us for four or five 'Eids at home, and it was thus a very joyful occasion to be all together, family and close friends, on this happy day. Ramzan and Aziza's servant, who had come to help, now went to the kitchen to assist Haleema Bhabi in making pilau and other dishes to go with the meat, and when this was ready the two servants roasted the chunks of meat on skewers over charcoal in the back courtyard, while the children played merrily about.

At this point I was feeling miserable with a full-blown cold. This as well as my thoughts about the goats whose lives we had taken made me very pensive and quiet, and while everyone sat in the courtyard eating, my mind was busy. Today, after years and years of eating meat daily without any particular thought about the matter, I had seen an animal slaughtered and dying for the first time. It had suddenly dawned on me with an intense realization what an awesome thing it is to take a life and why God requires Muslims to say upon slaughtering, "Allahu Akbar, Bismillah"— God is the Most Great, in the name of God. Without the remembrance of Almighty God when one takes a life, by His permission and to satisfy our legitimate need for food (for man, like all other living creatures, must live by taking the lives of other creatures, whether plant or animal), it loses its significance both as the bounty of God and as a living thing, one of His creations whom we are permitted to kill solely in order to meet our necessities; and without this consciousness it is easy to think of and to treat meat and other foods, as one tends to do amidst all the affluence of America, as if it were something to be taken for granted, something which is produced by man's effort alone, forgetting that it comes to us by God's permission and beneficence. This *"Allahu Akbar, Bismillah,"* and the *"Bismillah ar-Rahman ar-Raheem"*—In the name of God, the Beneficent, the Merciful—which the Muslim says when he begins to eat, together with the respectful attitude toward life and food which it engenders, makes every morsel of food—especially of meat—very precious and valued among Muslims, especially in lands where hunger is never very far away.

I thought too of the significance of this occasion, the commemoration of Prophet Abraham's total submission and obedience to God without question or reservation, which is an example for every Muslim to ponder deeply and try to emulate in his own life. I also thought of all those who were today involved in the observances of *Hajj* near Mekkah, where Prophet Abraham and his son Ishmael, peace be on them, had together raised the first house of worship of the One True God, known as Ka'aba.*

"The first house (of worship) appointed for men was that at Bakka [Mekkah], full of blessing and of guidance to the worlds. In it are signs manifest, (namely), the station of Abraham; whoever enters it attains security. Pilgrimage thereto is a duty men owe to God, for those who can afford the journey."**

---

* The cube-shaped structure in Mekkah which, as the first house of worship of God erected on earth, is the focus of the observances of the *Hajj* and the place which Muslims all over the world face when they pray.

** *Ale Imran* 3:96-97.

And I saw in my mind the Holy Ka'aba circumambulated by those hundreds of thousands of white-clad pilgrims whose minds were occupied solely with the worship and glorification of God Most High, and who had come together in that great international assemblage of Muslims from every corner of the globe, of every color, race, language and nation only for that single purpose. The patient *Hajis* we had seen at Ankara Airport would be among them, God bless them all, crying out in fervent unison with their fellow-pilgrims, *"Labbayk, Allahumma, labbayk!"*—Here I am, our Lord, at Thy service. For them as for all other *Hajis,* the men clad in the same two-part unsewn white garment and the women covered from head to foot with only their hands and faces exposed, there would no longer be any differences or distinctions to divide them—man-made distinctions at which God does not look—of black or white, high or low, rich or poor, educated or unlettered. All were equal before God, remembering and worshipping Him alone, and thinking of that awesome Day when all mankind would stand before Him, wealth and honors, status and prestige, forgotten, to be judged solely according to their actions and intentions in this life. And I wished and longed intensely for the day when, God willing, my husband and I might be able to stand among that vast gathering of pilgrims to God's house and share in the blessedness of that occasion . . .

After the meal was over, the dishes were stacked on the verandah by the kitchen door and the servants began to wash up at the outside faucet. Aziza and Haleema Bhabi had given each of them new outfits of clothes for *'Eid;* gifts of money or meat, or both, had been given to the sweeper boy, the gardener, the peons, the laundryman and others who rendered periodic service, and the equivalent of one goat and additional money had been distributed to the poor who came to the door until late afternoon and would continue to come the next day, to claim their rightful share in the charity of *'Eid.* May Allah accept our sacrifices and our charity, our prayers, and all we do for His sake . . .

The next morning there were more visits to friends and neighbors, and afterwards dinner with the Bhattis. Aziza, with the help of her servant and Ramzan, whom she had borrowed to help with the cooking, had prepared a splendid meal which we ate with enjoyment. Then in the early afternoon, taking along a basket of food, we set out on an expedition to see Warsak Dam in the mountains outside Peshawar, making a caravan with the three cars. Out into the lush green countryside, among fields, villages, the walled, fort-like dwellings, and villagers with their children attired in bright, colorful new clothes for the festival. Conditions of life here might be primitive and hard, but there was liveliness and color everywhere.

The dam was many miles outside Peshawar, a big installation set among the dark lava mountains bordering the Kabul River, with sentries posted here and there. Shakeel Sahib told us that the dam had been built some twelve years earlier by Canadian engineers, but, with the usual efficiency which characterizes many such projects in various parts of the East, there had been some flaw in its design and it was now partially silted up.

From here we went to a spot beside a river where, on this lazy early spring day, we sat basking in the warm sun, wisps of clouds flecking the blue, blue sky, chatting and eating the fruits, *halvah* and other food we had brought. At a nearby restaurant, a flock of teenage boys and girls danced to fast jazz music on the terrace, and presently they decamped to some spot a little way down the river. This was the first time I had seen members of the 'emancipated' younger set coming from the 'advanced' families of Pakistan, whom I had hardly expected to find in conservative Peshawar. Many of the girls wore the latest Pakistani fashion, a short tunic with straight or bell-bottom Western-style pants replacing the traditional *qamis* and *shalwaar* to make an outfit indistinguishable from the 'pant suits' now being worn in America, and their free behavior was certainly disturbing to observe among Pakistani young people. "What a way to spend *'Eid!*" Sharifa commented disgustedly. In the far distance, ancient rickety buses ambled along, heavily loaded inside and out with villagers coming from a fair which we had seen in the distance from the car. Clearly almost everyone was spending these days of *'Eid* as a holiday, each according to his own taste and means.

That evening Sharifa's family left by train for Lahore, taking along some of our luggage and leaving behind their car for our use, since a friend's car was at their disposal for the time-being. The house seemed suddenly very empty after they had gone, but we parted in the expectation of being with them in Lahore within ten days. Thus passed 'Eid al-Adha 1971, to be remembered always as the 'Eid on which our family was reunited after many years of separation.

The remaining days in Peshawar passed very quickly. Bhai and Bhabi took leave from their work as much as possible, and we spent hours and hours talking, during the day sitting out in the sun on the front verandah. We also did some shopping, visited friends of Bhai's, and received visitors. Many of their friends invited us; most of the men and some of their wives spoke English, but if they did not, my Urdu was by now again sufficient to manage. The ladies were all very pleasant people, friendly and hospitable to me, and I was naturally very happy to be received in such a kind manner.

We also attended a wedding, the first Pakistani wedding I had ever seen. The bride was a friend of Haleema Bhabi's, an educated girl, and the groom was a lawyer. As is usual in Pakistan, they did not know each other and had probably never even seen each other prior to the time of the marriage ceremony. In this type of arranged marriage the selection is made by the parents (or other relatives if parents are dead), who as a rule go to great pains to learn all they can about the prospective partner's background, personality, behavior, etc., from those who know him or her well in order to ensure the future happiness of their child; the final decision, however, is supposed to rest with the man and woman themselves.

We women and the girls dressed ourselves with care for the occasion and then all the family set out for the home of the bride, a modern, elegant mansion in University Town. Colored lights were festooned all over the top of the house and around the courtyard. On one side of the house, a large, colorful tent had been erected for the men's part of the function, for men and women usually do not mix in Pakistani weddings, and men outside the family ordinarily never see the bride.

The women's festivities—that is, the ceremony in which bride and groom would see each other for the first time—were set out on the back lawn, enclosed by walls and the colorful awnings. A group of women and girls had begun to assemble by the time we arrived; everyone was very well-dressed, with displays of jewelry and elaborate hairstyles. On the lawn, several young girls, relatives of the bride, sat together singing and playing a small drum. Gradually more and more women assembled; I found Aziza in the group, and Haleema Bhabi introduced me to her friends.

Now the bride, dressed all in deep pink, heavily garlanded with flowers and tinsel, and her face cast down and completely hidden under the fine veils which were pulled forward over it, was led out. She was seated, and the women gathered around to admire her and say soft words of affection and encouragement, lifting the veils and holding up her drooping face with eyes closed, for by tradition a Pakistani bride must keep her eyes down or closed as a sign of shyness and modesty on this occasion. Presently the bridegroom, so heavily garlanded that he could not see to walk, was led out and seated beside her. A thin veil of silver-and-crimson material was placed over the heads of the couple, while all the women crowded around them and the younger sisters of the bride teased their new brother in the customary manner. A Qur'an was brought, from which the groom read aloud under the veil. I was just behind them, looking on and taking photographs.

At length the crucial moment was at hand. A round, ornate mirror was brought and laid in the lap of the bride: the new husband would now see his wife's face for the first time in his life in the mirror. With gentle hands which must surely have trembled as a very vital part of his future unfolded before him, he put back the veils from the cast-down face and looked down at the reflection of the woman with whom he was to share his life.

There was such a crowd around the pair that I could see nothing at that point, but during the last five minutes all the romantic interest and associations of marriage to a person whom one does not know but which is contracted with implicit reliance upon the wisdom, judgment and love of parents had for me left the realm of theoretical knowledge and become empirical. The marriage is regarded as a binding, permanent, life-long relationship by both partners, and both enter into it with absolute commitment and devotion to one another and to their marriage, aware that it can succeed and be a source of satisfaction only if each puts effort into it, smoothing over difficulties, giving and forgiving and forbearing in good times and bad, and doing their utmost to make it a harmonious and happy relationship.

Although Islam emphatically prohibits the sort of dating practices and pre-marital intimacies which are so common in the West, still it does not require that marriage should take place without the partners having seen each other; indeed, the Holy Prophet, peace be on him, strongly recommended that they do see each other beforehand *in the presence of others*. However, marriages arranged by parents or guardians—whether the boy and girl meet beforehand or not—have been the recommended and customary way of uniting men and women throughout the centuries among Muslims, and this system has, on the whole, shown a remarkable viability and capacity for building successful and stable marital relationships due to the attitude of permanence, commitment and mutual responsibility with which both partners approach their marriage, strange as it always seems to Westerners accustomed to close association and intimacy before marriage. As Selim remarked, in a Muslim marriage, courtship and romance come after, not before, the wedding.

The bridegroom was led away, and then all the women crowded around the bride, lifting her veils and whispering words of encouragement; then she was led into the house. Immediately afterwards dinner was served separately for the male and female guests. When it was time to go, we rejoined our men-folk, whose part in the festivities had been very much less interesting and enjoyable, Jamal grumbling that Pakistani weddings were a hopeless bore and that he had not even seen the bride. I summarized my impression of the occasion by saying, "It's my feeling that a Pakistani wedding is enjoyable for everyone except the bride!" at which everyone laughed.

I had now been in Pakistan long enough to begin to have some thoughts about several issues. At present the hijacked Indian plane had become a critical problem. The two young Kashmiri hijackers had sat inside it at Lahore Airport under heavy guard, threatening to blow it up if any move were made against them, and although no move was made, on the third day they blew it up anyhow, slightly injuring themselves in the blast. There was now great support in the press for the 'heroism' of these Kashmiri 'freedom-fighters' who had resorted to such drastic action to draw the attention of the world to the oppression of their homeland by India. However, as tension mounted between India and Pakistan because of this incident—an entirely predictable result—I thought that they had behaved very irresponsibly, but hesitated to voice such an heretical opinion.

As a quite foreseeable result, India banned all Pakistani flights across its territory, and the link with East Pakistan now has to be maintained by means of flights via Ceylon, an extremely serious handicap in maintaining communications. If the hijacking were taken as the work of two private citizens acting on their own rather than of the government of Pakistan, this indeed seemed a very drastic and uncalled-for response, ultimately leading to speculations that this may have been a well-calculated move of the Indian government to put an end to communication between the two wings through the use of Indian air space, or even that India may have staged the hijacking and blowing-up of the plane in order to achieve such results.

There was rising fear of an outbreak of war as a result of this incident, as the Indian press and government reacted angrily and anti-Pakistan demonstrations flared up in various places in India, capital being made of the incident to the utmost possible extent. As the tension mounted, we saw that anti-aircraft guns had been placed around the military airport, on high buildings and in fields near it just off the main road leading west. Daily there were hours of breath-taking practice flying by Air Force Sabrejets, although I did not learn whether this was a normal routine or an effect of the crisis. In any case, the large garrison of military in Peshawar and, as we were to see later, in every town through which we passed on the way to Lahore, provided one with a sense of security—perhaps a false sense, as later events were to show.

As I wrote in Turkey, elections for a constitution-framing body, which was later to become the National Assembly of Pakistan, were held during the past December. Contrary to our hopes and expectations, the Jamaat-i-Islami Party headed by Syed Abul 'Ala Maududi, one of the world's most renowned Islamic scholars, thinkers and writers, was badly defeated, gaining in all only a few seats although in some areas it had a numerical majority. Instead, control was gained in West Pakistan by the Peoples' Party of Zulfiqar 'Ali Bhutto, who had been Foreign Minister during Ayub Khan's regime. Although he was himself a big landlord and a very wealthy man, he campaigned as a man of the people, depicted on political posters in the plain dress of a Pakistani villager with bare feet, drawing the votes of the common people through promises of a better life and pledging, under the strange, incongruous slogan of 'Islamic Socialism,' to give them 'bread, clothes and housing'. At the same time, in East Pakistan Mujib-ur-Rahman had won the election as head of the majority party primarily by playing up the inequalities between the east and west wings of Pakistan; he exploited the inferiority-feelings of Bengalis, who, although much more numerous than the population of West Pakistan, are considerably less developed economically, and promised them autonomy. It was now up to Mujib and Bhutto to get together with other parties to frame a new constitution within one-hundred-and-twenty days; otherwise, power would remain with Yahya Khan's martial law regime and a new election would be called.

It saddened us to hear that there were at present many so-called Islamic parties in Pakistan, with leaders whose very lives and characters could, in some instances, if the reports we had heard were correct, be called into question, each working for its own interests instead of all pulling together so that there would be a united Islamic party to unify and to polarize the votes of all concerned Muslims. As far as the Jamaat-i-Islami was concerned, we had read its Manifesto. It had appeared to be completely Islamic and also quite well-organized and thought-out in terms of planning and program, but somehow the Jamaat seemed to have failed to reach and command the votes of the common people, who had mostly supported Bhutto and his Peoples' Party. As for the upper classes, many of them were critical and hostile toward the Jamaat and their votes had been divided among several parties. However, it was obvious that, even with the unqualified support of the upper classes, the Jamaat could not have carried the election without the massive support of the common people, who had been led to give their votes to a leader of very questionable character through the usual politician's tricks—meaningless slogans, vague, unrealizable promises, and demagoguery.

It was clear then that for various reasons Pakistan as a whole had not chosen Islamic leadership and Islamic solutions to its problems, the one thing which could have united and bound up the frustrations and bitterness of this strange geographic anomaly and brought together its disparate elements if anything could. Nonetheless, whether the Jamaat-i-Islami won or lost, it had been one of the very few instances in modern history in which an Islamic group had formulated a political program and campaigned for election, and it had set an example of restraint by refusing to resort to the mudslinging and name-calling which had marred the campaigns of other party leaders.

One day Haleema Bhabi took me to visit Fawzia and Shireen's private school, and I was very well-impressed with the manners and behavior of the youngsters. As a rule, Pakistani children of educated families are extremely well-brought-up and well-behaved, indeed one of the most encouraging signs which one can see in any nation. At the same time, however, such good manners and behavior are often closely linked to a great degree of passivity and dependence, a lack of questioning and blind acceptance of any sort of authority, which results in a seeming stunting of normal personality development, leaving many people, even as adults, with the appearance of never having developed to their full potential as human beings. As I compared this with the aggressive independence and early cynicism of so many American young people, my mind searched about for that middle path between these two extremes which is required for the development of an Islamic personality and an Islamic society.

I had by now observed and thought much about the condition of women in Pakistan, both those who observed *purdah** and those who did not. In Pakistan, as in Turkey, Iran and the rest of the Muslim world, strictly religious, conservative women do not mix with men, even in their homes, unless they are family members or close family friends whose character and integrity are well-known. In practical terms, when a male visitor comes, he sits in the drawing room with the men of the house and the women carry on their own activities in other parts of the home, which is expressly designed for such a manner of living; tea and refreshments are sent in to the drawing room with a servant, or through the husband or a child if there is no servant. Outside the house and at any time when men are present, some type of loose, concealing wrap or coat is worn, for example, the *chaddor* in Iran, *çarşaf* or light coat and scarf in Turkey, *burnoose* in Morocco, *abaya* in Iraq, *jilbab* in Syria, *thoup* in Sudan, *burqa* or *chadiri* in Pakistan and Afghanistan. The type of *burqa* which is most common in Pakistan consists of two parts: a thin, loose coat of varying length, usually black, and a matching veil which covers the head and ties under the chin, with two thin face veils; one or both of them can be put back over the top of the head to leave the face uncovered, or they can be dropped down to cover the face at will, so that the wearer is able to see without being seen. As in Turkey, in Pakistan the observance of such dress and separation of the sexes is primarily a phenomenon of the middle class, which has retained Islamic values to a greater extent and with a truer understanding than other social levels; the upper classes of both countries have largely discarded it, and the lower class women, who work in the fields among men or as servants covered by their *shalwaars,* loose shirts, *dupattas* or kerchiefs, generally require no further covering.

Islam absolutely and unequivocally prohibits sexual relations and any expression of sexual interest outside marriage, and takes active measures to safeguard the purity and integrity of the Muslim society, the basis of which is the sanctity of the family. This is

* Refers to the separation of the sexes and the wearing of a covering type of outer garment when a woman goes outside her home or in any situation where men other than her husband and nearest relatives.

achieved by clearly defining the limits of the relationship between men and women, minimizing contact between the sexes, and through the various forms of Islamic dress of women. This dress, according to a clear *Hadith* of the Holy Prophet, peace be on him, should cover the entire body excepting only the face and hands (although the face too may be covered for greater purity if desired), should be loose, not transparent or revealing, and should not attract attention by its beauty.

It seemed to me as I thought about it that any sort of *via media* between total freedom of interaction and almost complete separation of the sexes is very difficult to maintain, for human beings will tend to move toward more and more freedom unless the limits are very clearly defined, understood, accepted, practiced and enforced on all sides. An example of this is Turkey, where up to the present, although there is virtually no separation of the sexes among most educated people, the behavior of most men toward women (barring the rough, amoral elements which flourish in the larger cities), and *vice-versa,* is very correct and respectful, coming as it does from the Islamic standards of decency and proper behavior of both sexes. Turkish men and women who have any respect for tradition, although they may not be very religious, know the limits and observe them very carefully, even without that strict separation of the sexes which is practiced by very religious or conservative Turks. However, as westernized ways of thought and behavior seep down from the 'liberated' segment of the population, and as the young generation of Turks who have been brought up without Islamic values and moral training grows up and propagates the increasing trend toward dating and pre-marital intimacy now little by little gaining a foothold in the big cities, all this has begun to change, for the clear definition of the limits has been discarded among them. Islamic restraints and conceptions of what is permissible and proper are gradually giving way to completely alien patterns of behavior, and that most admirable quality of integrity and decency which now characterizes the interaction of most Turkish men and women, like an invisible but clearly-defined barrier against exceeding the limits prescribed by God, is being lost; and a similar pattern of change is already well underway in other Muslim countries where the mutual acceptance by men and women of prescribed limits has been discarded.

In no case, however, can the effort to achieve correct relations between the sexes and to safeguard chastity be a one-sided affair, for purity and chastity are obligations on Muslim men just as much as on Muslim women; the same severe legal punishments for illicit sexual relations have been prescribed by Islam for both. Here in Pakistan, however, it appeared that a sizeable segment of the male society—those rough, lower class men who were to be seen hanging about in the bazaars, the counterpart of whom I had noted in Turkey—had relieved itself of responsibility for proper conduct. Thus it not infrequently happened that respectable Muslim women, even women completely covered by *burqas,* might become the object of attention of these coarse, depraved men, who might stare, pass remarks, or even attempt something worse. In Pakistan this had unfortunately become for some women—especially those who live in rough localities—the reason for wearing the *burqa* rather than a real understanding of and desire to implement the Islamic social system. Something was indeed drastically wrong with a society which claimed to be Muslim but in which large numbers of such men were to be found. On the other hand, in respectable and educated Pakistani families women generally held a position of high respect, whether they were single or married. And while Pakistani wives might be more patient and less aggressive in making demands than Western women and their lives might be much more centered on their families, clearly they had great influence on their husbands, fathers, brothers and children, and had their own unique methods of managing things.

Peshawar had left me with many things to think about. Here I had seen a city virtually unchanged, it would seem, for the past many, many years. I guessed that the Old City might not be substantially different today from what it had been a hundred years ago, apart from the addition of minimal electrification and sanitary facilities. It was a city with such a slow-paced existence that I wondered if life were not totally passing it by while its educated citizens went about their daily affairs and enjoyed its leisurely, quiet mode of life, leaving more important matters in the hands of people in other parts of the country for decision and action.

The month in Pakistan was now half over and it was time to go on to Sharifa in Lahore. We had tried to formulate plans for our trip back to Turkey, but as essential information about various matters was so far lacking, we did not yet know how we would travel and could only hope that the best plan would prove to be the one which involved going by bus from Peshawar to Kabul to Tehran through the interesting old cities of Qandahar and Hirat in Afghanistan and Meshed in Iran. Thus, with the hope of seeing them once more before returning to Turkey, we came to the end of our pleasant, happy stay with Bhai's family.

The children had had a delightful time with good health, thank God; Jamal's asthma had disappeared for the first time in several months. Firm, lasting bonds had been forged among the young cousins, and the love of family and sense of attachment to this new part of the Muslim world which we had hoped would come to flower in our children's hearts was a reality. Bhai and Bhabi had been immensely loving and kind and had done everything possible to make our stay happy and meaningful, and we could only pray and hope for our meeting again in the not-too-distant future, *insha' Allah.*

CHAPTER 11

LAHORE

On February 14 we were up very early preparing for the two-hundred-and-fifty mile drive to Lahore via Islamabad in Sharifa's car. Abdur-Rahman Bhai and Haleema Bhabi helped us with the last-minute arrangements, and Aziza and Shakeel Sahib came to the house to bid us farewell. We all parted from each other very, very sadly; only the vague possibility that we might meet again on our way back to Turkey provided a bright spot in our leave-taking. We turned our faces toward the Grand Trunk Road and Lahore, waving until the house and the beloved group standing by its gate was nothing but a wet blur before our eyes ...

✶ ✶ ✶

Nura was now fast asleep on the seat beside me on the jet, her yarn doll sprawled across her lap; we had two more hours of flying before we reached Beirut. Across the aisle, Jamal was reading one of the books he had brought with him for the third time, Selim had finished all the copies of the ''Jerusalem Post'' around him and was dozing, and Maryam had fallen asleep with her head on his shoulder. The departure from Peshawar was still fresh in my mind, a time of intense sadness for us all. Who knew when we would be able to meet again, and what lay ahead of any one of us ...?

✶ ✶ ✶

For a long while, as the car sped toward Lahore, I did not try to keep back the tears, for they *would* come; yet outside it was a pleasant morning, just beginning to warm up after the chill of the night. Everywhere green and lush vegetation, people walking by the road or in the streets of the small villages and towns we passed, droves of sheep, water buffaloes and camels of great height, creaking ox-carts, brightly-painted trucks and buses, children playing by the roadside, primitive fruit and vegetable stalls, dirt and dust everywhere, but in spite of the adverse conditions, an atmosphere both of liveliness and the peace which comes from acceptance of life on its own terms.

By ten o'clock we were in Punjab Province and had soon reached the outskirts of Islamabad, lying glittering and new in front of a range of hills with scrubby vegetation, a pleasant natural setting. It was a city unlike any other we had seen anywhere. A great many of its buildings, numbers of which were embassies and the residences of diplomatic personnel, were beautiful, elegant palaces tending toward futurism in style, with considerable non-functional architectural embellishment, one more magnificent than the next. We had seen fancy, rich homes in Karachi and Lahore previously, but this city contained such a profusion of them, so fantastic in their design and on such a grand scale, that it was hard to believe that Islamabad was actually a city of Pakistan; indeed, it did not seem to belong to the same country as the poor areas through which we had just passed, and we reflected on the appalling and unbelievable contrast between rich and poor in this land. (Later in Lahore we were to hear much about the illegal sources from which the wealth for the building of many of these glamorous mansions has come and shocking stories of corruption in high places which spread a taint of ill-concealed vice over the proud magnificence of the new capital city.)

We filled the gasoline tank and returned to the road. The plains of northern Panjab are hilly and the fauna thick and tropical, the temperature warmer than in the Peshawar area. These were the most fertile parts of West Pakistan, growing a variety of staple crops; fields stretched out on both sides of the road between the villages. The traffic was difficult and complicated, consisting of trucks, buses, occasional private cars, *tongas,* bicycles, ox-carts, all types of cattle and livestock, and pedestrians, and Selim constantly had to be alert and ready for quick action. The population gradually became more dense, and there were several larger towns on our way. Many of the men we saw wore *lungis,* a Panjabi dress consisting of a draped cloth tied at the waist; there were fewer women in *burqas* to be seen in the small towns we passed, for here many women wore shawls or thick *dupattas* on their heads, their faces uncovered.

When Selim's sister Sharifa had visited the United States, she had commented over and over on one of the most striking differences between America and Pakistan, namely, how few people and how many cars there were in the streets, for here the exact opposite was the case. The Panjabi towns through which we passed teemed with dense populations full of local color, living for the most part under very squalid conditions. Although Islam places such great stress on cleanliness, this aspect of the religion had suffered exceedingly here, under the impact of the extremely straitened circumstances of life, the appalling standards of hygiene, and the harsh climatic conditions. I thought of the scrupulous cleanliness of even the most humble homes in Turkey, wondering just how to account for the difference. To a large extent it must lie buried under the complex of historical forces which had shaped the life of the Muslims of the Indian subcontinent. Whatever the causes might be, however, what was urgently, desperately, needed here today was major governmental concern, effort and expenditure in the field of sanitation, public health and adult education.

Everywhere, almost at every corner, stood mosques, some of them very tiny and all having the same typical row of little ornamental minarets over the entrance or around the edge of the roof. From this fact, from the social system and the dress of the majority of women, from much else I had seen, it was very clear that Islam was a very strong influence in Pakistan. However, it was also clear that this influence was not unmixed with other elements which had no connection with Islam, and that, at the same time, there was an apathy and indifference to Islam as a way of life among the upper classes which one could hardly have expected to find in a country which claimed to have been established on the basis of Islam and where the name of Islam was on everyone's lips. I must try to understand all these strange phenomena more clearly in the time which remained . . .

We had now reached the outskirts of Lahore, after an area of heavy population; from the distance we could see the huge, commanding white domes of Badshahi Mosque, an impressive sight to greet the newcomer to the city. After crossing the Ravi River Bridge, in a moment we were in the midst of the city, its fantastic traffic swirling around us. Selim remembered directions very well, but in spite of this he took a wrong turn off Circular Road and we were lost for the moment in a whirl of *tongas,* bicycles, motor cycles, cars and the welter of pedestrians.

A sudden excitement swept over me as I felt the full impact of this great city of the East, unlike any other we had seen. It was just as I remembered it, although there had been some improvements and certainly a great increase in population since we had lived here many years ago; the middle class, it seemed, was somewhat better off, but the poor seemed just as poor as ever. As we threaded our way in and out of the traffic—now almost running into a cyclist, now stopping short as a *tonga* pulled abruptly into the street in front of us, passing crude fruit stalls at the side of a crowded, dusty street, the women wearing *burqas* or heavy shawls, men in *lungis, shalwaars* or Western-style shirt and trousers—my breath was quite taken away by the color and motion, the crowding, the teeming life. These were the sober realities of life in the second largest city of West Pakistan today.

I now recalled in fleeting glimpses how, several years earlier, we had tried to live here on a salary of about 375 *rupees* ($100) a month, as Selim struggled to earn extra money in various ways to supplement this meager income. How well I recalled the problems of living here: the wearing grind of daily life which absorbs so much of one's vital energies; the frustrations of not being able to work at one's chosen profession in a manner compatible with one's abilities and training; the inevitable illnesses, often serious, which one encounters in such a climate and under such living conditions; the perpetual sense of dissatisfaction with the leadership and government of the country which has been the lot of all honest, thinking persons in such a situation. Salaries were higher now, but prices too were high, and the government and condition of the country really did not seem to have improved materially; no amount of wishful thinking could change realities so bleak and so irrespective of good intentions. I now knew that if we or any other Muslims should in the future decide to return here from the world of the West, we must do so with full knowledge of the situation, not hiding behind a facade of unrealizable hopes nor afraid to face reality, but prepared to accept existing conditions with all the inherent frustrations in order to strengthen the cause of Islam and to help build the future of a Muslim country. For if this land were yet to be shaped by Muslims instead of by those who want to live and to rule by corrupt and non-Islamic systems, many, many committed Muslims would have to make this sacrifice, accepting whatever conditions were available for the sake of the greater reward which is with Allah in order to secure the future of Islam in Pakistan. The alternative was to spend one's life living in comparative luxury and ease in more prosperous parts of the world, but being forever without that true joy and satisfaction which comes from living by one's avowed ideals without thinking of material rewards, rendering them in many cases an empty profession rather than an actual way of life.

We had reached the entrance of Mall Road. Here was Kim's Gun; the old Panjab University; the Museum; the entrance of Anarkali Bazaar; the long stretch of Mall Road, with some obvious improvements in individual business establishments but on the whole with the same seedy, run-down look as formerly. We took many wrong turns in trying to reach Sharifa's house, despite a map made by Bhai, and lost ourselves completely in one of the large residential colonies of the city, wandering round and round, and passing scores of unbelievably ornate and magnificent houses, many of which must have cost hundreds of thousands of *rupees*. At last, after asking directions several times, Selim pulled into the driveway of the house for which we had been searching, with an *"Alhamdulillah!"* for our safe journey amidst the complex and difficult traffic of the Grand Trunk Road.

At that moment Asma stepped onto the verandah, exclaiming, "Ammi, Ammi—mother—they're here!" and ran forward to greet us. Sharifa was on the verandah and beside us in a moment, saying with obvious joy and relief, "At last you've come, thank God! How are you, Bhai, Bhabi?" cuddling the girls and Jamal into a warm embrace and leading us eagerly into the house.

This day on which Sharifa welcomed us to her home after our long years of absence was one of the happiest in her life, I am certain, for she was such a loving person that to have her brother and his family so far away and to see them so seldom was very painful to her. Our baggage was put into two bedrooms and everything arranged for our maximum comfort, while Asma brought food and tea for us. Jamal and the girls went to be shown around the house by Rafiq, their boy cousin. A little later Sharifa's husband Nizamuddin came home, with a hearty welcome to us all. We talked the hours away, catching up on all their news and describing our travels and experiences in Turkey in more detail. We were now temporarily part of a happy, harmonious family into which we fitted quite naturally and felt completely at home.

Before sleeping I reflected on the fact that our trip was now more than half over, for we would most probably return to Ankara in the early part of March. I wanted somehow to capture the time which was flying by so swiftly and to extend it so that the days would not pass by so quickly. Who knew when we might be able to come again? I wanted to see as much as possible, to understand this Pakistan better, and to leave here with a clear grasp of the situation affecting the land where we had such strong emotional ties, both because of our relatives and because of Islam—a land which was surely one of the most vital parts of the Muslim world and one on which Muslims all over the world had placed great hopes. Let me savor every moment which is left, I thought, and I asked Allah for the good of this experience, for understanding and for guidance, thanking Him for His uncountable and unlimited blessings to us all.

Sharifa held a position as a teacher at a girls' college and Nizamuddin was a university professor, an articulate, well-informed man who had educated opinions on all matters of common interest. Fortunately both of them were able to take leave from their work several times during our stay, and it was clear that they had some plans for us. Their daughter Asma was a student at a private high school, a charming, capable girl who was invariably helpful wherever she went, but yet was not too old to play and to spend time with our children. Rafiq was beyond the age of joining in their play, for he was a young adult, a student at an engineering college; but nevertheless he and Jamal enjoyed each other's company and spent a good deal of time together.

The house was a pleasant, modern one, simply designed for livability and convenience. There was one full-time servant, an old woman, very wrinkled but surprisingly strong and able, who lived in her own room just off the back courtyard; she did the dishwashing and preparation of food for cooking, and could also put a good meal on the table if need be without supervision. The preparation of food was quite a lengthy process, for spices must be gound, onions peeled and cut, vegetables washed and prepared, rice and *dhal* carefully cleaned and washed repeatedly, dough prepared and bread made from it, and so on, all time-consuming jobs. Sharifa did much of the actual cooking herself whenever possible, leaving the other tasks to the old *mai*. For cleaning there was a Christian *jamidarni* who came every morning. She swept the house and outside quarters with her short stick broom and afterwards wiped all the floors with a wet rag dipped in disinfectant, squatting as she worked; she also swept the courtyard and cleaned the bathrooms until everything shone. Besides these there was a woman who came to wash laundry daily, squatting by the faucet in the back courtyard as she soaped and rinsed the clothes, and a part-time gardener. As in every respectable household, a *dhobi* came regularly each week to take away the heavier laundry, which must be starched and ironed, and to bring back the crisp, fresh clothes and linen.

The first afternoon after our arrival, as Sharifa and Nizam had both taken leave from work, we visited Badshahi Mosque, the largest mosque in West Pakistan; Selim drove Nizam's car and Nizam that of an absent friend. The mosque was approached through the congested areas of Circular Road, its three great white domes visible from a distance in spite of the many trees and buildings surrounding it. It was a vast, impressive structure, flanked on one side by two old Sikh temples built during the period when Sikhs were dominant in Lahore, and on the other by the wall of the Old City. The courtyard of the mosque, surrounded by high walls and four tall minarets, was said to be the largest among the mosques in the world.

Built during the reign of the Moghal Emperor Aurangzeb in the seventeenth century, Badshahi Mosque was, like all the Moghal structures I had seen, somewhat massive, imposing and heavy; yet the white-garnished red stone mosque and its three beautifully-shaped white domes had a grandeur and beauty all their own, not to be compared with the deeply serene Ottoman mosques of Turkey or the exquisite, colorful mosques of Iran but appreciated according to their own unique qualities and merits. It is one of the glories of Islamic architecture that, like the varied cultures of different Muslim peoples, it has such a great diversity within an over-all unity. Each people, each place and period, have made their own unique and special contribution to it, each different in style and detail from the others, yet all tending toward the same object of glorification of God Most High and drawing the heart of the worshiper toward Him.

We entered the vast stone-paved courtyard, which is filled with tens of thousands of worshipers on the *'Eids,* through its ornate gateway, approaching the simple rectangular structure topped by the three domes, where the painted ornamental work had been restored and was quietly appealing. A steady stream of visitors flowed in and out of the mosque compound: old men with *henna*-dyed beards and turbans, sturdy Panjabi peasants in *lungis,* quiet women clad in *burqas* with their children.

At Nizam's suggestion, we decided to go to the top of one of the minarets which was open to visitors, with Rafiq as our guide. It was a hard climb, one which made me wonder whether *muezzins* had, throughout the centuries before microphones were invented, climbed up and down its two-hundred-and-sixty-eight steps five times a day to give the *adhan,* and what compensation could reward them for this labor of love save the pleasure of Allah Ta'ala. From the top we looked down over the city, spread out below in a maze of flat-roofed, reddish-brown or white buildings, the structures of the Old City nearest. Around the mosque itself lay an intersting panorama: the ornate Sikh temples on the left; the ponderous Moghal fort across the way, some of its kiosks and pavilions visible from this height; and just in front of the mosque the little tomb of the poet Muhammad Iqbal, who had inspired the Muslims of the

Indian subcontinent to think in terms of their Islamic identity and a homeland for themselves. But it was the magnificent view of the three white domes which was the real reward of our efforts, a picture of striking beauty from the high balcony of the minaret which towered above them.

Before returning home to Sharifa's house, we took a drive through some of the newer sections of the city, where I again marveled at the numbers of extremely expensive, mansion-like homes, wondering by what means Pakistanis were able to get enough money to lavish it on building such palatial homes and decorating them with all sorts of non-functional embellishments. Here and in many other parts of the city, I saw many 'modern' girls and women in the streets wearing outfits which were almost indistinguishable from the current American 'pant suits,' and at the new campus of Panjab University, where we next went to have a look around, I observed boys and girls pairing off, sitting together drinking tea or walking in couples, something entirely unprecedented and as yet very unacceptable in this society. Seeing all this, it was obvious that it was only a matter of time before, coming down from the upper, educated classes, vast social changes will spread over this traditional society. They may not, perhaps, spread very fast, for the upper classes are still quite small and will hardly influence the masses of the people under the present circumstances; but as the number of the educated and well-to-do increases and the presently-existing enormous gap between social classes lessens, the change in values and standards is gaining momentum little by little.

One of the major vehicles of social change, in Pakistan and throughout the Muslim world, is television, which is very popular. In Lahore television can be viewed every evening for a few hours; the price of a set is within the means of a middle class family and it is considered something very desirable. I was to watch a number of programs before we left. The majority were Pakistan-produced informative, cultural or religious programs, debates and discussions of political and other current topics, some of which were worthwhile, and Panjabi and Urdu dramas and films, many of which revolved around sex and cheap 'romantic' themes and featured vulgar actresses and music. There were also some foreign serials such as

"Saint," "The Lucy Show," "Star Trek," "Ironside," and other imported shows. Although among all these there were some programs of value, taken as a whole I could only wonder what the eventual impact of television on Pakistan, especially on its youth, could be expected to be.

Cinema had existed in Pakistan, as in almost all other parts of the Muslim world, for many years as the staple entertainment of the the masses, feeding them with a steady diet of indigenously-produced trivial nonsense and the equally absurd Hollywood version of life produced in the West; the tastes and interests of a great many Pakistanis have been moulded to an extent by this medium. However, viewing cinema requires bodily attendance at a cinema hall, which, for young people, is often restricted by parents. But today one can view the same things within the comfort of one's own drawing room, without the cost of a ticket, the effort of going to a theatre, and with the consent and even encouragement of parents, who are happy to be entertained, or to have their young people entertained, in this fashion.

Clearly when Pakistani parents, some of whom may be religious or at least relatively conservative, allow their youngsters to sit hour after hour before the television absorbed in trashy native-style romances or, conversely, with the social modes and manners of the Western world, with dating and free mixing of the sexes, casual Western-style family relationships, and classic TV violence (although television programs as well as films are previewed and censored before they are shown), they are by implication tacitly giving their approval to their children's learning and absorbing all this. Thus, the indigenously-produced fare of vulgar, sentimental rubbish which is seen day after day simply reinforces the naive, pseudo-romanticism of the empty-minded youth and adults who have been nurtured on native films, without taste for anything better. At the same time, the effect of the Western programs will obviously be a gradual acceptance of Western values and habits in a society in which social modes are anyhow changing quite rapidly among the upper classes. Add to this those Pakistan-produced programs which reinforce westernized attitudes and modes of behavior, especially as relate to women, and it becomes a powerful instrument for social change operating within the more affluent homes of the nation. Pakistani tele-

vision confirmed my opinion that while television possesses a potential for making a positive contribution to human society, in the long
run it is bound to do much more harm than good because of the
unthinking manner in which it is being used in many parts of the
world, particularly in Muslim countries. As for cinema, the adverse
effect it has had and is having on the Muslim world cannot be
overestimated, especially in countries such as Turkey where extremely harmful films are both produced and imported unthinkingly, side-by-side with better ones.

In this context there will be many, Muslims and non-Muslims,
Pakistanis and others, who will say, "Look here, now! This is
1971, not the sixth nor the sixteenth nor even the nineteenth century! Television, cinema, dating, unrestricted mixing of the sexes,
mini-skirts and all the rest are part of the scene and are here to stay.
Even if we concede that you are right, how do you think you can
protect young people from knowing about these things, enjoying
them and wanting to imitate them?"

This is by no means a new problem. Whether in the sixth or in
the twentieth century, it was and is the responsibility of Muslim
parents and the Muslim society to minimize rather than maximize
the exposure of its youth to whatever does not fit in with its frame
of reference and way of life. Apart from this, it is up to the Muslim
society to provide its young people with a sound and adequate Islamic education in the very broadest sense of the word—an Islamic
education which will enable them to evaluate not only their own society in a realistic and objective manner, but also the other major
societies of the world, so that they will not be carried away by the
supposed 'glamor' and 'superiority' of the other cultures—and this,
to my knowledge, is not being done anywhere in the Muslim world.
Where there is Islamic education, it is generally confined to learning
the principles and practices of the religion, often by mere rote and
repetition, without understanding of the vital fact that Islam is a
basic attitude and orientation toward all of life which must equip
the believer to evaluate and to deal with whatever he encounters
and subject it to the strict criteria of Islam, whether it pertains to
his own culture or to the ideologies, values and habits of other life-
systems, especially at a time when they are continually being forced

upon his notice. Moreover, in a society in which social change has already begun to take place in a haphazard manner, a group of far-sighted Muslim social scientists should be given the task of devising the means to retard rather than accelerate such change, for it is obvious that too rapid, unplanned social change and imitation of social patterns which have no indigenous development or connection, and which are contrary to all the accepted standards of the society, can have and are having disastrous effects on Muslim societies.

Television and cinema have a great potential as teaching tools for inculcating values and habits, and we Muslims should learn to harness this potential and use it for Islamic ends. Thus, if there are to be television and cinema in a Muslim country, only such programs and films could be produced and shown which have been reviewed and approved by a committee of reliable Muslim sociologists, psychologists, educators and religious scholars, and by similarly qualified persons from other religious groups if they exist in the country. Besides indigenously-produced programs and films of value, there are also excellent, very worthwhile ones produced by the hundreds in the West; these should be utilized instead of worthless or even downright harmful ones whose cumulative impact on the society will be felt all too soon. Muslims should and must strive to make their voices heard so that these media will take the direction which they want, for they will obviously be no more useful and beneficial to our societies than we determine to make them.

I continued to be very much struck by the weakening of the hold of Islam on the lives of educated upper class Pakistanis as a whole. To be sure, among some of them the *ibadat* aspects of Islam are still practiced; that is, they observe prayers, fasting, attend religious gatherings, and read the Qur'an in Arabic (usually pronouncing the words without understanding the meaning), but their very conception and comprehension of Islam has become nerveless and emasculated. All its dynamism is lost as they take worship, pious observances and some moral precepts to be the sum-total of the religion, not grasping the essential fact that Islam is a complete system to be practiced in every aspect of the individual and collective life, and that *ibadat* is the beginning rather than the end of a Muslim's practice of Islam. Others, although wanting their children to have some Islamic training, have themselves almost entirely given up any practice of Islam whatsoever. Thus, although almost all claim to be Muslims and take the name of Islam when convenient, to very few among the upper classes in Pakistan today does Islam seem to be the paramount value, the ultimate criterion, the truth by which they live, their all-in-all. When there is an appropriate occasion to mention it, it is piously mentioned. The rest of the time, like the Holy Qur'an which is considered so sacred that it must be wrapped in a silken cover and kept up on a high shelf so it will not be soiled, their Islam is put up in wrappings and forgotten until sickness or calamity, war or death, or the coming of another *Ramazan* at best, temporarily remind them once again of God and their religion.

But what does it signify that people are able to pronounce the sounds of the Qur'an in Arabic if they do not understand the meaning of it, if they do not *live* this Divine guidance? What does it matter that they have Muslim names and style themselves Muslims if they do not pattern their lives according to the Islamic teachings? It seemed to me more and more that an element of insincerity, of falseness, of downright hypocrisy, had crept into the attitude and practice of many middle and upper class Pakistanis toward Islam. Thus I found myself increasingly less and less able to identify with these affluent, 'advanced' people for whom Islam, if it is anything, is a mere social, cultural convention but nothing more. I continued to observe and to turn matters over in my mind in an effort to increase my understanding.

One afternoon we made an excursion to Shalimar Gardens. The way to this beautiful Moghal garden lay through one of the most congested and dirty areas of Lahore, where driving was a fine art as Selim threaded his way carefully through the maze of *tongas,* bicycles, cattle, automobiles, buses and pedestrians. We parked the cars outside the wall of the Gardens, and immediately several poor disheveled little girls rushed up, displaying small rattles made of plaited straw. *"Mem Sahib, Begum Sahib!"* they called out to Sharifa and me, pleading with us to buy. We told them repeatedly that we did not want their trinkets, but at last they tossed a couple of them into the car and Sharifa gave them a few coins. They were not satisfied with this, and when we got out of the car, one of them thrust one or two of the little toys into my hands, wanting me to give more money. At this, I lost my temper and threw them angrily on the ground after her, galled at such persistence, saying impatiently in Urdu, "I don't want them!" And then at once I was intensely sorry for what I had done: these were the poor of the world, and they had worked—or someone else had—to make these little straw trinkets; selling them was their livelihood, and it was a great sin to be so harsh and hard-hearted, especially when Allah had given me so very much. I went into the Gardens feeling deeply ashamed that I could so easily lose my temper and behave so unsympathetically toward these poor children, asking God to forgive me; for a long time afterwards I was to remember this incident with shame and regret.

Repairs and renovations had been made in the structures of the Gardens, built by Shah Jehan around 1637, since we had been there several years earlier. The Gardens were now beautifully kept, with magnificent trees. We strolled about, enjoying the greenery, Jamal excited because he has seen a vulture at last and Nura ecstatic about the flowers. Outside the walls of the Gardens the air had buzzed with flies, but inside, as if to symbolize the contrast between the affluent who enjoyed the good things of life and the poor who remained forever shut out from them, all was green, peaceful and very clean, the legion of flies stopped by the wall. May Allah admit His poor, who have not been admitted to gardens in this world, to His Garden in the Hereafter, and may we who have been tested in this world by affluence rather than by poverty not be excluded because of harshness or indifference to our brothers or sisters in need . . .

Afterwards we went to have tea with friends of the family who lived in a pleasant house with spacious grounds provided by the government. The lady of the house spoke fluent English and was very friendly; our children played outside with her children. We toured their garden while the men sat talking about political matters, the invariably favorite theme of conversation in any gathering of men. Along the roadway outside the thick hedge in front of the house, the squalid life of the poor went its way unnoticed; we were separated from it by the amenities surrounding us, although the house, that of an upper middle class government servant, was ordinary enough by American standards.

On the way home we stopped at the bazaar of one of the residential colonies of the city, where Nizam got out to make some
purchases and Selim and I to have a look at the shops. I could only
marvel at the vast variety of imported prepared foods available at a
small supermarket obviously much-frequented by foreigners—available that is, to those privileged few who could afford them. Clearly
if one had money all the amenities and luxuries of life could be had
here, perhaps even on a much grander scale than in the West.

Returning to the car, I found Sharifa engaged in a sort of running debate, of a kind which I was to hear again and again, with a
seller of apples:

Sharifa: How much are they?
Vendor: Four *rupees* a *seer,* * *Begum Sahib.*
Sharifa: That's too much.
Vendor: (polishing an apple on his sleeve and holding it up)
    Just look, *Begum Sahib!* Very good apples— first class!
Sharifa: Come on now, I paid less than that two days ago for
    much better ones. Your apples are very small and not that
    good.
Vendor: I'll let you have them for three-and-a-half *rupees* a
    seer, Begum Sahib.
Sharifa: No, that's too much, and I don't need any apples today.
Vendor (wheedling): First class apples, *Begum Sahib!*
Sharifa (laughing and motioning him away): No, no I don't
    want them.
Vendor: Three *rupees* a *seer, Begum Sahib!*
Sharifa (losing patience): Go, go—I don't want them!

At that moment, as the apple seller concedes defeat, takes up his
wares and marches away, a seller of bananas comes to the car and
the dialogue threatens to begin all over again. Nizam and Selim
come to the cars just at that point and we drive away, leaving the
banana seller calling, "Very fine bananas, *Begum Sahib!*" after us.

Although this sort of dialogue seemed something like a game or
contest to see who was the more shrewd or persistent, buyer or
seller, and there was a certain grim relish in it for both, nevertheless
I felt very sorry for these people, who somehow had to live by their

---

* A *seer* is a unit of weight, about two pounds.

meager trade. At the same time, however, their unbelievable persistence was extremely obnoxious; it was little short of begging, the only difference being that instead of begging for money directly, they begged to have their goods bought. I had never seen such behavior in Turkey, where merchants keep their dignity and do not importune to have their goods accepted.

Everywhere we had been in Peshwar and Lahore, real beggars had been at our side, and very often they did not take "No" for an answer. I do not like to refuse anyone who asks, but because in Pakistan most mercantile transactions are usually done in round *rupees* and coins are therefore rather scarce, many times neither of us had any coins and were then obliged to say, *"Maf karna, Baba, Mai"* (Excuse me, father—old man, or mother—old woman). However, often the beggar simply went on and on asking even after it had been said firmly several times.

The first time I gave to a Pakistani beggar was while I was shopping with Aziza soon after we arrived in Peshawar. I gave him a *rupee,* supposing from what I had been used to giving in Turkey that this should be the proper amount and overlooking the fact that the Turkish *lira* and the Pakistani *rupee* are not equal in value; Aziza was aghast at the large sum I had given him. But after receiving my donation, the man next turned to her, importuning. "What is this? Didn't *Begum Sahiba* just now give to you, much too generously?" she scolded. However, he was so persistent, buzzing around us like a fly and not leaving, that she finally gave him twenty-five *paisa* * just to get rid of him; but when he saw the small coin, he threw it indignantly on the ground, refusing to stoop to accept such a pittance after what I had given him! When I told this to the family, there was much teasing about my 'princely,' 'aristocratic' beggar. Apart from this, however, I had encountered countless old people and miserable women with pathetically thin babies in their arms, so many filthy and disheveled children, and all sorts of pitifully deformed, crippled or sick people begging whose plight hurt me, and Selim and I gave whenever we had coins.

* 100 *paisa*=1 *rupee.* At this time the official exchange rate was Rs. 4.75=1 U.S. dollar.

Entrance to Topkapı Museum, Istanbul, Turkey

Sultan Ahmet's Mosque, Istanbul, Turkey

Interior, Eyyub Sultan Mosque, Istanbul, Turkey

Sultan Ahmet's Mosque, Istanbul, Turkey

Courtyard of Eyyub Sultan Mosque, Istanbul, Turkey

Sultan Ahmet's Mosque, Istanbul, Turkey

A section of the old town, Ankara, Turkey

Atatürk Statue, Ulus, Ankara, Turkey

Manargat Waterfall, Mediterranean coast of Turkey

Old section, Antalya, Turkey

Muradiye, Bursa, Turkey

Small town near Göreme, Turkey

Tomb of Jalaluddin Rumi (left) and Ottoman Mosque, Konya, Turkey

Downtown Isparta, Turkey

HAYAL
PASTANESİ
İKİNCİ
NOTER
TÜRKİYE
EMLAK
KREDİ
BANKASI
TURKIYE
ÖĞRETMENLER
BANKASI

Atatürk poster during national holiday, Turkey

Masjid-i-Shah, Isfahan, Iran
Jum'a Mosque, Isfahan, Iran

The Madrassah Mosque, Isfahan, Iran

Jum'a Mosque, Isfahan, Iran

Old city, Peshawar, Pakistan

Badshahi Mosque, Lahore, Pakistan

Domes of Badshahi Mosque, Lahore, Pakistan

Lahore Fort, Pakistan

Mosque interior, Peć, Yugoslavia

Prizren, Yugoslavia

I had not thought much about the phenomenon of begging before, but now I grasped how degrading it is to the human spirit to live by asking people for money or other charity. As Prophet Muhammad, peace be on him, said, "It is better for one of you to take his rope, bring a load of firewood on his back and sell it, God thereby preserving his self-respect, than that he should beg from people whether they give him or refuse," by this and many other related *Hadiths* indicating that any kind of work, no matter how humble, is more acceptable and honorable than begging.

Many people both in Pakistan and in Turkey condemned beggars harshly. I had heard it said that most of them are fakes; that some actually live well and own extensive property; and that some are deliberately mutilated in childhood so that they can live by begging (an appalling situation totally condemned by Islam which unfortunately is known to exist here and there, but the blame cannot rest with the beggar himself since he had no say in the matter). This seemed to me to be a very hard-hearted attitude, for although there were undoubtedly abuses in the matter of begging and it was also clear that many able-bodied adults and youngsters old enough to work lived by begging instead of working, the majority of beggars were helpless women, poverty-stricken or orphaned children, the aged, the crippled and deformed, the chronically ill, the blind and all sorts of otherwise incapacitated persons. These were to be seen everywhere, in every sort of grotesque and pathetic form, often with unbelievable and shocking handicaps, those who in more affluent countries would be the recipients of government assistance or in institutions where they would be cared for; for them begging was an understandable and pitiful necessity, the only means of support available, and it hurt me to witness their endless misery.

Apart from beggars, even at a casual glance it was clearly apparent that there was a terrible social disease in this land where some lived in palaces (the money for the building of which was often known to be obtained by illegal means such as bribery, the use of influence, or the favorite trick of building a mansion with a loan from the government and then repaying the loan by huge rents charged to government servants whose accommodation was paid for by the government) and others barely had food to eat or a roof over their heads. There was, moreover, a great social gap between 're-spectable' people and the lower levels of the population such as I had not seen nor felt in Turkey, where social classes certainly exist but the distinctions are not nearly so glaring nor rigid, and where most types of work are considered respectable and compatible with human dignity. In Turkey, for example, a small shopkeeper, butch-er, tailor, etc., belongs among the middle class and is treated with dignity; in Pakistan, however, such tradesmen are not really regarded as 'respectable' although they may be earning fairly well. From what unIslamic source in the past or present had such artificial divisions among Muslims originated, I wondered.

I observed, moreover, that upper middle class people often treated the poor with considerable harshness of speech, had little concern about their plight, and seemed hardly able to perceive in them the characteristics of a fellow-human being, almost as if they were another order of creation which had no needs other than ani-mal ones and no feelings which could be hurt. There was, by and large, a strange, shocking lack of concern among them regarding the condition of this vast segment of the population. The relation of the poor to the affluent for whom they labored was solely in the capacity of those who were there to serve their needs, doing menial or difficult tasks for which their employers had either no time or energy, or which they considered beneath their dignity; and the more menial and less dignified the task, the less was the compensa-tion for it and the more those who performed it were looked down upon.

At the same time, it was clear that the poor were ignorant, dir-ty, disease-ridden, and that they lacked knowledge of proper man-ners and behavior. No way had been evolved to educate them or their children, the next generation of the poor; for, apart from the shortage of schools, since they must work from the time they were old enough to earn anything, they had a very meager and brief childhood indeed. Thus these two aspects went hand-in-hand to cre-ate and maintain the great void between classes, something so con-trary to the Islamic teachings of mutual helpfulness and responsi-bility among all members of the community of Muslims that it was hard to believe that it was happening in a 'Muslim' country. Perhaps it was true that the influence of the Hindu caste system or the discriminatory effects of British rule had played a part in encouraging such attitudes among the Muslims of the Indian subcontinent, but whatever the underlying causes, there could be no excuse of any kind for the perpetuation of such a state of affairs.

As for the middle class, those who had salaries adequate to meet their needs and to live decently without luxury or ostentation, it had taken them years and years of hard work—in many instances with the extra money which an educated wife could earn by working as a teacher or in some other profession—to reach their present level, and only after much time and slow raises in pay could they hope to own a refrigerator, a car, and ultimately to buy a house with monthly payments. Yet all this, barely average when compared with American standards, was so far above the standard of the masses of poor Pakistanis that no comparison was possible. For example, Sharifa's laundry woman, who also washed for a few other households daily, lived with her family in a tiny, squalid hut made of bamboo poles, two walls of which consisted of the angle formed by the two walls of adjacent houses, without amenities of any sort or even what are ordinarily considered the most basic necessities of life. In winter they would suffer unceasingly from the cold and wet; during the rainy season their hut might be flooded out and they would live in rain-soaked misery for days on end; and in summer they would broil and be a prey to disease, insects and other vermin.

But what was the solution? Clearly this extremely serious situation could not be dealt with only by scattered individual efforts or charities, essential though these were, but only by a concerted effort of the whole society. Yet it was obviously useless to hope that the government of a country so poor that it had barely enough resources to take care of basic administrative, defensive or other vital needs would, in the forseeable future, be able to provide help to the destitute, rehabilitation to the handicapped, or pensions to the elderly, unemployed and disabled or to helpless women and children as is done in the affluent countries of the West. Then what was the way?

Certainly it did not lie in the present situation, continuing unchanged almost since the inception of Pakistan, in which those who were already rich became still richer, often by underhanded or openly illicit means, indulging their appetites for luxuries and vices. It was essential that such inequity and the corruption which produced it should be cleared up, and severe penalties enforced for all illegal dealings at all levels without exception. Assuredly it also did not lie with blatantly materialistic ideologies such as socialism and communism, which opened the door to innumerable other, and perhaps far worse, evils in the society. Yet, although many people preferred to ignore it, a solution to poverty and social inequality through concerted community action had been given—given to Muslims fourteen hundred years ago by Almighty God, Who knows every aspect of the human condition far better than we ourselves can ever know it, in the prescription of *Zakat.* *

This obligatory poor-due, as well as the giving of additional voluntary charity to the extent each Muslim can afford, is repeatedly mentioned in the Holy Qur'an together with the obligation of five daily prayers. Indeed, the first Caliph of Islam, Abu Bakr Siddiq, declared war on a community which refused to pay *Zakat* while professing to be Muslim and continuing to observe prayers, thus emphasizing that this obligation is essential and inseparable from other Islamic obligations and *must* be met by those who claim to be Muslims. The paying of *Zakat* by all who are eligible to do so might not eliminate poverty and economic problems from the face of Pakistan, but it would obviously go a long way toward their alleviation; and it would assure a just sharing of the total wealth of the country by and among all its people, giving practical form to that sense of brotherhood and responsibility which Islam inculcates in Muslims, thereby eliminating the lack of concern on the part of the rich and envy on the part of the poor. It is the obligation of the government of every Muslim country to collect

---

* The fourth 'pillar' of Islam, the obligatory poor-due which is to be paid annually. It consists of a certain percentage due on cash savings, property not in use, minerals, business inventory, cattle, crops and other categories of property, to be distributed among the poor and needy in the community and for other uses "in the cause of God." (*Al-Tauba* 9:60).

and distribute the *Zakat* funds, and shamefully, since its inception in 1947, the government of Pakistan, a nation supposedly founded on the basis on Islam, had failed to do so.

While Islam encourages the acquisition of property by any lawful means which is of benefit to the society, permitting Muslims, both men and women, the benefits of their earnings and not prohibiting the enjoyment of the good things of this life, at the same time it asks Muslims always to remember that the Hereafter, not the present world, is their final goal. The true Owner of all wealth is God Himself, Who bestows it on men through His bounty and has defined the proper uses of it, so that the rich man is tested as much by his wealth as the poor man by his poverty; indeed, more is expected of him because he has been given so much.

The true Muslim, therefore, does not consider it his 'right' to use his wealth in any way he pleases and solely for himself and his family. It is to be spent in a moderate manner on whatever is needed, lawful and beneficial, but ostentatious displays of wealth to impress others, extreme forms of luxury and wasteful habits are not permitted, no matter how much one may possess. Besides *Zakat,* sharing, giving and acts of charity to the extent one can afford are enjoined over and over in the Qur'an and in the *Hadith* of the Holy Prophet, peace be on him, "in order that it [the wealth of the Muslim community] may not (merely) make a circuit between the wealthy among you"*—that is, so that it will be of maximum benefit to all, not only to a few, and so that all may share in God's beneficence, either through the fruits of their own labor or through the responsibility and concern of those to whom God has given more of the good of this world. For Islam aims at creating a balance between two extremes: between that poverty which degrades and wears down the body and spirit of a human being, imprisoning him in an endless cycle of frustrations, of basic material needs unmet, so that his whole existence becomes centered upon the search for his daily bread and a roof over his head, without time or energy left over for the needs of his mind and spirit or of his society; and between the other extreme, in which a man has so much that he be-

* *Al-Hashr* 59:7.

comes absolutely sated with material satisfactions and pleasures, while he slowly finds that nothing satisfies any longer because every material and physical pleasure has become meaningless in such a state of satiation, invariably accompanied by a great inner emptiness.

The basic physical needs of a human being are not very great, I reflected: food adequate to reinforce health and provide energy to meet the demands of life, a reasonably durable and convenient dwelling in which to live in a decent manner with one's family, and a few clothes appropriate for one's activities; but the poor of Pakistan obviously did not have an adequate diet by any accepted standards of nutrition, the most minimal standards of hygiene and cleanliness, nor a few changes of dress suitable to maintaining human decency. Is this a Muslim country where the fundamental obligation of *Zakat*—one of the five obligatory acts of worship on which Islam rests—is forgotten by all except the minority of the truly God-conscious and where the plight of the poor cries out to God? Is it a Muslim country where the rich live side-by-side with the poor but turn their backs on their needs in an endless race for more and more satisfactions for themselves, when the Holy Prophet, peace be on him, has said, "The believer is not the one who eats his fill when his neighbor beside him is hungry," and "The believers are like one man; if his eye is affected he is all affected, and if his head is affected he is all affected?" Oh, bring down the Qur'ans from the high shelf, take them out of their delicate silken wrappings and read, before it is too late, that

> "It is not righteousness that you turn your faces toward the east or the west, but righteousness is believing in God and the Day of Judgment and in the angels and in the Book [Qur'an] and in the messengers [prophets], and to spend of your possessions, for the love of Him, for your relatives, and orphans, and the poor, and travelers, and those who ask, and for the freeing of captives, and to be steadfast in prayer, and to give *Zakat,* and to fulfill the contracts you have made, and to be firm and patient in pain and adversity and during all times of panic. Such are people of truth, the God-fearing."*

Little by little I began to feel that Islam would survive in Pakistan not primarily because the more affluent people cherish it, nor

---

* *Al-Baqara* 2:177.

because the poor, ignorant and backward value it, but mainly because it is alive and strong among the middle level of the society—what I may call the middle of the middle class; those who live in a *via media* between two economic extremes, who have just enough for their needs and are content with what they have, who have a clear understanding of Islam, and to whom it means more than every worldly consideration. Slowly I began to feel drawn, as if by a magnet in the largely secular atmosphere around me, toward those whose love for God and for Islam is clearly demonstrated in their way of life. During this short stay in Pakistan, I was merely a visitor and an observer, not taking a stand on various issues but simply making an effort to understand; but I knew that if I should ever come to live here again in the future, I would take a position, and a firm one, and I began to gravitate inwardly in a clear direction toward those whose values were, both with respect to things inner and outward, the same as my own.

CHAPTER 12

TIME OF ACTIVITY

At this time we were visiting or having visitors almost every day. There were many invitations from Nizam's and Sharifa's friends, meetings with old friends we had known in America, and great kindness and hospitality on all sides. I had never been involved in such a social round, and it was very pleasant indeed.

The month of *Muharram* * was approaching, and now during these last days of *Dhul-Hijjah,* weddings were taking place everywhere, as marriages are not generally performed in Pakistan during *Muharram* even among the Sunni community. Daily we saw the rented *shamianas*—awnings or tents—and brilliant displays of colored lights at houses where weddings were taking place, and on the last Sunday before *Muharram* we must have passed some ten or fifteen marriage processions and houses decorated for weddings. The displays of colored lights, strings of them festooning the house, were often fantastic in themselves. It was estimated that the electricity—very costly in Pakistan—to illuminate a big house for only one night might cost as much as two or three thousand *rupees,* that is, roughly between four and six hundred dollars per night. The rental of *shamianas* and other essentials for the wedding, as well as the feeding of a multitude of guests, would be over and above all the expenses of clothing, jewelry, the dowry given to the bride, and the demands not infrequently made by the groom for money and

---

* The first month of the Islamic lunar calendar, during which in the year 680 After Christ, Imam Hussain, the grandson of Prophet Muhammad, was martyred, an event commemorated yearly by many Shi'ah Muslims.

other gifts. I though about the *Hadith* of the Prophet, peace be on him, transmitted by his wife 'Aisha, "The marriage which produces most blessing is that which involves least burden," in the face of these shockingly extravagant expenditures. To spend as much as one could afford (and often very much more) on a marriage was a social custom so commonly accepted and taken for granted that to criticize it was like attacking a foundation-stone of Pakistani culture in many circles.

★ ★ ★

We were very much disturbed one day to read in a newspaper that communist students had set fire to a dormitory at Hacettepe University in Ankara. This reawakened all my old anxieties, for we had been under the impression from the one letter we had received from Emine that the situation was relatively stable. It was now much easier to resolve that we should make plans to return to America as soon as we were back in Ankara. We were not in a position to contribute either to the society, to the University or even to our own interests, and there was no sense in living any longer with the fears for Selim's safety and the state of general anxiety and tension which had haunted us for many weeks.

The same evening two unexpected visitors rang the doorbell, asking for Selim. They were well-placed professional men with clear Islamic commitment, both of whom had studied in the United States; we had some friends in common, and they were much interested in hearing about the current activities of Muslims in America. There were many matters of mutual interest to discuss as we sat talking over tea. Before leaving they asked if each of us could give some talks about Islamic activities in the United States to various groups, and we gladly agreed; they would contact us later about time and place.

On the second weekend of our stay, there was an all-day outing to Lahore Fort and Jehangir's Tomb. The Fort, situated opposite Badshahi Mosque, had been constructed during the sixteenth and seventeenth centuries by the Moghal Emperors Jehangir and Shah Jehan, and was undoubtedly one of the most interesting Moghal forts or palaces in the Indian subcontinent. I had been in it once before during our previous stay and had been quite struck by the heavy, brooding flavor of its external architecture—Moghal style at its most 'Moghal,' bearing the traces of its Central Asian origin. Since then new areas inside it had been made accessible to the public and further restoration work was in progress.

In the bright spring sunshine we went through all the sections which were open, exploring the various pavilions and kiosks. In the Shish Mahal, a pavilion whose walls and ceiling were covered with mirror-studded ornamentation, a cleaning operation was in progress, and now at last one could see the original luster of the mirrors which had been crusted over with the grime of centuries. I took note of many of the very fine details in the ornamentation of the various halls and kiosks, still clear and beautiful, and made a number of photographs. Lawns with lovely trees and shrubbery surrounded the *Divan-i-Khas,* the emperor's audience hall, on three sides, and the pavilion was full of people of all social levels. I watched a brown, bare-bottomed baby struggling up the steps of the audience hall to the dais where once mighty emperors had sat on their thrones, and thought ironically that this was, after all, a fitting use for these symbols of their worldly pomp and power.

After completing our tour of the Fort, we had lunch in a restaurant and then went on to the tomb of the Moghal Emperor Jehangir* near the Ravi River; nearby were the tombs of Jehangir's wife, the Empress Noor Jehan, and her father. All the buildings in the compound were constructed of red-and-white stone; the largest, which had four minarets with a red-and-white zigzag pattern topped by the hat-like Moghal domes, housed the beautiful white marble-and-inlay sarcophagus. Here restoration work was underway to revive the now dull and faded painted ornamentation. Indeed, the whole area had been improved greatly since I had visited it previously in days when it was left to moulder and decay; the gardens and lawns within its compound were now beautiful and well-kept, and it was obvious that this was a favorite outing spot of Lahore. Simple villagers and educated city-dwellers alike strolled about, enjoying the spring sun and pleasant air, looking at the buildings or picnicking. It was a pleasant, happy day of sight-seeing for us, spent in the company of those we loved so well.

* Died 1627.

That evening the two men who had visited us previously paid another call, accompanied by their wives, both of whom wore *burqas* with their faces covered. We women went into one of the bedrooms to visit and have our tea while the men sat together in the drawing room. The ladies asked me to speak about Islamic activities in the United States to a women's Islamic circle three days later and I gladly accepted, happy with the opportunity of meeting these sincere Muslim women, the wives of well-placed professional men, and looking forward to meeting others of their kind.

One evening we went to visit Maulana Maududi, keeping an appointment with him at the Jamaat-i-Islami headquarters off Ferozepore Road. The aging Islamic scholar had been ill and hospitalized during recent days, but nonetheless he found time to talk to Selim and me for an hour or more. He was a commanding-looking man with a full grey beard, in whose face I read a total inner certainty and an inability to compromise on Islamic principles. He and Selim conversed in Urdu which I was able to follow to some extent about the conditions in Turkey, the situation of Muslims in America, and the Muslim world in general, and then I brought up some questions of my own, the talk changing to English.

After leaving him, I began to ponder, and I spent the next day in deep thought, turning over and over in my mind and talking with Selim about what Maulana Sahib had said, my own observations of the society around me, the situation of Muslims in Turkey and in America, the teachings of Islam, and my own personal feelings about various matters.

Ultimately a sense of the absolute purity of Islam and a profound yearning for this complete, unqualified purity, which could only be realized by living in an Islamic society and following the injunctions of Islam in their entirety, swept over me: that unconditional purity of life which Allah wants for all the members of the community of Islam. I felt a sudden, profound distaste for all things not in accord with this absolute standard, of wanting to rise above all worldly involvements which were tainted with anything contrary to it. A deep, poignant sense of complete acceptance of this pure and perfect system in its entirety took possession of me; for that moment, my whole heart submitted to God Most High and knew no other desire save obedience to what He had commanded. Yet at the same time I realized with a sense of sadness and loss that this total acceptance was by heart alone, not entirely by action, for due to my personal limitations and specific life situation, I compromise and fall short in innumerable ways. But now, nevertheless, in spite of this, for one single moment in my life at least, I had experienced the true meaning of Islam, of total submission to God. In that moment the standard of God, absolute and without equivocation, had been accepted in my heart, and I was able to grasp clearly the distinction between what God enjoins and what I myself, with all my limitations and feeble capacity, am doing. I prayed my prayers that afternoon with deep fervor and stayed apart in the bedroom, only wanting to be alone . . .

★ ★ ★

Now, sitting on the jet rushing away from that Pakistan where for one instant I had experienced that clear realization, deeply moved as on that day when this truth had come to me, I felt miserably that I was leaving behind the place where something immensely precious and meaningful had been glimpsed, something which I might never be able to experience again or to translate into action in my own life. That day after our visit to Maulana Maududi, when these thoughts and feelings had come to me, had been for me the climax of my experience in Pakistan . . .

★ ★ ★

It had been arranged that I would visit Sharifa's college the following morning. Accordingly, Selim dropped me there a little before noon and Sharifa met me at the gate. Like all girls' colleges, it was surrounded by a high wall and men might not come further than a little courtyard inside the inner gate. Within the college compound, the girls were completely free without the presence of any men except the staff of menials (who somehow were not counted as men); many of the students put on *burqas* whenever they left the college grounds for the outside world.

It was a pleasant scene: the red brick buildings and young girls everywhere, neat in their *shalwaar-qamises,* studying and socializing in an atmosphere free of the social problems and distractions which plague American colleges. I thought how difficult it might be to maintain this careful Islamic atmosphere of seclusion of girls in a college and at the same time keep them living in the world of real-

ity, that world in which they should take their places very shortly
not merely as women living entirely in the world of home and family, but as educated, intelligent, effective participants in shaping its
future, at the same time without losing anything of their status as
sound Muslim women who maintain their dignity and self-respect.

Sharifa showed me around the compound, taking me to see various class buildings and to the auditorium in which, impressively,
ornamental prints with Qur'anic inscriptions had been hung around
the walls instead of the usual art work or faces of 'great men' which
one sees in so many places. After a tour of the library, we went to
another building where a number of teachers were gathered. Sharifa
introduced me to her colleagues, and I was very pleasantly surprised when they greeted me with great cordiality, warm hand-
clasps, and even with the remark, "I've heard a great deal about
you from Sharifa."

I was then introduced to the Principal of the college, a lady of
great dignity and sweetness. I had heard from Sharifa about how
staunch a Muslim she was and how intent on preserving an Islamic
atmosphere in the college; as far as I could see in such a brief visit,
she had succeeded remarkably well. Making a place for me by her
side, she greeted me with, "Welcome, welcome! I'm so happy to
meet you!" At once I felt at home with her, and we began to talk
about some of the problems of Islam in Pakistan and Islamic activities in America. At length she asked if I could present a talk to
some of the students and faculty about the activities of Muslims in
the United States. I was extremely happy at that invitation, which I
accepted gladly, at the warmth with which she and Sharifa's friends
and colleagues had received me, and at the pleasant and congenial
character of the college.

"If you can maintain such an atmosphere for these girls, you
are doing a very great thing for the future of Islam in Pakistan. The
college truly has a beautiful quality about it," I told the Principal
as she, Sharifa and I walked to the gate.

"We are trying our best, with Allah's help," she replied, clasp-
ing my hand. "I am so happy to know you, my dear sister-in-Islam,
and I look forward to seeing you again very soon."

I bade her a warm goodbye. Selim was waiting for me beside the car as I came back through the college gate into the dusty outside world, filled with a deep sense of joy because of what I had seen and experienced behind those old red brick walls.

On the morning I was to visit the women's Islamic circle, I was ready and waiting when my acquaintance of the other evening arrived in an elderly chauffeur-driven car to fetch me. She took me to a spacious, very well-to-do home where a pleasant-looking lady in a *sari* greeted me. A few women were already gathered on the back verandah facing the garden and, as more continued to arrive, the hostess introduced me to each one. These were educated, articulate women of high social status with well-placed husbands, many of whom would have been able to hold their own anywhere in the world. Like many upper class Pakistanis, they knew English almost as well as Urdu and were familiar with the ways of the West; yet as we met together that day our common interest and bond was solely Islam.

Our conversation that bright spring morning began with a discussion of the problems of Islamic education in Pakistan. "Islamic studies are given some importance in the school program, no doubt," a serene older woman said, "but as the teachers are the same ones who teach other subjects, they are generally poorly-qualified and lack knowledge and special training in *Islamiyat.* * They often don't know how to present Islam in a way which is appealing and which can make an impact, especially on children from educated or well-to-do homes, and the *mullahs* who teach children in mosques are just as deficient in knowing how to present it in a way which will capture their interest."

"But another and even more serious problem," put in a pretty and vivacious matron sitting near me, "is the lack of observance of Islam in the home. There is simply no example for most children to follow except the very traditional observances, and they grow up without even knowing what Islam is."

---

* Islamic studies or knowledge.

"Just see," put in another young woman in a pale green *sari* on my right. "The Qur'an has come to be a book which you must have in your house if you are Muslim, but you read it—if you read it at all—in Arabic without understanding the meaning. In *Ramzan*, if you are a traditional Muslim, you will read it from cover to cover as fast as possible in Arabic for the *sawab*, * and after that it's put away until the next *Ramzan*. Our children are taught to read Arabic in parrot-like fashion by their *maulvi sahibs*, ** just learning how to pronounce the sounds of the words but knowing nothing of their meanings. They must be taught to understand Arabic as a language and to know the meaning of what they read," she continued earnestly. "Otherwise what is the value of just pronouncing the sounds? We think we will get *sawab* for it, but won't Allah instead hold us responsible for not understanding and acting on it?"

"The situation in Pakistan has become such that if a person is known to pray one prayer a day and to fast during *Ramzan*," another woman said with irony, punctuating her speech with gestures, "he is considered very religious. If he prays five times a day he is almost a saint, and if he goes for *Hajj*, why . . ."

"Then he is considered to be practically guaranteed Paradise!" I put in laughing. But there was nothing amusing about it. I had observed for myself how an upper middle class Muslim who fulfills the ordinary obligations which are the common duty of all Muslims was an object of comment and interest in Pakistan. Implicit in this attitude was a very confused, self-deluded way of thinking which was somewhat as follows:—"We are all Muslims because we were born Muslims and our ancestors were Muslims before us. We simply *are* Muslims, and we don't stop to consider the matter or question its implications. Islam enjoins certain obligations and we know that we're supposed to follow them, but we are a bit lazy and besides, they aren't too easy to follow. Moreover, we aren't quite sure

---

*   Reward in the Hereafter.

**   Teachers of religion and Qur'anic Arabic who, in Pakistan, generally teach the reading and recitation of the Qur'an, etc., to young people in their individual homes.

that it's really necessary to follow them in the twentieth century. Islam came to civilize mankind and it's done its work, so maybe for now it's enough for us to believe in Allah and His Prophet, *sallallahu alayhi wa sallam."* To 'believe' in Allah and His Prophet without obeying His laws and acting on the guidance sent through that Prophet—what does it mean? I personally have never understood and never will understand the nature of such a 'belief'—a belief in the 'theory' of a religious system without belief in the necessity of acting on its teachings—nor how human beings can delude themselves or be devoid of integrity to such an extent!

We were in the home of a family of considerable wealth and very high social standing. The house was in good taste which bespoke affluence without being showy and without any trace of vulgarity or ostentation, unlike many wealthy homes in Pakistan, for its owner, a very prosperous and prominent man, was a deeply sincere and commited Muslim. His wife, the leader of the group, had been blessed with a very strong and contagious faith, full of common sense and a mature wisdom which she communicated to those around her. I was very much struck by the potential of an educated, sophisticated woman having deep faith and Islamic knowledge to influence others, and realized that one person of this calibre could do more for the cause of Islam than hundreds of others who are passive or deficient in knowledge or understanding. As God says: God says:

> "Is one who worships devoutly during the hours of the night, prostrating himself or standing (in adoration), who takes heed of the Hereafter, and who places his hope in the mercy of his Lord (like one who does not)? Say: 'Are they equal, those who know and those who do not?' It is those who are embued with understanding that receive admonition."*

For I had by now realized that in this age we cannot estimate the strength or weakness of Muslims by their crude numbers; such statistics are relatively meaningless, if at any time in the past they had meaning. *Today only quality of faith and the action which that faith produces can be counted in a census of the Muslim population of the world, and we must accept the hard fact that our numbers are very small indeed. May God Most High increase them and help us in our striving in His cause.*

* *Al-Zumar 39:9.*

Presently we went into the drawing room and I talked about some of the activities of Muslims in America, illustrating them with color slides which I had brought with me to show to the family. The women were much interested, asking many questions. When it was time to go, an attractive, vivacious young matron named Zohra offered to take me home in her car; she was full of interest and enthusiasm.

On the way I commented to her that often Muslims return to their own countries from the West stronger in their Islam than they had been previously. She seemed very much struck by this statement. "How does this happen?" she asked. "What is the secret?"

"It's because Islam as a total concept and system of life, without division or compartmentalization, not just praying and fasting as many Muslims have been taught, is always stressed among us," I told her. "This is so different from the static, traditional Islam which many Muslims have grown up with, and involves the total personality so completely, that it reaches the hearts of people who have a good feeling for Islam, even though they may be weak in practice, and begins to activate them. This dynamic concept—the true Islam which the Prophet taught—was what drew people to Islam throughout its history. We have to revive this dynamism, to discard some of the so-called 'Islamic' traditions, which have in many cases become a substitute for the real Islam although they often aren't really Islamic at all, and return to the source and generator of this dynamism, the Qur'an and the *Sunnah* of the Prophet, peace be on him." I paused, thinking over other aspects of the question. "Another reason, of course, is that when these Muslims actually see the 'fabulous,' 'glamorous' world of the West for themselves, all the illusions they have built around it before coming are held up to the light of reality. Before very long some of them begin to realize that technological advancement and material superiority are not the real criteria for true civilization among human beings, and that perhaps it can be found more truly in their own ideology and its social system than anywhere else in the world."

Zohra was very much impressed by this statement, and I only wished that we could have had more time to talk together. As if reading my thoughts, she asked, "I wonder if it would be possible for you to give another talk about your activities in America."

"I would be very happy to," I answered, "but the time we have left here is very short, as we'll most probably be leaving for Turkey early next week."

"When would you be free?"

"Tomorrow morning, I think, is the only time left when something or the other is not planned. There are so many things happening, and so little time!"

"Well," she said, laughing, "that may be very short notice for some of the people I want to invite, but I think I can manage it. I'll issue the invitations for tomorrow morning right away and ring you up to confirm it. Is that all right?"

I agreed and we parted, happy in our new friendship, expecting to meet the next day.

That afternoon Sharifa, Asma and I went to Anarkali Bazaar with a friend to do some shopping. This was the main shopping area of the city. Its central section had not changed much during the past several years but there was a new and interesting extension of Bano Bazaar—the women's bazaar—with many types of beautiful merchandise. Although I wanted to buy a few items, I found to my dismay that at some shops the prices rose as soon as I expressed an interest. One shopkeeper said indignantly to Sharifa, of course unaware of our relationship, "Why did you bring this foreigner here and tell her the correct prices, when I could have charged her much more?"

We passed shop after shop where the richest, loveliest and most expensive of *saris* and *shalwaar*-suit fabrics for special occasions (notably weddings) were sold, many made-to-order with delicate embroidery and bead-work to suit the taste of the customer; each represented an outlay of several hundred *rupees*. Where, I wondered, is the money for all this coming from, while the poor get poorer and are more and more affected by the high cost of living, and the well-to-do, without compassion or sympathy for them, turn their backs on their plight and even try to claim that they are really well-enough-off with what they have? This indescribable inequality must ultimately have dreadful consequences of one sort or another for the whole society unless something is changed. In the elegant, showy mansions of Model Town, Gulberg and Civil Lines, and their counterparts in Karachi, Islamabad, Peshawar and other cities of Pakistan, where the rich go on enhancing their style of life by every means available while the poor around them can hardly find means for a bare subsistence, a catastrophe is being prepared in which it may fare very hard with the rich and powerful of the society who have, with relatively few exceptions, discarded Islam completely. The Holy Qur'an is full of incidents from the histories of earlier peoples who were steeped in one sort of vice or corruption or the other, narrating how God destroyed them for their misdeeds after they had been warned. Was I seeing in this modern era such a society, doomed by its own unending errors and its failure to learn the lesson of history, to destruction either suddenly and quickly, or to more gradual decline and fall?

Selim gave a talk about Islam in America, illustrated by slides, to a group of men that afternoon and was scheduled to give two more within the next days. Pakistan and Lahore itself had dozens of Islamic groups and associations. Unfortunately there seemed to be little connection or working-together among them, and while the members or workers in these groups were all educated people, they did not seem to be making much impact on the society. Many of the groups seemed to be lacking in dynamism, to be oriented toward 'Muslim culture' or Muslim nationalism rather than toward Islam, or to be apologetic in their approach. One of the outstanding exceptions was the Jamaat-i-Islami, which, as a movement spearheading Islamic revival long before it became a political party, was now in the forefront of the genuine Islamic revival in Pakistan, open and clear in its effort to call people back to a pure and pristine Islam without apologetics or romanticizing Muslim culture, calling for a total commitment to *living* Islam rather than being satisfied merely to be 'born Muslim' or giving lip-service to it.

Visitors followed one another during the remainder of the afternoon. The time left to us here was very short indeed, and we must somehow manage to include in the program of one day such activities as would normally have been spread over a much longer period. We had seldom been so busy or involved and I enjoyed it throughly while it lasted.

＊　＊　＊

Sitting in the jet on the way home to Ankara, I reflected on the tense atmosphere of political anxiety and instability—a big question mark about the future—which had gripped Pakistan during those days.

＊　＊　＊

When the movement for Pakistan, an independent nation for Muslims to be taken from that part of Imperial India having a Muslim majority, came about, several strands of thought went into its formation: the feeling that Hindus and Muslims were so totally incompatible in their beliefs, ways of life and habits that they could not live together as one nation; the determination of Indian Muslims not to be a minority discriminated against politically, economically and socially by the Hindu majority; and the desire for a separate nation where the Muslims of the Indian subcontinent could establish an Islamic state and live according to the Islamic *Shari'ah* both on an individual and a collective level. However, taken all-in-all, the formation of Pakistan was essentially a political rather than a religious move. The leader and prime-mover, Mohammad Ali Jinnah, was not himself a practicing Muslim. What he envisioned was simply a state where those Indians who had Muslim names could be free of Hindu political and economic domination or even persecution—in other words, a kind of Muslim nationalism rather than a true Islamic state.

During the twenty-three years since its birth, Pakistan had had a succession of leaders who had taken it further and further from the conception of an Islamic state (that is, one which allows no laws or practices contrary to the *Shari'ah,* while implementing legislation and encouraging behavior compatible with it), leaders who were primarily interested in maintaining their own power and the power of their cronies or relatives, and who were inefficient, corrupt and immoral. Since 1958 Pakistan had seen two military dictatorships, those of Ayub Khan and Yahya Khan, both hard-drinking professional soldiers trained in the Sandhurst tradition, and the promise of representation of the people, genuine democracy and an Islamic government had never been seriously implemented.

When in December 1970 elections were finally held to form a new constitution-making body (the previous constitutions having been arbitrarily set aside) whose members would later become the members of the National Assembly, Yahya Khan, as acting head of state, allowed the two majority party leaders, Mujib and Bhutto, one-hundred-and-twenty days to collaborate on the setting-up of the constitutional assembly. However, both leaders created problems. Mujib had campaigned and had been elected in East Pakistan on a platform consisting of six points, all of them having to do with Bengali autonomy, and he insisted that these conditions must be complied with before he would sit down to talk with Bhutto, representing the West wing. During the latter days of our stay in Pakistan, Bhutto had refused to agree to the six points; he had stated publicly that he would "break the leg" of any elected representative who went to the constitutional assembly and would "set West Pakistan on fire from end to end" if the assembly were convened. The situation was extremely threatening and serious, for it appeared impossible that an *entente* would be established between the two leaders before the expiration of the deadline. This raised the very grave question of East Pakistan's secession, a move which might also imperil the rather tenuous unity of the West wing, torn as it was by regionalism. There was also at present the tension whipped up by the hijacking incident, although it now appeared to have passed the critical stage.

What was it which, up to the present, had united a country separated by one thousand miles of hostile territory and made it a viable entity? It was only one thing, without which the idea of a nation composed of these two very widely-separated sectors appeared not only absurd but also impossible. This element of course was the common ideology and way of life, Islam. But both East and West had now elected leaders who have nothing to do with Islam (despite the repeated claims of Bhutto and his shrewdly having made use of its name for his political ends, appealing with that incongruous slogan of 'Islamic Socialism,' in which 'Islam,' the exalted religion given by God for all humanity, was made into an adjective modifying 'socialism,' to ignorant people lacking clear judgment, or to those who want only a smattering of Islam or merely the sanction of its name, and who are acting in ways completely at variance with it, the one leader a secessionist instead of an instrument of unity and reconciliation, and the other a man having a wide reputation for his personal immoralities who appears to have his own desire for power more at heart than the welfare of his people. Evidently the characters and motives of the candidates were never considered as relevant issues in the 1970 elections!

Thus, torn apart by perpetual divisions, a multitude of petty rivalries and hatreds kept alive and burning brightly by the manipulations of politicians and vested interests, the people of Pakistan had made their choice. It now remained to see where these leaders would take the people of this land and what would be the ultimate consequence of having selected them instead of sincere and upright Islamic leadership . . .

* * *

I gave my talk to the second group of women, Zohra's friends and neighbors among whom there was Islamic interest, called together at literally a moment's notice, the following day. They were sincere and interested, and Zohra's own enthusiasm for Islam was like that of a person who has suddenly come upon a shining jewel which has been in her possession all this time. I realized once again the value of such women—educated, thoughtful, full of zeal, familiar with the cultures of both East and West—and the influence which they could have upon the society, especially upon other women, once they consciously realize the inestimable value of the faith with which Allah has honored them and begin to communicate it to others, and I prayed that there would be many more such women in Pakistan in time to come. Obviously the complete acceptance of Islam as their criterion and total way of life would require many changes in their entire scheme of values and mode of existence, but if one were completely sincere in her conviction, such changes would be made gladly and without too much difficulty, as one exchanges a worse thing for something infinitely better and more desirable.

The talk at Sharifa's college also went well enough, thank God. I could only pray that the young women to whom I had spoken, who were being educated in the quiet, conservative atmosphere of the college, would retain its Islamic flavor throughout their lives and would somehow find ways to influence the society in which they live in the way of Islam.

As our visit here was drawing to an end, the following evening Sharifa gave a dinner for a number of friends. She was up at four in the morning to begin the preparations. Everyone stayed at home that day as there was so much work to be done, and Sharifa, her old *mai* and an experienced cook whom she had borrowed for the day worked steadily until late afternoon, with whatever assistance the rest of us could give.

It was to be a '*purdah* party,' the men sitting in the drawing room and the women accommodated in the other parts of the house. I had seen that mixed parties usually afforded no benefit, at least among nominally Islamic people, for the mixing created a stiff atmosphere, and women sat among and talked with women and men with men in any case; moreover, women who observed *purdah* generally did not attend mixed gatherings. Such parties had obviously become 'the thing to do' and a sign of 'modernity' rather than a convention which benefitted anyone.

At seven o'clock the guests began to arrive; the men went directly to the drawing room while the women were made comfortable elsewhere. To my great surprise some of them had brought me gifts; I was totally overwhelmed by the kindness and love which they expressed for me and could find no proper words to convey all that I was feeling.

At last the group was complete. Since most of the women were colleagues and close friends, it was a very congenial gathering. As we sat chatting over dinner, it was my privilege and joy to talk with women, several of whom I already knew and others who were new to me, whom I will never forget—sincere, loving people, some of them very deeply and fervently religious, whom I should have liked to know better and whom I pray to meet again. It was a beautiful, happy evening, shadowed only by the thought that we would very soon be gone from among them.

Everyone left quite early. As they were preparing to go, I asked the fifteen-year-old daughter of one of Sharifa's close friends, "Why are you leaving so soon?"

"It's late and we must go to bed," she replied.

"Tomorrow is Sunday and you can sleep late," I rejoined.

"We have to get up for *Fajr* prayer."

"Of course. But you can go back to sleep afterwards if you like."

"Afterwards we read Qur'an."

"Well, after that."

"After that we must have breakfast." She said it with such decision and self-assurance, as if it were obviously the only proper order of things and if anyone did it differently it was *his* mistake, that I was delighted with her. If there were large numbers of youth in Pakistan who had been brought up with such a clear sense of direction and commitment to Islam, its future as a Muslim country would indeed be no cause for concern!

I bade a warm goodbye to these friends. It had been a wonderful, unforgettable occasion, and I could only look forward to seeing at least some of them again on my next trip to Pakistan, *insha'Allah*. When it would be, God only knew, but I had hope and confidence that it would not be too long before we returned.

CHAPTER 13

RETURN TO TURKEY

Selim had had a letter from Enver a few days previously saying that the University was now open and examinations were in progress. He had inquired from Selim's department and had been told that he should plan to return just before the end of the examination period, that is, by about March 13. Accordingly, we had made our plans to return in a leisurely fashion by way of Peshawar, Kabul, Qandahar, Hirat, Meshed and Tehran, and had informed Bhai that we would be arriving in Peshawar on March 4 to spend two or three days before continuing our journey. Thus, when I joined the family in the drawing room on the morning of February 29, it was a most unpleasant surprise to find Selim holding a telegram which had just arrived from Enver saying that he must be back in Ankara for his examinations before March 5. There was thus no question but that we must fly back all or almost all the way; these were, then, the very last days not only of Lahore but also of this whole unforgettable trip. Since today was Sunday, nothing could be done about making travel arrangements, but tomorrow we must take care of them with utmost dispatch.

This sudden, unexpected change of plans left me feeling strangely upset, and I am sure all the others felt something of the same emotion. I was especially sorry that we would not be able to see Bhai and his family once more before leaving—yet how could I be other than infinitely thankful and grateful to the Beneficent God for the great abundance of good we had enjoyed? I began to pack books which had to be mailed and to take care of other essentials.

That afternoon we had tea with friends of the family and from there we went to another friend's where we were invited for dinner; as always the discussion of the men turned to political affairs, for matters of the utmost seriousness were at stake.

The next day, March 1, was very busy. We must leave Lahore by March 3 and all arrangements must be made very hurriedly. Everyone was dejected and grieved at our leaving in this abrupt manner. Although we had all known that we would be going soon, I don't think any of us would have felt it as we did if we had left as planned by way of Bhai in Peshawar. Now every moment left was the more precious to each one of us.

Selim and I spent most of that day in the city taking care of travel arrangements, in the hands of a ticket agent of doubtful competence. The best travel program which could be arranged was to leave on March 3 by way of Karachi, where we would visit relatives and spend the night, and the following day fly on to Ankara via Beirut and Istanbul. One day now remained to be with Sharifa's family, and that evening there was still another dinner invitation.

The next morning there was more rushing about the city on various businesses. I was very grieved at the prospect of leaving, taking a mental farewell of the now-familiar places until the next time we should come, God willing, whenever it should be. Selim and I had discussed the possibility of my staying on with the children for another two weeks and then flying back to Ankara, but I knew that if I stayed I would have no peace of mind with the indefinite situation in Turkey, nor any enjoyment without him here beside me.

I had developed a liking for this city and its life which I had not felt during the difficult period of our earlier stay, and I had also seen much more of it during this fortnight than I had during the fifteen months we had lived here previously, when we had moved about the city by buses and *tongas* only. At the same time, I was troubled by all the problems I had observed and thought about so much: the indifference toward Islam among the upper classes; the vast gap between rich and poor, and the lack of social concern on the part of the affluent; the corruption rampant in the society and the mentality which produced it; the political instability which now seemed so threatening; the unIslamic social changes which were gradually finding a foothold; the intellectual stagnation and bureaucratic mentality which kept new ideas and new approaches from producing positive changes. Still, with all these problems and defects, Pakistan was one of the very few countries in the world in which Muslims had almost complete freedom of activity, speech and movement; yet what had these Muslims, the fortunate possessors of what is so highly-prized and ardently sought-after by the Muslims of other lands where it is denied them, done with their freedom? What had they achieved for Islam . . . ?

The last day came. No one went to work or school that morning. I felt the heartache with which they saw us preparing to leave and knew the sadness which Bhai and his family would feel at our last-minute telegram informing them that we would not be coming to Peshawar after all. A bleakness and sadness touched all the faces, the children, in their frank way, able to give expression to what they felt far better than the adults who kept it all inside.

We bade the old woman servant farewell, took a mental leave of the house in which we had experienced such good days, and drove to the airport. There we waited, drinking tea in its restaurant to pass the time, a large group now with Sharifa's family and some old friends, although no one was in a mood to talk very much.

Presently the flight was announced, and then the hard moment was upon us, as we bade all of them, especially beloved Sharifa, a long and painful farewell. O God, how long before we will be together again . . . ? We walked out to the plane with brimming eyes. At that moment, as I turned my whole being away from Pakistan, I was most intensely thankful to God for one thing: that from here we were going back to Turkey, not to the world of the West.

We took our seats on the jet; Maryam and Jamal sat with Selim and Nura was beside me. She and I could see the family and friends standing in an enclosure where people wait, the slow tears falling on our cheeks as we sat silent. And then an old Irish melody

I had known since I was a child, a song of wistful, haunting sadness, was played over the public-address system of the plane. Somehow that plaintive melody unlocked all the grief which had been shut up inside me during those last days; I and the child held onto one another, shaken with weeping as the same emotion gripped us both and bound us together. I was filled with an indefinable sense of loss, an abrupt tearing away from something dearly-cherished.

The plane taxied down the runway and was airborne; we had left the city where we had experienced so much in such a short time. Nura and I sat speechless, our arms wound around each other, something in my throat feeling like a great stone for a long while.

Nura fell asleep soon after lunch; I was also miserably tired and tried to sleep. Toward the end of the flight I caught glimpses of vast stretches of sand below; a bumpy descent and we landed at the Karachi airport. There were tropical trees and vegetation everywhere, and it was several degrees hotter and more humid than Lahore. A face came forward out of the crowd and greeted us: a cousin whom we had informed of our coming. He showed us something of the city before taking us to his home, and we spent a very pleasant afternoon with him. At night we returned to the hotel where we were guests of the airline, and, very weary, slept immediately after our dinner and prayers.

I recalled how this day had begun—this day on which our great adventure would end, a day which would bring us abruptly from the depths of the East to the perimeter of the West.

We had been up by five and left the hotel on the airport minibus in the first light of dawn. There was a touristic-looking middle-aged American couple with us; I speculated on how and what a Westerner without any real contact with Pakistanis could understand about a culture so totally different and with such a different base. What could one grasp by seeing it from outside of the significance of five times a day prayer, of fasting in *Ramzan*, of marriages without dating, of the meaning of the *burqa*, for example? How much of this could and would be interpreted correctly even by the non-Muslim Westerners who wanted to understand it properly, let alone by those who did not have this interest and whose interpretations and opinions were based only on casual observation or misinformation?

We hurried toward the airport through dark, empty streets. At two or three mosques on the way I saw light and men praying *Fajr,* and we also prayed sitting in the bus. Farewell to this land in which God is remembered by many of the simple and pious, by the stable people of the middle class, and by that minority of the affluent who have grasped this firm handhold, and God bless the worshipers! At the airport, beggars came to us, and I gave them the last of our Pakistani coins. Flocks of birds—or perhaps they were bats, I could not tell—which roost in the trees beside the airport flew up and shot in swarms into the brightening sky. O God, preserve this country, and help it in the midst of the terrible evils which threaten it. O Lord, keep it safe from its enemies, within and without, and revive Islam in the hearts of its people . . .

A little later I sat on the plane overwhelmed by a deep sadness, Nura clasped in my arms. How hard to leave this Pakistan where, for a well-remembered moment, I had caught a glimpse of the purity of Islam, a glimpse which might have become a permanent vision if we had remained here, where I had felt so much at home among those who are dear to us and among those whose lives are directed to the same goal; tears burned sharply behind my eyes as I thought of them. The plane was up now, over the ocean, and then the desert, and back again to the endless dark blue water. O God Most High, bless those whom we love whom we are leaving behind until the next time You see fit to reunite us, and in Your mercy bring us back again to this land and to our people.

We were homeless now, the ties with Pakistan having been rudely and abruptly severed, and for the moment we were wanderers on the face of the earth . . .

Thus I sat in a deep reverie, turning over and over in my mind all the events and feelings of the last many days, and finally fell into a light sleep, awaking when the warning signs flashed on in the cabin and the plane began to descend. A brief stop in Beirut and back again into the sky, making for Istanbul. Two-and-a-half hours later we disembarked in the same dilapidated airport we had first seen just six months ago, feeling frustrated and troubled at being in this city which we had loved without being able to see anything of it; but we must reach home tonight. Now only the last leg of the journey, the flight to Ankara, lay before us.

Everywhere around us now, suddenly, Turkish was being spoken, and I realized with a shock that I had almost forgotten even the sound of it during the past five weeks, when I had gone from being unable to speak a word of Urdu to forgetting all my Turkish and being able to speak Urdu again. We sat wearily waiting for the departure of the plane in the midst of a group of Turks, including several overdressed women with a good deal of makeup. Well, I thought defensively, we are in Turkey now! All of us were silent, taking it all in and trying to cope with our many mixed feelings and impressions.

The hum of Turkish formed a background to our subdued English conversation as we took our seats on the Turkish Airlines' plane. Automatically we picked up the Turkish newspapers in front of us and tried to read without understanding much. The stewardesses, in their bright pink midi-uniforms, were friendly, typical in appearance and manner of the young Westernized women of today's Turkey; for me they underscored the abrupt change in environment very markedly. Yes, Pakistan and its atmosphere had been left behind, and now there must be a period of readjustment to Turkey, somewhere mid-way between a Muslim society and a Western one; we would have to 'debrief' ourselves of the world we had left that morning and return to the old Turkish frequency. An unnamed feeling of distaste rose up within me.

We reached Ankara's Esenboğa Airport, from where we had begun our journey so joyously nearly six weeks earlier, at dusk, all of us numb with fatigue, gathered up our luggage, and climbed almost automatically onto the airline's bus going to the city. I was so tired that I slept, very uneasily, almost all the way, waking every few minutes to peer out into the dark night and going immediately back to sleep.

The Kızılay Terminal at last, just the same as we had left it. A middle-aged taxi driver with a moustache and a kind, rugged face came forward. *"Taksi, efendim?"* he asked with a grave, courteous smile. He loaded our baggage into his car and drove us home through the familiar grey, smoky streets; he would never know how welcome and heart-warming his simple, polite Turkish sounded or how his kindly manner had touched me. But at the same time I was aware of strange, ill-defined feelings I had not anticipated: a dreary sense of coming back to all that we had left that was dull and oppressive, the bleak wintry Ankara atmosphere and all it had come to stand for in my mind.

All the way into the city on the bus in my half-sleeping state, a strong feeling of dislike for this westernized Turkey and everything it embodied in the way of destruction of Islamic values had been fomenting within me, and now, seeing the familiar, unlovely streets of Ankara, where nothing whatsoever had changed in our absence—was it possible, when *I* had changed, had learned and grown so much?—I was left with a miserable consciousness of having lost something very dear and precious in leaving Pakistan. Was it just a vague, imaginary, idealized notion which had no basis in reality, or had there really been something—something profoundly meaningful and important—which I had glimpsed there, apart from friends and family relationships? Had there been, in that country torn apart by political anxieties and social problems, something which my spirit had really encountered, and was there some real reason for this revolution within me as we drove down the familiar streets wreathed in perpetual smog, looking at the maxi-coated women walking arm-in-arm with their companions of both sexes in the night? All of us were completely silent, absorbed in our own thoughts.

The driver stopped at our apartment house, helping with the baggage in the darkness; no one was about and no one saw us come home from the other world where we had been. Selim opened the door of the apartment with his key; it was exactly as we had left it, with little deposits of soot which had blown in through the cracks by the doors and windows—the same apartment in which we had felt and experienced so much during the preceding months. I greeted it with that feeling of relief and belonging which travelers generally experience when they return home after a long absence, but at the same time with an odd sense of reluctance, of regret at what there was to return to.

I had not expected to feel like this. Surely it had been only a day or two before we left Lahore that I had told Sharifa that I love Turkey so much for all the good, Islamic qualities of its people, and I had really looked forward to returning—yet here I was feeling like this! What was this strange sense of disenchantment I was now experiencing? I rehearsed in my mind all the well-known, fine, admirable qualities of the average Turk—his profound dignity and self-respect, his striking honesty and integrity, his generosity and hospitality—and all that I had found here to love, but nevertheless I could not shake off the feeling that I had left behind me the most precious of all things. Now, this trip over, upon returning to the scene of our many earlier difficulties and problems, I felt that I was ready to go home; there was no longer any benefit for us here. The thoughts went around and round in my tired head and came back to the same point without any resolution as we prepared ourselves for sleep.

Thus, after five weeks and four days, the journey had ended and we had returned safe and well, *Alhamdulillah.* We had had very good, never-to-be-forgotten days and I had experienced much and learned much. With all my heart, I thanked the Most Beneficent God Who had given us all this good. And now, just as if we had never been away, the interminable laundry-washing and old daily round would begin again, even though there was so much in my mind and heart to occupy me at present. Again this evening, as on the first night we had stayed in the apartment, coal was dumped by the sidewalk and shoveled into the basement until far into the night. We said our prayers and went to bed, and all night long I had strange, disturbed dreams in which I saw the shapes of death.

Section Three

OF HATE AND LOVE

CHAPTER 14

THIS TROUBLED LAND

March 5: I awoke in the familiar pale pink bedroom at dawn to pray, immediately aware of no longer feeling as completely estranged as I had on the previous evening. This was home. The old surroundings and well-known belongings provided a kind of reassurance, and the settling-in process was underway.

As always, the sounds of a new day began in the street outside before it was completely light, as a few working men already on their way to their daily labor exchanged loud greetings and comments in passing. When everyone was up, Jamal was dispatched to a nearby *bakkal* for some groceries, and after we had eaten breakfast we set out for Enver's house, although we had not informed them of our return. Selim would stay for only a few minutes and then would go on to the University, where he would be occupied all day with his final examinations.

It was the same sort of a cold, cloudy, bleak Ankara day on which we had left and to which we had been accustomed throughout the winter; the smoke of thousands of chimneys formed a dense grey pall which hung over everything, the smell of it easily perceptible. The same streets of apartment houses; the *kapıcı hanıms,* dressed in their bright-colored *şalvars* and kerchiefs, doing errands or exchanging news with their neighbors; the *sucu* with his truck carrying the huge, heavy bottles of spring water from house to house; the *yogurtcu* with his home-made cart carrying an ice chest filled with containers of yogurt; the familiar, well-dressed, top-coated businessmen walking to the *dolmuş* stop; lower middle class matrons, still young but with the early lines of hard work and child-bearing indelibly printed on their faces, clad in scarves, coats and shoes which had seen better days, on their way to the city for shopping: the same bitter-sweet sense of simultaneous attraction and repulsion, a feeling of something artificial, meaningless, even worthless, and at the same time unique, beloved and with a sense of home. Oh, those dingy pavements of Ankara; I knew how well I was to remember their broken squares and bricks in time to come.

We rang the bell of Enver's apartment and waited; surely the mother would be there even if Enver and Emine had already left for work. At last Aynur Alba, clad in a familiar house dress and slippers, opened the door, with an exclamation of glad astonishment at our unannounced return. She welcomed us very warmly, bringing us inside and asking about our healths and our journey. When we asked about Enver and Emine, she replied that they had gone to Istanbul and would probably be back tomorrow; yet to grasp even this much of what she said required a considerable effort, and I realized with extreme dismay how poorly we were now able to handle Turkish, for we could barely understand anything she said or speak even a few words ourselves.

Feeling somehow shy and awkward with her as communication was now virtually impossible, although she was a dear and valued old friend, we left very soon. Selim went to the University; the spring semester would begin, we supposed, in a week or two after a brief post-examination break. Meanwhile the children and I returned home, feeling peculiarly lonely and ill at ease, like utter strangers in a half-familiar place.

The girls started to put their room to rights, while Jamal was similarly occupied. Now, instead of returning to school, the children would spend some time each day working with the school books which we had sent from America until we returned home. I eyed the heap of luggage and began to unpack it. It was full of mementoes of Pakistan and our travels: the clothes we had worn, gifts which loving people had given us, the beautiful things I had bought in Isfahan, Tehran and Peshawar, all of which brought back so vividly the memories of what we had left behind. It hurt me to look at them now, and I unpacked only the things which we would need here during the coming months, apart from a few ornamental things for our house and gifts for our friends, leaving all the rest in the valises which I shut into the closet, as if shutting away with them memories which were now painful. Then I began to attack the soot and dirt which had blown in through the cracks.

At that moment I heard the key turn in the lock, and before I could investigate, Selim walked in. Astonished at his quick return when he had expected to be at the University most of the day, I asked, "What's happened? Why are you home so soon?"

He put down his briefcase wearily. "I went to the bus stop to catch the bus for the University," he said. "There I met a student I know, and he told me that I could not go to the campus. The army has occupied it and a full-scale battle is raging!"

I put the broom away and leaned against the wall, my head on my arm, utterly defeated. It was for this, then, that we had put aside all our desires and plans and had returned in such a hurried manner from Pakistan! The children gathered around, each one talking and asking questions, but Selim had no further information. Jamal was sent to bring a newspaper and returned running.

The headlines in the Ankara "Daily News" announced: "TERRORISTS KIDNAP FOUR U.S. AIRMEN: ASK $400,000 RANSOM." The relevant portions of the feature article read as follows:

"An extremist group calling itself the 'Turkish Peoples Liberation Army' kidnapped four American airmen yesterday and threatened to shoot them if 400,000 dollars is not paid by 1800 this evening.

"American officials said the four radar technicians were kidnapped by five armed Turks while driving in an official car from a radar and communications base outside Ankara to their billets in Ankara.

"Police said they later arrested a youth. . . He reportedly confessed to having participated in the kidnapping and said that the rest were Deniz Gezmiş and his friends who were being sought for the Ankara bank robberies. [The youth arrested is] a former student at Middle East Technical University whose campus adjoins the road where the kidnapping took place.

"Several hours after the kidnapping, three armed youths appeared at the semi-Official Anatolian Agency. They handed the night editor a three-page ransom note and the identity card of [one of the airmen]. They demanded the note be published and left.

"Copies of the note were also left at the Turkish state radio (TRT) with demands it be broadcast.

"The ransom note was signed by the 'Turkish Peoples Liberation Army,' (THKO) the first time the group has surfaced."

What follows is a verbatim and unabridged translation of the relevant portion of the ransom note as it was reproduced in the "Daily News."

"Officers, students, technicians: Use the arms and knowledge that you possess for the liberation of the motherland. Stand up to the commanders who are under the order of NATO and the American-fed traitors [i.e., the Turkish armed forces and government].

"Small artisans, small tradesmen, orphans, widows and retired people: You need to live like human beings and to be treated like human beings. Dire poverty is rotting your backbones more and more every day. You view your tomorrow with horror. Your salvation and the salvation of all our people are not different things. We will not rest easy until all traitors are done away with.

"All patriots: Because of the United States and the traitors under its order we have been reduced to the position of stepsons in our own motherland. Don't leave the motherland to the coming generations in this position and . . .

"The Turkish Peoples Liberation Army claims responsibility for all the activities it has undertaken in its short period of activity and makes its first announcement to the public.

"1) The riot police in front of the U.S. Embassy were shot at on the night of December 29. This incident has given a feeling of security to the revolutionaries and the people, and for the first time there was an encounter with a serious revolutionary terrorism.

"2) On January 11 the Emek Branch of Iş Bank was robbed and TL 124,000 was taken. The aim of the robbery was on the one hand to undermine the working system of banks which are a tool for the continuation of the mechanism of exploitation and on the other, for [money for] arms so as to be able to fight more effectively. And it is because of this that after the robbery the enemy [the government of Turkey] increased its pressure on our fighters and the people with a savagery not experienced in the past. After a full month of pursuing, the enemy has failed to catch our fighters but on the contrary has helped them to become heroes in a very short time.

"3) In mid-March an American motor was bombed.

"4) On February 20 the riot police was shot at Istanbul at Edirnekapı.

"5) On the night of 21 February we entered the Balgat [Air Force] base of the Americans [in Ankara]. For four hours the base was under the control of our fighters. We could not find arms in the depots that we entered or on the guards. While they were leaving, our fighters took with them an American sergeant who was on guard and changed their minds about placing him before a firing squad when they saw that he was a Negro. He was set free after the necessary information was extracted from him.

"These incidents show this:

"The enemy [the NATO- and U.S.- supported government of Turkey] is cruel and more cowardly than he appears.

"He is weak in spite of the fact that he appears strong. We are the ones who are strong, courageous and heroic. For one and a half months the police organization of the treacherous government has been brought to its knees by a handful of fighters. In spite of all the pressure and terrorism (the police) were unable to arrest not even one of our fighters but have caught and tortured revolutionaries who had nothing to do with the incidents so as to appear successful and to deceive the people."

I was thunderstruck by this sudden, totally unexpected precipitation into terrorism and revolution, so immediately after our return, which nothing had led us to anticipate; for during our stay in Pakistan we had had no news or information indicating that matters were in such a bad way in Turkey, and had also largely forgotten how serious the situation had been before we left. To see Turkey in the hands of an unchecked terrorist gang, with its vicious and immoral tactics, its garbled ideas and inflated rhetoric, and a government which appeared to lack both authority and interest in maintaining security and order, filled me with unutterable dismay, complicated by the recurring question of our own immediate future.

Already before Selim had come with this news, I had been in a state of great inner turmoil continued from the previous evening, as the aversion which I now felt for Turkey burned on within me undiminished. And now this! The present state of chaos was simply the obvious outcome of turning away from Islam, of the open hostility and systematic efforts to discredit and destroy it which we had seen on the part of the Turkish government and people in high places, and the filling of the ideological vacuum with whatever ideas—no matter how wrong—had taken hold among the dominant segments of the population. I cannot express the feeling of anger against Turkey, the sense of despair, which I now experienced as I observed the shocking dilemma of a once-noble people turned toward other, worthless and extremely harmful values; even Maryam expressed the same feelings as I silently pondered over my own. Now, with this latest news, although the present situation was merely the logical culmination of the forces which we had observed building up during the past months, our own personal situation was also affected and some concrete action was required. I hurriedly advised Selim to wind up his affairs here immediately; we should not stay on under such dangerous and difficult conditions, for there was obviously no benefit in it. That was clear.

In the afternoon, while we were still trying to digest these matters, Aynur Abla, together with Enver and Emine, unexpectely appeared at the door, to our great joy; they had returned a day earlier than anticipated. With their coming, all of us suddenly felt very much better, and things fell into some sort of focus once again. We went with them to their house to discuss the grim events of the day, to hear their news and give ours. Enver merely confirmed whatever we had read in the newspaper and could say nothing more until the outcome of the situation became clear. Jamal was again having trouble with asthma, both he and Nura had sore throats and upset stomachs, and all three children were coughing. This is Ankara! I thought bitterly as I looked out into the grey, polluted dusk.

At that time a news bulletin on the radio summarized the day's events, Enver translating for us. As the newspaper had stated, the kidnappers were the same Dev-Genç gang, headed by Deniz Gezmiş, which had committed all the terrorist activities mentioned (some of which we were hearing about for the first time and others well-known from the weeks preceding our trip), including the bank robbery because of which M.E.T.U. had been closed prior to our leaving. A confession had been extracted from the member of the kidnapping ring who had been caught; he had stated that the kidnappers were hiding at M.E.T.U. The police and army had gone to the campus, and the students had opened fire. A full-scale battle between army and students had followed, the students utilizing the complete array of weapons stored up in the impressive arsenal which had been accumulating at M.E.T.U. during these months. One soldier and one student were dead, some others wounded, and a large number of students had been rounded up in the University's stadium for searching and interrogation while the dormitories were evacuated and searched. Not only were M.E.T.U. and Ankara affected by the terrorist activities, but several other parts of Turkey as well, with serious disturbances in several other cities. Today yet another bank robbery, one of a series, had been committed by the terrorists. We looked at one another unbelievingly and asked what might come next.

Enver paced up and down the room with clenched fists, angry as I had never before seen him. "We have to take drastic action against these people!" he exclaimed. "There is no other solution! They are traitors, trying to destroy Turkey and Islam with their criminal terrorist tactics and wicked atheistic ideology, and we must get rid of them once and for all!" The talk continued until far into the night, all of us burning with the same fierce anger against these criminal revolutionaries who now dominated the country, our recent travels and experiences (and theirs as well) entirely forgotten in the face of all these more immediate events. Yet when I thought of Pakistan, of all that had happened to us so recently *(had we really left Pakistan only yesterday morning?)*, I felt an indefinable sting of regret and sadness . . .

March 6: This morning's "Daily News" only confirmed what we had heard on the radio. I went with Selim to a neighborhood shop where he tried to telephone his department at the University. Although after a long while a University telephone operator answered, there was no answer from his department's number and the operator told him that the University was closed.

Feeling a great need to talk over the situation further, in the afternoon we went to visit Bahadir Bey, leaving the children at home. He and Deniz Hanım welcomed us warmly and asked about our travels. The latest news was that the army had occupied the M.E.T.U. campus; all students had been expelled from it and numbers arrested. Although our friends were concerned about the situation, naturally they were not as disturbed as we, who were a part of the University community and whose immediate future depended on what would happen there, our sense of shock at these events, moreover, increased by our absence and unpreparedness. Talking to Bahadir Bey, a sensible man having a deep feeling of history and the context of things, restored us to a sense of perspective and proportion again. His objective attitude and wise words helped us to realize, as we should have from the beginning, that this was only one incident—perhaps not even a very important one, large as it now seemed—in the history of a nation struggling to find itself.

It was, nevertheless, necessary that we take some action or at least make a decision about ourselves. If the University were to remain closed indefinitely, there was no sense in staying on, Selim without any occupation and drawing a stipend for non-existent studies while his work waited for him at home. However, when we asked Bahadir Bey whether at this point he would advise us to return home or to stay on in the hope that the University might reopen soon, he replied that there was at present no way even to guess when it would open, and that under these circumstances whatever we decided would be the right thing. And then I asked him the question which I had asked myself so many times before, the question which had silently troubled me so much: if the University reopened, was there a real personal danger to Selim, who was known to be a practicing Muslim? To lay down one's life purposefully in the cause of God, accomplishing something with one's death, was one thing; but to remain in an exposed situation in which one was unable to contribute anything either to Islam, to Turkey or even to oneself, and risk being killed in an incident like today's or by terrorist scoundrels to no purpose was something else, I felt. Bahadir Bey shrugged. "Marian Hanım," he said, "There is no answer to this question. You must simply put your trust in Allah."

I did not say anything more. After this, it seemed to me *kufr*—non-belief, denial of God's power and sovereignty—to worry like this. All the wives and families of practicing Muslims at M.E.T.U. and other institutions which were affected must be living under the burden of this same nagging anxiety, this continuous sense of fear, but we were simply in the vortex of an historical maelstrom which must run its course. Although under these conditions I knew I would be uneasy every time Selim went to the University, every time he did not come home when I expected him, we would nevertheless stay and do our work. I would trust in God's infinite wisdom and mercy, knowing that every human being has a term of life appointed to him which can neither be extended nor shortened by circumstances no matter what one does or does not do, and would pray for whatever was best.

My debate within myself about the state of things in Turkey continues. Now after having been in Pakistan, I realize much more clearly that, although there are sincere, devoted Muslims in every sector of Turkish society, some of whom are deeply concerned about the situation of Islam (and this would be far more obvious outside the larger cities, which are justifiably notorious for their unIslamic, westernized atmosphere), still Turkey cannot possibly by any stretch of the imagination be considered a Muslim society. In Turkey today Islam is barely tolerated—more accurately, is severely repressed—by the leaders of the society and the government.

The process of westernization begun in Turkey in the eighteenth century, developed during the nineteenth, and brought to its climax during the dictatorship of Kemal Atatürk, followed by that of Ismet Inönü, is being continued and expanded by their successors, the Kemalists of present-day Turkey. And yet, although Atatürk and Inönü dealt Islam almost a death-blow, so that it is indeed almost a miracle and a proof of its God-given vitality that it has survived at all in this land, nevertheless, I now realize, what is happening here today is not solely the fault of Atatürk, Inönü and their successors in materialism and disbelief. It is the responsibility of every single human individual to think and to decide for himself what the goal of his life is and how he should live it. Very few of today's educated Turks have lived up to this responsibility; they gladly let others, no matter how evil or misguided, do the thinking and deciding for them, without caring for the disastrous consequences of their ignorance and indifference. To me this ignorance and indifference are unforgivable sins, rather crimes, leading to the destruction of everything good and worthwhile in the society, and I am bitter and angry against them all because of it—so angry and bitter that I cannot even express it!

The thing which has disturbed me more than anything else in returning to Turkey from Pakistan is the sight of the imitation-Western women and girls, strolling about with their male or female companions or in mixed groups, clad in the latest, sometimes quite *outré,* European styles. It has been extremely difficult for me to come back from Pakistan, where my wearing an opaque shawl over my head and breast was at best a moderate rather than an extreme and unusual form of dressing, to this Ankara, where any woman who tries to dress according to Islamic standards is looked upon as belonging to those reactionary or ignorant groups who still cherish outmoded, obsolete traditional values. What, what has happened to this society? One has only to recall that two or three generations ago, until after the founding of the Turkish Republic in 1922, covering the whole body, the hair and even the face was common to all respectable Turkish women.

Time and again I have thought over the question of women's dress and talked it over with my Turkish friends. A response perhaps fairly typical of today's educated upper middle class Turks was that of Deniz Hanım, who has a good feeling for Islam and is conservative in attitude but quite westernized in dress, and who defends this by saying, "But, Marian Hanim, form is not everything in Islam."

No, certainly form is not everything in Islam, but, as I understand it, it cannot be divorced from its inner spirit; the two are one and inseparable. As the Prophet, God's peace and blessings be on him, has said, "Faith is that which is inscribed in the heart and corroborated by deeds." The *Shari'ah*—the law of God which was given to guide the life of the Muslim individual and society—has both a spirit and a form; they are essential and complementary, form being the concrete, external expression of the spirit. If we accept even for a moment the idea that spirit is independent of form in Islam (most of the forms coming to us directly from the Holy Prophet's example and teaching), then we have a basis for deciding to modify or eliminate the prescribed forms, and thus eventually to modify Islam and in its final stages to do away with it altogether, which has been the thinly-disguised ultimate aim of all attempts at 'reforming' Islam. These outward forms—the dress and manners and limits on the behavior of Muslim men and women— are of vital importance, as they are the tangible expression of that concept of personal purity and social relations which is basic to the Islamic society, and they cannot be separated from its spirit. And their observance is not a matter which only concerns the individual privately. Because what each person does or does not do ultimately affects the entire society, every human being must bear the responsibility for how his behavior affects other individuals and the society in the long run, and will be held accountable for it by God.

In the big cities of Turkey today, societal pressure is so great that it is extremely difficult, often almost impossible, for an educated Muslim woman or girl to wear an Islamic type of dress, and especially to cover her hair. Her scarf and modest dress are taken as a badge of backwardness, reaction and even fanaticism, so strong and unquestioned is the Western influence among most upper class Turks; and if she persists in wearing it, it is very improbable that she will ever attain any position of responsibility and authority in the society, particularly in any official capacity. It is a clearly-stated requirement of the secular Turkish Republic that its female employees must be free of these 'backward' religious influences and must conform to the principle of secularism even in appearance, thus subjugating the requirements of religion and conscience to the arbitrary requirements of the state. How true is the saying of the Holy Prophet, peace be on him, that "Faith and modesty are companions; when one is taken away the other is taken"—taken both individually and collectively!

Thus, whatever is left of the noble conception of feminine modesty in Turkey today cannot influence the society in any way. The uneducated city women who had prayed beside me at the Sultan Ahmet and Eyyub Sultan mosques in Istanbul, whose counterpart one sees in every city of Turkey with their drab Western-style raincoats and scarves tied under the chin—the final faded, undistinguished remnant of that outward dignity of form which was once the Turkish Muslim woman—are nothing of consequence; and as for the unlettered women of rural Anatolia or its towns who still wear the black *çarşaf,* the beautiful head coverings, the *şalvar* and other Muslim dresses, they are considered fit only for housework, manual labor or menial service, not as an example of feminine modesty for the rest of the nation.

A change in the dress of the middle and upper class Turkish Muslim women can come about only if respectable, educated women who are convinced of its rightness undertake it, if possible on a mass rather than an individual scale, with the certain conviction that careful adherence to the requirement of modesty of dress is a vital part of their Islam, and also as an expression of their God-given right to exercise free choice concerning their dress. It will not be easy, for they will meet with resistance and rejection, even from their sincere Muslim sisters who have been wearing the prevailing Western dress all their lives without thinking about it and as a result view it as perfectly proper. But here and there, even in Ankara, it is possible to see occasional individual respectable women and girls, some of whom are educated and are the wives and daughters of educated men, who are wearing various types of Islamic dress despite the strong social pressures; and I believe that their number will *insha'Allah* continue to increase as Turkish Muslim women reassert their inherent right to dress according to their convictions.

There may be many, both Muslims and non-Muslims, who will react to this by saying, "But we see so many Muslim women from Arab countries and other parts of the Muslim world in Western dress. Is this matter then really so very important in Islam?" Indeed, I have pondered over this question time and again, and have come to realize that the answer to it is clear and unequivocal: Yes, it surely is, quite regardless of what Muslim women may or may not do, for without proper regulation of the relations between men and women, of which dress is an integral part, there cannot be a stable and balanced society, which is the aim of Islam. As I have gradually come to a clear understanding of the Islamic social system, with its continuous emphasis on safeguarding the purity of the individual, the sanctity of the family, the integrity of the Muslim society, and on maintaining relationships between human beings based on truly human and   brotherly behavior, not merely on instinctive behavior which is common with animals, I have come to appreciate and value the Islamic injunctions concerning dress more and more, for they rest, with infinite logic and wisdom, on premises which take into consideration the real nature of human beings.

Islam regards sex as a God-given and potentially wholesome and positive aspect of man's existence, but at the same time it is permitted expression only within the marriage relationship, that is, with the assumption of clear and binding responsibility on both husband and wife before God and the human community; satisfying the sexual drive without the assumption of such responsibility is absolutely prohibited.* To maintain this standard of purity, there

---

* The existence in Muslim countries of such social evils as premarital sexual relations, prostitution or homosexuality has never been and will never be sanctioned by Islam. These are considered as not only being among the greatest of sins but also as crimes for which very heavy legal punishments are prescribed by the Islamic *Shari'ah*.

must be a clear understanding of the nature of the sexual urge. Islam recognizes the obvious fact that when men and women mix with each other freely, latent sexual feelings may be aroused and seek ways of expression. Thus it prescribes the non-mingling of the sexes, or at least the observing of clearly-defined limits and restraints, properly understood by both men and women, between them if they do mix, and the concealing by women of their personal attractions, in adherence to the simple principle that it is easier, more sensible, dignified and effective to prevent temptation than to control the expression of sexual feelings once they have been aroused.

Since I have been away from the United States, how often I have compared this with the pattern of social relations and the conception of womanhood prevalent in America, where, from childhood, a female is expected and desires to be ornamental, charming, attractive, and to enjoy and covet the admiration of men; where, indeed, in many cases, the attractiveness and social finesse of the wife is considered as a definite asset for her husband's work or advancement, and its lack a handicap. While Islam recognizes that the possibility of sexual attraction between men and women is ever-present and that it seeks ways of expression unless it is neutralized in both sexes by the fear of God, in American-style social relations, on the other hand, people often try to pretend that this attraction is quite innocent, that it is limited only to good-humored 'kidding,' to dating, or to 'harmless' sex play. At the same time, it is so often a very obvious undercurrent in the action, words, looks and appearance of men and women, as expressed in the covert glance, the joking, the innuendo, the pat on the back, the compliments, the loaded speech; even in the most casual mixing of men and women (indeed, *because* of its very casualness) unmistakable sexual overtones are commonly present in the background. Thus there is a perpetual demeaning and debasement of American women under a great many circumstances in which they mix with men because the limits and restraints of relationships are neither clearly-defined nor accepted, and because they are always viewed in relation to their sexuality, which is, moreover, cynically and blatantly exploited by commercial interests to add still another dimension to their overall degradation in American society.

While the American woman's worth and value, and indeed her ego and self-esteem, are inextricably tied up with her sexuality and its attributes—her dress, appearance, charm, social grace and skill at simultaneously attracting and keeping at arm's length—the Muslim woman's worth and self-esteem are entirely independent of these attributes of her sexuality; on the contrary, she is valued for her scrupulousness in concealing these attributes, which are only for her husband's appreciation and enjoyment. This difference in attitude can be illustrated by a simple example. If a Muslim woman is complimented by a man on her appearance or charm, both she and her husband will be offended and angry that a man who has nothing to do with her is paying her such attention; on the other hand, if an American woman receives a compliment from a man, both she and her husband will be pleased and will accept it as a fitting tribute to her effectiveness as a woman.

As the Muslim woman grows older, she loses none of her value and self-esteem; indeed, as she grows in maturity and experience of life she is respected even more, since her worth has never been tied up with her sexual attractiveness and youthful charm. The American woman, on the other hand, often feels that she has lost much of her status and value as her good looks and charm decline with age. Who has not seen the pathetic elderly American woman with their dyed hair, all-too-obvious make-up and too youthful mode of dress, who are walking advertisements of their conviction that their value as human beings is inseparable from youth and physical attractiveness? Because the American woman, from early adolescence until middle age, is on display and is convinced that her value depends to a very great extent on the appearance she makes, it is easy to understand why many American women are so preoccupied with their appearance and why they use such a startling array of aids and props to keep it up, well-aware that without that appearance in many circles their value will be very much reduced.

And I ask myself: Is this, then, the ideal to which my Muslim sisters are aspiring when they adopt Western dress, a dress which has evolved from concept of womanhood and the standard of social relations prevalent in Western society, shaped as these have been by the rapid deterioration of religious values and the consequent changes in morals during recent years. By adopting it, the once-distinctively modest dress of the Muslim woman has been exchanged for the right to display her attractions in public in order to be considered 'modern' and 'emancipated'—emancipated from being protected by her dress from being considered that sort of a 'sex object' against which American women are now up in open rebellion, from having her sexuality exploited and her femininity degraded! Certainly the women of the West are much more 'free' than Muslim women in their dress and behavior, but they can never experience such a total sense of human dignity and self-respect as does the Muslim woman who observes propriety in her dress and manner, and who thereby insists on being respected by all who see her as a human being rather than as an object associated with sexual interest.

March 7: Cemile came to visit today and we talked for a long time. Prior to our leaving for Pakistan we had become quite close, and now she was very much interested in all our adventures, keen to share in our impressions, and very deeply concerned about the future of Pakistan, as are all knowledgeable Turkish Muslims.

There is no news of the kidnapped airmen so far, but voices have been raised in Turkey saying that the kidnapping is a slur on the honor of the nation, which owes hospitality to its guests. There is a report that the *Rektör* of M.E.T.U. and other University officials may be indicted for their complaisance in communist student activities, a move long overdue. It is clear that the militant communist movement is firmly entrenched and getting stronger day by day, encouraged by the inaction of the government and the exploits it has been able to manage thus far. It cannot be expected just to die down or go away by itself, and only the worst is to be expected from hardened criminals and terrorists.

From the moment we landed in Istanbul on our way back to Ankara we realized how very much of our Turkish we had forgotten. We can actually no longer communicate, and I now feel very much ashamed when I meet anyone I know since I cannot understand, much less speak; not only that, but I have also lost my once-keen and passionate desire to speak and understand. My heart is completely hardened and bitter against this Turkey which has sold out to meaningless systems and values, which has betrayed its religion and its God. Yesterday evening we were invited to tea at Enver's. Some of our old friends were visiting, meeting us with kind words and affection as always, and of course not remotely imagining anything of what I was feeling. We could hardly speak a word to anyone, so completely has our Turkisn left us, and as I faced my dear Emine, Aynur Abla and the friends who have been so kind and hospitable to us, I felt a deep sense of shame toward them because of this, and because of my bitterness and disgust with their country. Were they then to blame that I should feel angry even with *them?*

March 8: Yesterday Selim managed to go to the University, which is very strictly guarded by military, to take his final examinations, and returned this morning to complete them. Leaving the children at home busy with their lessons, in the afternoon I went to visit Aynur Abla, wanting to overcome the shyness and strangeness I was feeling toward her and everyone else I know. There is of course no question of resuming my formal Turkish studies now under these indefinite conditions, but while we live here we must be able to communicate, especially with those who are so dear to us, and cannot continue to remain cut off in this way language-wise and, more importantly, emotionally.

Emine was also at home, as she was sick, and she and I had a good long talk together, pouring out our hearts. Late in the afternoon, Selim, knowing that I had planned to go there, dropped by their house on his way home, his work completed. We sat down to drink tea, as we had done so many times before, in their sunny dining room. I was very eager to have his news.

"It seems that the University is closed indefinitely this time," he reported. "There is considerable damage to dormitories and other buildings from the fighting. No one knows how long it may take to repair it, and of course it will be impossible to reopen the University until the work is finished. Some radical changes will also have to be made in the administrative set-up as well. I think," he said, turning to me, "that under these circumstances there is nothing more we can do here and we should go home as soon as we can."

I put down the glass of tea in my hand, overcome at this statement. That morning before he had gone to the University, upset by
the unsettled conditions, I had wept and insisted that we must return home. Now, when he concurred in my decision, by a strange,
unaccountable maneuver of the human heart, I backed away, unable to accept it, feeling that we simply could not leave Turkey like
this. We who had come with so much enthusiasm and interest, who
had found here so much to value and to love—were we now just to
pack up and leave for home like hopeless creatures beaten by adverse circumstances, without having contributed anything worthwhile, without having really understood Turkey or having even seen
anything of it? For to have spent a few months in Ankara was not
to have seen Turkey; it is the Turkey which is outside this place,
altogether different, I am certain, which we have come to see and to
know. And there, before Aynur Abla and Emine, and Enver, who
had just come home, I sat and cried. Emine knelt down beside me,
her soft eyes filling in sympathy. She put her arms around me and
consoled me with great tenderness, while Aynur Abla asked over
and over what was the matter, trying to comfort me with a great
many Turkish words of which I could understand almost nothing
but her kindly manner, as she searched for something which would
reach me. And this made it only so much the worse, for to go will
be to leave them, whom we love and value so greatly, and Cemile
and all our other friends.

Who can explain this strange about-face, this unpredictable conduct of the heart? When the time for decision came, I forgot the
personal risks and frustrations, my anger and bitterness against this
unIslamic environment, and could not bear the idea of leaving it!
Was it just because when we go our interesting trip will be all
over and I will have to settle down and adapt myself to American
life again; or because after two or three days here I have again adjusted to the old familiar conditions here, which, although bad, are
nonetheless much better to me than conditions in America, since
they are leavened with the Islamic qualities and traditions which
live on among a vast segment of Turks? Yes, all these factors played
a part, no doubt. Besides this, I had also recovered sufficient objectivity to realize that only *some* Turks—not all or even most—are
guilty of the betrayal of their religion and traditions, and that to be

angry and condemn everyone indiscriminately was harsh, unjust, childish, and left out of consideration all that I had loved and valued here.

March 9: Our neighbor Güneş Hanım came over this morning to tell us that the American servicemen had been found safe. Working together with the U.S. Embassy, the Turkish government had decided that no ransom should be paid, and a dragnet of police and intelligence personnel had been on the trail of the kidnappers. They had been traced to a locality of Ankara where they had been hidden among sympathizers, and when the police finally closed in they fled, leaving the airmen behind unhurt. (Later we learned that this had made the news in the United States, where many people heard for the first time—*perhaps because it affected Americans*—that something unusual was happening in Turkey, a natural enough situation as there is so little coverage of events in this part of the world in much of the American news media.)

Again Selim and I talked about what we should do and discussed the matter at great length with Enver and Emine. We finally decided to wait until the University opens and then see what seems best; surely it cannot be too many weeks before it opens, for otherwise the entire spring semester will have to be postponed. The turn of events at that time must dictate our course of action, for none of us is prepared to leave now in this defeated fashion.

Now I have again become used to this Ankara and its lack of Islamic values and atmosphere, so familiar to me after all these months. Everywhere in the city one encounters large numbers of university students on holiday, with their immature, insolent expressions and long, drooping leftist-style moustaches, for all the universities and *fakültes* in Ankara are now closed due to the communist disturbances.

March 12: These have been tense days, the political problems continuing. Dr. Erdal Inönü, M.E.T.U.'s *Rektör,* has resigned. The Faculty Council of M.E.T.U. has been dismissed and the Board of Trustees given charge of the University; however, a spokesman for the leftist-oriented Faculty Council stated that they would not step down and would continue to run the University. After this, the

Council was barred from entering the campus, which is guarded very strictly by the military, and the University was officially pronounced closed indefinitely without any indication of when it might reopen.

Today Prime Minister Süleyman Demirel resigned at the insistence of the military leaders, who, it seemed, were using all their influence to keep the entire military from initiating a full-scale military *coup* due to the inaction of the government against the terrorists; the possibility of such a *coup* had been anticipated at any moment. Demirel, pleading that the Constitution did not empower him to take strong action against the terrorists, and, it is widely believed, hoping that the rightist (nationalist) guerillas would do the job of finishing off the communists for him, has taken no effective action in a situation bordering on anarchy and has thus forfeited all claim to the support of Turkish citizens. It has been announced by the new government that the Dev-Genç the revolutionary communist group consisting mainly of students, is to be outlawed and many leading communists are to be sentenced.

As for ourselves, we are just waiting and passing time. If we are to travel in Turkey, now is the time to do it. Certainly we must, if possible, visit the Mediterranean coast, Konya, Bursa and any other places we can manage as far as time and money permit; too, Cemile's family in Isparta, situated between the Mediterranean coast and Konya, has been waiting for us to visit almost since the time we came to Turkey. Bahadir Bey is planning to make a trip to the Mediterranean coast in the vicinity of Antalya within the next few days on business and has suggested that we accompany him; on the way back we will be able to stop in Isparta and possibly also in Konya. None of us is in the mood for another trip just now, not having yet digested the previous one, but as it will be very helpful as well as pleasant to travel with him, we will probably decide to go.

March 14: Today is cold, with scattered snow. Tomorrow we are to leave for the Mediterranean coast with Bahadir Bey.

Yesterday he and Deniz Hanım came to tea, bringing a tape recorder with tapes of Turkish classical music. By now I have become quite familiar with many kinds of Turkish music, for music is everywhere present here as part of the background of one's consciousness, and I have developed a great appreciation of much of the religious and classical music. As I sat listening to the tapes, I asked Bahadir Bey if this were religious music, since its style was very similar to that of some Turkish religious music I have heard. "No," he replied, "but when this music was written in the fifteenth century, there was no distinction between sacred and secular. Everything was part of a unity without division."

I pondered over this statement, thinking of the current vulgarization of taste in the arts in Turkey, moving so far from this conception and this type of music, which one can hear only seldom on Turkish radio or in live performances. All about us in Turkey today we can see the fruits of this division, this compartmentalization, this lack of comprehension that man is a total human entity, not merely an animal or at best an organism divided into body and soul which are at war with each other and go different ways, which comes from the loss of Islam, whose task it is to blend and fuse together man's spiritual and physical aspects through the medium of God-ordained laws which give spiritual direction to the fulfillment of his physical and material needs. Yet this is the false and dangerous notion upon which the Turkish concept of 'secularism,' the guiding principle by which Turkey is ruled, rests. By it religion is relegated to the mosques or occasional religio-traditional observances, while the rest of life is governed by another set of principles, such as 'progress,' 'modernization,' 'good of the Fatherland,' etc., which are alleged to have no connection with it.

One day, perhaps after many years of struggle between the forces of God and the forces of materialism in Turkey (whether they are called 'communism,' 'atheism,' 'Kemalism' or 'secularism,') it will finally be understood that it is impossible either to 'secularize' or to 'religionize' a human being and a society, and that the unnatural attempt to create a division between the various aspects of the human personality, which together represent an organic whole, has resulted in the diseases of fragmentation, alienation and disintegration—the utter personal, social and moral chaos and confusion which has beset Turkish society in our time.

CHAPTER 15

A GLIMPSE OF ANATOLIA

March 15: Today we began our journey to the Mediterranean coast with Bahadir Bey—began it with a certain feeling of holding back, a reluctance which was not very surprising in view of the fact that we had just completed a major trip only ten days earlier and there had been neither peace of mind nor time enough to integrate all the impressions which it had left with us, apart from being just plain tired of traveling. Yet it was a good opportunity for us and we must try to make the best of it.

We met Bahadir Bey at a very early hour at the big Ankara bus depot from where innumerable buses depart daily for various parts of Turkey, and took our places in our five reserved seats of the bus. Another trip had begun. The itinerary this time was quite complicated and involved much traveling in a very short time. We would leave the bus at Antalya on the Mediterranean, where Bahadir Bey would plan some sight-seeing for us in the vicinity, and toward the end of the week we would travel to Isparta, where we would visit Cemile and her family, after which we would return to Ankara by way of Konya.

The way led out the M.E.T.U. road, through bleak, ploughed land on which the faintest green of a new wheat crop was beginning to appear; in some places snow covered the ground, increasing further on. In this area southwest of Ankara, the villages were not nearly as poor as those we had seen in the central and eastern parts of Anatolia. Little by little trees appeared and gradually became more numerous. High snow-capped mountains formed the background in many areas and the landscape became increasingly gentle and appealing, the area near the road, lying in a valley, always cultivated up to the slopes of the hills or mountains. The number of trees continued to increase, fruit trees with early flowers of white or pink among them, a lovely sight to our winter-weary eyes. The villages gradually became more prosperous and pleasant, and there were scattered small towns which had a charm peculiarly their own, at one of which we stopped for lunch. Now the journey began to be really interesting to me, although I was still aware of that pulling back within myself, as if it were a trip which should not have been made just then—but we had no choice. The time at our disposal was short at best, for if the University reopened we would have little free time for traveling, and if it did not we would undoubtedly return home soon; and in any case we must be back in the United States by mid-summer because of Selim's professional commitments.

An informal, friendly atmosphere which I liked prevailed on this bus. The passengers were mostly quiet people of the middle class, and I felt at home and at ease among them. Several people showed their friendliness with a few words, a smile. Someone gave an apple and a bag of dried chickpeas to Nura, and when we got out of the bus in Antalya, an older woman who had been sitting across the aisle from us came up and spoke a few words to me. Although I could not follow what she said, there was such kindliness and goodwill in her manner that I clasped her hand, as Bahadir Bey interpreted between us. In one spot where there was spectacular scenery, the driver very thoughtfully stopped the bus by the roadside so I could take photographs. From time to time he turned on the radio and played popular music—what Nura called 'sour songs' because of their plaintive, minor-keyed character, so similar to that of Arabic music—and then turned it off when he had had enough. It was a very pleasant trip indeed.

A fantastically winding stretch of road with a series of switchback curves brought us from a high plateau onto the Mediterranean coastal plain. Here the topography and climate changed completely. Everywhere I saw twisted, spongy-looking rocks and an entirely different vegetation, with many olive trees and colorful wild flowers. In the distance, high, jagged mountains, the Toros range, rose abruptly, and as we approached Antalya through an area of increasing population, we caught tantalizing glimpses of the sea from various points along the road.

Opposite the Antalya bus station was a weather-beaten Osmanlı mosque with a single minaret, and all about stood the four-wheeled, horse-drawn carriages which are called 'faytons,' which one sees with some variations in many Anatolian towns. Two of these were hired, to the children's delight, and they took us through the town —a town wonderfully different from Ankara, charming and picturesque, situated at the edge of the blue Mediterranean, with old mosques and a slow-paced life—to the office of a relative of Bahadir Bey's, a contractor, where we sat drinking tea while the men conversed.

Bahadir Bey had some official matters to transact for which he must now go to a small town in the vicinity. We would accompany him, spend the night there, and the next day we would do some sightseeing in the area together, after which we would be on our own for a couple of days. Afterwards we would return to Antalya, where we would meet him again before continuing our journey.

Accordingly, we took a mini-bus dolmuş, a type of public taxi which runs within and between towns all over Turkey, to our destination. The countryside here was wonderfully green and wild flowers bloomed everywhere, a lovely landscape indeed. A young village woman wearng a şalvar and white kerchief, with a baby suspended from a sling on her back and a small son, climbed in after her husband and sat down beside me. Although she was still quite young, the cares of life had already etched lines in her white forehead and around the corners of her mouth, and I could only speculate on what burdens her life might hold. From time to time our eyes met and she smiled a faint wisp of a smile in answer to my own.

The place where we got out was hardly more than a big village. Bahadir Bey went to find the person he had come to see, and when the two men returned together, they took Selim along to find a hotel for the night. I would be thankful, I thought, if this tiny place had any reasonable accommodations.

We stood by the curb of the main street, an obviously foreign woman and three children, with our baggage. People passed by, including school children in their black uniforms and white collars, looking at us covertly but not offensively, and I felt quite uncomfortable in this situation. A few men who stood about nearby quietly discussed us among themselves in a discreet manner, and I caught the word "Pakistan;" they had seen Selim and had drawn the obvious conclusions. At that, chairs were brought and set on the sidewalk for us, and we sat down gratefully; the men had called me "kardeş"—sister—and I now felt perfectly safe and at ease near them, although Islamic reserve did not permit them to speak to me directly.

Selim and Bahadir Bey presently returned and took us to one of the town's tiny hotels on the main street, the best which was available. There in a small cubicle which served as an office sat a profoundly unenlightened youth who managed to conduct us up to bare, primitive rooms, but, when asked for clean sheets, had no idea where they were kept, and when asked by Bahadir Bey, who was by now rather angry, for the manager, could not accommodate us in that article either. At length the manager was located and at Bahadir Bey's request replaced the grey, obviously much-used bottom sheets on the beds with clean ones (the top sheets being pinned to the quilts in the usual Turkish manner). Due to a wide-spread power failure there was no electricity in the town that night, and an oil lamp was hung up and lighted for us. As we were going out for supper, Selim asked the manager for the keys to the rooms. "No keys," he said, but he casually removed the door handle and presented it to Selim, who just as casually pocketed it instead of a key. Our things should be perfectly safe here—that is, unless it occurred to some thief to take an identical handle off one of the other doors and open ours with it!

Bahadir Bey took us to a nearby restaurant, and seeing that we were able to look after ourselves, left us to take care of business matters; we agreed to meet at the same place the next morning. After supper, we groped our way down the dark street and up the hotel stairs in the chilly night. Before sleeping I turned over in my mind the events of the day.

At last we had caught a glimpse of the real Turkey. My bitterness against the spoiled westernized Turkey which was almost all we had known so far had faded away in the goodness of what I had now experienced, and once again I knew that I had and would always have a deep love for this land. Today we had seen some of the good agricultural land of rural Anatolia, where men and women alike worked the soil. I considered the meaning of this soil to a peasant and the love which he must feel for it. Perhaps, I thought, the divorce of urban man from the land, from seasonal phenomena, from the natural products of the earth through which one realizes his total dependence on God and His all-encompassing power, is really the divorce of man from his very self, for man is intimately and inextricably tied up with the land and with natural forces; they are an inseparable part of him and he of them, and much of his inner life, his sense of relationship with God and with the universe comes from maintaining the deep ties with them.

Today I had realized that in the way of life of the people of rural Anatolia, close to the soil and to the products of their labor, there is a reality, a vitality and a goodness which makes the artificial westernization of cities like Ankara seem the more meaningless and intolerable, for it is not connected in any way with the indigenous culture of this land and has no significant internal development among its people. I had also realized that in its small-town and rural population lies much of Turkey's real strength; yet despite this fact, the unlettered villagers and townsfolk have little awareness of the issues and problems confronting their country and very little voice in the shaping of its affairs.

March 16: In the morning Bahadir Bey, who felt that we were his guests and who was very eager to make our trip enjoyable and interesting, told us what he had planned for today. We would go first to see the Roman amphitheatre at Aspendos some kilometers distant, afterwards to visit a famous waterfall at Manavgat, and finally to the village of Side where there were more ruins, from where Bahadir Bey would return to Antalya and we would spend the night.

Leaving our luggage with his associate, we entered a taxi and sped away into the lovely, peaceful green countryside, punctuated by cedars and wild flowers. It was the middle of spring here (the winters would be quite mild in any case), and there was a remarkably bright, vivid quality in the greenness which I had never seen anywhere else. The taxi turned from the highway onto a side road, where scattered ruins and peasant cottages stood grey against the bright verdure, entirely unspoiled by any commercial establishments. At the end of the road we came upon the vast Aspendos amphitheatre. Although externally plain and completely unimpressive, the mingling of its ancient grey-brown stone with this unbelievably beautiful Mediterranean springtime setting produced a remarkably lovely effect. Central Anatolia in winter had been endlessly drab and bleak, but now we were surrounded by currents of burgeoning life and color—how precious and welcome a sight! All the problems of Ankara and its life dropped away from me. They would come back in good time, I knew, but for now, for today, there was nothing but pure contentment in this surpassingly beautiful spot.

For the next hour or so, we clambered up and down that ancient structure, thinking of nothing in particular, our minds free, just taking in and trying to store up the scene in our minds with the help of our cameras, while the children climbed about and explored joyfully. The amphitheatre was built against a green hillside, and all over the hill and down the slope wild flowers bloomed in profusion. Nowhere else had I seen the scarlet or purple anemones with black centers edged in white, which, lovely beyond description, bloomed all over that green hill; shy children who lived nearby brought tiny nosegays of these sweet blooms to us, to Nura's great delight.

From the top of the amphitheatre we looked out across a broad valley: jagged mountains in the distance, fields and trees close at hand, crumbling ruins on one side of the amphitheatre, and on the slope below us, a small whitewashed peasant cottage beside which a woman stood churning butter in a goatskin suspended from poles. Delicate wild flowers and small plants grew among the crevices of the ancient stones forming the top of the amphitheatre's wall; Nura ran about with a small bouquet in her hands, joyously admiring the flowers she loved so dearly. I drank in, as one with an immense thirst, the moving beauty of the scene—the distant mountains, the endless brilliant green of spring near the warm sea, the bright flowers—which reached straight to the heart.

An unkempt boy had approached us earlier, intimating that he had antique Roman coins to sell, and he now reappeared. Jamal by now had a small interesting collection, although without value, and Selim was willing to buy the coins for him if the price were reasonable. When we asked Bahadir Bey about it, he said that he did not know what the proper price should be but that if we wanted we should buy. I hesitated. "Is it possible," I asked him, "that someone might be manufacturing these coins somewhere?"

"No, I don't think you should worry about that. The boy says they were dug out of his father's field, and they seem genuine enough," he replied. Selim dickered over the price and finally bought the five coins for 75 T.L., to the joy of Jamal who was highly elated at this grand addition to his collection.

But the taxi driver was waiting, and there were other places to visit and other things to do today. We returned to the little town, where we drank tea with Bahadir Bey's associate before collecting our luggage and continuing on our way. Everything was done in a very leisurely manner, as if we had the entire day to sit over tea, that sense of hurry and pressure which so often characterizes activities in America pleasantly and conspicuously lacking.

Presently we and our luggage were stowed in a *dolmuş* going to Manavgat, a town at some distance, where we would see one of Turkey's most celebrated waterfalls, the Manavgat Şelalesi. After depositing all the other passengers in Manavgat, the *dolmuş* driver agreed to take us to the waterfall, where we would have a picnic lunch, and he, Bahadir Bey and Selim went off to buy some food, returning presently with several packages of eatables.

The waterfall was on a side road outside the town, its entrance beside a teahouse; since it was very early in the season, we were the only visitors present. The grey-green water of a deep, rushing river descended in heavy sheets over a low, circular gorge, flowing swiftly away to the sea; a snow-capped mountain rose in the distance behind the river and trees with new, pale green leaves unfolded in the foreground, a lovely sight. Terraces had been built out into the river where the water was quiet, and here one might clamber about and find a small private land of one's own to inhabit for a while. Selim, always liking water, had his shoes and socks off in a moment and went exploring with his trousers rolled up, making *wudu* in the rushing water, and Bahadir Bey followed him; I sat on a rock while the children played about, absorbing the scene and the atmosphere in a state of utter happiness.

When it was time to eat, the packets of food were opened and spread on a rock, and the driver invited to share our repast. The fresh ripe tomatoes, Turkish bread and white cheese, followed by bananas and *baklava* and then tea, were indescribably delicious in that setting. The manager of the tea house then invited us to sit and watch the scenery from a platform overlooking the waterfall, where he had placed a table and chairs for our use in a typical Turkish gesture of hospitality. As we sat on the platform enjoying the wonderful sight of the rushing, foaming water with its majestic background, the children of various ages threw sticks into the current below, watching as they were whirled out to sea. These were timeless, precious moments, thanks be to God, an island of peace and absolute contentment in the midst of the cares of life. It was one of those times which come only very rarely in most of our lives, when all experiences tend toward inner harmony, when thought, emotion and sensory experience flow together in a single unblemished stream to produce that unalloyed sense of joy and peace which the heart always yearns to experience in its journey through this world. . .

At length it was time to go. We returned to the *dolmuş*, asking the driver to drop us at the village of Side, famous for its Greek and Roman ruins, which was only a few kilometers distant. Ruins of aqueducts and buildings rose on both sides of the road, set amidst the unbelievable greenness to form a picture of indescribable loveliness with its blending of ancient grey stone and the bright verdure of early spring near the sea. We passed a vast structure, the amphitheatre, with an archway spanning the road, and then reached the center of the village, a square around which were grouped a post office guraded by a bust of Atatürk, restaurants, discothéques and other businesses, and beyond, the blue, blue Mediterranean. Here we would stay tonight.

Bahadir Bey found rooms for us in a pleasant *pansiyon;* in its garden fruit trees bloomed and ripe yellow lemons hung down from heavily-laden branches. To my eyes it was too lovely to be real. And the sea was only a minute's walk away!

We went out at once, taking our cameras. Down a lane, past a wall, through a field, and then we were at the beach. It was covered with a curious sort of dry, grey seaweed which looked like wood shavings and with rocks having a strange spongy appearance. Three small fishing boats rode at anchor in a tiny bay nearby, and in the distance the roofs of houses and the minaret of the village mosque rose up toward the dull grey sky, pregnant with rain.

To me the sea sometimes brings a kind of pensiveness, a brooding sense of being alone within myself to ponder over the mysteries of God's creation, all that lies within the sea and beyond it, and the waves sweeping in an endless series since the beginning of the earth, connecting the land upon whose edge I stand with other lands at the far reaches of the globe; and the blue Mediterranean, breaking upon the coast of Turkey which I loved so much, next to a little village with grey ruins along the shore in the distance, evoked this mood like a spell. I left the others, wanting to be alone, and wandered slowly along the beach in the grip of this mood, watching the waves break in a high spray of white foam upon a pile of rocks in the sea. Is there something in the ocean itself, I wondered, some deep, unfathomable connection with the human consciousness, which draws a man toward it and makes him thus quiet and pensive? In His Book, God Most High says, "It is He Who has created man from water."* Has this water, then, in some subtle way which no one can grasp, an undercurrent of connection with each human soul. . . ?

Nura came running, in raptures over the few small shells she had found, and I returned abruptly to the world. Selim, Bahadir Bey and Maryam walked on an old wall of conglomerate rock, presumably from Greek or Roman times, which jutted into the sea and during high tide was covered by it. Jamal forged ahead down the beach toward the grey ruins which could be seen amidst profuse greenery in the near distance.

* *Al-Furqan* 25:54.

The rest of us followed him slowly 'down the beach to a promontory of land where green creepers had twined themselves over ancient battered grey stone walls. We were standing at the site of a Greek temple, perhaps, its marble columns fallen centuries ago and so much weathered as to have lost their shape, the flutings now smoothed over and their roundness melted away into a flat shapelessness as wind and weather had their way with them; Maryam pointed out a well-known frieze of Gorgon's heads which lay nearby at our feet. Around this point of land the sea washed, breaking on one spot so forcefully that the wind blew the fine spray upon us. A villager wearing a vizored cap walked slowly along, grazing a cow, oblivious to our presence.

Jamal wandered among the ruins of arches and out the other side, and we slowly followed along a path leading to the village; only a short time now remained before Bahadir Bey left us on his business, for he must reach Antalya by late afternoon. He asked directions to the amphitheatre, the major structure of historical interest, of various people along the way. By way of a reply, an elderly man joined our party and accompanied us up the hill, explaining what we were seeing for our benefit, although we could understand very little. Small, clean, picturesque houses, many with big fig trees and huge, tree-like cacti, lay along our way.

We soon reached the vast grey rock amphitheatre, very different in style from that at Aspendos, even in the texture of its rock. Where a stage had once been, a veritable forest of fallen, broken white marble columns lay strewn over the ground in a haphazard manner, as if tumbled about by some giant hand. The old man led us up, up, up to the top of the vast structure, past row after row of stone seats, telling us that an earthquake in the eighth century had toppled the columns. Selim rejoined by reciting in Arabic the Qur'anic verse, "Say: 'Travel through the earth and see what was the end of those before (you). Most of them worshipped others besides God,' "* and the old man nodded assent, understanding. Thus had the glory of those peoples vanished with all its pomp and power, and thus too would all the works in which contemporary man takes such pride be folded up one day.

* *Al-Room* 30:42.

Side had been occupied successively by Greeks, Romans and Byzantines, and had been the chief slave market of the Mediterranean area in Roman times. From the top of the amphitheatre we looked down over a museum and an extensive cluster of ruins which gave an indication of the size of this place during ancient times. The dark sea stretched behind us, the village nestled on a tiny bay touching it; the sky arched above us like a grey dome, rain imminent. I caught brief glimpses of Nura and Maryam on the other side of the vast amphitheatre, running in bright flashes of color among the grey-brown stone seats and a colonnaded passage which bisected the structure.

But Bahadir Bey's time was now up and he must return to Antalya. We climbed slowly down among the fallen remnants of another age, glimpsing Greek inscriptions cut into the grey-white grain of marble, and out onto the green land, dotted with bright flowers, as light rain began to fall. Bidding us farewell for the present, Bahadir Bey caught a ride with a car which was just leaving from the village square, and we were on our own for the next two days. The five of us sat by the square drinking tea, under shelter from the rain; when it began to pour down heavily, we ran back to the *pansiyon*. We were confined there by the downpour until night, when we ventured out for dinner in a restaurant by the square and returned in the pouring rain. Here too in Side there was no electricity and it was quite damp and chilly indoors.

This place was indeed a veritable Paradise on earth, with the blue sea and its beach, the coastal atmosphere, lovely vegetation, quaint houses and ruins. People here seemed on the whole softer and more gentle than in our part of Anatolia, where perhaps the bleak climate, topography and living conditions had affected the outlook of the countless generations reared on its soil; yet everywhere we had found people very kind and willing to be helpful, always and invariably without any thought of a return or even of thanks, for Turks do not consider effort or cost in showing hospitality or helpfulness, and there can never be any question of a material or monetary return of a kindness.

When, in the beginning, I had tried to return money spent on us by Enver or Aynur Alba—for example, a *dolmuş* or taxi fare— Enver would say reproachfully, "Marian Abla, now you're acting just like an American!'' and I came gradually to realize that spending for others without thinking about it is a basic part of friendship and hospitality in Turkey, as in other parts of the Muslim world, traits in which calculation or keeping accounts have no place. Later I was amused when, on a couple of occasions, we had tea somewhere with an American acquaintance, and he, American-style, had offered to repay Selim the 25 *kuruş,* mentioning the cost of that simple refreshment as if it had been an important matter. By now such manners had come to appear uncivilized, almost barbarous, to me. Here there was no price nor repayment for hospitality or for kindness, and money was not permitted to become the object of discussion among friends or even strangers in this land. I noted instance after instance of this sort of disinterested helpfulness on this trip whenever we had occasion to ask something or needed help of any kind, and it seemed to me one of the finest traits I had observed anywhere, having, like so many of the excellent and endearing qualities I had remarked among Turks, its origin in Islam and being common among Muslims of every kind.

March 17: During the night I heard rain pattering on and off, and when I awoke at dawn to pray it was very damp and chilly. I do not usually occupy myself with the state of the weather, but this time I prayed to God, Who has asked us to come to Him with all our needs no matter how small, for a fine day. Our time here was so short, and if it rained all during this precious day . . . ?

To our joy, the morning, after all, turned out clear and beautiful. As I looked out into the garden with its rich wet soil, blooming fruit trees and waxen-leaved citruses, at the bright sky with its fast-scudding clouds blowing along on the brisk south wind, I realized anew that the sense of peace and cosmic unity which man so often derives from contact with nature is one of the ways which the Beneficent God has provided to human beings to come close to Him. Indeed, the Holy Qur'an repeatedly exhorts man to ponder over God's creation, to try to understand the Creator and man's place in the universe through it. And what thoughtful person is there who, earnestly seeking to understand, would conclude after seriously studying this immense reservoir of knowledge, or after observing his own wonderfully-functioning body or the entire scheme of natural relationships, that there is not an All-Wise Power behind everything Who gives it purpose and meaning? As God says:

"Behold, in the creation of the heavens and the earth, and the alternation of night and day, there are indeed signs for men of understanding; men who celebrate the praises of God standing, sitting and lying on their sides, and contemplate the (wonders of) creation in the heavens and the earth (with the thought), 'Our Lord, not for nothing hast Thou created (all) this. Glory to Thee! Then save us from the penalty of the Fire (of Hell) .' "*

Another approach to God, I considered, has been through various forms of art. It is evident that the arts of man can serve either to lead him toward God or away from Him. One can perceive the truth of this statement very clearly by analyzing the music and graphic art which flowered in the West during the 'Age of Faith' and declined during the 'Age of Reason,' when it became excessively pre-occupied with material forms and the egos of its producers, utterly losing it spiritual emphasis, and now, during the Age of Materialism and Disbelief, has deteriorated beyond the point of recognition as art, serving merely as a mirror of man's inner disturbance, emptiness and lack of faith.

Indeed, to many people in the West, 'art' is regarded as a form of human activity beyond moral and spiritual considerations, yet having almost the flavor of a religion. At the same time, what to many people passes for 'religion' is often dominated by popular culture and 'art' instead of guiding it, and many of the expressions of what is considered 'religion' in America today have become the vehicle for expressing the average (or below average) man's way of thinking and feeling instead of raising him up toward a higher and nobler level. Thus, for example, we find many sincere contemporary Christians who, still holding to the belief that religion should set the standard rather than following the demands of the people, today are left confused and hurt, their spiritual needs unfulfilled and outraged by such bizarre phenomena as religious services set to 'rock' music in many churches, prayers and other religious expressions couched in contemporary slang ("Are you running with me, Jesus?"), and an increasing array of 'artistic' expressions of so-called religious feeling (such as the much-publicized musical work, "Jesus Christ, Superstar") in which the spiritual concept underlying religion and the dignity which has traditionally characterized expressions of religious feeling are totally subordinated to the so-called 'popular culture.'

* *Ale-Imran* 3:190-91.

In Islam neither the arts nor any other form of human endeavor can ever be divorced from its basic conceptions and values. Thus, the notion of 'art for art's sake' or art which is 'above' moral considerations is completely alien and meaningless. Among Muslims the function of the arts should be to reflect and support the belief system; otherwise they simply become an instrument for the destruction of Islamic values, the precursor of trends leading Muslims away from God, and toward the immense self-absorption and self-glorification which we see today among Western artists, whose productions are, in so many cases, a true reflection of their empty, self-engrossed lives, out of which nothing of spiritual depth or real meaningfulness can come. While in the past Islamic attitudes and feelings, as I have seen, produced the great, profound, devout art, architecture, music and poetry of the Muslim world, one of the many expressions of the totality of the Muslim's submission to God and his love for Him, today attitudes and art unregulated by Islamic values are producing in the contemporary Muslim world a mere blind imitation of Western art forms, including those grandiose depictions of national heroes which are idolized on public occasions and venerated as only God should be.

Finally, another way through which man has searched for and found nearness to God is through the guidance and insight of men of great devoutness and pure faith, whose hearts burned with an inner certainty beyond doubt or error, mirrored in their words and deeds. I am not referring here to the prophets, peace be on them all, who, appointed by God as His messengers to mankind, are entirely unique and apart from the rest of humanity, but to those righteous and devoted servants of God whose pure perception of the truth and whose living Islam has been instrumental in spreading Islam since early times. Anatolia has bred many such great Muslims, whose inner light has been a beacon drawing men to Islam since its beginning in this land. In our time these lights have become dim as the lessons taught by these noble men have become distorted and elements not from Islam have crept into their movements, as materialism and disbelief gain a treacherous foothold; yet there are still thousands of Muslims who follow the teachings and discipline imparted by one or another of these saintly men. It is one of the rallying points for Islam in Turkey even today, and please God, nothing will destroy it.

Although quite chilly indoors this morning, it was warmer outside, with a pleasant hearty breeze, and by now some of the rain which had fallen during the night had dried up. After having breakfast we went back to the beach, the children running joyfully through the lane in front of me, swept along by the wind. It drove the waves up on the sand, the foamy breakers leaping higher than usual. Now the fallen wall on which we had walked the previous afternoon was lashed by waves, the high foam breaking upon it. I walked along the beach filled with that same strange sense of peace and inwardness, looking for shells and finding many pieces of stalactite rocks with crystalline formations and, to my delight, a small sponge.

But time was running out. We had enquired earlier about transportation to Manavgat, from where we would get a *dolmuş* to Alanya, the next city east down the coast where we would spend the day and night, and we must hurry now. Reluctantly we turned back from the sea, collected our luggage, and presently took our seats in a three-wheeled mini-*dolmuş* going to Manavgat. In my heart I bade farewell to one of the loveliest of all the lovely places I have ever seen, watching the bright verdure and grey ruins recede into the distance behind us. I wondered sadly what time and the tourist trade, that insidious vehicle for introduction of alien manners and habits, would do to create another kind of ruin in this fair spot,[*] and whether we would ever see it again. How beautiful a thing it would be to come here, I thought, if God spares us, when Selim and I are elderly and can no longer participate in the affairs of the world, and buy a small, modest house, to live out our last days here among the ruins and greenery, the sound of the waves a lullaby at night and the sight of the blue water the constant delight of our eyes as we watch weathers come and go across the sea—days of calm, days of storm. I knew within myself that this dream of Paradise on earth could never be realized for me, and that I left a part of myself behind in Side forever . . .

[*] A note in the "New York Times Review" dated June 29, 1971, reads: "Introduction of electricity, movie theaters and seaside 'Diskotek' brings problems of modern inconveniences to ancient town of Side."

At Manavgat we took our seats on a mini-bus *dolmuş* bound for Alanya, sixty kilometers distant, almost at once, Selim and I in front and the children in back. Half-empty when we left, the *dolmuş* was presently so full that there was no space to possibly squeeze another human being; in all there were nineteen passengers, five more than there was seating space for, and I prayed that nothing would happen due to this reckless overloading. There was much quiet curiosity concerning the foreign travelers among our fellow-passengers; some of them plied Maryam and Nura with questions concerning our place of residence and nationality, but none of them addressed us directly.

Much of the road led along the beautiful coast, past sandy beaches where the blue water danced and foamed, unmarred by any commercial establishments, past hills and sand dunes and banana plantations, past road cuts exposing more of the stalactitic rock. At last we neared Alanya, a town of twelve thousand population which is approached from the west side around a big hill jutting into the sea. On the eastern side of the hill castle ramparts going up to the very top, an ancient red stone tower with battlements standing next to the sea, and a mosque with a single minaret near the top of the hill, were visible; houses were built nearly all the way to the top within the outer citadel walls, a very picturesque and lovely sight. On one side of the town were limestone hills covered with greenery, on the other the sea.

We were shortly installed in a pleasant hotel and spent the next hour or so by the sea; the children and Selim waded in the gentle surf while I looked for shells. After lunch at a nearby restaurant, we decided to go up the hill to see the castle, and a taxi was called. Its pleasant, well-groomed driver was one of that increasingly rare breed of Turkish chauffeurs who are courteous, gentlemanly, intelligent and informed, and with whom it is a pleasure to ride. He talked to us continuously on the way up the hill under the impression that we understood Turkish far better than we did, while we made such replies as our limited linguistic skills would allow.

The *kale*—castle—of Alanya had been constructed by Seljuks in the thirteenth century at the top of its hill, which commanded a sweeping view of the sea, on the remains of a much earlier Roman structure. The road leading up to it was rough and bumpy, but our driver took it with as much dash as if it had been a modern highway. Houses clung to the hillside all the way up and people trudged along the rocky road, which grew increasingly steep, winding and narrow, affording a spectacular view of the town below us set on a curving bay with the blue sea at its edge. The ancient ramparts of the castle zigzagged all the way up the hillside; we passed weathered gates and finally reached the top, where we paid admission, the driver accompanying us inside as our guide.

Exquisite pale blue wild iris bloomed here and there among the grass forming the floor of the castle. Little was to be seen here except crumbling grey stone walls and ramparts, and the remains of an old church, a trace of whose faded frescoes was still visible in its interior. There was no remnant of any dwelling of ancient or more recent times on this wind-swept hilltop, exposed on every side to the weather in all seasons, but while there was little to be seen of the castle itself, the view on every side was spectacular.

The southern rampart overlooked an almost vertical cliff, a very beautiful vista but quite frightening; here the cliff was so steep that I sat down to photograph it, afraid I might lose my balance and fall if I stood, concentrating on the camera, to take the picture. Below the cliff, the water was an unbelievably deep, translucent blue, a color such as the artisans of the Isfahan mosques might well have taken as the inspiration for their glowing turquoises.

At the wall overlooking the west side of the mountain, a rough ladder led up to the ramparts from the ground. Mounting on them, to our right we saw a small village situated perhaps a third of the way down the mountain, in the midst of which stood the mosque which we had seen from the town. Immediately below us lay a sheer cliff, and beyond that the bay sloping to the west and a vast blue expanse of sea. I had never seen anything like the clear, vibrant color of that water and, wanting to capture its vividness, was very busy with the camera.

When we turned to come down from the wall, a group of cheerful-looking girls clad in the bright garb of villagers, with kerchiefs

on their heads, stood before us; each of them held an assortment of
long rectangular silk scarves in lovely soft colors which they were
selling. As I came down the ladder, they all turned toward me,
showing their handiwork. I began to talk in my elementary Turkish.

Me: *Esselâmün aleyküm, kardeşlerim. Nasılsınız? (Assalamu
alaikum,* my sisters. How are you?)
They: *Ve aleyküm selâm. (Wa alaikum salaam.)*

Perhaps it will seem rather strange to reproduce here this simple
exchange of greetings, but to me it was very meaningful. The expression *"Esselâmün aleyküm"* was, among the Turks who love Islam, a kind of magic key to communication (although in Ankara
and other westernized places it was considered backward and reactionary by many people), almost a password, opening the door to
understanding and acceptance among them with one stroke, and after this we could continue our dialogue. No problem of being a
non-Turk or foreigner; I was one of them, a *Müslüman kardeş.*

The beautiful silk scarves were thrust into my hands, some in
solid colors, some striped. I did not really need a scarf, but for their
sake I could not refuse. So . . .

Me: *Çok, çok güzel. Ama pahalı. Bir tane istiyorum, param az.*
(Very, very pretty. But expensive. I want only one as I don't have
much money.)

In spite of this exceedingly primitive Turkish they understood
me easily, and each girl naturally wanted one of *her* scarves to be
the one which was selected. One of the group was a little more as-
sertive and the colors of her scarves simply melting; so I selected a
lovely one of hers with stripes of white, lavender, pink and pale
green.

Me: *Kim yaptı?* (Who made them?)
They: *Biz.* (We.)
Me: *Aferin, çok güzel yaptınız. Çok teşekkür ederim.* (Bravo,
you made them very nicely. Thank you very much.)

I knew I would always treasure my new scarf for their sake. Selim paid the money, and then I asked the girls if I could take their photograph. When two of them hesitated I reassured them, saying, *"Ben de Müslümanüm"* (I'm a Muslim too—like you, and you can trust me with your picture); the driver chided them and pushed them among the others for a group photograph. I thanked them heartily and said goodbye; a few minutes later I saw them walking toward the gate, and we waved at each other from the distance in passing.

As we left the castle, another group of tourists had entered the gate, and the girls with their scarves now stood quietly near the entrance, waiting for an opportune moment to approach them. I exchanged greetings with two or three village women who also offered handiwork for sale; when I said I had already bought, they did not insist. One of the women, with a very sincere look, came to the taxi to bid us goodbye. As we were leaving I said to her, *"Bu en güzel bir yer, maşallah!"* (This is the most beautiful place, *masha'Allah!*).

"Yine buyrunuz!" (Come again!), she said heartily, smiling and showing gold teeth, and I thought that I would never forget that woman and her sincerity at that ancient mountain-top castle.

Those who read these lines may well wonder—as I did myself— how anyone could feel so happy at a few simple, commonplace words or greetings exchanged with strangers and why they had so much meaning for me. And I asked myself, Am I so much in need of acceptance and approval that the merest casual word from a passer-by can give me so much satisfaction? Have I over-reacted to or romanticized these simple chance encounters which were after all of a very limited nature? As I pondered over these questions, I finally came to realize that in the answer to them lay the key to all I had come to feel for Turkey during these months.

These are surely questions which could easily occur to someone who had lived all her life in a society where the majority of human contacts have very little personal significance, where a few polite phrases exchanged with a stranger or in a business relationship pass as meaningless and unnoticed formulae. All these years I had been used to American-style casual relationships, in which personal services might be rendered and many words exchanged without anything being said which carried genuine feeling, without a real human-level encounter; yet here, under these circumstances, simple words which seemed ordinary enough were precious, and brief meetings and conversations with individuals for whom I could feel a sense of fellowship became dear in my eyes, for there was an unmistakable genuineness and sincerity in the faces and in the way the words were spoken which reached from heart to heart. Although I was a foreigner, a stranger, one whose poor, childlike Turkish hardly admitted of conversation, nevertheless I felt this sense of relatedness, of being at home among them in spite of it. And this was not only because, with their earnest friendliness, they appreciated the fact that I had taken the trouble to learn a little of their language, but more importantly because they and I were both Muslims. We might come from different countries, cultures, backgrounds and social levels; but the primary identification between us was common, and it forged a strong, sure bond of sisterhood between us which made our tiny momentary communication meaningful, which made their sincere words and looks precious in my eyes.

And this is the effect which Turkey had on me—on all of us—ultimately. Aspects of life and of human relationships which up to then had been casual and without significance were transformed into something profoundly meaningful, something worthwhile and valued, and a certain softening and mellowing came to me with all this which I now realized was among the most valuable lessons Turkey had taught me. The Islamic elements of the environment— the consciousness of God and obedience to Him which is a tangible quality among Turkish Muslims, the mosques with their *adhans* and devout atmosphere, the sense of being a part of Islamic history in this land, and the Islamic habits and manners so evident among the people—all these contributed to this softening, this receptiveness to deep spiritual and human influences.

And now the softness of speech, the thoughtful, courteous manner which I had noted from the beginning among many Turks were no longer something which I imitated; they had become part of me, the way I felt within myself, as I learned over a period of several months to respond more readily with sincerity and warmth to sincerity and warmth in others. I did not realize it at the time, but I had been learning a new sense of values, one in which the spiritual dimension was becoming more deeply a part of my life and in which human relationships were becoming increasingly meaningful, permeated by this quality of warmth and sincerity. Time too had a different value. One did not need to be busy every moment of the day 'doing' something. Here there was time just to *be,* to sit and think without the necessity of being occupied with anything else, and time never hung heavy on my hands nor did I wish for its quick passing as long as I was in such an atmosphere.

Yet at the same time as these new ways of feeling and responding were becoming established within me and more and more precious to me, I knew that I must soon leave all this behind and return to the old American way of life, with its empty, superficial interaction and relationships. And it was largely because I valued these newly-learned patterns so greatly and realized that they were something which Muslim Turkey had given me which could not, would not, stay with me in the spiritually empty, harder, more business-like society of the United States, that I came to dread so greatly our return to the world of the West. There this deep inwardness, this continual contact with the things of the spirit, this sense of the meaningfulness of human relationships, this deep sincerity and quickness to sense sincerity in others, this profound courtesy and softness of manner, had been virtually lost, and I knew that I too would almost certainly lose it when I left Turkey; for one almost *had* to lose it merely to survive in a world which was so hard and so business-like. Little by little I had come more and more to love and value these qualities which I saw among so many Turks and to regard them as the living expression of Islam, inseparable from the unique life and soul of the people and this land, taking concrete form in their relationships with other individuals and very much inherent in the loving and pious idioms of their language. Turkish is a very warm and sweet tongue, full of expressions reflecting reliance on God, compassion, concern and kindliness. Even in today's impoverished Turkish, there are dozens of expressions, most of them having a counterpart in Arabic and consisting largely of 'Arabic' words, for expressing this dependence on God and this sense of compassion and fellow-feeling for others, many of which I have already mentioned. Some others are:

Allaha ısmarladık - God go with you, i.e., goodbye.

Ellinize saḡlık - Health to your hands (which prepared the food or did the work), said by guests to the woman of the house.

Kusura bakmayın - Please don't look at my faults (forgive any mistakes I may have made).

Afiyet olsun - May you be healthy (said when someone expresses appreciation for food).

Allah'a emanet olsun - May God protect you.

Allah kabul etsin - May God accept (your prayers or deeds).

Allah rahatlık versin - May God give you comfort, i.e., goodnight.

Allah bereket versin - May God give you abundance.

Allah razı olsun - May God be pleased with you (for the good thing you have done).

How I have loved this language, with these beautiful, heartfelt expressions of reliance upon God and of deep human goodness. I pray that I will not lose it when we leave Turkey and that there may yet be many occasions to remember and to use it in the future. For suddenly now, on our own without any English-speaking interpreter, all of us had begun to regain our Turkish quite rapidly. The extreme awkwardness I had felt in Ankara about being able to communicate, making me almost ashamed to face the old friends who loved us sincerely after the past several months of hard work on both our parts to establish communication, had now begun to diminish noticeably. And even more importantly, with these travels in Anatolia, the fierce anger I had felt against Turkey and Turks, which had been coupled with this sense of shame at being unable to communicate, had also eased away, *Alhamdulillah.* I had seen the real Turkey at last, and although it could by no stretch of the imagination be called really Islamic, nonetheless I now knew with renewed certainty that Islam was still dearly cherished and a very vital force among many of its people, and that all that was best among them had its origin in Islamic habits and traditions. Now the effect of the ability to communicate once again and the fading away of my bitterness restored to me the very real joy which I had felt previously about my ability to communicate in Turkish, and now I valued that joy, too!

We stopped briefly at the little village part way down the mountain to see the small square Seljuk mosque, with its almost severely plain red brick minaret and ancient Kufic inscriptions carved on the heavy wooden shutters of the windows. The driver continued to talk to us. When he began to discuss the problem of communism in Turkey, we laughed and said that we knew all about it. Selim then told him that he is a student at M.E.T.U., at which the driver whistled under his breath and exclaimed in sympathy. He reported that during our absence from Ankara, Deniz Gezmiş, the ring-leader of the Dev-Genç kidnapping gang, had at last been captured—very happy news to us, naturally.

In the evening we walked through the darkening back streets of the pleasant little seaside town, looking in antique shop windows and then having our dinner in a hotel. As we returned to the *pansiyon* in the dark near the sea, the movingly solemn strains of the day's last *adhan* called Muslims to the remembrance of God Most High from nearby mosques, and I knew that I left another part of my heart here in Alanya, as in Side and Aspendos, forever . . .

March 18: We had booked seats on a bus leaving at midmorning for Antalya, where we would rejoin Bahadir Bey. Before the bus left, we strolled through the same streets where we had walked the previous evening, returning to browse in one of the antique shops. While we were there, a villager came in to show an old coin he had found, for which the proprietor offered him 50 *kuruş*— half a *lira.* When Jamal showed him the antique coins we had bought at Aspendos for 75 T.L., the proprietor gave the merest cursory glance and said, without considering the matter further, that they were counterfeits. We were extremely taken aback at this, but when he held out to us some real ancient coins encrusted with clay and streaked with copper oxide, we were able to realize at once how gullible we had been in mistaking these round, polished, clean coins with clear impressions for ones which had been buried in the earth for hundreds of years. I recalled having asked Bahadir Bey whether it was possible that the coins were being manufactured locally for unsuspecting tourists and his rather emphatic denial, and felt relieved that it was not only foreigners who could be thus deluded. As we exchanged glances, Selim cautioned the children never to reveal to Bahadir Bey how he and we had thus been taken in and cheated.

Within half-an-hour we were on the bus, returning to Antalya by the same route by which we had come—past the stretches of sandy beach and blue sea, the road going off to Side with a glimpse of its grey ruins, and the deep, dark green of the countryside around Aspendos. We found rooms in a pleasant hotel, had our lunch and took a long rest, all of us tired from traveling. In the late afternoon we went for a walk which took us through a part of the commercial district of the town to a spot overlooking the sea. Three or four ships rode at anchor in a small bay; tall apartment buildings rose behind them, and in the distance the spectacular jagged peaks of the Toros range which we had seen on our first arrival appeared to rise abruptly out of the sea, snow-covered near the top and wreathed in clouds, a scene of breath-taking beauty. We remained there until day drew to a close. Darkness came down on the peaks and water very quietly. For a few minutes there was a wonderful spectacle of grey clouds and grey water mingling, the last golden rays of the sun piercing the clouds and the lights of a ship glimmering on the shadowy darkening sea . . .

March 19: Selim telephoned Bahadir Bey at his relative's office this morning and presently the two men came to the hotel to fetch us. We would first go with Bahadir Bey to see some old parts of the city, and then the men and Jamal would go to *Jum'a* prayer; later his relative, Erol Bey, would take us to lunch and then for more sight-seeing. I marveled at his courtesy. We had not come as his guests nor even as Bahadir Bey's but merely as tourists who were traveling with Bahadir Bey; nonetheless, with typical Turkish hospitality, he felt that we were in some sense his guests also and that he had obligations toward us.

While the morning had been chilly, now as we set out on our excursion with Bahadir Bey it was warming up, the first really clear, bright day of the trip. After some walking, we reached one of the ancient Roman walls of the city, passing through the arched Hadrian's Gate with its well-preserved decorative details into one of the town's old sections. It had that indescribable charm so typical of old Turkish neighborhoods, with its picturesque asymmetrical two-storied houses, some of them painted bright blue, and ruins from various times. And then suddenly as we came out of the narrow streets, we were greeted by a wonderful view of the shimmering unbelievably blue sea, with the ship in the foreground and a backdrop of grey, snow-capped mountains, a glorious sight indeed. I was thankful for the sun at last, for what had one seen of the Mediterranean coast if he had not seen it on such a bright, golden day as this? And what a sun! The clothing in which we had been cool earlier in the day now suddenly seemed much too heavy.

We reached the confines of a pleasant park and stood by a parapet overlooking the sea, drinking in the surpassing beauty of that scene. But it would not do! We were not people, any of us, to be satisfied with standing there and looking on; we wanted to be going somewhere, down to the sea itself! And surely enough, a tiny path led along the cliff and down to the water. Among the stalactite rock, the springtime vegetation flourished profusely, a brilliant and lovely green interspersed with delicate wild flowers. The path was extremely steep and rugged. Selim, being more agile than the rest of us, reached the bottom of the trail first, climbing on rocks in the water; Jamal was close behind him, and he and Bahadir Bey took off their shoes and socks and went exploring. The girls followed more slowly, and I came last, filling my pockets with snail shells and bits of rock, and trying to capture some of the lovely flowers and the unbelievable color of the sea with my camera.

Huge chunks of stalactitic rock with beautiful crystalline formations exposed here and there lay at the bottom of the cliff, half-in, half-out of the shallow, clear water. I had never seen such rocks elsewhere, and it seemed that much or perhaps all of the Mediterranean coast of Turkey was made up of them. The color of that water was oh! such a brilliant, translucent, vibrant, melting blue that I only wanted to store it up in my heart and carry it away with me; glints of sunshine quivered in shining pools among the rocks of the tiny cove which was ours, for that moment, in all its loveliness. All along the coast as far as we could see there was no sign of a beach, only cliffs—but then, what need for a beach when one could go right down to the water among such magnificent cliffs as these?

(As I sit at my typewriter in the United States with my diary, remembering, I think of that shimmering sea of most brilliant blue. It still dances and gleams in the sunshine before the rocky cliffs of Antalya. The castle in Alanya is still there without change, windswept throughout the endless cycle of days and nights with the villagers who are a part of its life. At my Side, the unending waves lap at the shore and atom by atom reduce further the point of land on which once a Greek temple stood and the projecting rocks at its shore. The world goes on turning and day follows night and night follows day without alteration, all held in the beneficent keeping of Him Who created and sustains it all, until the time shall come when days and nights shall have their end.

(The forces of nature continue to move men and nations and to shape the surface of the globe, the stage for the small drama of mankind. Human beings are born, after nine months of gestation and the pangs of birth, each one of them reaching this world through the same insignificant and humble origins and by the same laborious process. They live out their tiny course on the surface of the globe, attain consciousness and a sense of identity, do at most a very few acts for which they may be remembered for a moment in the span of time, and then pass on and return to their Source and their Origin, God Most High.

(We are like specks of dust blown across the face of the universe, less than that even. We come, naked and alone, helpless and utterly dependent, and we leave this life, taking with us nothing more than what we brought, with no mementoes of our passage except our own deeds. Then what is man, that he should have such an overweening pride in himself and in the glory of his accomplishments; for no man makes himself nor gives himself the power to do the smallest thing, even to the lifting of his finger or the beating of his heart. None of this will go with any man to his grave, where he will be alone and will, alone, have to give an accounting of his deeds to the One Who gave him the capacity to choose between good and evil. May God Most High guide me to live the short and quickly-passing span of life which remains to me so that I may leave behind nothing which has harmed any of His creatures, and so that my accounting before Him may be light . . .)

We lingered at the bottom of the cliff for a while, marveling at the surpassing beauty of the day and place, and at length clambered back, hoping, if it please God, to return one day to that unforgettably lovely scene. At the top of the hill we re-entered the well-kept, pleasant park and walked back toward the center of the town, but in my heart I felt sorry to come back to 'civilization.' Although Antalya was a small, conservative town compared with Ankara, the signs of westerninzing influences were present and disheartening nonetheless; and it is a characteristic of medium-sized Turkish towns, as well as of the big cities, that a large proportion of the population which is not distinctly westernized is not Islamic in aspect either, but is characterized by a drab, monotonous nondescriptness which defies any type of classification.

A fluted Seljuk minaret of red brick stood opposite an old mosque with a clock tower at the intersection of the main streets of the city, forming a wonderful scene with the sea and snow-capped peaks in the background. It was now time for the *Jum'a* prayer, and Selim, Bahadir Bey and Jamal would go to the mosque; in the meantime the girls and I would go to the archaeological museum nearby where the men would meet us after the prayer. However, when we reached the museum I found to my dismay that it was closed for lunch. What was I to do with the two little girls for the next one hour or more? After walking about among the now-closed shops to pass time, I decided that we would explore the old section of town below the mosque and museum, which evidently led down to the sea, an area full of ruins, arches, broken walls and the picturesque, asymmetrical old houses which one sees in the old sections of all Turkish towns, which I always found somehow lovely and full of a unique charm peculiarly their own.

I was conscious that we made an odd picture walking along in that quiet, out-of-the-way old corner of the town, two young girls and a woman who was obviously foreign but wore a Muslim type of dress. We greeted each of the several women we passed standing by the doors of their houses or walking in the street with *"Esselâmün aleyküm;"* they glanced at us, wondering what breed of people we might be, and returned my greeting, and one of them told us, *"Hoş geldiniz."* I asked directions to the sea of one of the women and followed her instructions, enjoying the atmosphere of age and serenity of the staid, picturesque old houses, which had seen many a birth and death in their time.

At the bottom of the hill we came to a small harbor where a few small ships were moored; trucks went in and out and men loitered about. I would have enjoyed sitting there and watching the activity, but it was no place for women. We returned by the way we had come, greeting the women we passed in those pleasant, shaded old streets. On one side, above a cliff and ruins of walls covered with green creepers, I could just see the tip of the Seljuk minaret and its neighbor, the minaret of the nearby Osmanlı mosque where the men had gone for prayer, nodding at each other, as it were, with a white flowering fruit tree in the foreground forming the link between them. It was a lovely sight, one which spoke volumes in its simple way of the continuity of Islamic civilization in Turkey throughout the centuries. As I exchanged greetings with a group of şalvar-clad women who stood by their doorsteps chatting, I heard one of them comment as we passed by, *"Turk galiba"* (She is probably a Turk), and felt very happy.

After the prayer we rejoined Bahadir Bey's relative, Erol Bey, who was devoting the afternoon to our entertainment, first by taking us for an excellent lunch at a pleasant restaurant, then to a beautiful recreation site outside the city where a man-made waterfall had been ingeniously constructed, and finally to tea at his apartment, where we met his wife, a pleasant, modern young matron. Erol Bey's kindness was entirely unexpected and unmerited, for we

were nothing to him; but kindness and hospitality were so customary everywhere in Turkey that perhaps to him it was nothing out
of the ordinary.

We had thus far seen none of the Antalya beaches, which, it
turned out, did after all exist, and we now drove out in the direction of the jagged Toros range. Here, indeed, was a beach. On one
stretch of it had been erected hundreds of small, plain square
wooden cabins for the occupancy of summer visitors, each numbered and identical except for variations in color; as they were built
in three parallel rows with fronts facing the sea, they presented a
very depressing appearance, destroying the serene beauty of the
scene with their monotonous uniformity. When Bahadir Bey pointed
out that, because of the existence of such inexpensive facilities,
Turks who could not afford better accommodations were able to
enjoy the sea in summer, I imagined how the beach looked covered
with bikini-clad bathers not having the remotest semblance of privacy from one another, and thought silently that Turks would surely have been much better off without such facilities. As for the
beach itself, it was quite ordinary; however, instead of sand it was
covered with small symmetrical pebbles as smooth as silk which delighted Nura, and we collected pocketfuls of the best specimens we
could find to take home with us, commenting on the varied beauties
of God's wondrous creation.

The two men then returned us to our hotel; we would leave
early the next morning by bus for Isparta and Cemile's home, while
Bahadir Bey would not return to Ankara until some days later. We
bade them goodbye, with warm thanks for all their kindness, had
our supper and returned to the hotel, very tired, to pray and sleep.

CHAPTER 16

A NEW LOVE

March 30: At dawn I heard, as in a kind of dream, the most beautiful chorus of *adhans* coming from the mosques of Antalya, like several strands of pure melody interwoven into a single strain, harmonized without any effort at creating a harmony between them. We prayed *Fajr,* readied ourselves for the journey, and were on the bus a short while later.

We left the city by the same route by which we had come. Now farewell to the beautiful Mediterranean coast which we had loved so much; up the winding, serpentine road, leaving behind the stalactitic rocks, the olive trees, the lovely warm coastal greenery, and the bluest of all blue seas, into an area of blossoming fruit trees, still beautiful, with mountains, often snow-capped, in the distance. Somewhere the road branched off to Isparta, and we reached the center of the town by half-past ten.

Cemile was to have come from Ankara the previous day, and as it had been impossible to know exactly when we would be arriving, we had agreed to go straight to her house by taxi. We had no clear idea of what to expect from her family, for she had not talked very much about its members to us. Her father, we knew, was a high school teacher, and there was her mother and a younger sister who was married; as was common in Turkey, the parents, alone now that Cemile spent most of the year in Ankara, shared the same house with the young couple. I somehow expected them to be religious in a stiff, dogmatic way, or perhaps—another possibility—

in the usual semi-traditional Turkish manner, without real understanding of Islam. Well, we would soon see.

The central part of Isparta was crowded and not very noteworthy in any respect. A taxi took us to a quiet residential area where the apartment houses were considerably smaller than is the rule in Ankara, stopping at the address Cemile had given us in front of an elderly building. A second floor window over-looking the street flew open and Cemile's face appeared. With a flash of a smile and wave of her hand she vanished and was at the street in a moment, hugging the girls and me tight, saying with a hearty *"Hoş geldiniz"* to Selim and Jamal, and conducting us into the house with our baggage in flurry of joy.

Two men—one tall and middle-aged, with greying blondish hair, her father, and a younger one, his son-in-law Lûtfi, who worked for an engineering firm—came out to receive us, embracing Selim and Jamal affectionately; they had both taken leave from work this morning in honor of our visit. They were followed by her mother, a slender woman wearing a snowy white muslin kerchief on her head, who embraced the children and me with ineffable tenderness. As she took my face between her hands, saying words of endearment and kissing me again and again, I looked back into a countenance whose beauty, serenity and inner light were not dimmed in the least by the effect of years of hard work and struggle, and I loved her at once, feeling that she must be someone very precious and good. And then her daughter Fatma! As soon as we entered the simple, immaculately clean apartment, a sweet-faced young woman of about twenty-two, wearing a silk scarf, came forward to greet us. She welcomed me as heartily as if I were an old friend whom she had not seen for years, winding me in her arms, and took the children to her heart from the first moment, loving them and commenting over and over how dear and good they were, and the children, from the beginning, returned her love just as warmly.

There was no need for anything else. We were all completely at home here at once, feeling that we had come into a unique and wonderful household, wanting to know each member of the family well and to understand the secret of its immediately-perceptible special quality.

We were made comfortable, and glasses of tea were brought and refilled as we sat down amid many interested enquiries about our trip, Cemile translating. Presently the men and Jamal went to a nearby mosque for *Dhuhr* prayer while we women prayed at home. When they returned we sat down to lunch in the pleasant dining room, getting further acquainted. Afterwards we went for a walk with Cemile, Lûtfî and Amca Bey, as we were to call Cemile's father, seeing a section of the town and returning at the time of *'Asr* prayer, which the men prayed in the mosque. Later we sat around the dining table talking together through the interpretation of Cemile over glasses of sweet, strong tea.

It had by now become unmistakably clear that a common belief, a similar way of thinking, a kindred pattern of life brought together and motivated all of us, although we came from the opposite ends of the earth. Each member of the family was deeply religious and had that mature, true understanding of Islam which is possible only to those who also have deep knowledge, living their Islam, valuing it above everything else, and searching for ways to bring its light to others. We talked about the situation of Islam in Turkey, exchanging comments and observations. At the same time, they were also very much interested in knowing more about the situation in Pakistan, the activities and problems of Muslims in America, and our life in the United States. Amca Bey was altogether so keen and alive mentally that we were delighted, while Lûtfî spoke little but appeared to be thinking deeply about what was said, and Fatma and her mother took part in the conversation with interest as they were able during the cooking of supper. As far as possible we tried to speak in our limited Turkish, but as the subjects we were discussing were highly complex, most of the time we had to resort to our translator, who took obvious pleasure in bringing our thoughts together, putting in ideas of her own as well from time to time.

After supper, a delicious, hearty meal at which the two sisters waited on us solicitously and lovingly, and *Maghrib* prayer, two colleagues of Amca Bey's came to visit. The men sat together in the drawing room, which was closed off by doors from the rest of the house with a separate entrance of its own, and the children and I sat with Cemile, Fatma and their mother in the dining room talking about matters of common interest. The sisters took tea and refreshments to the door of the drawing room, which was used only when visitors came, but did not go in, handing the tray to Lutfi or to their father, not associating with men they did not know but admitting into the sanctuary of their home only those who were well-known and trusted. It was a deep honor for us to have come among them not as strangers but as familiar, cherished friends, for they had heard so much about us from Cemile that it was as if we were old acquaintances. Beloved Cemile! She had become so close and so dear to us as the weeks and months passed; she loved each of the children so well, spent much time playing or talking to them when she visited us, and Selim was like her own older brother. As for the two of us, we had become like real sisters through our common belief and commitment, the many ways of thinking and feeling we shared, and the deep love we felt for one another. Now at last we were in her home and she was sharing with us everything that was most precious in her life, and I believe—as she said— that these were among the happiest days of her life.

A great joy in being with this family, a part of its life for this brief time, and a great love for them all, grew up within me. The two sisters were so lovely, so completely pure in their looks, manner and behavior, and the mother, although work-worn, had the most beautiful serene face I had ever seen, a 'nurlu' face—full of light—as Turks often say. I had never seen people so deeply, tenderly loving and sincere, with such a glowing warmth and goodness. Although I struggled to communicate all I was feeling in my poor child-like Turkish, it had never seemed so inadequate; for the things I wanted to say here were not the ordinary, everyday matters for which I had a sufficient vocabulary but deep things which went straight from heart to heart.

We prayed 'Isha and sat up after the visitors left until quite late, talking about matters of mutual concern, feeling the deep and total commitment to Islam which ruled this household. At length when it was time to sleep, the whole house was re-arranged for our comfort as the family gave the best of everything to us without any thought of themselves. Fatma and Cemile eagerly took care of our needs, delighting in doing everything for us and every little while coming to embrace the girls or me. O loving hearts, so soon to be parted, savor every moment of these few precious hours together, and give your treasures, to be cherished and remembered always, while you may, into each others' keeping . . .

Before I slept I thought over what I had seen today. There was a kind of wonder in my heart and a great contentment as I thought of this family; I had never been in a household like it and tried to understand the reasons for its uniqueness. It took me many days and long conversations with Cemile, who did not seem to realize that her family was different or special in any way (indeed, she said she knew many other families like her own), to grasp the whole of it.

What was evident first was that there was no disparity between what they professed and what they practiced; for them belief and action were neither separated nor separable. This imparted an atmosphere of great integrity to their way of life such as I had not seen in any other family, and it was not a matter only for the men or only for the women; no, all of them had this same quality. One expression of it was the immaculate cleanliness, order and simplicity of their house and persons. There was no pretension or ostentation, nothing showy or luxurious, no excess of things or clutter, but whatever was needed was provided and was valued, cared for and kept as nicely as possible. The small things of daily life made up the greater part of the world of the mother and Fatma, who, although young and beautiful, was not spoiled by too many things or the desire for thing. I was struck by the quiet industriousness of the mother and daughter, for they were extremely hard-working, knowing all the skills necessary and desirable for women, including sewing, knitting, crocheting and embroidery, which they did with obvious capability and enjoyment. It was at once their duty and pleasure to care for the needs of the men who were so precious to them, and they in turn were equally cherished and valued by the men.

I had also noted that everyone was very scrupulous about the observance of prayer, getting ready for it deliberately and carefully as soon as the *adhan* was heard as if it were something special and enjoyable, and not being rushed by other business so that there was no time to do it properly. The obvious love of knowledge and interest in learning which prevailed among them were also very noticeable. Each member of the family was educated to the level his or her temperament and interests required, each was very well-informed and articulate, had clear understanding of current issues, enjoyed reading, and was obviously used to discussing all matters among themselves. There were many books in the house, especially on Islamic subjects, each one treasured and cherished, and in the many questions which Amca Bey had asked, I detected an alertness and intellectual vigor which is found in few people, the desire to grasp the very essence of a topic and to get at the fundamentals of relationships and events. Each member of the family could also read and write Arabic. Cemile said that her parents had taught her when she was a young child; hence she and the rest of the family could read the Qur'an in Arabic and could also read Ottoman Turkish, something uncommon among younger Turks.

This was indeed no ordinary family; its entire way of life represented the translation into concrete form of the clear, pure, true understanding of Islam of each of its members. As I tried to grasp all the elements which made it so unique, I realized that one primary reason was because it was headed by a strong yet loving father whose wife, with her quick mind and common-sense wisdom, was his equal, even though she had not had the formal education which he had received. It was the combination of the influence of the father and mother which had shaped the young people; one parent alone could hardly have done it. And this made me aware of a very vital aspect of the present situation in the Muslim world about which I had not previously thought in depth, but about which I now began to ponder a great deal.

March 21: The men went to the mosque for *Fajr* prayer at dawn, while the rest of us prayed in the house. We must leave with Cemile in the early afternoon for Konya so that we could reach Ankara by tomorrow night, for our situation was so indefinite that we could hardly prolong our absence any longer, and Cemile must also return to her university, having taken time out from the research she was conducting in order to be with us here.

The time we had had together was so very short; none of us could bear the idea of parting with no hope of meeting again before we leave Turkey, and thus when Lûtfî suggested that we could perhaps return to Ankara by way of Isparta if we go to Bursa (a trip which we hope to make soon), we were all relieved that there was at least a *possibility* of meeting again. Although it would involve an extremely long journey, it would be the only chance, and the prospect gave us hope. I sat with the mother on the sofa for a long time, our hands clasped, wordlessly communicating all we felt for each other, thinking of the great love which was in her—in all of them—and wondering if we would ever meet again in this world after we leave Turkey.

Here, perhaps for the first time in my life, I was seeing a completely pure Islam lived, without any contradiction or discrepancy between belief and practice. Here were no compromises or half-measures, only a great integrity which encompassed everything about them, from the spotlessness of their home and persons, deep sense of discipline and regularity, judicious use of money, unflagging industriousness, scrupulous honesty, great love of knowledge, modest dress and restrained relations with the opposite sex, to the deep love and sincerity which were a tangible quality among them. During the short time we had been together I had observed that each member of the family treated the others as himself, sacrificing for them individually and for the whole household, and when we were their guests, they made no distinction between themselves and us; whatever they had was also ours and whatever was needed was shared. Their hospitality was without limit, measure or calculation, for they felt us to be one of themselves.

We ate an early lunch. The mother sat by the table with an expression of deep sadness on her serene face as the time for our departure drew near. The previous evening Amca Bey had given expression to what we all felt when he said, "We almost wish we had not met you, since you are leaving us so soon." As we left the house, Fatma and I wept and clung to each other, feeling that we were separating from one another forever; the mother and I embraced again and again, unable to tear ourselves apart. Only Cemile was able to say brightly, "I would be just as sad as they if I were not going with you." As I said a last farewell to the mother and her daughter at the street in front of the house, taking a final long look at them through blurred eyes, I could only thank God with all my heart for our meeting and pray that we might be together again one day.

Amca Bey and Lûtfi accompanied us to the bus station. Before Selim could say or do anything, Lûtfi had given the bus tickets for .our trip to Konya (which he had purchased the previous day without our knowledge) to the driver. When I tried to remonstrate, Cemile said, "Marian Abla, there are some things we do not discuss," in such a way that nothing more could be said; for them it was evidently the most natural thing in the world that they should thus take care of our travel expenses. Amca Bey and Lûtfi came into the bus with us and said the warmest of goodbyes, embracing Selim and Jamal heartily, wishing us a good journey and commending us to God, and then stood outside until the bus left.

The tears ran unheeded down my cheeks, for I knew that I had never before seen and perhaps would never again see a family such as this. A last glimpse of them as they stood smiling gravely with hands upraised in farewell, and we were gone. And so, among the many parts of myself which I had left here and there on this journey through Turkey, the most important part remained forever with those whom we had come to feel were our very own family in Isparta. . .

Thus we left them. Cemile sat with Maryam and Nura, who were quite broken-hearted at leaving, and I with Jamal, our hands clasped as we wept together, for he too had felt a great love for all the members of that family. A little later we changed places, and my dear Cemile, intensely happy and joyful to be traveling with us even on this very brief trip, came and sat beside me, trying to cheer me up with her unfailing good humor. I asked her many questions about her family, trying to understand more fully the nature of the deep Islamic qualities which were so evident among them. She also told me many things about Konya, which she had visited several times before.

The countryside was not remarkable until we reached a vast lake on one side of which was a town called Egridir with an old mosque; the rough, unpaved road went on around the lake, requiring an hour or more to complete the circuit, a serene view of distant mountains whose snowy peaks were mirrored in the smooth water forming the background. There was little population in this area; in one place I pointed out to Cemile a solitary peasant woman making the prostrations of prayer in a field. We stopped at a miserable little town to eat a hurried lunch at a very poor *lokanta,* and presently entered a dull, bleak landscape without any colors visible other than those of the grey rocks, red soil, occasional green trees and blue sky. Then began the volcanic zone of which the Ankara region is a part, with endless vistas of lava rocks and hills, and the journey became quite tiring and monotonous. At length we reached a pass on a hill in the midst of this volcanic desert from which we looked down over the plain on which Konya lay. It was quite a large town with some industry, a very old town, the Iconium of the New Testament, whose Islamic heritage dates from Seljuk times. Minarets of mosques rose in all directions, as well as scattered peaked Seljuk tombs.

Together with Bursa, Konya is known to be the most religious and conservative of Turkish cities. Our primary interest here was to get a glimpse of its atmosphere and to see the tomb of the great Muslim mystic and poet, Jalaluddin Rumi, whom Turks call Hazret-i Mevlâna Celâleddin-i Rumi. Mevlâna Rumi had dwelt here during the thirteenth century and established the Mevlevi (or Maulawiya) order of dervishes: his tomb continues to attract large numbers of visitors to Konya annually.

A dervish (otherwise called a *mureed* or *shagird*) is a follower and disciple of the Sufi leader who heads a *tariqat,* literally meaning 'way,' that is, a way of life, thought, discipline and devotional activity based on the concepts and teachings of Islam. While there is neither precept nor example for *tariqats* and many Sufi practices in the Holy Qur'an and the *Sunnah* of the Prophet, peace be on him, they have traditionally been a way of bringing Muslims closer to God by means of purification of heart, and the noble example of the great Sufis—for example, Abdel Kader Jilani in Iraq, Sayyed Ali

Hujwiri and Moinuddin Chishti in India, and many others—had a great impact in spreading Islam in early times.

Unfortunately, although many of the original Sufi leaders were true, deep Muslims wholly devoted to God, who preached a pure Islam and followed the *Shari'ah* very strictly, in later times what passed for Sufism throughout the Muslim world became, in many cases, a mockery and distortion not only of the teachings of Islam but also of the original teachings of the founders of the Sufi orders. In some parts of the Muslim world today, 'Sufi' or *'derveesh'* connotes a ragged *sa'in* or *qalandar* with matted hair and beads, often engaging in para-normal practices, having the word *'Allah'* and pious phrases on his lips but without any shadow or substance of Islam in his way of life. The ignorant masses are easily taken in by such charlatans; they also flock to the tombs of *pirs, shaykhs* and *walis,* ask them to intercede for them with God, beg them to grant favors, and come very close to actually worshipping them, practices which are utterly condemned by Islam as being tantamount to associating others with God's divinity, which is considered the greatest of all sins and the lowest possible form of degradation.

Thus the true message of submission to God, striving to come near to Him, and attempting to purify the hearts of men which the orignal Sufis brought has in many cases become distorted, and in many respects the so-called 'Sufism' has become a burden and a curse to the Muslim world, bringing people to the very border of man-worship and the pagan practices which Islam came to abolish, and taking them from the realm of actively trying to live Islam and striving to improve the society to sitting about repeating pious formulas by the hour or engaging in other activities which, if not accompanied by a sincere attempt to improve the condition of humanity and to strive in the cause of God, are at best useless and at worst harmful and wrong.

I had come to view with deep mistrust and horror those so-called 'Sufis' I had met or heard of in America who have not the remotest conception of Islam, for whom 'Sufism' was simply another pseudo-religious fad among the many current today in the United States, a gimmick for possessing some of the trappings of 'religion' without any commitment or responsibility; for there are many self-styled exponents of 'Sufism' today who claim that one can be a Sufi without being a Muslim either in belief or practice, going so far as to state that Sufism has no relation to any particular religion and that a Sufi can belong to any faith or even have none at all. These allegations are entirely, unequivocally false and without substance, and anyone who makes such a claim concerning Sufism is falsifying the spirit and principle of *tasawwuf,* has not understood it, and can under no circumstances be considered a Sufi. Such people have simply exploited and used for their own questionable purposes a well-established term in a sense which has no relationship to its original and accepted meaning; for without exception the true Sufis always believed, taught and emphasized that there was no *tariqat* without the strictest obedience to the Islamic *Shari'ah,* that is, without very faithfully following the laws, injunctions and practices prescribed in the Holy Qur'an and the *Sunnah* of the Prophet, peace be on him, both as relate to acts of worship *(ibadat)* and to practical matters *(mu'amilat).* This obedience and discipline must be perfected first; only after one had established a pattern of life of faithful and strict adherence to these basic Islamic requirements could one come to the next step, the striving for purification of heart and drawing nearer to God with practices additional to the prescriptions of the Qur'an and *Sunnah* which do not deviate in any respect from them but rather strengthen and reinforce them.

In the past many *tariqats,* notably the Nakşbandi, Mevlevi, Bektaşi, Kadiri and Ticani orders, had a vast following among the people of Turkey, as well as in other parts of the Muslim world, but the *tariqats* were banned by Atatürk and their *tekkes* turned into museums. Today in Turkey, although on the surface the *tariqats* appear to have all but vanished, their activities and followings have merely diminished and gone underground. While it is unlawful for any *şeyh* to gather around himself followers who live in a community of brothers, the movements still continue in a semi-secret manner. Those who want to learn about and affiliate themselves with a *tariqat* can find the way to do so without any great difficulty, and these officially non-existent movements exert a considerable influence on numbers of Turkish Muslims even today.

A taxi took us from the bus station to the hotel which Amca Bey had recommended. I had time to observe that here one saw many more traditional dresses and far fewer westernized women; many older women wore black *çarşafs,* seen only rarely in Ankara, the Turkish counterpart of the *burqa* and the *chaddor.*

After a rest, we went for a walk in the city and then had a pleasant dinner together. We slept early that night, very tired. We would have only the next morning to see whatever we could of Konya and must make the best possible use of the time, for by tomorrow evening we must be back in Ankara.

March 22: At five in the morning I awoke to the very soft sound of literally dozens of *adhans* coming from the numerous mosques of Konya, which evidently use no amplifiers; I opened the window to hear them better, the most beautiful and incredible harmony on earth, I verily believe, coming through the pale dawn. Indeed, the Turkish *adhans* are particularly beautiful and moving, and in the dawn seem almost sublime, especially when there is a chorus of them, the sound rising and falling, blending and interweaving into an inadvertent harmony more delicate and perfect than the greatest master could ever compose.

Later, with Cemile showing the way, we set out to visit Mevlana Rumi's tomb.* It was straight ahead at the end of the city's main street, fifteen minutes' walk from the hotel, at once recognizable by the striking blue dome which is one of Turkey's best known landmarks.

The architecture of the *tekke* of which the tomb is a part is complex and interesting: twin circular domes, that of the mosque and an adjoining chamber; the celebrated dome, a cylindrical structure with fluted walls covered with turquoise mosaic and topped with a fluted turquoise cone, under which lies the tomb; a number of smaller domes, outlying structures, and a single high minaret. On top of the outlying buildings stood a row of small white chimneys topped with black cones like hats, somehow a sweet and touching

* Built around 1274 A.C.

sight. I had seen similar chimneys on the outbuildings of various old mosques, but this black-and-white was somehow especially appealing, perhaps because the rest of the structure had a certain sublimity and depth, while those small humble chimneys, which reminded one of a white-clad Mevlevi dervish in a conical cap, spoke of the simple human needs of food, warmth and shelter of the people who had lived and remembered God there.

The tomb and *tekke* of Mevlâna Rumi was now a museum where, surprisingly, one had to pay admission to enter. From inside the compound, I noted with distaste that the galleries on top of which the pious chimneys stood, where once Godly men had lived together to remember their Creator and purify their hearts, were now the offices and exhibit halls of the museum.

Like everyone else, we were asked to deposit our shoes outside with a custodian (although no area inside was used for worship). An antechamber where beautiful framed works of calligraphy were displayed led into the dimly-lighted main section. On one side, in great dignity, stood the solemn tombs of a number of pupils and followers of Mevlâna Rumi. Beyond them, one sarcophagus stood by itself in front of a wall decorated with ornate Arabic calligraphy in relief, the resting place of the body of Celâleddin-i Rumi.

Many people went in and out—mostly simple folk, women in black *çarşafs,* laboring men in caps with vizors—stopping to pray *al-Fateha* at the tomb, some of them obviously very much moved. As I repeated the opening verses of the Qur'an and prayed for God's peace and blessings on Mevlâna Rumi's soul, the tears ran down my cheeks unheeded, for the remembrance of one who had spread the blessed light of God in this world could not but move me deeply. But I was aware that at the same time I wept for something else as well, wept for it in bitter anger. My first glance had shown that in front of this tomb of one of God's servants who had called people toward Him, as if placed there deliberately in order to mock it, were displayed two or three ornamental tables on one of which stood an old clock, with signs identifying their historical backgrounds, while other articles associated with the communal life of the dervishes were displayed, as in any other museum, in this room and throughout the rest of the building, including the chamber which had once been a mosque.

Mevlâna Rumi's grave, then, was the main exhibit, the 'masterpiece,' in this museum, at which people might come and look as a relic of an ancient, dead past! Waiting quietly in front of the tomb until almost everyone had left, I made a photograph of what I saw: the tomb of a devoted worhipper of God turned by government decree into an artifact among many others in an ancient history museum, but done in such a manner that, together with such acts as leaving the shoes outside, it satisfied the simple and pious, while at the same time it subtly emphasized and underlined that what was dead and buried here was not only a man but also a way of life, a way of thought and feeling belonging to a dead past, to another time and frame of reference now extinct—the way of devotion to God Most High. With angry tears burning in my eyes, I stood and prayed, beseeching God that the light which He had kindled among those whose graves were now transformed into a mockery of their mission might not be allowed to go out in His earth. Indeed, I reflected as I left the place, the Islamic prohibition against constructing permanent tombs is a very wise one, for either they may be made into places which are accorded a completely unIslamic exaggerated respect and reverence by the ignorant, or they can be mocked at and used by vested interests to manipulate people's attitudes, as Mevlâna Rumi's tomb was obviously being used.

In the outer buildings, under the humble chimneys, there was more of the 'museum,' with models of dervishes in various dresses, displays of old costumes and rugs, and many other things in which none of us had any interest; we went through part of it quickly and then turned away in disgust. Cemile, quick to understand what I was feeling, took my hand and said, with her never-failing objectivity, "Ablacığım, don't care so much about this. There are many, many more important problems for Islam in Turkey!" How right she was, indeed! The simple people of Turkey might safely be kept busy visiting tombs or praying at special mosques, under the impression that they were doing something very Islamic, yet all the while, in any aspect requiring action and movement of Muslims, Islam was being systematically rejected and suppressed. As we were leaving, it occurred to me that perhaps the devout chimneys with their black hats were the most real and honest things there. . . .

After a visit to the adjacent Sultan Selim's mosque where we prayed *nafil salat,* we made a few purchases in nearby handicraft shops in which much tasteless rubbish was sold together with some better things, and then walked to the Alaeddin Tepe, a hill on which a modern park with memorials had been erected, no doubt as a deliberate counterbalance to the thirteenth century Seljuk structures which still stood in its vicinity, with their appealing simplicity and architectural integrity. Nearby, as if to punctuate the scene with its irony, stood two schools bearing names and titles of Atatürk.

As I looked at them, thinking over all the conflicting and con- tradictory things I had. experienced this morning, I realized once again how, among all except a few committed people in Turkey, all the dynamism and life-giving force of Islam have been set aside, so that today only the worship aspects, at best, remain. Thus, as long as Islam is not seen as an all-inclusive system embracing every as- pect of man's existence, it cannot be expected to guide the life of the society, appearing to substantiate the claim of the critics and enemies of Islam that "Islam does not work." Obviously no system under the sun can "work" unless it is conscientiously applied, and since Islam as a total system of life has been almost nowhere ap- plied during the last many, many years, those who make such claims against it can never vindicate them unless they first sincerely try to understand and to apply it in entirety. The narrowing-down of Islam to acts of worship, obligatory and essential though they are, and traditional pious observances, has been a very deliberate, calculated policy, not only in Turkey but in every part of the Muslim world; for the vested interests in whose hands power lies today know well, as did the Quraish of Mekkah in the sixth century when they faced the revolutionary call to truth of God's Messenger, peace be on him, that Islam, faithfully believed in and lived with all its dynamism, is an irresistable force which nothing can withstand. In order to weaken it, to destroy its hold on the society, it has been necessary thus to isolate it from life, leaving only the worship as- pects and a few moral injunctions, just enough that the people will be pacified into thinking that they have Islam and that their morals will not deteriorate absolutely. And how well has this policy succeeded, as Muslims, without thought or reflection, allow themselves to be herded toward alien values, attitudes and habits, without ever realizing upon how great and inestimable a treasure they are thus turning their backs!

Cemile put her arm through mine, bringing me back from my reverie with a start. Praise be to God, as long as there were people like her and her family left in Turkey—and there must be many, many of them—there was yet hope for its future as a Muslim country, *insha'Allah*. For each Muslim who holds these values in his heart and lives by them, wherever in the world he may be, is like a brick in a wall, a link in a chain, a strand in a rope—the "rope of God"* to which Muslims are asked to hold fast and keep united—by means of which the hearts of Muslims which are confused and wavering may yet be reclaimed from following unIslamic values and habits and restored to the way they have left, and through which the message of God may be spread throughout the world to those who have never even heard its call. Our task is only to strive, to do our best, never to cease working as long as we live with whatever resources of time, energy or means Allah has given us, and then to leave the outcome with Him, for He has promised to safeguard His religion against destruction until the Day of Judgment. I pressed Cemile's hand warmly, and then Selim, who had been walking along in silence with the children thinking his own thoughts, turned us into the doorway of a restaurant with his unfailing practical good sense, saying good-humoredly, "Come on here! Hadn't we better have some lunch now?"

During the time which remained before we must leave for Ankara, we visited a few old mosques and prayed *Dhuhr* and *'Asr,* combined and shortened in the manner of travelers, in one of them. In the early afternoon we took our luggage from the hotel and returned to the bus station. The passengers on this bus, which was completely full, seemed to be mainly university students, an entirely different breed from the pleasant, conservative people among whom we had traveled to Antalya. Yes, we are going to Ankara alright, I

---

* *Ale Imran* 3:103.

thought acridly. A young man and woman—although not *that* young—occupied seats across the aisle from us; they caressed and kissed each other passionately in a totally unashamed and uninhibited manner throughout the entire journey of several hours, oblivious to everything. No one except ourselves seemed to pay any attention to this behavior or to be bothered by it, but poor Cemile, extremely ashamed on their account, kept repeating, "Can they really be *Turks?*" I also did not like the loud, swaggering manner of the driver, who drove too fast and inflicted vulgar popular music on the passengers, many of whom were asleep, suddenly and very loudly at intervals. The entire route was bleak and empty. We passed the time in chatting and changed places occasionally so that no one would be left alone, reaching Ankara at about six o'clock in the evening.

After a quick dinner, Cemile parted from us reluctantly to return to her university, and we took a taxi home. Well, it was the same old apartment. A few minutes later we were on the way to Enver's house.

Welcoming us warmly, the family sat us down at the table for tea and sweets. The news of the capture of Deniz Gezmiş had been correct.* Besides this, four top M.E.T.U. communists had been fired, the new government of Nihat Erim was in the throes of trying to organize itself, and it appeared that a full-scale army *coup* had been averted by the army's pressure on Demirel to resign.

---

* He was subsequently tried and hanged.

CHAPTER 17

ANOTHER ADJUSTMENT

March 23: If we had left Ankara with the least hope that during our brief absence there might be some real improvement or change in conditions, we were now to be disappointed; but I don't think any of us had really cherished such unrealistic hopes. The situation remained just as we had left it, and we must now make the decision which had been postponed since the end of January.

Our extended trip, begun two months earlier, was now finally over. We had left for Pakistan, despite the disturbed situation here, with light hearts, full of joy in the adventure before us, had had very happy experiences, and then had returned home five weeks later in a very hurried and abrupt manner only to be faced with a state of crisis. Because of our travels outside Turkey, during this period I had come to realize even more fully what this land had lost and had felt deeply angry and bitter, unable to reconcile with the situation in spite of all I knew of the good qualities of countless numbers of Turks. And then there had been the trip which we had just completed, during which I had found an unsurpassed loveliness in the natural aspects of a part of Anatolia, a deep and profound goodness among the people, and in Cemile's family a living embodiment of a pure Islamic way of life; had grown to love this land even more despite its defects and had been the more grieved by its turning away from Islam; and surely had not wanted, despite all the problems, to leave it so soon. But the traveling and pleasure were now over; we must settle down to deal with the sober and disheartening realities of the situation and to resolve the problem of our immediate future.

In the afternoon I went with Selim to the University, waiting with a heavy heart while he discussed his situation with his advisor. He recommended that Selim make his own arrangements and do whatever he felt best, for conditions were completely uncertain and he could give no promises of any kind; the University remained closed and there was no indication of when it might reopen—it could be a few weeks or several months. Apart from the problems in the administration and faculty which must be resolved, the March 5 damage to the dormitories and other buildings must be repaired before the campus was in operable condition. Selim showed me bullet holes and other damage in various buildings from the fighting; I could only think about all that might have occurred and thanked God.

In the meantime the thought of Cemile's family did not leave my mind. The next afternoon I wrote a letter to all of them expressing what we felt, to be translated by Cemile; I put it in my purse and left everything else to visit her at her university. She was not there. Imagining I knew where she might be, I returned home and found her, as I had anticipated, in our drawing room talking and playing with the children. We talked about our trip, her family, and tried to formulate some plans for visiting Bursa in the near future, for it was the one place which Enver insisted we must see before leaving Turkey, even if we saw nothing else. Cemile told me that it had now been officially confirmed that many of the Turkish communist revolutionaries are being trained by Arab communist guerillas and that Deniz Gezmiş himself was a graduate of their revolutionary leftist training. These Arab communists, who pretend to support the movement to liberate Palestine from Israeli occupation, are in fact cooperating with Israeli communists; their sole aim is to foment communist revolution throughout the Middle East under cover of the Palestine liberation movement, in which they have played no significant role.

While Cemile was here, a lengthy telegram arrived; it was from her father, and she translated it to me. It said in very brief but moving language that all 'the family thanked God for having met us, that they loved and respected us very deeply, rejoiced in the closeness which we felt for one another, were very much grieved at the

prospect of our leaving Turkey, and finally that they offered heartfelt prayers to God for our future; I turned my face away to conceal
how much affected I was. Late in the afternoon I sent out my letter
to the family, with Cemile's translation. These were but words, yet
I hoped that they might nonetheless be able to convey some of the
great love and respect which we felt for them, which, if our days
here were not so closely numbered, we might have had many future
opportunities for expressing. But that, obviously, is not to be . . .

March 28: There is shocking news from Pakistan. Mujib-ur-
Rahman has declared East Pakistan independent and has announced the creation of 'Bangladesh;' there is serious trouble in the
East wing, of which we are not getting clear news. Yet this was predictable and inevitable in some form or the other; the departure of
Pakistanis from Islamic values is now being paid for—in blood,
chaos and terror.

It is spring, and this Ankara has taken on a better look than we
have seen so far. The grass is growing green, trees are blooming
everywhere, and the parks are all decked out in loveliness, although
the days are still quite cloudy. One could *almost* like it here at this
season . . .

For us, these are strange days of waiting to see what will happen. We consulted at length with Enver and Emine about what it
was best to do and came to a tentative decision. Although they were
very much grieved and hurt on our account at the way things have
turned out, they could not reasonably suggest that we ought to stay
on under present conditions, and Selim has now written to his
sponsoring agency about the situation here and asked for its recommendations. We are nearly sure that they will advise him to return
home, in which case we will leave as soon as possible so that he can
get back to his work in the States. Emine and I wept together over
his decision, so hard to reach and yet even harder, under the circumstances, not to . . .

The past days have been extremely difficult as I contemplate
our return to America, trying to imagine myself there and to adjust

to living there in anticipation. But now the bitterness and sadness which I have felt have ebbed away and I feel alive once more; my spirit is moving and good experiences are coming to me again. For as long as I live here I am a part of the life of this place, and whatever I experience and observe, whether good or bad, will never cease to interest me. Although I know that we will probably be going back soon and that I must detach myself emotionally, day by day I cannot help becoming more and more involved.

When we returned from Antalya, Enver at once remarked, "You have gotten back your Turkish!" and the improvement was indeed very noticeable. I no longer have to feel embarrassed about not being able to speak, and I go everywhere and manage very nicely with this Turkish, poor as it is, for people are very generous in making allowances, and I hope to continue to make some slight progress on my own as long as we are here.

Nura and Maryam also continue to become more fluent. Each day they play outside with their friends of the neighborhood, all Turks, and they have picked up a rapid, colloquial style which I can hardly follow, even though their vocabularies are quite limited. Their life is leisurely and unstructured: a while of lessons each morning and then play with each other or with their friends, reading, drawing, visiting, going on errands with me, and so on. They are very close to Emine and to Cemile, who are like older sisters to them. By now they have lost most of the 'Americanisms' which all my efforts could not prevent their acquiring and which used to grate on me so much, replacing them with a more polite, gentle form of speech and manners, and they have also learned a far greater perceptiveness and sensitivity to other peoples' feelings and needs since they have been here, in the atmosphere of love and tenderness we have found among our friends.

As for Jamal, he has little trouble with asthma now unless he is around people who are smoking. He spends most of his time reading or working on various projects of his own, for unlike the girls he has not found any friends or companions in our neighborhood; nonetheless, something vital has taken place within him for all his seclusion. He has become more clear and definite in his Islamic

feelings and now prays all the prayers regularly without any reminder from Selim or me—the same boy who six months ago had to
be reminded two or three times a day. His identity as a Muslim
seems somehow to have crystallized, he has come to have a deep
sense of belonging to the Muslim world, has been affected deeply,
as we all have, by the Islamic elements in the environment and by
the atmosphere of warmth and sincerity which is about us here, and
is on the way, *insha'Allah,* to becoming a young Muslim man.

March 30: Yesterday afternoon I had errands at Kızılay, where I always enjoy going to shop and to see the people, although often and
often I have come back angry and upset by the crassly materialistic
atmosphere which characterizes it, the majority of people in its busy
streets, offices and shops so totally westernized as to be completely
unidentifiable in terms of religion or nationality. Toward evening
this center of the city is extremely crowded with shoppers, people
going home from work or simply out walking, and these days a vast
number of unoccupied students whose universities are all closed,
making it almost impossible to find a place on a bus (the alternative
to which, standing in an endless line waiting for a *dolmuş* or spending on an often almost non-available taxi, is nearly as bad).

That afternoon as I walked down the main street amidst the
throng of pedestrians on my way to a shop at some little distance, I
began to look at peoples' faces, trying to find some individuals in
the crowd who looked as if they had something within, some spiritual or good human qualities. As I glanced from face to face in
that crush of hurrying people, I saw almost no one whose features
reflected such vital inner qualities or who could be distinguished
from an inhabitant of almost any city of Europe.

This, then, is what one may expect to see today in the westernized sections of large Turkish cities, and one can only ponder over
what has happened to these people and their faces when one thinks
of the countless numbers of Turks who, because of what they have
within, possess such decent, open countenances, abounding in sincerity and often 'nurlu'—with an inner light. With the adoption of
alien values, habits and dress has come an alien outlook, destroying

all the goodness and loveliness in the spirit, which is mirrored, as God intended it to be, in the face of every human being. It was not the first time, and will not be the last, that I came home from Kızılay feeling angry and hopeless . . .

April 6: During the past several days I have been able to satisfy my curiosity to see something of contemporary Turkish cultural activities, namely, television, opera and theatre productions, which were very interesting.

One evening recently we were invited to a friend's for dinner followed by television-watching; it was the first time I had seen television in Turkey. The evening's program was as follows: a short concert of Mozart's music; a brief feature about the latest styles in women's shoes and hosiery (both foreign-produced); and a Turkish-produced program about yoga exercises, which featured two women clad in skin-tight black leotards, one of whom narrated while the other demonstrated the exercises, assuming postures which, for a Turkish (and presumably 'Muslim') girl were exceedingly improper and indecent. Next came a program of Turkish music, both of the decadent modern variety and a more classical type, performed by a *prima donna*-ish man and a buxom, vulgar-looking female 'artiste'; then news, sports and weather, followed by a British mystery movie which was relatively harmless.

As in Pakistan, I was amazed to see how such programs can be accepted and indeed very much liked—a matter of pride to invite friends to come to watch—by Turks who have retained the smallest sense of Islamic values. It is clear that pride of ownership of a television set—Status Symbol Number One among upper middle class families in Turkey today—has blinded many to considerations of values, decincy and appropriateness, adding to the already great degree of cultural confusion in this country. As Turkish television is known to be controlled by communist elements, it can certainly be expected to be, by and large, a questionable and harmful form of entertainment—especially for people who have ceased to exercise any critical or reasoning faculty.

For months I had wanted to have a look at Turkish opera, just for the interest of it, as the whole idea of opera in Turkey seemed a very strange and incongruous thing. At last a few evenings ago I was able to persuade Deniz Hanım to accompany me to the State Opera House in Ulus.

The work was a very mediocre and vulgar one, Lehar's "Count of Luxemburg." While the production itself was reasonably adequate, the thing which made it strikingly interesting was that it was performed in Turkish. A performance sung in Italian, French or German would have been one thing, but a European opera sung in Turkish struck me as somehow very funny. However, Turkish-izing it had the effect of eliminating much of the strangeness and foreignness from it, making it into simply another form of Turkish cultural activity, a deliberate move to popularize the art among Turks, although it is said that is has never taken hold on a large scale in spite of this. We exited after the first act, having had enough of the boisterous music and rowdy can-can dance sequences, and I commented on the way in which, at the insistence of Atatürk himself,* the Turkish government's budget is burdened with this very pointed attempt to make Turks identify with the culture of Europe, especially when it is comparatively rare and unusual (even in the capital city) to find live performances of Turkish classical music and dance.

The following afternoon I went to the theatre with Cemile. For some time I had been asking her to take me to see a performance of something she thought would be of interest. Since she was not really too aware of what was current in the Ankara theatrical world, she chose a play which was then being widely discussed without having much idea of what it was.

It turned out to be an *avant-garde* leftist production, staged in a small theatre in Kızılay where the front row of seats was just at the edge of the stage, giving the performance an unusually immediate effect for those who were seated near it. The work was on typical communist lines: a glorification of the movement to liberate Turks from 'enslavement' (in this case to their Ottoman rulers and Muslim

* See Note (27).

leaders, who were portrayed with terrible venomousness), and of the 'liberators' (Atatürk and others) themselves, depicted in scenarios interspersed with choral readings by the small cast of male and female actors, who stood before us, their mouths opening and closing, with the heightened effect produced by makeup and the glare of lights, in a strangely menacing and ugly manner. I became suddenly keenly aware of the fact that the actors and also undoubtedly most of the audience (which was, however, very small) must all be communists or communist sympathizers, and that we two women, with our Islamic dress and English conversation, were not n a very congenial situation. Cemile shared my anxiety, for she had not realized previously how strongly communist-oriented the performance was, and we were therefore quite relieved when it ended and we returned to the outside world without any incident. Thus passed my first and last exposure to Turkish theatre, after an interesting and not altogether unsuspenseful afternoon.

April 8: These are very, very hard days for me. As one day follows another, I struggle with myself because of what lies ahead, trying to find some way to resolve the dilemma of my life and finding none, and knowing deep down inside that there is no solution except to accept the situation with patience and dignity as befits a Muslim, and to prepare myself for the change which is undoubtedly coming to us all too soon.

This morning I had an errand in Kızılay. When I reached home I was astonished to see Gül Hanım sitting desolately on the steps of our apartment house, her face red and swollen with weeping. When I asked a woman from our building who was with her what was the matter, she said that one of Gül Hanım's children, a boy of three years, had been hit by a car; his father had taken him to some hospital—Gül Hanım was not sure which one—and she had no idea about his condition, nor even whether or not he was still alive.

Well, much of the rest of the afternoon was taken up with this situation. I tried to comfort the unhappy woman, and Maryam and Nura fed her other children, who were wandering around outside completely neglected. When I asked Gül Hanım what she wanted to do, she replied that she wished to go to the hospital where she supposed the boy had been taken, but appeared to have no idea where the hospital was nor how to get there. As no one else seemed ready to take her, I presently fetched my neighbor, Aysel Erbulut, and the three of us went to the hospital together. Gül Hanım was told that the child had indeed been seen there earlier, but as he was not seriously hurt he had been treated and sent home with his father. However, when we returned home, they were not there nor was there any news of the boy, and Gül Hanım became very anxious and upset.

Gül Hanım, who has been coming once a week or so to clean for me, has come to like me very much, and knowing that we may be going back to American soon, has said many times, "*Gitme, gitme, ağlayacağım!* (Don't go, don't go. I'll cry!), telling me in all earnestness that in America there are '*gâvurs*' who will cut our throats, illustrating her statement with a meaningful gesture across her throat. Time after time I had explained to her that we had come to Turkey for a limited time only, that Selim Bey's permanent job was there, not here, and that the *gâvurs* are very friendly and very good in many respects, but she was never satisfied about it. Now I brought her to our apartment, fed her whatever I could find to eat, and made her lie down on my bed to get some much-needed rest for a little while. Later in the afternoon when I went down to her apartment on the bottom floor of the building to see if there was any news, her husband had returned with the information that the boy was in no serious trouble and would come home the next day after spending the night in the hospital. I made supper for them together with ours and took it down to them, very thankful that the boy had received no serious injury.

Although this day had brought much suffering to the *kapıcı's* family, it had been very beneficial for me, for in the depth of my involvement with this situation, I had realized all at once that everything would not end for me when we leave Turkey. The life and movement in my soul were part of me and would be with me wherever on God's earth we went, if He willed; going back to America, away from the Muslim world which had so richly stimulated my mind and heart, could not take this from me except insofar as there would be far fewer stimuli to produce this inner movement, and many sources of conflict and inner disturbance which might occupy my mind. Mine was the precious gift of savouring life and its small experiences, praise be to God. I wondered, as I had done many times before, why any human being should need the stimulus of alcohol or the distortions of reality which come from the use of intoxicating drugs in order to be able to relish life and the small and great things of which it consists. It is, I think, to a large extent because in the West life is largely so empty and meaningless, and human relationships so cut-and-dried, so business-like and lacking in feeling, that there is very little to produce currents of joy or involvement in the heart. I prayed two *rak'ats* of thanksgiving after *'Isha* prayer in gratitude to God for the boy's safety and for my own return, although it might be temporary, from my preoccupation with what lay ahead to the value and interest of the present.

Today had also given me something else to think about. I had observed that in this difficult situation, the women in our building who knew Gül Hanım well and who should have been the ones to help her had treated her to some extent more like a *kapıcı hanım*—a person of a lower social order—than like a fellow human being whose capacity to feel and suffer was equal to their own, although her socio-economic status might not be. It had hurt me to observe that no one did anything practical to help the distressed woman but largely limited their assistance to verbal enquiries and expressions of sympathy. It had also hurt me that on the way home from the hospital, Aysel Hanım, a *hanım effendi* like myself and my social equal, had taken my hand as we were walking, leaving Gül Hanım to walk alone, so that although *she* was the one who needed sympathy and affection, she was excluded from this gesture of friendship; but would a respectable, modern middle class Turkish woman *ever* walk publicly hand-in-hand with a *kapıcı hanım,* no matter how much her situation might require such an expression of support? I wondered how much more kindly, by way of contrast, the neighbors would have acted toward any of the 'respectable' women who live in this building if such a thing had happened to their children. Thus, while there was no actual hardness or lack of concern such as I had seen in Pakistan, I had not expected to find this sort of social discrimination in Turkey. This, it seemed to me, was another manifestation of the recent deplorable trends apparent among the spoiled half-traditional, half-westernized Turks among whom we were living, for I knew that among truly Islamic people there would not have been the lack of concrete help and support I had observed.

Thus it is: when people come to value others for their wealth or social status, it is a clear indication that they have lost the true criteria for judging, namely, the character and conduct of a person, and, without correct standards and values, are on the way to accepting financial status and social position—their own as well as the other person's—as the ultimate values. They have also lost that sense of brotherliness and fellow-feeling which should impel them to give help to their fellow-Muslims and to anyone else in all situations of difficulty and need, translating into concrete terms the Holy Prophet's saying, "You see the believers in the mutual pity, love and affection like one body. When one member has a complaint, the rest of the body is united with it in wakefulness and fever."

I have felt a great love for these simple people of Turkey, for they have a quiet goodness of heart and a deep sincerity; they have not been spoiled by the inner malaise which comes from the forgetting of Islamic and traditional values, and I have felt close to them when I could not feel anything for the more affluent, westernized people around me. When I was coming home on a crowded bus today, I happened to stand beside a couple of village women wearing immaculate white kerchiefs. Seeing them, I thought, They have not yet been tainted by sophistication and worldliness—and then caught myself wondering what had just gone through my mind.

Are culture, education and possessions elements which easily subvert and destroy spiritual and human qualities? Can it be that the modern urban civilization which we have developed is to a large extent artificial and distorting, producing non-direct, non-human responses in people and marking them with some corrupt and unnatural element which is not there in the original human constitution? Indeed, I can never accept the idea that to be educated, to know the ways of the world, to possess material abundance, should or must result in one's becoming spoiled or bereft of true spiritual or human values; in fact, it should have just the opposite effect through broadening the mind and spirit. But what I am observing is that unless that mind and spirit are ruled and guided by non-material, transcendental values which come from God, unless one is able to live in the world without living *for* it or allowing himself to be dominated by its demands, such corruption can and does occur all too readily.

April 9: Yesterday evening Selim and I went to visit a Pakistani whom he had met recently; he had lived for several years in the United States and has a very modern American wife. The husband, nominally Muslim, appeared to be without any identifying characteristics—neither Muslim, Pakistani nor American. The girl, however, seemed sensible, and I could not blame her for anything; in remaining a typical American she was simply being what her upbringing and environment had made her, as her husband had offered her no alternative values or way of life. Although we did not discuss anything personal, for my own interest I asked her, "What have you done about the question of religion?" in relation to the upbringing of their children. The reply: "Neither of us is religious, so I don't think our children will be either. When they are old enough we will tell them about both religions (Christianity and Islam) and they can decide for themselves."

This was just one more disheartening addition to the legion of Muslim men married to Western women in our time. In the majority of these marriages, one sees a man who is drifting between cultures, who has little or no identification with Islam because he has never understood nor practiced it as a total system of life, and often not a great deal even with his home country, although he seldom misses opportunities for associating with his countrymen wherever he finds them; he belongs nowhere but can fit in and adapt very nicely anywhere. Thus he and the Western woman he has married are generally able to be relatively compatible without major areas of cultural conflict, since as a rule the wife also has no strong beliefs or values which could be the cause of significant differences between them. In a number of such marriages, I have observed that the girls were good people, undoubtedly having the potential of becoming excellent Muslims if only their husbands were firm believers who could affect them. Unfortunately, this is all too rare, and thus in such a family neither husband, wife nor children have any particular identity; they merely get absorbed, due to lack of resistance and any alternative values, wherever they may happen to settle down.

How sad, I thought, to be a *nothing* and to have no identity!

This afternoon the *kapıcı* and his wife went to the hospital to bring home their son. In the evening I went down to see about the injured child; he lay pathetically in bed with eyes half-closed, bandages covering the deep lacerations on his nose and forehead. Thank God, his injuries had been very slight. I rejoiced with them that it was nothing worse and told them once again, "Allah is merciful," which they fervently repeated over and over. Yet, I reflected, it could very well have turned out differently. If he had been very seriously injured, crippled for life or killed, would we still have had the same unfailing conviction of Allah's mercy and believed in Him just as certainly?

When we say, "I believe in God" or "I have faith in God," I pondered, what do we believe *about* Him? What does having faith *in* Him actually mean? Does it mean that because we have faith God will not permit anything bad to happen to us; that is, that we or those whom we love will never experience trouble and misery, incur any major loss of possessions, be the victims of injustice, tyranny, violence or natural disasters, suffer from any terrible accident, painful disease or major handicap and ultimately death; or that, alternatively, if such things do happen to us or to our dear ones, we will be convinced that God does not exist, or that He has abandoned us or does not care about us, since if there were a God and He did care, He would not permit such things to happen?

If by 'believing in' or 'having faith in' God we mean this, we are surely very likely to lose our faith sooner or later, as a great many Europeans did after the devastating calamities and atrocities of World War II, for such 'faith' rests on the foundation of a profound misunderstanding of the way in which God operates and the nature of the physical world. Since man is just as much a part of that world as the rest of God's creation and just as equally subject to the operation of its laws and to death, sooner or later every human being and his dear ones are bound to suffer from trouble of one sort or another, and sooner or later he and they will die, since this is simply the way God has ordained the present life. For God does not promise Muslims, or any other people, that because they believe in Him, or because they love Him above everything and may even spend all their time, energies and resources striving in His cause, He will never permit anything which they feel is bad to happen to them. In fact, such committed people are the most likely to experience suffering, for they do not try to avoid the consequences of their commitment and spend themselves without stint in the way of God, concerned about the quality of their life instead of its ease or duration. They view death not as a tragedy or an evil but rather as the natural end of this temporary life by which they return to their Source, not clinging to life nor trying to keep death away, but knowing that it will come, unfailingly, when God decrees and that nothing they do or do not do will change the time of its coming. Thus they try to live their lives in the best and most meaningful manner possible no matter what their circumstances and conditions, without concern for whether its duration is to be long or short.

To a Muslim or to anyone else who truly believes, then, belief in God and His attributes must be totally independent of all circumstances, unconditional and unchangeable in all situations, without reference to what happens to individual men or to mankind, for no one can seriously believe in a God Who is limited or bound by the temporal affairs of His creation. When a Muslim says that he 'believes' in God, therefore, he means that he believes in His Oneness and in His absolute sovereignty, that there is no authority over the universe and men except Him, and that no matter what happens—to himself, his dear ones, his community or nation or even to the entire world—he has perfect trust that He is in control, that He knows the end of all things which he himself, with his limited faculties and understanding, cannot know, and that it is He, the Source of all meaning, Who gives meaning to his life, to both the suffering and the joy which he experiences. And when insurmountable difficulties and problems come his way, the Muslim—that is, the one who submits to God—is able to accept them with patience, for he knows that whatever happens to him is decreed, by God, Who alone decides the end and outcome of all things, just like a child who has perfect confidence in the goodness and sound judgment of his parents, although he knows that they may at times deny him something he wants very much or expose him to difficulties in order to train or to test him. As God says:

> "Be sure that We shall test you with something of fear and hunger, some loss of goods or lives or the fruits (of your toil); but give glad tidings to those who patiently persevere, who say, when afflicted with calamity, 'To God we belong and to Him is our return.' They are the ones on whom (descend) blessings from God, and mercy, and they are the ones who receive guidance."*

The Muslim's task, therefore, is to do the best he can with whatever God has given him; to be moderate, humble and generous in days of affluence; to be thankful for all good, whether great or small; and to show patience and dignity in difficulty and suffering, seeking God's help not necessarily through the agreeable resolution of his difficulties but through the strength and courage which He gives to those who trust and hold fast to Him to meet trouble and pain with fortitude and resolution. For him, this world is not the ultimate destination but only a preface and a preparation for his final goal, the world of the Hereafter, where no one will be dealt with unjustly and where he hopes for the mercy of his God and a place in His *Dar as-Salam*—The Abode of Peace.

> "But God calls to the Abode of Peace; He guides whom He pleases to a way that is straight. To those who do right is a goodly (reward)—yes, more (than in measure). No darkness nor shame shall cover their faces. They are the companions of the Garden, and therein will they remain (forever)."**

Thinking over all these things, I have tried to express them more meaningfully in a poem.

> Nothing am I, nothing in this world,
> but a traveler, going on a journey;
> hearing and seeing on this journey many things;
> striving always on this journey at one clear task:
> to reach my Home.

---

* *Al-Baqara* 2:155-157.

** *Yunus* 10:25-26.

Many hands reach out to detain me, clinging;
offering the delights of this world, crying,
"Stay, these are yours!"
Many a time my soul has lingered, saying,
"Let me stay for a while savoring these treasures,"
yet deeply knowing: the journey's end is not here;
I cannot take these Home.

Sometimes I have been hard-pressed and worn
in the effort to go on, step after step;
sometimes wholly spent in toiling
along the steep roads of the journey
until I reach the Home which is my goal.

For I am a traveler, going on a journey.
For me there never can be rest nor peace
until the Master of the Journey calls me to its end;
until I stand before Him, with all my striving,
all my good and all my ill,
seeking from His infinite mercy forgiveness
for all the wrongs of my journey toward Him;
asking from His boundless goodness acceptance
of my small and feeble efforts on this journey;
and coming at last to my Home in the Hereafter,
through the fullness of His limitless grace
in the blessed light of His ineffable countenance.

April 10: During the past days we have been meeting some new people and exchanging ideas concerning the future of Islam in Turkey. I noted much earlier that there are many Muslim groups in Turkey today. Perhaps the strongest of these are the Milli Nizam Partisi (National Order Party), which is currently under severe attack by the government, and the Nurcu movement, comprised of the followers of Said Nursi, a twentieth century reformer, writer and scholar who has had a great impact on the Islamic revival in Turkey, whose followers are continuously subject to arrest and harassment although the charges against them have been dismissed time after time.

It is clear and obvious that no one who speaks openly for the ordering of political, economic and social affairs in Turkey today by the Islamic teachings can expect anything other than the loss of his job and prestige, the scattering of his forces, trial, persecution and even imprisonment or exile, and hence any sort of Islamic movement or effort is almost bound to be pushed into oblivion or suppressed under present conditions. At the same time, taken together, the members of all the Islamic groups are enough to form a substantial and effective force for Islam if their efforts were united and coordinated; but at the present time there is no cooperation, not even mutual respect among them. The end result of this is that their efforts and resources are scattered and isolated rather than being unified around one common goal, and as nothing concrete can be accomplished without a united, concerted effort, the harassment and suppression of Muslims by the government and other elements continues.

What can bring together the Muslims of Turkey in a common meeting ground and organization, with a common leadership, so that they can have the necessary impact on the society to bring about some fundamental changes? This is a question which needs deep and earnest study by the Muslim leaders and thinkers of this land, who must evolve a plan of action and strive to implement it among their followings. It is also obvious to me that communication with the common people and activating them Islamically is an absolutely indispensable ingredient of any success which Muslims will have in Turkey; for clearly Islam in Turkey rests on the backbone of the great mass of ordinary Turks, who love it and value it but remain totally inactive and unable to take any part in shaping the destiny of the nation without firm support and guidance from the knowledgeable and educated Muslims. Thus the Islamic leadership in Turkey must make a simultaneous effort not only to bring the various groups together to work (although by different approaches and methods if desired) for the common goal, but must also find a way to communicate with, to train and to mobilize the common people for Islamic commitment and activity, despite the repressive policies of the government which makes use of the issue of 'secularism' whenever Islamic elements raise their heads. Without this, I am certain that the Islamic movements in Turkey will continue to remain largely static and without the impact necessary to bring about the changes necessary to keep the society from being lost completely to Islam.

April 13: In a week we will *insha'Allah* go with Cemile to Bursa, for she will have a long holiday them. Fatma is now there visiting her husband Lûtfi's *hala,* * and we will be seeing her again at the *hala*'s house, to our great joy.

April 18: Selim received a reply from his sponsoring agency yesterday. As anticipated, they decided to terminate his fellowship and asked him to return home if the university did not open by April 15 or soon thereafter, and at present there is no indication of any sort that it will reopen in the near future.** The irrevocable step, then, has been taken; the bridge which connected us to Turkey and the possibility of staying longer has been burned behind us, and it is now definitely certain that we will go soon.

And the painful struggle within me continues. Without doubt very difficult days lie ahead, with deep and wrenching feelings of grief, loss, depression—that is certain; for, in spite of all that I have disliked so intensely here, Turkey has come to seem like a home to me, a place of belonging for my mind and spirit, where I have experienced something which was missing throughout all my previous life and which I may perhaps never find again. May Allah my Sustainer give me strength and courage for what lies ahead and help me to be patient. For wherever He has seen fit to place my life, that is where I must continue my efforts for Islam, regardless of my personal feelings or of conditions and circumstances . . .

Thus the days here draw to a close. One last spurt of joy before we leave in the form of the trip to Bursa with Cemile, and then a hard push to do what must be done and have it over with. In the days and months and years which stretch ahead, I will remember even the very paving stones of Ankara on which we have walked in all seasons, God knows with what love and longing. Turkey has disappointed me, has hurt me, has done me great good and filled my heart with love. It is not Turkey's fault that we happened to

---

* Paternal aunt.

** The University ultimately reopened in August 1971, delaying the beginning of the spring semester by about five months.

come here at such a difficult time and with the expectation of finding it as it was in another era and with qualities which to a large extent it no longer possesses; this is entirely my mistake, for we were told repeatedly what me might expect. Let me praise God that I did yet find here so much that is precious and of value, the stock of which, still left, is continuously being eroded away by rough forces devoid of respect and love. I pray for the day of the triumph of belief in God, of truth and decency which still burn like a flame in millions of Turkish breasts, and for my return to this beloved land when Allah in His infinite mercy shall see fit to permit it . . .

CHAPTER 18

MORE GLIMPSES

April 20: This morning we met Cemile by pre-arrangement inside a small shop by the bus station; she greeted us with the greatest enthusiasm and joy. These days were holidays for the Children's Festival, the Çocukların Bayramı. Now we are all going on a trip together, a happy, delightful prospect; but I must not let myself forget: I must now de-involve myself emotionally with Turkey and must not let it leave my mind that we will be returning to America soon.

Ankara had been cold and unpleasant and it was good to get away from it; it had snowed the previous day and we all wore winter coats. Cemile sat between the girls during the first part of the trip; they were very happy and excited to be traveling with her, loving her so dearly, and the three of them carried on an animated conversation without pause.

The first stretch of the road to Bursa was the same as that on which we had traveled to Antalya, and this time I was surprised to see that even these bare treeless hills could be pretty with the tender green of spring on them. The terrain presently became more rolling and the countryside very green, with a profusion of trees, and in some places the road was quite winding and tortuous. We passed through several small towns as well as villages, pleasant and picturesque amid the lovely early green of spring and the flowering trees dotting the landscape; school children in uniforms and men and women in traditional dress added color and human interest to the scene. In a very green, moist area we saw numerous storks, which live in many parts of Turkey during the summer months, standing alone or in flocks, and an occasional one on the wing. I had not imagined that any of the interior parts of Turkey would be so beautiful; I was reminded of my childhood home and I thought that I had seldom seen such a lovely countryside.

It was early afternoon when we reached Bursa—green, beautiful Bursa, a city of about three hundred thousand population nestling against a snow-capped mountain, the famous Uludağ, at the top of which, we knew, was a ski resort. Bursa (Brusa) had been the first Ottoman capital during the years 1326–1453; it is known as one of the most religious cities of Turkey and as a unique and beautiful place of great historical interest.

We went to a pleasant, modern hotel which Enver had recommended, left our baggage in our rooms, and set out by taxi for the home of Lûtfı̂'s *hala,* where Fatma was expecting us. Here we were welcomed cordially by Asim Bey, the *hala's* husband, a man in early middle age, as well as by Gönül Hala herself, a plump, homey-looking woman—and there was Fatma, even dearer and more beautiful than I had remembered, beaming at us and hugging me so tight in her joy at seeing me again that she almost lifted me off the floor.

Since Asim Bey spoke no English, Cemile served as interpreter. His family consisted of a 'teen-age boy and girl, both very attractive, well-dressed and quite westernized in manner and appearance. The contrast between these children and their mother struck us all forcibly from the very first moment. She was a simple, hearty, uneducated woman who wore a kerchief and pyjamas with her dress as many unlettered conservative women do and who spoke but little, and I was at once at a loss to grasp how she could possibly be connected with these handsome, modern children. The apartment and its furnishings decidedly bespoke affluence, for Asim Bey was a flourishing businessman, and everything was elegant and expensive.

Asim Bey had taken the afternoon off so that he could accompany us on a tour of the city together with Fatma and Cemile. We were much impressed by his hospitality to us as complete strangers and indeed found it somewhat embarrassing, for we had no connection nor relationship with him except through his wife's niece by marriage, and were not in a position to repay his kindness in any way.

We traveled about the city by *dolmuş*, and I had an immediate impression of an exceedingly pleasant and lovely town, the old and new areas and structures intermingling to give a sense of unbroken continuity between past and present. We went first to the area called Yeşil, going through an archaeological museum containing for the most part Greek and Roman artifacts, housed in what had formerly been the *medrese* of the Yeşil Camii built in 1421; nearby was the beautiful Yeşil Türbe—the Green Tomb—in which fifteenth century Sultan Mehmet I was buried. A visit to the Yeşil Camii completed our tour of the area. The older Bursa mosques were quite different in basic architecture, even in the shape of the cupolas of their minarets, from the later, classical mosques, a feature of considerable interest to me.

Afterwards Asim Bey took us for tea at an outdoor teahouse overlooking one of Bursa's lovely hills on which stood the venerable Osmanlı mosque of Yıldırım Bayazıt with its vast cemetery. Fatma, Cemile and I were full of joy at being together; the two sisters kept Maryam and Nura close to them, loving them, talking to them and making them as happy as possible. Although Fatma did not understand a word of English, my scanty Turkish together with Cemile's interpretation was quite sufficient; for we had loved each other from the very first and there was a tacit understanding between us which came from the outlook and commitment we shared, often making a single word, look or gesture suffice.

Asim Bey then took us by *dolmuş* to a very old, picturesque part of the city called Muradiye, where stood the house in which fifteenth century Fatih Sultan Mehmet—Mehmet II, known as the Conqueror—was born. Beside it, within an enclosure stood a mosque and a series of tombs of a family of Ottoman sultans. The grounds of this compound were very beautifully arranged with flowerbeds and many kinds of trees, including palms, and the total effect was one of great serenity and peace, with a unique and unforgettable flavor. We visited the mosque and prayed *al-Fateha* at some of the tombs, enjoying the quiet, staid atmosphere of the place. It was a beautiful, happy, memorable time as we wandered hand-in-hand, Fatma, Cemile and I, with the girls, among the sheltering trees.

Afterwards we returned to the center of the city, where stood a statue of Atatürk on horseback before which a kind of grandstand was being erected for the observances of the approaching Children's Festival. Although the town was quite large population-wise, still it had the atmosphere of a small town because its sections were rather spread out and decentralized. Both because of its lovely natural setting and its historical places, it possessed a special, indefinable charm and personality, so totally different from that monotonous modern uniformity which characterizes New Ankara, which I had not found in other Turkish cities excepting some sections of Istanbul.

Asim Bey did not permit Selim to spend even one *kuruş* on this outing, and we were in the difficult position of accepting hospitality which we could never hope to repay. We now returned to his home to have tea, followed presently by dinner, talking with him through the interpretation of Cemile, while Fatma helped her aunt in the kitchen, and our children and Asim Bey's found some common interests.

It was impossible not to be struck by the great contrast which existed between this household and that of Cemile's family, for Gönül Hala seemed more like a housekeeper than the respected mother whose work for the benefit of the family was valued and shared by the younger people. Although Asim Bey himself was half-modern, half-traditional, the children were distinctly more 'modern' than their father, who, it was clear, had strong Islamic interest and feeling, and they seemed entirely without any connection with the simple, uneducated, decidedly unmodern mother who took care of all their needs, kept the lovely apartment with its elegant and costly furniture so beautifully for them all, but who herself seemed very much out of place in such a setting. The apartment was immaculately, shiningly clean, the work of one pair of hands alone in this case, I surmised, for I saw that the young people hardly offered to help their mother and seemed to protest if asked to do anything. I could not imagine how that mother could affect her children in any way—indeed, it was all too apparent that she could not—and I guessed that even the influence of the father, due to whose efforts, by the beneficence of God, all this affluence had come to them, might not be very great. I wondered if the children, who were nearly young adults, ever prayed or even knew how to pray, and if Islam meant anything more to them than simple tradition, for they were students in private schools—that is, among other young people as affluent and 'advanced' as themselves, which in turn probably meant weak Islamic values, in spite of their father's clear Islamic ties. It was not the least among the many contradictions and inconsistencies which we had observed in Turkey that a man who held strong Islamic values might totally neglect to pass them on to his own wife and children, observing prayers and other obligations but not teaching and guiding his family to do the same nor making sure that they understood Islam properly, and feeling satisfied that he was doing his full duty as a Muslim.

After dinner we chatted for a while with Asim Bey and then took our leave, with many thanks, promising to visit the next day, and returned to the hotel, full of thankfulness to God for the very happy experiences of the day.

April 21: This morning, after seeing some other places of historical interest, we decided to visit the ski resort at Uludağ, reached by a cable car going up the mountainside, just for the interest of the thing.

A young moustachioed taxi driver chauffeured us about. When we questioned him about going to Uludağ, he reported that the *teleferik* to the top of the mountain was not functioning. He could, however, drive us there, wait while we looked around or had lunch, and bring us back; and after a little dickering about the price we accepted his offer, under the impression that we were going to a place well worth seeing. The driver, who brought along a friend of his own careless, swaggering type "in case of snow" (he said) or other emergencies, was a youthful individual with a huge mop of black hair, of a highly romantic turn of mind which revolved on a lost beloved, although he had just been married. Depending from the rear-view mirror, where other drivers hung religious ornaments or other trinkets, was the touching emblem of his inner condition: a wire heart with a couple of brilliant blue, affectionate-looking love birds sitting together on a single perch absorbed in mutual adoration, while the radio poured forth the most doleful Turkish love songs available to serve as fuel for his inner fire.

The way to Uludağ lay through one side of the town. The day was quite cloudy. A very winding road went up through a belt of beautiful greenery to higher elevations whose slopes were covered with pines; at last there were patches of snow, and soon more snow, very soft-looking, covered the ground. We drove among clouds which flowed past and at length reached the top, where the pavement ended abruptly. The road was a sea of mud, and off the road there was soft, dirty snow. Various hotels and restaurants were scattered around the area, a touring bus stood waiting, and a handful of people was about, some on skis; the skiing season was almost over and the summer tourist season had not yet begun.

Walking about here without boots was out of the question because of the thick mud; we therefore asked the driver to recommend a restaurant where we could have lunch. He took us to a crude-looking place which he said had good food, but when we entered we heard the sound of loud jazz music and saw that people were dancing and drinking, although it was only noontime. A little way up the road we tried another establishment of similar appearance, and although it was not prepossessing, at least it was quiet and would have to do. It was empty except for two or three couples who sat about eating and drinking beer. The only food served here was *pirzola*—lamb chops—and bread, plus *ayran* or beer for those who wanted it. We ordered food, and the chauffeur and his companion, at another table, requested a beer apiece.

Although very expensive, the restaurant was primitive, and Cemile and I felt very much out of place in its atmosphere; I was only glad that Fatma was not with us. After a totally hopeless lunch of Turkish bread and very tiny chops which were mostly fat and bone, for which the bill was an outrageous 57 T.L., we returned to the taxi still hungry, the driver angry that the guests he had brought had been charged such high prices and that he and his friend had themselves paid for their beers at the inflated rate of 5 T.L. apiece.

Since there was nothing more to be seen here, and in any case one could hardly move because of the snow and thick mud, we drove back down the mountain through the same fog in silence, broken only by the 'sour songs' on the radio, the driver turning off the engine and coasting downhill to save gas whenever possible. The trip to Uludağ had offered no satisfactions of any sort to any of us. Although new for Cemile, apart from its unpleasantly vulgar atmosphere, it was an ordinary enough place compared with other ski resorts we had seen; but to find such a place with such an atmosphere in Turkey—and close to the venerable city of Bursa at that— had been interesting and at the same time depressing. When I heard it said that Uludağ was supposed to have been Mount Olympus in ancient times and that pagan priests and priestesses had used it as a resort, I thought that no good was to be expected from it after such an association.

Later in the afternoon we visited Asim Bey's house and then went to the covered bazaar and other shopping areas of Bursa to look for the ornamental wooden articles for which the city is justly famous, accompanied by Fatma. There was a pleasant flavor here, and I saw many women, especially older ones, clad in black çarşafs and other types of conservative dress. We returned with Fatma to Asim Bey's house for tea, and later went back to the hotel, where Cemile and I sat up talking until late into the night.

April 22: All during the night I heard rain dripping, and it was still raining in the morning. Asim Bey had invited us for an early lunch in a *kebap salonu** which he said was the best in Bursa, and after-

---

* A restaurant specializing in *kebap,* a savory meat preparation.

wards we went to the Ulucamı, the vast old mosque in the center of the city, for the *Dhuhr* prayer.

This fifteenth century mosque was quite simple, a great square or rectangle in shape; in the center of its interior stood a fountain for making *wudu,* something not uncommon in some of the older Osmanlı mosques. The ornamentation consisted mainly of many different styles of Arabic calligraphy lettered on the walls, a feature for which the mosque is famous. Afterwards we made some purchases of small religious articles from the little stalls near the mosque compound, many of which were closed during prayer time while the proprietors went to pray.

Later we took a *dolmuş* to the aged mosque of Yıldırım Bayazıt beyond Yeşil, beside which a vast cemetery, with old tombstones of interest, sloped down the hill, and here we walked in the soft drizzling rain. *Bursa in the rain . . .* I wonder if Bursa in fair weather can be as lovely. It gives the city a flavor all its own, a kind of melancholy which becomes it so well. I had not seen any other Turkish city I liked as much, for here much of the old had not yet been destroyed and replaced by ugly and soulless modern structures; old and new were delicately and unobtrusively blended, producing a very lovely and unique effect, and appealing in a quiet manner to one's Islamic feeling and sense of Islamic history. Asim Bey had said that Bursa had about three hundred mosques; as we had seen on the first afternoon here, on a fair day one could look out across the city from hill to hill, the slendered tapered columns of minarets intersecting the horizon in every direction. I thought over and over how lovely a place it would be to live in and how happy I might be here.

But time was becoming short. Fatma and Cemile had asked, so earnestly, if it might be possible for us to return to Ankara by way of Isparta so that all of us could be together once more before we leave Turkey, and although it was so much out of our way, our own hearts pulled us strongly in that direction. As Fatma was to have returned home now in any case, her leaving her aunt's house with us at this time would not be a problem; Lütfi had given her his unqualified permission to travel with our family in case the possibility arose, and this arrangement would also spare her the necessity of making the long trip home alone. It was decided that this afternoon we would go to Yalova, a small town on the Marmara coast two hours' drive from Bursa, to have a glimpse of the sea, and the next morning we would leave for Isparta, from where we and Cemile would return to Ankara two days later.

Accordingly, we went to Asim Bey's house, where Fatma explained the situation to him and Gönül Hala; they could not help feeling happy that since she must return home now in any case, she would not have to travel to Isparta alone. When she was ready, we took our last leave of Asim Bey and his wife, thanking them heartily for their hospitality, and joyfully went toward the center of the city. We would have three beautiful days together before returning to Ankara!

It was early afternoon when we dropped into a small *lokanta* for a bite to eat. Fatma was full of joy at the prospect of traveling with us, and we were equally happy at the unexpected way in which things had worked out. But as we sat at lunch chatting pleasantly together, I began to reflect on the fact that this trip was now half over and that we would very soon return to Ankara to begin our preparations for going home. Although I did not want to spoil the pleasure of the others, I could not help myself; I sat at the table silent and dull, almost unable to eat and unable to conceal what I was feeling from the perceptive, loving eyes of Cemile and Fatma, who did their best to comfort me although they themselves shared my regrets so keenly.

The modern hotel for ultra-westernized Turks and foreigners to which we now returned to fetch our baggage was something completely new for Fatma, who was very much interested in all she saw. I had observed her habits and ways of reacting, and, apart from the deep love which I had felt for her from our first meeting, had come to have a profound respect for her completely clean, pure, fastidious ways. She had not acquired great experience of the world in her short, sheltered life, but still, whenever any matter requiring an opinion or decision arose, I saw that her judgment about it was clear and faultless; for she judged solely by Islamic standards and was not confused, as worldly people are apt to be, by other considerations. It was a part of her nature to observe, to think over matters, and to evaluate everything by the sound Islamic criteria which were a part of her very being, and she passed carefully over anything which fell short of the pure and pristine standards by which she lived. I was so thankful and happy for her and her sister's love, and loved them so dearly in return; yet there was no respite from the perpetual nagging awareness that we must part so very soon.

We got a bus almost at once for Yalova, traveling through beautiful rich countryside to this small town on the Marmara Sea. We spent the afternoon at the beach, happily walking along the edge of the water, in which the children played, looking for shells, and later seeing a little of the town which was in no way interesting and indeed rather dingy and depressing. We found rooms in a plain, simple hotel and in the night Fatma, Cemile and I sat up talking together until very late.

April 23: The next morning we set out early. We had made our reservations the previous day for the first leg of the journey from Yalova to Eskişehir, a town midway between Bursa and Ankara where we would change buses for Isparta, and Cemile had arranged that reservations for the Isparta bus be made by telegram as well. As a rule Turkish buses are very efficient and are easily available, but to find seats on this same bus for so many people without having reservations might present difficulties.

Today was the first day of the Children's Festival, one of the national holidays instituted by Kemal Atatürk, and the streets were full of people. After we had finished a poor breakfast in a crude eating place, the parades of elementary school children for this occasion began, and we stood watching among the throngs of people as class after class marched down the street. The youngsters of each class all wore a particular dress or costume which was different from that of all other classes, and some carried banners or pictures of Atatürk. Although it was obvious that many of the children came from very poor homes, almost everything they were wearing had been made or purchased especially for this occasion. Those who were wearing ordinary street clothes could of course wear them again, but many wore special costumes which could be used only for this particular function. Little girls, who generally wore their hair, if long, in plaits, today marched proudly along with flowing or curled hair, self-conscious at being the focus of all eyes. I thought of how poor parents must have sacrificed to make this possible, and how many of them must be viewing the spectacle of their marching children not with pride but with a justifiable bitterness at having to spend their precious cash for such a purpose.

The counterpart of this festival for youth from middle and high schools will be observed in about a month, on May 19. On that occasion, youngsters of both sexes from *orta okuls* and *lises* parade and perform gymnastics in public. They are without exception required to wear shorts for this occasion, and the participation of everyone selected is compulsory. If they refuse to participate, even on grounds of religion or conscience, they receive failing marks in physical education, which means that, under the Turkish educational system, they will fail and have to repeat the entire school year, no matter how well they may have done in academic subjects. Clad in their mini-shorts, they perform gymnastics (which often include lying on the ground for leg-raises or push-up exercises) before large audiences in a public arena such as a stadium, something absolutely unthinkable for Turkish girls who have been brought up to value their modesty.

With this background of encouragement—rather insistence—by the government of institutionalized immodesty and enforced lack of shame, it is hardly surprising that so many of today's Turkish girls have not developed and do not value such qualities. Obviously this policy is quite deliberate. It is hoped that by pushing Turkish girls (and boys as well, for no religious or conservative Turkish adolescent boy would willingly be seen in public in shorts) to wear such a dress and participate in such exercises, they will become isolated from and forget the Islamic standards of modesty, and perhaps indeed all of Islam, in order to become 'modern' and 'emancipated.' Apparently no one in high places cares to realize that the matter does not end here, and that gradually many Turkish girls will be encouraged by such activities to pass from immodesty of dress and behavior through the intermediate steps leading to illicit sexual relations unhampered by any considerations of morality or shame, as so many have done in the West—or perhaps this is the ultimate aim of requiring such a dress and participation in such a festival!

I took photo after photo, standing among the adults along the side watching the spectacle of marching children. In dozens of towns in Turkey today this parade would be duplicated on a smaller or larger scale. A grandstand had been set up nearby for public ceremonies, and throughout the country millions of flowers would be sacrificed to make beautiful wreaths and floral arrangements to place before images of the national 'idol' who had instituted this holiday. As we traveled during the day, we saw Turkish flags flying or draped on buildings in various towns along the way, statues of Atatürk before which offerings of flowers—expensive wreaths—had been placed, and the usual huge, hideous cloth posters depicting his scowling face in livid colors hung on public buildings. It did not in reality appear to be the Children's Festival as much as a holiday for the national deity, like all national holidays in Turkey!

After the parade was over, we went to the bus station. Since it had been impossible to find seats for all of us on the same bus without waiting until afternoon, we made the first leg of the journey to Eskişehir on two different busses; Selim and the children were waiting at the Eskişehir station when the bus carrying Cemile, Fatma and me arrived. We had a wait of an hour-and-a-half there during which we had lunch and went for a walk, but at last we were all seated on a bus for the second, longer portion of the journey to the home which we loved so much. The seven of us occupied the back row of seats, Nura first sitting on our laps and later asleep across a row of laps. I sat by Fatma, our hands clasped, wordlessly bound together by deep love; none of us was in a mood to talk very much. From time to time the radio played the sad, lilting popular songs which are everywhere present here, somehow evoking, with the plaintive, haunting melodies which form a subtle background wherever one goes in Turkey, the very mood of Anatolia itself.

Later, as people left the bus at various places along the way, we were able to get better seats, and I went to sit in front with Jamal, taking photographs from time to time. Again the same pleasant countryside, the villages, the rural people—this beloved land.

Seeing a bullock cart creaking slowly up the road ahead of us, Jamal remarked to me that mechanization of farming must come to Turkey and that it would improve living conditions greatly. "That's true," I replied, "but you know that technological change also changes the values and living patterns of a society. Therefore technological change must be planned, not haphazard, so that the value system will not be destroyed and disruption of the social fabric won't result."

Jamal considered this for a minute. "I guess that's pretty important," he said thoughtfully. "Technology must be made to conform to values, not values to technology." Startled by his concise way of putting it, I sat there astonished at his grasp of a matter which has so far apparently eluded the combined understandings of the leading 'experts' and social planners of the entire Muslim world, namely, that a society must first establish and define its goals and values—not merely goals of material advancement but, much more importantly, spiritual and moral goals and values which can give direction to its material aspects in a clear-cut manner—and that technological changes must conform to and implement them.

"Very well put," I told Jamal approvingly. "But the question is how to go about it. Technological change is of course essential and must come. But before major steps toward industrialization and technological development are undertaken in any Muslim country, there should be well-thought-out planning at governmental levels by a corps of dedicated Muslim sociologists, educators and social planners, as well as technical personnel. In that way, Muslim social scientists and scientific and technical personnel would all work together with their common Islamic frame of reference to build, from the ground up, a sound society governed by Islamic principles. Without this, changes will be completely random and can do great damage to social and moral values. But such planning hasn't been done anywhere in the Muslim world as far as I know, and I'm afraid the result is going to be some very serious disruption of the society and its values."

Making sure Jamal understood, I continued. "There is another point which is very important. We Muslims have fallen so far behind much of the rest of the world in developing our science and technology that we must now get our knowledge and experience in these areas from those who have them. But it simply doesn't follow that because Turkey and the rest of the Muslim world want the benefits of modern science, industry and technology, we have to accept along with them the values and behavior patterns of the technologically-developed countries where they conflict with our own; for we believe that since the guidance which Islam gives is so greatly superior to any man-made system, no one else can be our example or teacher in the realm of beliefs, morals or behavior, and that we are to be the leaders and teachers, not the other way around. So today we have to do two things: to acquire modern skills and knowledge from the West, always taking great care not to bring in with them all the undesirable, destructive values and behavior which have gone hand-in-hand with them in the West, and are now doing such great harm to its spiritual and social life, and at the same time to try to impart the Islamic beliefs and values to it."

Jamal turned this over in his mind. "All right," he said, "but what I don't understand is why people in the Muslim world don't know all about the West and the things that are wrong with it. If they did, it seems to me they wouldn't want to copy it. Why do they think it's so great?"

"You see," I replied, "Muslims generally know about the West only from a distance and through a haze of glamour. Many of them actually get their ideas about it from what they see in Hollywood movies—the high standard of living, wonderful industry and technology—but they don't have any clear idea about its moral, spiritual and social problems. So it's the job of knowledgeable Muslims who are informed about these things to tell others. I think one of the things the Muslim world needs most urgently today is to develop the discipline of sociology with an Islamic frame of reference. There should long since have been numbers of knowledgeable Muslim sociologists who informed the Muslim world about other cultures, especially about the West—its ideology and the meaning of its behavior patterns, its good points and its bad ones. If this had been done, Muslims would have understood the philosophy and value system underlying Western civilization, and they would not have been so ready to accept its values and imitate its behavior patterns just because they seem to go hand-in-hand with material progress.''

"Well," Jamal said, "that may be true, but I think another reason is that a lot of Muslims don't seem to know much about what Islam is either, and so of course they're bound to be confused."

"Quite right," I said, "both of these things are major causes of the problem. A proper education for Muslims is essential if the trend toward acceptance of non-Islamic values is to be stopped—an Islamic education which tells them what Islam *really* is, and which also tells them what other cultures are so that they can evaluate them realistically and know how to react to them, starting from first grade."

Jamal nodded, understanding. Although only thirteen years old, he was already a thinker. Out of his experiences of recent months, away from the pressures of American society and the need to conform to it, in an atmosphere from which he had drawn the Islamic elements for which he had been searching, as well as our long discussions about many serious subjects, had grown a new awareness and comprehension rare in one his age. How excellent a thing, I thought, is correct understanding in the mind of a Muslim no matter what his years, observing and judging solely by the standards of Islam.

It was this same clarity of understanding which I had observed in Fatma, over which I had pondered a good deal. What the world said, thought or did had no influence with her; her vision was purely that of a Muslim, judging always by Islamic criteria, and hence it was sound and true. Time after time in talking with her on this trip, either with my scant Turkish or through Cemile's interpretation, I heard her voice opinions, saw them to be wise and sound, and to be arrived at easily, immediately and by the most direct route. Leaving my place at Jamal's side; I now went to this dear Fatma and we sat with our hand clasped, neither of us speaking. I thought sadly for how brief a time it would be my privilege to be near her, Cemile and the rest of the family, yet I was boundlessly thankful to God for that privilege, short-lived though it might be. She was as bright and lovely as a flower, the cheerful, loving ornament of the home in which she filled the vital role of wife and daughter, strong and healthy physically, clear and straight mentally, with well-formed, mature judgment and common sense, and eminently capable of guiding the development of the children she would insha'Allah have one day. Although she had not had a highly-advanced formal education, nevertheless she was an avid reader and was completely aware of all issues—political, economic, religious, social—as these were discussed between her and her husband and with her parents and sister, and on such matters as on all others, her ideas were clear and sound.

I had thought so much about her family during this trip, especially about her mother, whom I could not help comparing with Gönül Hala, a woman of about the same age but utterly simple and evidently incapable of joining any discussion or doing anything other than housework. I recalled with what interest Fatma's mother had listened to our discussions whenever she was not busy elsewhere, her comments clear-sighted, completely Islamic and full of mature understanding. Cemile had told me that her mother read Islamic literature almost daily, including the Qur'an in Arabic. Her mind was well-formed, keen and disciplined, and it was very clear from what I had seen and from what Cemile had told me that the minds of her children had been shaped by her wise and sound training just as much as by their father's. She was in every way a fitting companion and partner for him and matched his Islamic zeal and purity with her own.

The fact that it had been the joint effort of both the parents which had trained and guided these two excellent sisters was of great importance in my mind. It was clear that the father or the mother alone could not have achieved this result, and their combined influence was also the reason for that very strong sense of cohesion, cooperation and selflessness which I had felt among them.

The *hala*'s children, on the other hand, had been brought up largely by a father who had not seen to it that his children shared his Islamic values; and his lenient upbringing, his showering them with things, and above all, his not bringing his wife up to his level but leaving her, like the household servant, to fill no role in the home other than that of carrying out the domestic work, had had a marked effect on them. How could such 'modern' children as these, tutored by their father's indifference to inculcating in them Islamic values and by the one-sided educational system of which they were the product, respect, sympathize with or possibly even act dutifully toward such a mother? Thus, while the uneducated women of Turkey might be wonderfully goodhearted and pious, they were often totally without understanding of any matters beyond those pertaining to household work, and therefore able to have little or no influence on children growing up in the rapidly-changing world of urban Turkey, subjected to all sorts of societal influences and pressures which their mothers could not even grasp and certainly could not expect to counteract.

Everywhere I had gone since coming to Turkey I had observed women of all types. For example, I particularly noticed on this bus a woman who wore a scarf in a very careless manner and took it off when she decided to sleep—for her a convention rather than something integrally bound up with her conception of herself as a Muslim woman. Her husband sat by her side reading one of the many ugly tabloid newspapers of Turkey which specialize in stories and pictures of film stars and semi-nude women. Perhaps such a woman took it as a matter of course that her husband should be interested in this type of reading matter; this was the way men were, undoubtedly, in her conception. I had now come to realize with great impact that a considerable part of the plight of the Muslim world today is due to the appalling fact that very few Muslim women (and, for that matter, Muslim men as well) have had any true and correct training in Islam, apart from, at best, very traditional approaches. Generally lacking any sort of education in observing, thinking, analyzing, reading, studying, improving themselves, or feeling responsibility for any aspects of life other than housework, looking after the physical needs of their children, and satisfying the often arbitrary demands of their husbands, most Muslim women know neither their rights, duties nor responsibilities, nor how these should be carried out.

This lack of education of Muslim women has in effect resulted in one-half the population of the Muslim world—undoubtedly the more important half as far as the basic training of children is concerned—ceasing to play an effective role in shaping the society and its future. Thus, lacking the strong example of and training by one or both parents, without a meaningful and adequate Islamic education, and influenced by the unIslamic attitudes and practices prevalent in the society, it is hardly any wonder that Muslim children today grow up very vague or even totally ignorant concerning the basic message of Islam, their obligations as Muslims, and how these are to be fulfilled. And when they in turn become parents, can we be surprised that they are unable to impart Islamic values to their children and have also ceased to have a clear conception of how to bring them up?

Thus, as generation succeeds generation, the understanding and practice of Islam in the total society is steadily diminished, a phenomenon which is illustrated in a striking manner in Turkey and other parts of the Muslim world. In the same family there may be a pious and devout elderly grandmother wearing a *şalvar* and kerchief, who never mises a prayer and spends much time reciting *dhikr* with *tesbih* in hand and reading *du'as* in Arabic or Osmanlı Turkish. Her daughter is likely to be a modern, well-dressed young matron who seldom if ever prays and whose Islam is confined to *Ramadan*, the 'Eids or the occasion of a death; and in the next generation, her grand-daughter, in mini-skirts and with very westernized ways, may not even know how to pray, Islam being for her a mere occasional social convention which is related, in some remote and rather unintelligible manner, to special festivals and to the habits of the elderly. Certainly it is not very unusual to find in the same Turkish household today a devout elderly Muslim whose son or daughter is a Kemalist and whose grand-child is either an ardent communist or Kemalist.

Now in Cemile's home I had seen, in the truest and purest form, a family in which children had been raised in the real spirit and tradition of Islam, their minds having been cultivated with care by the joint effort of both their parents—and most importantly in my mind, by a mother who had not abdicated her role and responsibility as the educator and guide of her offspring. Although up to this time I had not been clear how this could be effected in a society like that of present-day Turkey, I now had a concrete example and embodiment before my eyes, and I knew that, apart from the great happiness which their love and friendship had given us, our meeting with Cemile's family was one of the most important things I had experienced in Turkey—an example of the personification of the Islamic teachings and way of life in a concrete family. And Cemile assured me that her family was by no means unique, and that there were many others whom she personally knew who were very similar.

Now with this great love in my heart for them which every one of us shared, we would see them again only to leave them, this time perhaps forever, for who knew when in the changing paths of this vast world, we might meet again. The mother, with her earnest, loving manner, had had a heart big enough to take me in and love me as her own daughter, and I had called her *"Annecigim,"* the Turkish diminutive for 'mother,' from my heart when we had parted. I would always think of her by that name, and of each one of them as our own beloved family members . . .

The journey occupied the entire day, taking us through country most of which we had seen on the way to Antalya, and was entirely uneventful. We reached Isparta after dark, our arrival announced by a telegram which Cemile had sent from Yalova. And there at the well-remembered house was Anne, her face alight with joy at having her daughters back home and at seeing us once again. Amca Bey bade us a hearty welcome, greeting Jamal and Selim like his own sons; Lûtfî came back from visiting a neighbor, equally warm in his welcome, and then the circle was complete.

As we sat down to a very late supper, the two sisters narrated the highlights of our trip, with many interested comments and questions from the other members of the family. We did not sit up long to talk tonight, as all the travelers were extremely weary from the

long journey, and by half-past eleven, our prayers completed, we
were all asleep.

April 24: I was awakened by the stir of the family preparing for
Fajr prayer in the early dawn; Selim went with Amca Bey and Lûtfî
to the mosque, and we women prayed together in the house. When
the men returned, Amca Bey read aloud from the Qur'an in Arabic,
all the family gathered to listen. A simple breakfast followed; we sat
around the table in an atmosphere of utter contentment, hardly able
to believe that this precious gift of another whole day together was
ours, by the mercy of God.

The morning was spent in a pleasant, leisurely walk with
Cemile, her father and Lûtfî through the center of the city; on the
way home we passed by the school where Amca Bey was a teacher.
When we sat down to lunch amidst the spotless cleanliness of the
sunny dining room, Amca Bey talked about the school, Cemile
translating as necessary. Here in conservative Isparta children were
on the whole better behaved, with fewer discipline problems than
we had observed in Ankara, but nevertheless, he said, the weakening of home controls and standards during the past years was quite
noticeable. He was much interested in educational methods current
in America, and I promised to leave the children's workbooks from
their American school with Cemile when we go so that he can, with
the help of her translation, study the methodology and approach.
He asked many further questions about conditions in America and
our life there, trying to form a clear picture of it, and again I was
struck by his unusual intellectual vigor and alertness.

Afterwards Fatma, Cemile and their mother conferred among
themselves. It had been decided the previous evening to invite a
small group of women after dinner, most of whose men-folk were
also coming to meet Selim. Lûtfî, Amca Bey, Selim and the children
then departed to convey verbal messages to the persons who were to
be invited, while Cemile and I went to town on an errand or two.
Thus the afternoon passed all too quickly in the company of the beloved ones with whom these few precious hours were being shared.

Soon after dinner the visitors began to arrive, and the men retired to the *salon*. Cemile had said to me, *"Ablacıgım,* you have told me many times that you think our family is special and unique in Turkey. I'm sure that after you meet these women tonight you will know that this is not so, and that there are so many other Muslim families like us." Indeed, this proved to be wholly true, and at the end of the evening I could only thank God for another very important and meaningful experience which had strengthened my certainty that Islam in Turkey is, by His mercy, a very strong and vital force, which has not been in any way impeded by all the difficulties and repression which it has faced but may in fact have been strengthened by them.

A series of young women, close friends of Fatma and Cemile, all wearing various types of modest dresses, coats and head coverings, arrived one after another in the course of the evening, accompanied by three or four babies and small children. As we sat down together after the initial greetings and embraces, Cemile told them in a few words about me; their eyes held me with looks of great love and sympathy. Then Fatma introduced them one by one. Several were well-educated; one was a graduate of the *Ilâhiyat Fakültesi* (Religious Faculty) in Ankara and two others of other faculties, while two were currently university students, now on holiday like ourselves. Some were married. All gave the impression of being conscious, committed Muslims who took their responsibilities toward Islam very seriously.

We began to talk together without any shyness or reserve. After many questions had been asked concerning Islam in America and our personal situation there, it was my turn to ask questions, Cemile translating as necessary. During the last days I had been turning over and over in my mind the problems of Turkish Muslim women, searching for answers to the questions I had framed. Now, *Alhamdulillah,* I was at last among a group of young, obviously committed women who seemed to have found some answers for themselves, and was eager to share their ideas.

Safiye, a girl who was studying at a university in Ankara, seemed the most articulate of the group. I therefore asked her what she felt to be the most serious problems of Turkish Muslim women. After considering for a moment, she replied, "First of all, ignorance. Most of our mothers are illiterate. At the very most they may pray and fast but they will probably not do anything more than that. They will certainly not be able to affect the society, but it will be able to affect and to spoil them. We have to find a way to change this ignorance into knowledge—not just religious knowledge alone, but knowledge which will help us to understand modern problems, to change Turkish society and bring it back to Islam."

"This is very right," I said, struck by her clear analysis of the situation. "But how can it be done? What is the method?"

"That is the important question," she replied. "You see, the problem of girls' education in Turkey is a very serious one. Many Muslim families don't allow their girls to go on to middle and high school because they are afraid that the experience will spoil their daughters' morals, especially as almost all schools are co-educational. Besides that, there is the matter of dress, since girls are not allowed to cover their hair in school."

"This is a very big problem," said a very sincere-looking girl who was a graduate of the *Ilâhiyat Fakültesi.* "Even in my institution, the place which is supposed to train Muslim leaders, although we could cover our hair, people still bothered us about it, including some of the teachers. But still it was much, much easier there than in any of the other *fakültes* and schools."

How well aware I was of this! Although there were some extremely courageous girls attending various higher educational institutions in Turkey who kept their Islamic dress and hair covering, perhaps Allah alone knew how much this simple matter of putting a scarf on their heads was costing them. May He help all those who have the courage to take this very brave step as an integral part of their identity as Muslim women whose modesty is an uncompromisable part of their faith.

"It is very difficult," Safiye went on. "Some Muslim girls who are trained as teachers don't teach after they graduate because they can't cover their hair. For example, these two sisters here"—she indicated the girl who had spoken previously and another girl—"are graduates of the *Ilâhiyat Fakültesi*. They are well-qualified and could be *deen* teachers in the best high schools, or even become assistant principals. But because in Turkey a teacher is not allowed to cover her hair, they have decided not to teach and are sitting at home, without any use for the knowledge which it took them years of hard work to acquire."

"Not without any use, Safiye Abla," one of them remonstrated. "You know that I want to teach and that I know how important it is, but I just can't feel that it's right to uncover my hair to do it. It is compromising modesty, which is a basic principle of Islam. So I'm trying to find some other ways of being useful by teaching Islam to groups of children privately."

"That is the next best thing," I told her.

Another girl took up the thread. "I wanted very badly to continue my education after elementary school, but because of this problem my family wouldn't allow it. They wanted to send me to a Girls' Institute where I would learn domestic skills, but," she smiled ruefully, "I wasn't interested in it. What I really wanted was to study at an *Imam-Hatip* school,* but there again I couldn't cover my hair. So we found another solution. I am now studying the *imam-hatip* course at home, and when I finish it I'll take the official examination and will have the same qualifications as if I'd studied at the school, but without having had to compromise my modesty."

"What will this type of education qualify you to do?" I asked.

"I plan to work among women, teaching them Islam and trying to help them understand their Islamic responsibilities."

We smiled at one another. "That is a wonderful work, my sister," I told her. "May Allah help you."

---

* An institute at middle and high school level which trains both boys and girls in Islamic knowledge, Arabic, etc., preparing them to be *imams*, readers of the Qur'an, religious teachers and preachers.

Two other girls, both of whom were married and the mothers of young children, said that as their families were convinced of the value of a higher education and had trusted them not to get spoiled by going to school, even with uncovered hair, they had completed high school. They had married soon after finishing school and had begun to wear a complete Islamic dress at that time.

"What about you?" I then asked Safiye, curious to know how she handled the problem. "Do you go to your university with your hair covered?"

"No," she replied, after a moment's hesitation. "It is simply impossible to do it at my university, which has so many anti-Islamic students and professors. You would be taunted and mocked at by everyone, the teachers would despise you and treat you like dirt under their feet, and they would do all in their power to see to it that you got poor marks and bad treatment—and even worse things might happen. My life would have been made unbearable if I had worn a scarf on campus, so I put it on when I am away from the university and take it off before I return. It is the only way to survive there."

I nodded, understanding the magnitude of the problem which confronted her.

"Actually," she continued, "in the beginning my mother was very much against my continuing my education. But my father is quite a strong person, a fighter. He realized that I would be much better able to serve Islam if I got an education which would prepare me to hold some good position, even if it had to be done without a scarf, than by staying home and leaving all the important posts to unIslamic people. Marian Abla," she went on, looking at me with great sincerity, "this is the big dilemma for women in Turkey today. We want to live Islam but are unable to. All of us, as students or as teachers, are facing the same difficulties. Leftist teachers are preferred, and ideas and dress must conform to the secular ideal. But although it's very difficult, we have to go on struggling, and *insha'Allah* we will be able to do something for Islam."

"*Insha'Allah,* my sister," I rejoined warmly. This was indeed a difficult and distressing situation; yet in the course of our discussion several possible solutions had been mentioned, although each presented difficulties of one sort or another and none was ideal. Still, until a permanent, really adequate solution to this question was worked out in Turkey, women could follow one of these or possibly other alternatives with the intention of pleasing Allah and serving Islam in the best way possible; for where one's sincere desire and intention is to serve Islam, solutions can be found to problems far more pressing than these.

Fatma and her mother now brought tea and pastries for the men to the door of the *salon* and handed them in through Lutfî, and we also had our share. Thus the talk among us went on and on into the night, ending in an exchange of ideas for dresses and head coverings. All these girls were dressed in a way which clearly denoted their Islamic identity and which was, for the most part, also contemporary and appealing. How different a breed of Turkish women these were, I thought, from the simple, good-hearted, uneducated and unaware women of the villages and towns. These were dynamic, alive people, consciously committed to Islam; this quality of aliveness and dynamism shone in their faces as they spoke of their conviction that Islam was the greatest thing in life and that they must help to bring its light to others.

At last a knock on the door which divided the *salon* from the dining room where we sat broke up the group. While their husbands, fathers or brothers who had gathered in the drawing room waited for them outside, they put on their scarves and coats, and said goodbye to each of us in turn. The embraces of farewell were long and meaningful to me, as I held these girls close, aware of the commitment which we shared half-way around the world, sisters in faith and in mutual love, and tears shone in more than one pair of eyes as we parted. After they had all left, I brought myself back to the every-day world with a sigh, recalling what I had for the moment almost forgotten—that tomorrow morning we must return to Ankara with Cemile.

April 25: We were up for *Fajr* prayer with the family and spent the next few hours together talking. It was exceedingly hard to contemplate saying a final goodbye to them all, so lately become beloved and familiar to us; yet I knew that it was only one of the many difficult and bitter moments ahead of me. Our last journey before we turned homeward was coming to an end, and within a short time the entire trip would be over.

It was an extremely sad and painful parting for us all, this time without any hope of meeting again in the foreseeable future. The mother and daughter whom I loved so dearly stood waving goodbye to us with wet eyes at the street, as I strained for one last, treasured glimpse of them before the taxi turned the corner. Amca Bey and Lûtfî came with us to the bus station; they saw us seated in the bus, and for the last time bade us a hearty, loving farewell, commending us to God's protection.

The children and I did not try to keep back the tears, for they *must* come. We had seen Bursa and other parts of Turkey, but for me that was a secondary matter, enjoyable and interesting though the trip had been. The main thing was that we had seen Cemile's family once more and members of several others like it, and had reaffirmed our faith in the fact that even in the Turkey of today, so spoiled and distorted by evils which have assaulted it from within and without, there are Muslim families living pure Islamic lives; it *can* be done and it *is* being done. I thanked God with all my heart for having brought us together from the opposite ends of the earth, and prayed that the love which is between us may last until our final breaths, *insha'Allah.*

Cemile sat with the girls, talking gaily and joking with them to make them forget their grief, and I was with Jamal who, as usual on buses, was having trouble with asthma because of the cigarette smoke and lack of ventilation. Uneducated men sat engrossed in reading the same shabby, shameful tabloid newspapers. This, I thought acridly, is what the minds of many Turks are formed by, perhaps almost the sole use of their limited literacy. The crystal clarity of judgment which is possible to a well-trained, well-informed mind like Fatma's is destroyed, confused and covered over by a welter of ideas coming from various directions, like so many poisons, to distort judgment and reason, to subvert morals and behavior, to render men an easy prey to those who want to manipulate them for their own nefarious ends, and, equally bad, to render them an easy prey to their own baser desires and feelings. For the average non-Islamic Turk is like that today: without mind, without purpose, without faith, without integrity, he has been taken over and mastered by those who are experts in destroying the true values of human civilization, whether they are political leaders, business interests, the controllers of mass media, or the distorted educational system, and made their slaves.

The net result of all this? That that particular vitality, those splendid human qualities which have characterized Turks throughout the centuries, are being attenuated, weakened, sapped, by the lack of direction and sense of true identity, and thus the contemporary non-Islamic Turk is nothing: not recognizable as a real Turk, certainly not a part of Europe, hardly a Muslim, perhaps not even a decent human being—in short, an ideological, cultural, cipher having no real contribution to make either to his own society or to the world community.

My reflections on the way home were bitter, and I wondered how, after seeing the glorious countryside around Bursa, I could ever have found any beauty in this bleak landscape around Ankara, although it was now pale green instead of only earth-colored. Truly the countryside leading to the capital is as stark and unappealing as the city which has sprung out of the desert around it, with its endless streets of characterless, faceless buildings belonging neither here nor there, as if symbolic of the many identity-less Turks who inhabit them.

Thus we returned from our last trip within Turkey. Gül Hanım was sitting on the front steps of the house when our taxi drove up, and her son, almost completely healed now, was playing nearby; she bade us a hearty, *"Hoş geldiniz."* Cemile spent the evening with us and then returned to her university after the bright glory of these few beautiful days together which none of us would ever forget.

Now all our efforts would be directed toward the winding-up of our affairs. But the heart does not let go so easily of what it has called its own and of what it has deeply loved and cherished. Although Turkey may contain elements of everything worthless and wrong at this time, still to me it has become dearer than any other place on earth by virtue of the loveliness and goodness which are stored up, in a less obtrusive and noticeable fashion, within it. What I have observed of what remains of the vitality of Islam in this land is merely a shell, or at best a dimmed mirror, of what had once been. Nevertheless, in what is left, one who views it with understanding and with the eyes of love can find precious traces of characteristics, qualities and traditions which are purely Islamic, many of which are common throughout the Muslim world, coming as they do from one common source. One who approaches it with love can find such sincerity, such goodness of heart and such uprightness among many of its people, such inestimably valuable qualities and characteristics, that the heart almost breaks to think of the destruction of all this noble heritage. Turkey is a land and a people to capture the imagination, stir the heart, and kindle the fires of love for what Islam had imprinted upon the lives of its followers in the past and could do again in the future, with the help of God, if Muslims are firm and sincere in striving toward this goal . . .

One last word before I close the book of pictures which remains in my memory of this trip. I cannot forget the image of Cemile's mother, whom I also call *Anne,* as she prayed *'Isha* in her house but one night ago. I had come and prayed beside her, reciting the shortened prayer of the traveler, said my brief *du'a* and *dhikr,* folded up the *seccade* and went out of the room. Seeing her totally absorbed in her prayer, completely oblivious to everything around her, I knew that under that roof there were hearts which feared no one except God, which were completely centered on Him and contented with Him, and which no power or persuasion on earth could change or subvert. Because of such true hearts as these, I do yet have great hope for the future of Islam in this land, although at times the picture may indeed seem without hope. Let me close this chapter by praying for a faith as deep, true and unwavering as that beloved mother's faith before I come to the end of my journey in this world, and for a heart as unswerving from truth and righteousness, by the grace of God.

"The believers, men and women, are protectors of one another. They en-
join what is just and forbid what is evil. They observe regular prayers,
practice *Zakat,* and obey God and His Messenger. On them will God pour
His mercy, for God is Exalted in Power, Wise. God has promised the believers, men and women, Gardens under which rivers flow, to dwell there-
in, and clean and good dwelling places in Gardens of everlasting felicity.
But still greater is the pleasure of God; that is the greatest achievement."[*]

.

[*] *Al-Tauba* 9:71-72.

CHAPTER 19

THE CLOSING OF A CHAPTER

April 27: The preparations for returning home are underway. Knowing this, I have felt a curious sensation within myself, of which I was aware all during our Bursa trip, of the cutting-off of my emotional involvements here and a sort of hardening which at first I was at a loss to identify but which I have now recognized; it is no stranger. It is the precursor of that hardness which one must have, and which certainly to a great degree I myself have had, in order to live in the America of today. Indeed, a great part of what I feel about returning home is due to a dread of reacquiring this hardness which I dislike so intensely.

It is this hardness which often makes Eastern people seem strangely simple to Westerners, as indeed they are; for this hardness is antithetical and opposed to simplicity and the acceptance of life on its own terms. It is the product of a social environment in which human beings, in defense of retaining even their bare individuality in an ever-increasing ocean of depersonalization and mechanization, have had to develop a sort of protective shell in order to survive; but the cost of maintaining that shell is a steadily-rising tide of emotional disorders, social ills and an enormous deterioration in the quality of one's inner life and interpersonal relationships.

For this hardness is the antithesis of love. Because of it an individual becomes increasingly able to accept as 'love' many things which merely masquerade as love; the quality of selfless concern and affection by which true love is characterized becomes tainted with self-interest, and calculation and manipulation are interwoven into the better feelings. Thus relationships with other human beings are characterized by a progressive loss of warmth, sincerity and intimacy, and by a 'handling' and 'dealing with' people as if they were things.

Such hardness is the exact opposite of the disinterested sincerity which I have found here among the non-westernized Turks, and during our stay here I have found myself losing it little by little, replacing it with a softness, gentleness, courtesy and consideration for other human beings which surely was not there earlier. May God keep me from becoming hard in my relations with other people, whether they are themselves hard or not, for they cannot help it, I know; it is in the very air they breathe there, permeating many of the attitudes towards other people, both individual and collective. And oh, so earnestly I pray for it, may He bring me back to live the rest of my life, somehow, somewhere, among those who still have the sweet grace of simplicity, the blessed ability to love unselfishly, the clear light of faith, which are His most precious gifts.

For faith, too, is intimately connected with this simplicity and lack of hardness—not the simplicity of credulity or unawareness, but that simplicity which is a reflection of openness of heart, the opposite of cynicism: the capacity to believe and to trust in what is beyond the limited grasp of the senses and of human reason, but what the heart, with its clear, innate grasp of truth, *knows* without doubt. And while this faith, a complete and unreserved trust in God's wisdom and the ability to accept whatever He sends, becomes the focal point of the personality of the one who possesses it, guarding him against bitterness, rebellion and despair, those who have this hardness, like a covering grafted on their hearts, *cannot* believe because the vital ingredient which makes belief possible has lost its hold on their being, stamped out and crushed by that cynicism and disillusionment which they attempt to disguise by high-sounding words such as 'realism,' 'intellectual honesty' and 'facing the facts.'

During these months I have been both a participant in and a spectator of the process of becoming adjusted here, for I have simultaneously lived it and observed my living it. How easy was that adjustment compared to that which lies before me now! As the confusion of the early days gave place little by little to understanding, a kind of deeper inner life, nurtured by the various Islamic elements in the environment, grew up about the new experiences and emotions, opening windows of the heart which had never been opened before, and beckoning me to look into them and submerge myself in them. I can look back now upon my early days here, read what I wrote then, and understand what I could not grasp at the time. But although the judgments and impressions of that period may be partial and incomplete, they still retain their interest and validity as early parts of an experience in maturing in understanding which, if we had been able to stay on, would undoubtedly have continued to increase in depth and breadth.

I continue to turn over in my mind all I have observed and experienced during these months. It seems to me that in what I have seen both in Turkey and in Pakistan, a pattern is to be discerned from which it is possible to learn much.

Among the attributes of a true Muslim are the love of God and His Prophet; the cherishing of what is right and the abhorrence of what is wrong and sinful; the desire to preserve and transmit Islamic values and to live, strive and fight for them; a great degree of self-discipline and self-control; and the love of knowledge, valuing and propagating it. From what I have observed, it would appear that these values are transmitted largely by one particular segment of the population; that is, neither by the extremely poor who, although they love Islam and may be capable of being activated to work for it, are mostly too burdened by the struggle for survival and too ignorant to be its real carriers, nor by the extremely wealthy, who by-and-large are too preoccupied with the world to give attention to other aspects of existence, but by the middle and upper segments of the 'middle class'.

Many among this group prize their Islamic standards, their integrity and self-respect above every worldly consideration and will not compromise in matters of conscience. They know how to value material things and how to conserve them, as they come in limited quantity and are obtained by hard work and effort, but at the same time they are not so pinched that they cannot maintain a clean and decent living standard, acquire learning, travel, and so on. They do not spend money for ostentatious displays or keeping up with others but rather on obtaining the best possible quality and value for the money they have to spend, on providing a suitable home atmosphere, on having wholesome food and proper clothing, and on education and self-improvement. They do not spoil their children with too many possessions or enjoyments but expect them to manage with what there is, to be helpful and to assume responsibilities according to their capacities without overburdening them, and at the same time they are willing and able to encourage them in suitable skills and interests and to provide them with wholesome activities. Above all, they know how to love, and infinite tenderness, an unselfish spirit, helpfulness and kindliness, together with firmness, consistency and unswerving adherence to Islamic standards, go into the training of their children, who, with this secure foundation and positive example, early absorb and reflect this love and these values in their own behavior as they mature.

This group is, unfortunately, rather small everywhere in the Muslim world at present. Pressures are being exerted on it from various directions; yet because of its deep inner certainty, it is kept intact by the very vitality and basic rightness of the values by which it lives, and its standards are indeed suitable to be emulated by those who are more affluent. (I have observed that although many lower middle class Turks are nominally Islamic, they often lack the knowledge, discrimination and understanding for making correct choices. For example, as I mentioned earlier, while literacy has given them the ability to read, their minds lack the essential judgment and sense of values for making correct choices about *what* to read, and hence it is open to question whether, without such understanding, they would not be better off remaining illiterate. Their way of life is often tainted with vulgarity and with an emulation of the affluent on a cheapened scale. Among the very affluent, the same vulgarity and questionable taste is often present but in a more expensive form, and so many choices are available to them that, without sound and pure Islamic criteria, they often make extremely wrong ones.) Thus, while the number of those to whom Islam is the dearest value is at present quite small in any 'Muslim' country, nonetheless I believe it is this relatively small group which by and large will carry forward and transmit true Islamic values, as those who belong to it are able to understand and to exemplify them in their lives in a correct and sound manner.

A reflection on this will demonstrate what excellent qualities moderation in living standards and habits is able to produce among human beings, qualities which the economy of superabundance has failed to produce even in the most advanced countries of the West, and will point to the great desirability of maintaining such moderation, which is also compatible with the Islamic idea of a "middle way."* We can see the validity of this conception very clearly today as the United States, the leader of the wealthy nations, gradually discovers the very high price it must pay for an extreme, unhealthy affluence in terms of an upset ecological balance which it is extremely difficult if not impossible to restore; air and water pollution which pose a very serious threat to health and even to life; depletion and spoilage of irreplaceable natural resources for the over-production of consumer goods, many of which are unnecessary or even actually harmful; and such huge amounts of waste products that it is less expensive for the time-being to dispose of them than to recycle them, while at the same time it becomes more and more difficult to find ways to dispose of them. And on the human level, the introduction and perfection of stream-lined methods, mechanization and the thousand-and-one latest devices which fall under the heading of 'efficiency,' have resulted in the loss of interdependence of human beings on one another, replacing it with dependence on machines and gadgets, and producing a kind of aggressive independence which has little room for anything other than self, or self and immediate family at best, without even realizing the immense preoccupation with self which exists. Moreover, the great and menacing degree of personal 'freedom,' which is more like moral and social anarchy, is also very highly correlated with this unhealthy excess of material comforts, coupled with an appalling loss of moral direction. Thus the technology of the West—the technology of superabundance toward which Muslim countries are looking as toward a

* That is, balanced between extremes; al-Baqara 2:143.

kind of Paradise on earth and longing desperately to realize for themselves, as if material abundance contained the secret of man's ultimate happiness and well-being—today has become its master, and its people are now anxiously searching for a way to deal with the side-effects of these improper uses of it before it is too late.

We Muslims do not want to emulate this, and the day is now dawning when, *insha'Allah,* our people will cease to desire and to blindly accept whatever they see in the Western world at face value, chasing madly after it like hollow people who have nothing of their own to offer to themselves or to the rest of humanity; for our moral and spiritual goal is to be the leader of mankind through Islam, not the camp-follower of others. At the same time our economic goal must be a *via media* between the two extremes of too little and too much:—a decent living standard, not copied from Hollywood but rather based upon a realistic assessment of the actual needs and wants of human beings and their *optimum* rather than their maximum satisfaction; beyond this lies the way to dangerous excesses and to the deterioration of the society through too great a portion of its vital energies being channelized into material preoccupations. Such a realistic and viable policy should be the goal, both immediate and long-range, of all socio-economic planning in the countries of the Muslim world.

April 28: Today a state of emergency and martial law was declared in eleven provinces of Turkey, "as [according to a cabinet proclamation quoted in the 'Daily News'] it has become clear that the attitude of interest groups and anarchic behavior and activities which have been observed in our country for a long time are no longer directed at damaging public order and security, but have been transformed into a powerful and active uprising directed at ideological aims and against the basic order of the state, the integrity of the country, the motherland and the secular state."

While this is directed primarily against the leftist militants, obviously it can also be equally applied to any activities of Muslims which can be interpreted as being against the "secular state." Ankara is one of the areas, which include large portions of Turkey, now under martial law. Cars and buses entering and leaving the city are being stopped and searched, and large numbers of military police as well as the usual *jandarma* are on patrol in the streets, walking in pairs. The Diyarbakır area, with its heavy concentration of Kurds among whom there is strong communist-inspired and supported agitation for an independent Kurdistan, and the Hatay area bordering Syria, from which, according to the "Daily News," Turkish leftists have been leaving for Arab communist guerilla training areas, are also under martial law administration.

As far as we personally are concerned, for the first day or two after we returned from our trip, my mind was still with Cemile's family. Cemile came to us the following day, the wholesome flavor and scent of home seeming still to cling to her. She as much as ourselves is preparing for our leaving and what will follow, for we are scheduled to leave Ankara and Turkey in about two weeks for home.

I came here eight months ago a stranger, but I could not remain one; I became involved and gave my heart. In order to leave here and return to the world of the West, the opposite of this process must take place; in order to accomplish it, something precious and of great value which has grown up within me must die, or at least must be put away for a time. Please God, the loves I have formed here will never die, nor the bright lights and insights I have gained, the things which have happened to me inwardly here which I never want to lose. O love! Must there be limits and boundaries for you, must there be adjustments and adaptations so that you are no longer felt to burn so brightly? Cannot the heart be left alone in the grace of its feelings, wherever it is able to find you?

That heart is torn in two . . .

April 29: Today we went with Bahadir Bey—as I had promised myself we should before leaving—to see the Anit Kabir, Atatürk's mausoleum. It is built on a low hill (whether natural or artificial I do not know) at some little distance from the center of Ankara; its well-kept grounds cover quite a large area and are planted with trees, shrubbery and flowers. The mausoleum itself is an immense square or rectangular structure of sand-colored stone supported by many square columns; friezes decorate the walls below it, and an avenue of large, modernistic sand-colored statues lines a drive leading to it from one side. The area is patrolled by *jandarma* in every direction, I suppose lest someone should attempt to harm it, or perhaps in homage to the deceased *Ebedi Şef* (Eternal Chief), or both. What a terrible waste, I thought, to pre-empt for such a use this large parcel of land in the midst of a populous city and to erect such a costly tomb over the body of a single man, for the internment of whose remains, like any other mortal's, only six feet of earth is required. I suppose it is one of the largest mausoleums in the entire world, beside which the tombs of the Ottoman *sultans,* who ruled a vast realm, all appear minute and insignificant.

The interior of the mausoleum is quite plain, almost severe, in style and ornamentation, its floor made of very dark gleaming marble. A single rectangular block of pale marble forms the sarcophagus; before it lay a few wreaths and floral arrangements. I had seldom seen such a cold building and thought how fitting it was, indeed, for the hard, ruthless man who had wrought such devastating changes in this land. This was one grave at which Selim and I did not think of praying for the soul of the dead, and I left that stark, frigid tomb hoping that the day would come when the land on which it stood would be taken over for better uses by a free people, who had at last shaken off their intellectual and spiritual bondage to the one buried there whose super-image had, for a time, enslaved the minds of millions of Turks.

May 1: About a week remains to us to live in this place; we are to leave by ship from Izmir on May 12. I have been extremely busy —doing errands, shopping for gifts, making travel arrangements, and so on—with a very heavy heart. The sorting out and packing of our personal effects is underway, our furniture has been sold to various people, to be delivered just before we leave, and there has been much activity in our apartment in recent days as we wind up our affairs. Cemile has come whenever she was able, and we have been spending as much time as possible with Emine and Enver.

I have been lying in bed trying to sleep after a very tiring day, during which I paid a last visit to my dear Çikrikçilar Yokuşu in Ulus, the one part of Ankara which I have really loved. Lying here wide-awake, I have been thinking of home, of our city, and of a highway in our area on which we have traveled very often on the way to and from a neighboring town. Soon *insha'Allah* we will be going on that road again, and if God wills it will be our destiny to travel it many times in the future: sometimes in snow, when the sky is a flat, leaden grey; sometimes in storm when the clouds are piled black and angry above us; sometimes when it is sunshiny and beautiful like these late spring days in Ankara, when even this unappealing city, with little beauty of nature or man's handiwork to enliven it, has become joyful with the warm weather and flowers and trees, all the city seeming to be alive again and its inhabitants out-of-doors after the grip of the bleak winter. Yes, we will travel that well-known road, and traveling it I will *insha'Allah* think of Ankara and of all our travels in Turkey and beyond.

Will it all seem unreal and like a half-forgotten dream? Will it all be written off later as a year of interest and adventure which now no longer seems important? Will Alanya, Side, Bursa, Isparta, İstanbul and even Ankara, and Peshawar, Lahore and Isfahan, eventually become nothing more than the memory of something which I once experienced but which has now ceased to be meaningful to me? Yes, I am sure it will and must—and should—happen ultimately, for if we live in the past instead of the present, we lose our reason or become dead while we are still alive. A Muslim must carry out his commitment to Islam wherever he is, not living his life in the vain pursuit of memories and longings but in an effort to strive in God's cause with whatever talents and resources he may possess, and contributing to the Islamic community and movement nearest to him. Then what will be left to me will be my memories, a very few dear and cherished relationships, and the sure knowledge, triumphing over the loss of reality which comes with the passing of time, that if I ever come again to the lands where Muslims live, please God I will not act differently but will again give my heart; and each day I will pray and long for opportunities to be with these lands and peoples once again . . .

May 2: The communist terrorists' activities have accelerated once more after a breathing spell while everyone waited to see what the new government's policies would be. Everywhere now one sees military police and *jandarma,* with their strange, robot-like appearance. The new government has already taken quite a number of steps to deal with the problem, using its emergency powers. The Dev-Genç and the rightist organization of Alp Aslan Turkeş have been declared illegal, various newspapers (several communist-oriented ones as well as the Islamically-oriented *"Bugün")* which allegedly criticized the new government have been closed, and many arrests are being made.

Much of this was essential and long-overdue; yet I am certain that these diseases of the spirit in Turkey will continue. For the heart of every human being needs some *ilah,* a deity, someone or something to worship and give its allegiance to; and if one does not worship and obey God Most High, it is certain that he will find some other object of worship—some man-made system or ideology, material things, desires or even himself—before which his heart prostrates and to which it gives its devotion. Thus, while it may be possible to crush communist activities *per se,* as long as Turkish hearts remain devoid of allegiance to their Creator as their Lord and to Islam as a way of life, communism will continue to spread like a deadly infection among those whose hearts are void of true values, faith, virtue, and by and large even of softening traditions and influences.

It has often been said that the Muslim world will never turn to communism as long as it has Islam. This is unquestionably true, as the two cannot co-exist, if they are correctly understood, within the same breast; but now that the people of this Muslim world in general and Turkey in particular are progressively and rapidly losing their Islam, they can learn to accept communism—or other -isms —in their desperate, frantic search for something—anything—to fill their inner emptiness. Let the world of the West, which so much fears communism but which seems equally to mistrust and fear Islam without knowing anything about it or having any basis for this feeling except the misunderstood legacy of medieval history, take note of this fact: *that only Islam, with its tremendous dynamism, its revolutionary ideology of human brotherhood and social justice, its capacity to motivate human beings to strive for the highest and noblest of aims, the clear, definite righteous way of life it prescribes, and its bringing the human heart to bow in submission to the One in comparison to Whom all created things are minute and insignificant, can effectively resist and contain communism in this part of the world today!*

Today was our last Sunday in Ankara, a sunny, warm spring day. We planned to spend the afternoon at the pleasant zoo at Atatürk Orman Ciftliği with Cemile and the evening with Enver, Emine and Aynur Abla.

The afternoon was lovely, and the zoo was full of people who were picknicking, looking at the animals, and generally enjoying themselves. In one spot a few elderly men offered their prayers, and a solitary woman also prayed in a secluded place in the tall grass. Most of the people there were villagers or simple townspeople, and I felt happy and at peace among them.

We had brought a picnic lunch, and after eating and praying together in an area away from the crowds, we went to see the animals; Cemile and I walked hand-in-hand, the continuous prick of imminent parting sharpening our enjoyment of these last few precious days together. Selim made a photo of Cemile, the children and me standing under the pale blue-purple clusters of wisteri. hanging down around the zoo's entrance; I think for the rest of my life purple wisteria will bring back the wrenching bitter-sweet ess of this day when so much joy was mingled with the dull pair which is now never absent from my mind . . .

Cemile returned to her university, having work which must be finished by tomorrow, and we went to Kızılay so that I could take some photographs to record the scene which I had disliked more than anything else I had seen in Turkey, feeling the sharp contrast of it all: hating so much and loving so much, but love always returning as the dominant emotion, especially away from this *kalbsız, muhabbetsiz*—heartless, loveless—Ankara. I felt that my home, my roots, my very life, were here, almost as if I must have been born and lived always in this land, a very part of its soil; leaving it seemed to me incredible, impossible, and completely wrong . . .

We passed the evening at Enver's, where for months we had been almost like part of the family. How we would miss them—and they us! Their love and friendship had made Ankara seem a home to us from the very first moment, and without them this time here would have been poor and barren—and under the difficult circumstances, quite miserable indeed. Emine and I sat together on the sofa with our arms wound around each other, Aynur Abla sharing in our grief, and wept for our coming separation, so soon, so soon!

May 3: It has been a hard day, for our belongings went out today. Earlier the house had been littered and messy as I did the packing; afterwards it was empty and naked but clean, with almost nothing left except the bare furniture and whatever we would carry with us. On the walls were light patches where pictures or ornamental plates had hung. There was a dull, numb resignation within me, a heavy, stifling burden of sadness, as our days here draw to a close.

During these days we have had many visitors and invitations. Cemile brought a letter from her father expressing the great love which all the family feels for us and saying that they want very much to come to Ankara or Izmir to say goodbye to us. In reply she sent off a telegram conveying our heartfelt love and prayers for them all but asking them not to come, for she knew that already, without meeting and parting from them again, it was more than enough for us all. Two days later she came again, bringing precious gifts which her family had sent for us which we knew we would always dearly cherish.

The children have been wonderfully loving and helpful to me during these very difficult days and weeks when I—and they—must pull our hearts out by the roots and return to the place where these hearts cannot find a home, consolng me so kindly, trying to understand and to comfort, and we have been very close to one another. Each of them in his or her particular way would have been happy to remain in Turkey and none really wants to go home, but thank

God the adjustment is not so difficult for them, as they are too young to understand the full implications of it all and have also shown a great flexibility in adjusting themselves to changing conditions. At the same time, I pray that they will not forget either, for if any of them is able wholeheartedly to adapt and feel entirely at home in the society of the United States after this, I will surely feel that all our training of them and this experience have not served their purpose. It is of course very difficult for children to be unadjusted to the society in which they live, but for a Muslim it is infinitely more desirable to bear maladjustment to the surrounding society than to accept maladjustment to the standards of God.

In this atmosphere of sincerity, love, simplicity and lesser preoccupation with material things which we have found here, each of them has experienced that softening, warming and deepening of the personality to which I referred earlier. Each of them in his or her own special way has tapped some internal reservoir of love, of tenderness, of feeling for others, of inwardness, of deepened religious feeling, and of coming nearer to the Beneficent God through these benign influences. For although this country cannot and does not claim to be Islamic, nevertheless, like all Muslim countries in the world, it still rests on the premise (held by the Muslim majority, of course, not by the materialists or atheists) that God exists and that He is the Sovereign and Ruler of mankind, that every human being is His creature, and that the relationships of His people with one another should be characterized by fellow-feeling and kindliness. Although that influence is much attenuated now, these pre-suppositions still permeate the life of this land, so that those who have broken with the mainstream of the society and do not believe, must consciously and deliberately get away from these basic premises in order to live according to their convictions of materialism or atheism, as I saw in the case of my teacher, Zeynep Hanım; for it is implicit in the traditions, the morals, the manners, the living habits, the very air one breathes here, an inseparable part of Turkey and its people, and of the excellent and remarkable qualities which still characterize many Turks today.

May 6: In three days our home here will be no more. The kindness of our friends of the past months has graced these last days; tonight we are to have dinner with Bahadir Bey and his wife, who have been so very hospitable and kind. Enver, Emine and Aynur Abla have been dropping in and out, helping with arrangements, being so good to us. Cemile has come on each of the last few afternoons, trying to act as usual and to keep inside all that she feels about our leaving, but her emotions cannot be so easily disguised and I know all she is feeling, just as she knows what the children and I are feeling. It is hard—so very, very hard!—to think of being separated from these very dear ones, who seem like an integral part of our very life, hard to imagine living somewhere without them. But I am almost numb now. This time of grief is as severe and difficult as if I were losing what I love best—as indeed I am—and I can only pray for the help of Allah in getting through it.

Is it wrong for a Muslim to feel so about a place or a country? I don't think so. The Holy Prophet himself, peace be on him, who is the example for all mankind, was deeply attached to Mekkah, his home; for the heart of man has been made by God to form attachments and to put down roots, and it is very natural for one to have strong ties and affection for a place where his spirit feels at home, and also to feel grief at leaving it. But if that attachment to a specific place or people keeps one from the greatest bond and allegiance to the entire Muslim *ummah,* if it prevents him from doing his duty or engenders rebellion, if it causes him to remain fixed in a particular place when he is needed elsewhere for the cause of Islam, it becomes destructive and wrong, exceeding the limits of what is permissible for a Muslim, and has perhaps indeed become a rival to God in his heart. I pray that I may not be guilty of such things. To me Turkey will always stand for the realization, partial though it must be because of all the contrary elements, of my dream of finding a home for my heart in this world, the place I have loved more than any other I have seen so far, and where, indeed, it would have been the greatest blessing and satisfaction to pass the remainder of my life . . .

May 7: Today I worked very hard and cleaned the house as thoroughly as possible. By afternoon the electricity in the apartment had been disconnected and the gas would shortly be as well. Cemile came, restrained by the great love and consideration she feels for us from expressing her own sense of grief and loss. Later Selim and I went to say a last goodbye to Bahadir Bey and other friends, while she stayed at home with the children she loves so dearly. We have been at Enver's for dinner several times in succession during these last days, their boundless love and hospitality making these final days easier—and at the same time so much more difficult.

Tomorrow—the last day here, as we had a last day in America before coming here and will have a last day in this world. O my God, I pray for the strength to live moment by moment through the days and weeks which lie ahead . . .

Let me draw the curtain of silence over the day, our last day in Ankara, which followed, for the heart is entitled to its privacy. But I will recall one incident which occurred on that final afternoon.

Various people had been coming in and out all morning to take away the furniture which they had bought from us, last-minute visitors had come and gone, Emine, Enver and Aynur Abla had been with us, and Cemile and I had gone out together for one or two final errands. She was with us now, and later we would all go to Enver's house for supper.

As she and I sat talking together, both trying to say and not to say all we felt, Gül Hanım came accompanied by her elder daughter. She had been to see us in the morning, and I knew well how much she loved us and how sad she was at our leaving; she had told me over and over during the past days, "Please don't go! Please! I'll cry!" Now she sat on a chair facing us, her daughter on another chair, both completely silent, their faces red with weeping, and Cemile and I, sitting together on the sofa with our arms wrapped around each other, wept silently with them.

As a dull grey dusk fell over the city and the trees and houses of our neighborhood, we spread a sheet on the floor for *Maghrib* prayer, and our family, Cemile and Gül Hanım prayed together, Selim leading. And somehow it was like the solemn sealing of a bond between ourselves—Cemile, the simple, good-hearted woman who had been one of the most real people I had known in Turkey, and our family—that the blessed ties of Islam which had brought us close during these past few months would be our common bond and our guide wherever we might go and under all circumstances. Then Gül Hanım said goodbye to us with many words of sincere love, as we embraced each other over and over again, and went away, the tears flowing down her cheeks.

CHAPTER 20

ADHAN OVER ANATOLIA

May 9: I was up, weary and unrested, at a little past four in the morning. Faintly the solemn, moving strains of our mosque's *adhan* floated out to me, unforgettably, from the distance for the last time as a dark, cloudy day dawned. I knew then, with a sudden shock, that the worst part of what I had yet to experience lay ahead, making the leave-taking seem an easy thing in comparison. For here in our grief we have been surrounded by loving, sympathetic friends who have cared and shared our sorrow at parting, and we have still been in the place which I have learned to love so dearly; but after this we will go from the Muslim world, returning to a world of entirely different concepts, relationships and patterns of life—a world which has become totally foreign and strange to me during the past months.

Thus it is: in his homeland the Muslim is often beset by hostile forces trying to suppress Islam and his efforts in its cause from every side, for they know the great power of God's religion. Outside, in lands where he has freedom to propagate and to work for Islam, he encounters such completely alien patterns of life and thought, such an emotionally empty and sterile climate, that his very soul is bruised and torn by the separation from the deep tender ties which are so essential to him and which provide the food for his spirit. O my God, if there has ever been a time when I needed Your help—I and my children—it is in the days which lie ahead of me now. O merciful God, give me strength and courage to go on, for I have no helper and no support except You. . . .

I will not recount here the details of our leave-taking and departure from Ankara. Those loving friends who said goodbye to us at the bus depot will not forget it, a   either will we. Our life as residents of Turkey had drawn to a close, and as we took our seats on the bus bound for Izmir, we were now American tourists on our way home. My last memory is of beloved Emine, her lips trembling as she looked up at us for the last time through her tears, and of dear, dear Cemile, for all our sakes waving gaily and managing to smile valiantly as long as we could see her face . . .

Physically exhausted and spent with grief, I recall nothing of the early part of the trip except a stop for tea at a roadside restaurant somewhere, and the fact that all the countryside, even around Ankara, was now a luscious green; everywhere wild flowers, among them the tulips and poppies which I love so much, nodded brightly among the grass. By the time we were half-way to Izmir (the first part of the route the same as the way to Antalya and Bursa), flourishing orchards and fields of vegetables and poppies appeared. Peasants labored in the fields in groups, including women in colorful *şalvars,* working or sitting together; in one place I saw a row of women praying together in a field. Here were the rural people of Anatolia and their good land, living close to it, depending on it after Allah, and undoubtedly loving it as a part of their very selves.

After all the experiences of the last few weeks, worn with our emotions and our tears, all of us were weary and numb; yet the realities, both of our concrete situation and of our personal feelings, must be analyzed and dealt with. As I sat with Maryam, my arm around her and our hands clasped, both of us remarked on the same strange, unexpected feeling—a sense of distinct relief now that the terribly difficult ordeal of leave-taking, the first step of our return from the Muslim world, was over. The actual parting with the dearest friends and the dread of that parting now behind me, I did not try to think of what lay before us, for I did not dare to, and I also could not see clearly what might be ahead; this was not the time to anticipate or to think of the future, but to live day by day as circumstances dictated. Now, I asked myself, not unnaturally, what was left to us of this past eight months, and Maryam and I pondered over this question together as glimpses of the green Anatolian landscape flashed swiftly by.

We were returning to the old *milieu* which we knew inside and out, and would fit back into it like an old work-horse going willy-nilly back into its traces, I supposed. We now no longer belonged to Turkey nor could claim to be part of it; our home was there, not here. Yet nothing had really changed with the change in the physical location of our home. We were Muslims; our home was anywhere on God's earth where we happened to reside, and no consideration such as nationality or citizenship had meaning for us in the universal brotherhood of Islam. But—the question repeated itself insistently in my mind, requiring an answer—what would now be left to me of all this experience, especially of the feelings and insights of these last weeks, of the love and yearning I had felt for this once-blessed, God-centered country, on whose face the traces of its Islamic heritage were still, in spite of everything, so abundantly visible?

I am not a person to dwell in the past, nor am I one to merely exist; I must live and experience my life to the full, good or bad. What was past was over. The home in Ankara, with all the movements of the mind and heart which had accompanied it, now belonged to our history as individuals and as a family. Yet *something* must be left to us besides memories, a very few dearly-cherished lasting relationships, and some tangible mementoes; but what?

First of all, I think we now have a much clearer understanding of the forces of equilibrium and change at work in the Muslim world and of the problems which are affecting it. We have seen for ourselves some of its people, their lands, their cultures, their practice of Islam, their assets and their areas of difficulty, and have come to identify ourselves with it much more deeply. We have observed the processes of social stability and social change working simultaneously upon it, at once to retard and to accelerate new patterns coming into the society, and have seen a note-worthy example of the sort of confusion and disturbance which comes to a Muslim society when it is forcibly cut loose from its Islamic base. We have noted some of the efforts to destroy Islam, to weaken its influence, to mix it with present-day, man-made systems and values, and also some valiant efforts to preserve it without compromise and spread it in the society through Islamic movements; in short, we have observed at first-hand the methodology of its enemies and also of its faithful followers. All this has been for me a living proof of the innate, God-given vitality of Islam. Because it is the sum-total of life for the true Muslim, even when it is suppressed, misunderstood, misapplied or neglected on a mass scale in the society, it is not lost nor destroyed; and even if only traces of it remain, this is enough to leaven the whole society to a certain extent and to preserve many of its Islamic characteristics both individually and collectively.

Besides this, even in the face of such opposing forces and values as we have observed during the past months, here and there we have seen a true and pure Islam lived. We have learned that there is still a kingdom of the heart, a realm in which spiritual and human values are yet paramount among a portion of the people—*and there is surely no Muslim away from his home who reads these words who will not understand what I mean:* a part of the world where still there are some people who love and fear Allah Subhanahu wa Ta'ala above everything else, are centered upon Him and strive to please Him, and who, out of love for Him, are habitually gentle and compassionate, with a pure, disinterested openness of heart, approaching other human beings with a sincerity and kindliness undistorted by preoccupation with self. All these qualities and values are a vital part of Islam, the translation of its concepts and injunctions into concrete human terms as a complete and inclusive way of life for Muslim individuals and their society.

Thus, in the Muslim society, the total love and kindness which an individual has to give is diffused to a wide circle, its radius extending outward from the self to all with whom one comes in contact, as I have experienced myself in this land. This is in marked contrast to the pattern prevailing in American life where, although the amount of love latent within the individual is quantitatively no doubt the same, it very often reaches no further than one's own immediate family members or personal circle of friends at best, while the greater part of its energy is applied to oneself in various forms of self-absorption which are the very antithesis of generous and selfless love and concern for others. Thus its scope is very limited—rationed as it were—and little of it passes out into the society at large to be shared among all its members.

As an example, while in the West many of those who are involved in service to others or in the healing arts may initially be motivated by humanitarian considerations, with effective training they are often taught to work not primarily in the frame of reference of compassion and concern for their fellow human-beings but as a means of getting a necessary job done, putting maximum efficiency before the feelings or even the well-being of those whom they are supposed to serve. Similarly, many aspects of contemporary Western society, such as the drive for social justice, care for the needy, aged and handicapped, etc., which are so excellent and laudable and which are an integral part of the Islamic system although Muslims today have largely lost them, are due much more to abstract, theoretical humanistic conceptions, and undoubtedly to a very profound sense of guilt on the part of the better-placed members of the society, than to a real sense of personal care and concern for other human bengs. Thus it is not unusual to find persons in the West who talk endlessly about the worth of all human beings, who are ever ready to work for humanitarian causes or to send money each month to support an orphan in India or Viet Nam, but who do not know the names, faces and needs of their nearest neighbors and who are unable to get along with the members of their own families. Thus in the West, by means of the preoccupation with 'humanity' at large, with people in the abstract rather than with concrete, specific individuals, love is depersonalized and its object made into an abstraction. At the same time, the obsession with romance, 'fulfillment' and the channelizing of so much of one's potential for loving into heterosexual relationships (which are often a form of extreme self-absorption) causes love to be confined rather than diffused, so that a great deal of what passes for 'love' is rather an attempt to bolster up a faltering ego by identifying oneself with another person who enhances one's self-image through intimacy with sexual overtones, while the greater part of one's relationships remain loose, casual, often meaningless and devoid of responsibility.

Here in Turkey we have learned what love is, a disinterested love flowing out from oneself to any and all who come within one's sphere of contact, whether friend or stranger: the love of a Muslim whose obligations are prescribed by Allah to a widening circle of relationships, governed by the Islamic attitude that relations among human beings are to be characterized by meaningfulness, sincerity and a sense of mutual responsibility and concern:

> "Serve God and do not join any partners with Him; and do good—to parents, relatives, orphans, those in need, neighbors who are near, neighbors who are stranger, the companion by your side, the wayfarer (you meet), and what your right hands possess; for God does not love the arrogant, the boastful, (nor) those who are miserly or enjoin miserliness on others, or hide the bounties which God has bestowed on them . . ."*

In Turkey, as in other parts of the Muslim world, these mutual obligations have become traditionalized throughout the centuries in such moving and tender ways that the very manner of thought and the structure of the language mirror the flavor of this love and sense of mutual responsibility. Please God, no amount of legislation or governmental repression will ever remove this from the lives and hearts of the Turkish people, who have absorbed these gracious and lovely qualities with their mothers' very milk!

The countryside two-hundred-and fifty kilometers west of Izmir was very beautiful. After this, Izmir itself, a crowdded, ungainly city which seemed full of rough elements, was something of a shock. At the bus station two porters quarreled over our baggage and charged 50 T.L. to take it to a hotel which had been recommended to us. All of us were exhausted; Selim had the beginning of a cough and cold, while Jamal was having trouble with asthma.

As the girls and I sat in the hotel room talking over the experiences of the day, there was a natural reaction and we wept together; nevertheless, the great burden of leave-taking was now behind us, and I did not yet look ahead to what was to come. After we could pull ourselves together sufficiently, we went out into the evening to look for a restaurant where we could have dinner, feeling now like wanderers without a home. All we could manage to find was a dis-

* *Al-Nisa* 4:36-37

mal place with a bar on a dirty, ugly street somewhere near the hotel, and we were asleep before ten o'clock.

May 11: Yesterday morning Selim woke up with a fever, but later, as he felt better, we hired a taxi with a dour, silent driver to take us to Efes (Ephesus) and Meryemana, the site which is believed to have been the home of Mary, the mother of Jesus, may God's blessings be on them both, some seventy kilometers south of Izmir.

The part of Izmir through which the road to Efes lay was an unattractive, congested, sprawling section; the city seemed to have grownup haphazardly and traffic was heavy. But in the very fertile and beautiful countryside beyond the city, we felt refreshed and at peace. Men and women labored in the fields, hoeing and setting out plants; wild flowers of great loveliness bloomed everywhere and an occasional stork was to be seen.

After a time the countryside changed in character, becoming hilly with a scrub type of vegetation. After stopping for lunch in a small town, we presently left the highway for a side road leading to Meryemana. The road wound up a mountain at the bottom of which grew the same scrub, but as we went higher the bushes became trees, and toward the top there was a wonderful green forest in the midst of which was set what is popularly supposed to be the site of Mary's house.

We left the uncommunicative driver waiting at the entrance of the Meryemana compound. It was a beautiful, serene spot where the heart of the mother, if she had indeed lived there, must have found peace amidst the forest with its wild flowers and, in the distance beyond a hill, a glimpse of the blue Aegean Sea. The building which is supposed to mark the site of her house was a Christian shrine, a simple church of stone constructed in the shape of a cross, in which stood an altar bearing a cross and a bronze statue of Mary before which candles burned. The guide, a French priest in street clothes, explained to us that a very early Christian settlement was known to have existed at nearby Efes and in this immediate area, and legends and other evidence suggest that Mary had come to live at this spot in her later years.* He told us how the site of the house had been discovered and what had led to the assumption that it was Mary's home, something which evidence made possible but by no means certain.

We walked down a path to the spring of Meryemana, to which miraculous properties are ascribed, and drank of its cold, clear water. In this place my thoughts turned much upon the mother of

---

* With regard to Jesus (Isa), peace be on him, and his mother Mary (Maryam or Meryem), Islam teaches that Jesus was the prophet who came immediately before the last Messenger of God, Muhammad, whose coming Jesus foretold:

"And remember, Jesus the son of Mary said: 'O children of Israel, I am the Prophet of God (sent) to you, confirming the Law [of Moses] (which came) before me, and giving glad tidings of a Prophet to come after me, whose name shall be . Ahmad [another name for Muhammad]...'" (al-Saff 61:6)

Muslims revere and love Jesus, peace be on him, very greatly as a prophet and a messenger of God and cannot tolerate any disrespect to him. At the same time, to consider him as more than a prophet and a man is a very grave sin, for it involves negation of the Uniqueness and Oneness of God and attributes to a man— a created being—a share in His Divinity and Godhead. The Holy Qur'an contains numerous passages referring to Jesus and his mother in which God categorically denies that Jesus is His son, emphatically stating that it is incompatible with His Divinity to have a son (or any other 'relatives'), and proclaims that to call Jesus or any other human being His 'son' in tantamount to blasphemy and shirk: |

"Indeed, Christ Jesus the son of Mary was a prophet of God...so believe in God and His prophets.... For God is One God. Glory be to Him, (far exalted is He) above having a son. To him belong all things in the heavens and on earth.... Christ does not disdain to serve and worship God..." (al-Nisa 4:171-172)

"They do blaspheme who say, 'God is Christ the son of Mary.' But Christ said: 'O children of Israel, worship God, my Lord and your Lord.' Whoever joins other deities with God, God will forbid him the Garden, and the Fire will be his abode. For the wrong-doers there will be as one to help. They do blaspheme who say, 'God is one of three in a Trinity,' for there is no deity except One God.... Christ the son of Mary was no more than a prophet: many were the prophets who passed away before him. His mother was a woman of truth. They both had to eat their (daily) food. See how God makes His signs clear to them, yet in what ways they are deluded away from the truth!" (al-Maida 5:75-76, 78)

(continued on next page)

Jesus, who is mentioned so movingly in the Qur'an as the prototype of a pure, devout woman;* I returned to the building which is believed to mark the site of her home to pray *al-Fateha* for her, may God bless her and be pleased with her. As I was leaving, a flock of middle-aged foreign tourists, wearing sleeveless dresses and big colorful straw hats, brushed past me and entered the church.

The waiting driver now took us down the mountain to the entrance of the site of ancient Ephesus; since there was no road through the area, he would drive around to the exit side and wait for us there. Here too were the inevitable tourists in various kinds of typical touristic garb, photographing one another posed against the ruins and exlaiming in admiration. Yes, we were tourists ourselves now, but my world could never be theirs nor theirs mine. Although we walked among scenes which had charmed many and many a visitor with the lovely blending of ruins and exquisite scenery in that bright, sun-drenched spot, none of us had any heart for such sight-seeing and we did it automatically, almost as a duty because we happened to be there, our minds preoccupied with other matters and unable to summon up any real pleasure or interest. Nevertheless, I could not be insensible of the beauty around me, and the delicate, lovely wild flowers blooming among those broken

---

The Qur'an also denies that Jesus was crucified:

"...They did not kill nor crucify him, but it was made to appear so to them; and those who differ in this matter are indeed confused, with no knowledge and following mere conjecture, for of a surety they did not kill him. No, God raised him up unto Himself; and God is exalted in power, Wise." *(al-Nisa 4:157-158)*

"And behold, God will say [on the Day of Judgment]: 'O Jesus son of Mary didst thou say unto men. "Worship me and my mother as deities besides God?"' He [Jesus] will say: 'Glory to Thee! Never could I say what I had no right to say....Never did I say to them anything except what Thou didst command me to say, namely: "Worship God, my Lord and your Lord."'" *(al-Maida 5:119-120)*

In Islam there is neither concept of Original Sin, Vicarious Atonement, Resurrection nor Redemption. Each human being is born pure and sinless and is responsible to God for his own actions, according to which he will be judged, for there is no intermediary between any human individual and God.

Ale Imran 3:35-51; Maryam 19:16-36.

marble columns only made my heart ache the more. When shall I forget those scarlet poppies, so dear to me, nodding on their slender stalks in the brilliant sunshine beside the ancient marbles of Efes? I picked a small bouquet of flowers, one of every kind I found, and carried them, folded and dried between newspapers, back to Izmir as one of my dearest possessions.

(I wonder whether the mechanism of love does not give a superlative sort of beauty to whatever is touched by it, indeed. Two days later, traveling by car in Europe, we passed through what I know was very beautiful countryside, where wild flowers including the poppies I love so much, bloomed everywhere. But I seemed to have become temporarily insensitive and immune to beauty; and as for the flowers, they could not charm me, they were nothing to me, for my heart was not present among them. I had left it, heavy and full of grief, among the wild scarlet poppies blowing in the mellow sunshine of the Turkish Aegean coast...)

After leaving Efes, the driver took us to Kusadası, a lovely little seaside resort which only increased our sadness. Here were a big grand hotel and a beach where bikini-clad women lay beside men in the sun, and everything in the town itself seemed to be geared to tourism, an element whose adverse influence has been so marked in Turkey and other parts of the Muslim world.

However, just off the shore lay a tiny island on which stood a small, beautiful castle, connected to the mainland by a causeway on which various men and boys lounged about. We were at once attracted by the charm of the scene—the little castle of pale-colored stone with a square tower at its center, steps and walks laid out neatly in all directions, with borders of exquisite cultivated flowers and shrubbery. However, when we went inside the tower, we found that it was being remodeled and fitted with barrel-shaped bar stools, with a terrace for dancing overlooking the bay adjoining it. This was, in short, a pleasure spot, lovely indeed but in such an atmosphere combining the greatest beauty with forbidden things, we could only feel sad and sorry. We rode back to Izmir in silence, Selim now feverish again, and the ugly, teeming city seemed terrible to me after our last glimpse of the peace of the villages and the countryside. We paid the driver for his services and returned to the hotel.

Selim was now sick in real earnest, with a high fever. I gave him aspirin and covered him with blankets, and by evening he felt well enough to go to the hotel's restaurant for dinner. Before going to bed the children and I talked together, commenting to one another on the strange, almost unbelieveable fact that only yesterday morning—could it really have been?—we had had a home in Ankara!

Selim awakened me in the night, shaking with severe chills. I wrapped him in another blanket and gave him more aspirin, and presently he slept. In the street below, although it was past 2 a.m., loud, vulgar music blared up from a crude coffee house or tavern; I could hear the shouts of men and there was still much traffic in the street. It was indeed a rough city.

Today was a terrible day. Selim continued to be sick with high fever and a very bad-sounding cough, and it was clear that he needed medical attention. I told the attendants at the hotel desk that my husband was quite ill and needed a doctor; they promised to send someone right away, but the hours passed one after another and no one came.

By early afternoon, I too had begun to ache all over and realized that I was also ill; but far worse than being unwell was the terrible feeling of being utterly alone and homeless which possessed me. Although the hotel people knew that Selim was sick, they did not offer help of any sort and the doctor did not come. A simple middle-aged cleaning woman who was about for most of the day was solicitous and kindly, acting as one would expect from a Muslim and a Turk. To me at that time she was the only source of human sympathy and support, and that plain, hardworking, kindhearted woman—may God bless and reward her!—will never know how much she meant to her Muslim sister who was at that moment without a home and so heavily-burdened. How sad, I thought, how ironic, to feel so passionately about Turkey and to be stranded, ill and solitary, in a hotel in Izmir without any human helper except a humble janitress! But so it will always be: the poor are God's people, close enough to the trials of life themselves to be sympathetic and compassionate, while the affluent easily pass by those who are

in difficulty, too busy or absorbed with other matters to care. I
thought too of the days when Muslim individuals or an entire community had built *karvanserais* for travelers for the love of God,
when caring for their needs was felt as an obligation on the entire
Muslim community and service to them was considered an act of
worship, and reflected on the sharp contrast between then and
now . . .

At mid-afternoon the doctor came at last. Selim had bronchitis
and needed an antibiotic, he said, and I too needed medication.
When I returned to the hotel after buying the medicine, the attendants at the desk asked me solicitously why I had gone myself to get
it; I could have sent my children or asked them. They advised me
not to go out, to let them know if we needed anything, and wished
us good health. A little late, I thought bitterly.

I returned to the room, gave Selim and myself the medications
and collapsed in bed, aching all over. While Selim slept, I lay
thinking.

This was our last day in Turkey, the final remaining hours
before our departure, for tomorrow at this time we would
insha'Allah be on a ship sailing for Europe. I knew now, hard as it
was for me to accept the fact, that it was almost out of the question
that we would ever come back again to live in Turkey, much as I
loved it; this was, in effect, our final and permanent farewell.

I thought of Cemile and her family, the recollection of whose
love for us and whose pure Islam will be a part of me as long as I
live, God willing, as will their joys and sorrows, the very thought of
them giving me strength; of Enver and Emine and Aynur Abla, the
kindest and most loving friends we could ever have had, whose care
and concern had made of our stay in Ankara the profoundly memorable experience it had become; of the *kapıcı* and his wife, of
Bahadir Bey and Deniz Hanım and all our other friends in Ankara;
of the home we had broken up just two days earlier; and of how
much of myself I had given to our life here, as if it were to be permanent. Now we would go home, take up the threads of our life

there, and continue the existence which we had left behind during these past months, unless or until it pleased God to make some change in our condition.

The little hotel room with sky-blue walls had been turned into a sick room, but from my bed I could see the roofs of buildings in the sunlit street, I could hear the continuous blaring of cheap music from some restaurant or coffee house nearby, I could look up at the row upon row of small colorful houses on the hill where Izmir's old *kale* stands. The noise of traffic was continuous, the streets teemed with life:—illiterate laborers, peasant women from the countryside, mini-skirted city girls, suited businessmen, and occasional older women in black *çarşafs.*

This is Turkey. This is the land which, in all our other travels within its borders, has been, as it were, ours; we had had our home here and it had belonged to us. Now we no longer belong and it is no longer ours. It is behind us, a memory, a mixed thread of delight and sorrow running through these middle years of our lives.

As I listen to the notes of almost the last *adhan* I will hear in this Muslim world for a long time to come—or will hear for the rest of my life if the All-Wise God sees fit that I should not return—coming from the old hill in front of me which has seen so many lives come and go, so much evil and so much good, where at night the lights of the small colored houses wink and blink like tiny jeweled eyes, I know that I cannot see ahead clearly. God knows what the rest of my path may be, but I, weak and finite, can barely see one step ahead to tomorrow. He then knows my road, and the roads of all His creatures, which lead back to Him, I pray for his guidance, His help and mercy as I leave this beloved Muslim world with which my heart is so bound up and try to re-establish my life away from it.

Although tomorrow at this time we will *insha'Allah* be at sea, all this will go on. Ankara too goes on, our street and our house go on, the *kapıcı hanım,* Enver and Emine, Cemile and her family and all our friends go on, sustained by God's mercy for as long as He wills, and we too go on. Certain things have changed necessarily, but please God our hearts will never change. Wherever on God's earth we may be, *insha'Allah* our hearts will hold the love of all this that we have cherished, as we strive in His cause, until the end. . .

"Say: 'Truly, my prayer and my service of sacrifice, my life and my death, are for God, the Sustainer of the worlds....' "

(al-An'am 6:162)

CHAPTER 21

IN RETROSPECT

May 12, 1971: It is a year to the day since we left Turkey, since the terrible day when I stood on the deck of a ship with such dry misery burning behind eyes which had wept until the head ached and until it seemed there were no more tears to shed, as the shore of Turkey which I had loved so dearly receded in the distance. An immense sorrow and sense of loss, as at the death of one's best beloved, overwhelmed me; but indeed, as I was soon to realize, this grief was the easier part of what must be experienced, for now I must come to terms with the world of the West where God had placed me, the world which was both totally familiar and totally strange, which was completely inimical to almost everything I valued, and of which I was a part but to which I could never truly belong.

During the days which followed—on the ship when I was ill and burning with fever, when we traveled in Europe with a very sick child who had caught the illness, when we were on a jet speeding back toward home, and when I looked around me at the America in which I had lived all my life—I was like an absolute outsider and stranger to what had formerly been my own world. Watching the thousands and thousands of cars speeding along the expressways of a vast American city like so many over-grown mechanical toys having no connection with human beings, observing the legion casual, unkempt boys and girls with streaming hair, their sex often a matter of guess-work, meandering along together in their careless way, I asked myself, "*Do* people—*can* people—really live like this? They must be utterly mad to do so!" Everything seemed very, very strange and altogether wrong. And all the old simple routine things to which I had been accustomed for years and years were, in the beginning, seemingly beyond my comprehension and grasp. My feet had forgotten how to use the pedals for driving a car, I could not find anything I wanted in a super-drug store because of the bewildering array of too many things, and the entire system and way of life seemed as foreign to me as if I were returning home after an absence of many years or as if I had dropped from another planet.

This stage, difficult as it was, was, thank God, soon passed, and as we settled into the old routines of life, the intense dislike I felt for many of the patterns of life around me (although I also found much to admire: the cleanliness, order, comparative lack of poverty, hard work and fruits of industry) subsided into a permanent, dull conviction that, although there were good and decent individuals everywhere, I and the society of which I was a member and in which I had lived all my life were, in basic and essential ways, totally imcompatible and irreconcilable, and a sense of being spiritually more a foreigner here than I could be in almost any other place on earth grew up within me.

Under these circumstances, I was the greatest mercy of God that my tenderest memories and emotions did not continue for very long at a peak stage, for human beings must and do adjust themselves to every sort of condition. We had returned and were here to stay; I must accommodate myself to the environment whether I liked it or not, and must, with God's help, try to keep alive all that had grown up within me during my sojourn in the Muslim world and utilize it in His cause.

While Selim returned to work and the children to their usual activities, I settled into the routines of housekeeping and my writing. At the same time we immediately involved ourselves in Islamic activities and re-established our ties with the Muslims in our city and in other areas of the country; for this was the vital community of believers, our link with the beloved world of Islam, which both supported us and to which we lent support in living Islam and striving to spread the light of its truth.

Turkey has not, as I imagined it might, come to seem like a passing dream for me, and I think it never will. Indeed, what I experienced there has in many ways more reality and validity for me than anything else I have known. And although I have had to put it away in a deep, not-easily-accessible corner of my heart for the time-being in order to keep the recollection of it from being too painful and in order to live fruitfully in the present, it will be part of my life and thought until my last moments, please God; for I have lived and breathed its atmosphere, good and bad, and have loved it dearly. To be sure, my old dream of a country, a place where I could find among Muslims a home for my unattached heart, has necessarily been put aside just now; but as I think of the Turkey which I have loved, where day after day the clear notes of the *adhan* ring out over the towns and cities of Anatolia, I know that the love and warmth, the sincerity, the inner life, the clear, pure blessed traditions of Islam which are so much alive among its people and will *insha'Allah* continue to live among them, burn with undiminished brightness in the hearts of all those who shared those months with us—we here and they there—and that nothing can take from me the rich and precious inner treasures which I brought back with me.

With all my heart, I thank the Most Merciful God Who bestowed upon us all this good, Who let it penetrate into our minds and souls, and Who returned us to our home to work and strive in His cause, for the great abundance of blessings which has been ours.

THE END

GLOSSARY OF FOREIGN TERMS

Some spellings have been used interchangeably in the text (e.g., *shalwaar and şalvar, Ramadan, Ramazan and Ramzan,* etc.), as the spelling varies from country to country. Most Arabic Islamic words or terminologies are also common to Turkish, Persian and Urdu. Where there is a difference in spelling and pronunciation, particularly in Turkish, I have given both in the Glossary.

Turkish words are spelled phonetically. I have tried to render Arabic, Persian and Urdu words as close to their pronunciation as possible; however, some sounds, such as 'gh' (*al-Ghaib*), do not exist in English and the reader will have to approximate them for himself. Symbols used: (T) = Turkish, (A) = Arabic, (U) = Urdu, (P) = Persian.

A

abaya (A)

Outer dress of Muslim women, worn in Saudi Arabia and Iraq.

abla, ablacığım (T)

Older sister, and its diminuitive.

used for one's real sister and also for older girls or women who are not related as a term of respect or affection.

adhan (A), *ezan* (T), *azan* (P, U)

The Muslim call to prayer, given, with its translation on page 486.

agabey (also *abi*) (T)

Older brother, used in the same manner as *abla* for older boys and men.

ahlâk, ahlâksız (T), *akhlaq* (A)

Morals; *ahlâksız* = without morals.

al-Fateha (A)

Literally, "the opening," i.e., the opening verses of the Holy Qur'an.

al-Ghaib (A)

The unseen or unknowable things e.g., God, His attributes, the angels, the Hereafter, man's soul, and any events or things outside the reach of human experience or perception.

Alhamdulillah (A), *elhamdulillah* (T)

Thank God.

Allah (A)

God.

Allah Subhanahu wa Ta'ala (A)

God Most High (Praised and Exalted).

Allahu Akbar (A), *Allahüekber* (T) God is the Most Great.

Amca Bey (T)

Amca = uncle, *Bey* = mister. Amca Bey is a title or expression of affection used for an older man who is not necessarily a relative.

Amerikan emperyalizm (T)

American imperialism.

ammi, amma (U), *umm* (A), *anne* (T)

Mother.

Anadolu (T)

Anatolia, i.e., the Asian part of Turkey.

anne, annecigim (T)

Mother, and its diminutive.

'Asr (A) prayer, *Ikindi namaz* (T)

The third prayer of the day, performed in the latter part of the afternoon.

assalamu alaikum (A), *esselamün aleyküm* (T)

"Peace be on you," the Islamic greeting.

ayran (T)

A drink of yogurt and water, popular in Turkey.

Azeri (Azerbayjani or Azerbeycani)

A dialect based on Turkish and Persian, spoken in Turkish, Irani and Russian Azerbayjan.

B

baba (U,T)

Father; in Pakistan it is also used as 'old man.'

bakkal (T), *baqqal* (A)

Grocery store

baklava (T, A)

A dessert made of thin layers of dough, nuts and sugar or honey, popular throughout the Middle East, Greece, etc.

bardak (T)	Small glass for tea.
Bayram (T), *'Eid* (A)	Festival
begum sahib(a) (U)	Servants' or tradesmen's title for the lady of the house.
Berat Kandili (T), *Baraa* (A), *Shabe Barat* (U)	The Night of Reckoning, one of the holy nights of the Islamic year.
bey (beg) (T)	Mister.
bhai (U)	Brother, usage same as for *agabey.*
bhabi (U)	Older brother's wife, usage same as for *abla.*
bir şey değil	It's nothing, don't mention it.
Bismillah; Bismillah ar-Rahman ar-Raheem (A)	"In the name of God," "In the name of God the Beneficent, the Merciful," said by Muslims at the beginning of Qur'anic recitations and at the starting of all actions.
börek (T)	A Turkish dish consisting of thin layers of pastry filled with ground meat or white cheese and parsley.
burnoose (A), *bornuz* (T)	Outer dress of Muslim women, worn in Morocco, having an attached hood; also used in many parts of the Muslim world as a towel for the bath.
burqa (U)	Outer dress and face-covering of Muslim women, worn in Pakistan.

C

caliph = *khalifa* (A), *halife* (T)	Temporal and spiritual leader of the Muslim *'Ummah.*
cami (T), *jam'i* (A)	Mosque.
canm (T), *janum* (P, U)	Literally, "my life or "my soul," a term of endearment and affection.
chaddor (P)	Outer dress of Muslim women, worn in Iran.
chadiri	Outer dress of Muslim women, worn in Afghanistan.
Cuma (T), *Jum'a* (A)	Friday.
Cumartesi (T)	Saturday.
Cumhuriyet Bayramı (T)	Republic Festival of Turkey.

Ç

çarşaf (T)	Outer dress of some conservative Muslim women, worn in Turkey.
Çarşamba (T)	Wednesday.
Çocukların Bayramı (T)	The Children's Festival of Turkey.
çok güzel (T)	Very pretty, beautiful or nice.

D

Dar al-Islam	Literally, "the abode of Islam," i.e., the place which is ruled by the Islamic *Shari'ah.*

Dar al-Salaam (A)	Literally "the Abode of Peace," i.e., Paradise, the state of bliss in the next life.
deen (A), *din* (T)	Religion or way of life, i.e., Islam.
derveesh (A), *derviş* (T)	Member of a Sufi order.
Dev-Genç (T)	Name of Turkish communist terrorist organization.
dhal (U)	Collective name for the family of dried peas or pulses.
dhikr, or dhikr Allah (A) *Zikir* (T)	Literally "remembrance" (of God), in particular the recitation of phrases of glorification of God.
dhobi (U)	Laundryman.
Dhul-Hijjah (A)	The twelfth month of the Islamic calendar during which pilgrimage to Mekkah *(Hajj)* is performed annually.
Dhuhr (A) prayer, *Öğle namaz* (T)	The second prayer of the day, performed in the early afternoon.
diskotek (T)	Discothèque.
Divan-i-Khas (P, U)	Special audience chamber in a king's palace.
diyanet (A, T), *Diyanet İşleri* (T)	Integrity or peity; Diyanet İşleri is the Turkish Religious Affairs Ministry.
dolmuş (T), *servees* (A)	A collective taxi shared by several people going along the same route.
du'a (A), *dua* (T, U)	Supplication to God.

dupatta (U)	A long scarf or veil worn with the *shalwaar-qamis* by Pakistani girls and women.

E

Ebedi Şef (T)	The Eternal Chief, i.e., Atatürk.
efendim (T)	Literally, "my sir," used in the sense of Sir, Madam.
'Eid (A), *Bayram* (T)	Festival.
'Eid al-Adha (A), *Kurban Bayramı* (T)	The Festival of sacrifice at the time of the pilgrimage to Mekkah.
'Eid al-Fitr (A), *Ramazan Bayrami* or *Şeker Bayramı* (T)	The Festival of Fast-Breaking at the the end of the month of fasting, *Ramadan.* It occurs two months and ten days before *'Eid al-Adha* each year.
'Eid mubarak (A)	*'Eid* congratulations, or Happy *'Eid.*
emanet (T), *amanat* (A)	Literally, "trust" or "that which is entrusted." As used in text, it refers to the sword and mantle of Prophet Muhammad which were entrusted to those who succeeded him as head of the Muslim state and community *(khalifa).*
esselàmün aleyküm (T), *assalamu alaikum* (A)	See *assalamu alaikum.*
estağfurullah (T), *astaghfirullah* (A)	"I ask forgiveness of God." In Turkey and the Arab word this expression is also used to mean "You're welcome" (i.e., I ask God's forgiveness for expecting or receiving thanks).

evkaf (T), *awqaf* (A)	Religious trust or foundation.
ezan (T), *adhan*(A), *azan* (U)	See *adhan*.

F

Fajr (A) prayer, *Sabah namaz* (T)	The first prayer of the day, performed between dawn and shortly before sunrise.
fakülte (T)	Faculty, i.e., college or department of a university.
farz(T,U) *fard* (A)	Obligatory, i.e., those Islamic practices which are an obligation on Muslims.
al-Fateha (A)	See under *al-*.
fayton (T)	Phaeton, the four-wheeled horse-drawn carriage used as a taxi in many Anatolian towns.
fez (T)	High brimless hat formerly worn in Turkey and other parts of the Muslim world.
futbol (T)	Football.

G

gàvur (T), *kafir* (A)	One who denies or is ungrateful to God, i.e., a non-believer or heathen.
Gazi (T), *ghazi* (A)	Literally, "the victorious;" as used in the Notes, refers to Atatürk.
gecekondu (T)	Literally, "night-built," i.e., houses which are built in one night, assuring ownership and tenancy to the builder under Turkish law.

geçmiş olsun (T)	Literally, "may it be past," most often said in relation to illness or any calamity.
al-Ghaib (A)	See under *al-*.
gharara (U)	Girls' and women's dress worn in Pakistan and India, consisting of a very full, gathered split skirt with tunic and *dupatta*.
gün aydın (T)	Literally, "bright day," i.e., good day..

H

Hacı (T), *Haji* (A)	One who has performed the pilgrimage to Mekkah.
Hadith (A), *Hadis* (T, U)	Sayings and actions (the Tradiions) of Prophet Muhammad.
Hajj (A), *Hac* (T)	The pilgrimage to Mekkah.
Haji (A), *Hacı* (T)	See *Hacı*.
hala (T), *Khala* (A.P.U.)	Paternal (T)/maternal (A.P.U.) aunt.
Halk Partisi (T)	The Peoples' Party, formerly the political party of Atatürk and İnönü.
halvah (A, U), *helva* (T)	Literally, "sweet," the generic term for many different kinds of sweets throughout the Muslim world.
hamam (A,T)	Public bath.
hanım (T), *khanum* (P,U)	Woman or lady; also used as a title signifying Miss or Mrs. in Turkey and Iran.

hanım efendi (T)	A respectable woman of the upper classes.
harem=*haram* (A), *haramlık* (T)	Literally, "sacred" or "prohibited" (from violation) ; refers to the part of the house where women lived away from contact with outside males in former times.
Havagaz Ofisi (T)	Gas Office.
Hayirle Bayramlar (T) *'Eid mubarak* (T)	See *'Eid mubarak*.
henna (A, U)	A red dye used for dyeing the fingers or palms of hands or feet for marriages and special occasions, or for dyeing the hair or beard.
Hijrah (A), *Hicret* (T)	The emigration of Prophet Muhammad from Mekkah to Medina, which marks the first year of the Islamic era. *Hijrah* Day (1 Muharram) is the first day of the Islamic year.
hodja=*hoca* (T), *khwaja* (P)	Teacher or religious instructor.
hoş bulduk (T)	Literally, "happily found," said in response to *hoş geldiniz* (T)
hoş geldiniz (T)	Literally, "happily you came," i.e., welcome.
hutbe (T), *khutba* (A)	The sermon which accompanies the *Jum'a* and *'Eid* prayers.

I

ibadat (A), *ibadet* (T)	Worship.
iftar (A)	Breaking one's fast after sunset with water, a light snack or meal.
ilah (A), *ilâh* (T)	A deity, that is, anything or anyone who ·is worshipped, to whom ultimate authority is ascribed and allegiance and devotion are given.
ilâhi (T)	The religious chanting or music of Turkey.
imam (A)	Literally "leader;" as used in the text, one who leads the congregational prayers.
Imam-Hatip School (T), *imam khateeb* (A)	Turkish schools for training boys and girls as religious functionaries.
insha'Allah (A), *inşallah* (T)	If God wills.
'Isha (A) prayer, *Yatse namaz* (T)	The fifth prayer of the day, performed during the night.
Islamiyat (U)	Islamic studies.

J

jahiliyyah (A), *cehalet* (T)	Literally, "ignorance;" in a specific sense, ignorance of the Divine guidance. Also refers to the period of the ignorance of truth and God's guidance before the mission of Prophet Muhammad.

Jamaat-i-Islami (U)	Islamic movement and party in Pakistan.
jam'i (A), *cami* (T)	See *cami.*
jamidar[ni] (U)	Menial servant (*'jamidarni'* is the feminine form) in Pakistan.
jandarma (T)	*'Gendarme,'* the Turkish military personnel who also perform police duties.
jihad fi sabeel Allah (A), *cihad* (T)	Striving in the way of God.
jilbab (A)	Outer dress of Muslim women, worn in parts of the Arab world.
Jum'a (A), *Cuma* (T)	See *Cuma.*

K

kabab (U)	A meat preparation.
kahrolsun (T), *qahr* (A)	Wrath, i.e., "damn him!"
kalbsız (T)	Heartless.
kale (T), *qal'ah* (A)	Castle.
kalorifer (T)	Furnace or central heating.
kalpak (T)	Tall turkish hat usually made of fur.

kandil (T)

Literally, "lantern" or "light;" specifically, the holy nights of the Islamic calendar.

kanun(i) (T), *qanun* (A)

Law (canon); as used in the text, refers to Sultan Süleyman the Magnificent, noted as a law-giver.

kapıcı, kapıcı hanım (T)

Literally "doorman," i.e., the caretaker—janitor of a building,— and his wife.

kardeş (T)

Brother, used for real brother and also for "brother-in-Islam;" also used for "sister" in the latter sense.

karvanseray (P),
   kervansaray (T)

Hotel for travelers in the Muslim world in old times.

kebap, kebap salonu (T)

Same as *'kebab,'* and the place where it is sold.

khalifa

See 'Caliph'.

*Khodaigon Shahinshah
   Aryamehr* (P)

Title used by the present Shah of Iran, meaning "God, the King of Kings, the Sun of the Aryans."

khutba (A), *hutbe* (T)

See *hutbe.*

kiralık daire (T)

Apartment for rent.

Koka-kola

Coca-Cola.

konak (T)

A mansion of old Turkey.

Koran = Kuran (T), *al-Qur'an* (A) The Divinely-revealed scripture of Islam.

kuaför (T)   Coiffeur or hair-dresser.

kufr (A), *küfr* (T)   Disbelief or denial of belief in God.

Kurban Bayrami (T), 'Eid al-   The Festival of Sacrifice, 'Eid
'Eid al-Adha* (A)   *al-Adha.*

kuruş (T)   Unit of Turkish currency; 100 *kuruş* = 1 T.L.

L

Labbayk, Allahumma,   One of the *talbiyyah* (devotional
labbayk (A)   calls) recited by pilgrims during the *Hajj*, meaning, "Here I am, Our Lord, at Thy service."

La ilaha illa Allah,   "There is no deity except God,"
Muhammadu Rasul Allah (A)   Muhammad is the Messenger of God," the basic creed of Islam.

Lailat al-Qadr (A), *Leyle-i Kadir* The Night of Power, a holy night
or *Kadir Gecesi* (T)   of the Islamic calendar, on which Prophet Muhammad received the first revelation of the Qur'an, observed on the night preceding 27th day of *Ramadan.*

lira (T)   Turkish monetary unit, about 1/15th of U. S. dollar.

lise (T)   *Lycee,* i.e., high school.

lokanta (T)   Restaurant or cafe.

lungi (U)	Pakistani garment covering the lower half of the body, usually worn by men and also by some women in the Panjab.

M

madrasah (A), *medrese* (T)	School, often in the sense of religious school.
maf karna (U)	Excuse me.
Maghrib (A) prayer, *Akşam namaz* (T)	The fourth of the five daily prayers, observed between sunset and dark.
mai (U)	Mother; also used for elderly women, especially servants.
masha'Allah (A), *maşallah* (T)	Literally, "as God willed it," an expression of appreciation of some good quality or agreeable happening.
maulana (A), *melvana* (T)	Literally, "our patron" or "our leader," a man of religious learning and eminence.
maulvi sahib (U)	Religious teacher.
medrese (T)	See *madrasah*.
mem sahib (U)	Literally, "madam *sahib*," a title formerly used for British women in Imperial India, now used for Western or Westernized women in Pakistan.

merhaba (A,T)	Greeting used in Turkey and Arabic-speaking countries, literally meaning "Welcome."
mersi (T)	The Turkified *"merci."*
mevlàna (T), *maulana* (A)	See *maulana.*
Mevlud (T), *Moulud* (A), *Milad* (A)	Literally, "birth," i.e., the celebra of the birthday of the Prophet Muhammad. In Turkey *Melvùd* also refers to a long narrative poem in praise of the Prophet which is recited for many different occasions.
minbar (A), *minber* (T)	The pulpit in a mosque from which the sermon is delivered.
Moghal (U)	Mongol peoples from Central Asia and a dynasty of kings who ruled India during the 16th-19th centuries.
mu'amilat (A)	The duties of a Muslim which relate to practical matters
müdür (T), *mudir* (A)	Official, director.
muezzin (U), *muedhdhin* (A)	One who gives the call to prayer *(adhan),* usually an officially-appointed functionary.
Muhammadu Rasul Allah (A)	"Muhammad is the Messenger of God," the second part of the Islamic creed.
Muharram (A), *Muharrem* (T)	The first month of the Islamic calendar.

muhabbetsiz (T)	Loveless.
mullah (U)	Teacher of religion.
mureed (A)	A student or follower of a religious guide.
Müslüman kardeş (T)	Muslim brother (or sister).

N

nafil salat (A)	Supererogatory or optional prayer.
nafs (A)	Spirit or soul.
ney (T), *ny (A)*	Wooden flute, often used in Turkish religious music.
nurlu (T)	Literally, "with light," i.e., having the quality of inner-light or radiance.

O

orta okul (T)	Middle school.
Osmanlı	Ottoman, i.e., of the dynasty of Othman, the 12th century founder of the Ottoman Empire.

P

paisa (U)	The smallest unit of Pakstani currency.
pansiyon (T)	Pension, a small hotel.

pasaj (T)	"Passage," that is, a building housing a complex of shops, an arcade.
paşa (T)	Military general.
Pazar (T), *bazaar* (P, U)	Bazaar; in Turkish *Pazar* also means Sunday since this is the day on which local produce markets are most commonly open in Turkish towns.
Pazartesi (T)	Monday.
peri bacası (T)	"Fairy chimneys," the Turkish name for the strange geological formations of Göreme and other areas of Anatolia.
Perşembe (T)	Thursday.
pilau (P,U), *pilav* (T)	A rice dish.
pir (T,U)	A saintly Muslim who is accorded much respect.
pirzola (T)	Lamb chops.
purdah (U), *hijab* (A)	Literally, "curtain;" refers to the concealing dress of Muslim women and their separation from men.

Q

qalandar (P,U)	A recluse or man who gives no importance to worldly matters.
qamis (U)	Pakistani dress, similar to a European frock, worn with a *shalwaar* and *dupatta*.

Qur'an (A), Kuran(T)	See 'Koran.'

R

Raj (U)	Rule; as used in the text, it refers to British rule in India.
rak'at (A)	Unit of Islamic prayer which is repeated two, three or four times during the prayer. In each *rak'at* recitations from the Qur'an and glorification of God are said, and the worshipper stands, bows, prostrates and sits at specified times.
Ramadan (A), *Ramazan* (T), *Ramzan* (U)	Ninth month of the Islamic calendar, during which fasting between dawn and sunset is observed each day by Muslims, accompanied by increased devotional activity.
Ramazan Bayramı (T), *'Eid al-Fitr* (A)	The "*Ramazan* Festival," *'Eid al-Fitr.*
rektör (T)	Rector or president, specifically of a university.
riyal (P)	Unit of Irani currency.
rupee (U)	Unit of Pakistani currency.

S

sahib (U)	As used in text, means "Mister."
sa'in (U)	Beggar.
salat (A), *namaz* (P,T,U)	The prayers observed five times daily by Muslims, as follows:

(1) *Fajr,* observed between dawn and sunrise;
(2) *Dhuhr,* observed between noon and mid-afternoon;
(3) *'Asr,* observed during the late afternoon;
(4) *Maghrib,* observed between sunset and dark;
(5) *'Isha,* observed during the night.

Salı (T)	Tuesday.
sallallahu alayhi wa sallam (A)	"The blessings of God be on him and peace," said by Muslims when mentioning Prophet Muhammad.
salon (T)	Drawing room.
sari (U)	Dress worn by many upper class women in Pakistan, consisting of 6 yards of draped and pleated fabric.
sawab (U), *thawab* (A), *sevab* (T)	Reward in the Hereafter.
seccade (T), *sajjada* (A), *ja namaz* (U)	Small rug, used during prayers so that the worshipper may be sure of praying on a clean surface.
seer (U)	Unit of weight, approximately two pounds.
selâm (T), *salam* (A)	Literally, "peace," i.e., salutation.
Seljuk	Pre-Ottoman Turkish tribe and dynasty.
shagird (P,U)	Pupil or student; as used in text, of a Sufi leader.

Shah, Shahinshah	King, king of kings; as used in text, the ruler of Iran.
shalwaar (U), *şalvar* (T), *sarwal* (A)	Wide trousers worn throughout the Muslim world by women and in some areas also by men.
shamiana (U)	Tent or awning, used for housing wedding festivities, cultural gatherings, etc., in Pakistan.
Shari'ah (A), *Şeriat* (T)	Literally, "the way," the legal system of Islam derived from and based on the injunctions of the Qur'an and the *Sunnah* of the Prophet.
shaykh (A), şeyh (T)	Leader, specifically a religious leader or guide.
Sheriat	See *Shari'ah*.
Shi'ah	The section of the Muslim community believing in the succession of leadership through 'Ali, the cousin and son-in-law of the Prophet.
shirk(A), *şirk* (T)	Associating others with God's divinity, whether deities, human beings, etc.
sigara (T)	Cigarette.
simit (T)	Sesame-seed covered pastry ring, very popular in Turkey and the Arab world.
Subhanallah (A)	Glory be to God.

sucu (T)	Water seller.
Sufi (A), Sufism	Muslim 'mystic,' 'mysticism.'
suhoor (A)	Pre-dawn meal taken on days of fasting in *Ramadan* and at other times of fasting.
sultan (A)	Ruler or king.
Sunnah (A), *Sünnet* (T)	Refers to what the Prophet used to do, i.e., what is desirable and recommended but not obligatory for Muslims, following the Prophet's example, including also the portion of the daily prayers which are called *sunnah*. In Turkish *Sünnet* also means 'circumcision.'
Sunni	Short for *"Ahl al-sunnah wal jama'a,"* that is, people who follow the Prophet's *sunnah* and his community, i.e., the majority of Muslims

Ş

şalvar (T), *shalwaar* (U)	See *shalwaar*.
şarap (T), *sharab* (U), *khamr* (A)	Wine, or in a generic sense all alcoholic beverages.
Şeker Bayramı (T)	The "Festival of Sweets," *'Eid al-Fitr*.
Şeriat (T), *Shari'ah* (A)	See *Shari'ah*.
şeyh (T), *shaykh* (A)	See *Shaykh*.

T

taksi (T)	Taxi.
Tanrı (T)	The pre-Islamic Turkic word for God.
taqwa (A), *takva* (T)	Consciousness and fear of God.
tarawih (A), *teravi* (T)	Supererogatory prayers said at night after *'Isha* prayer during *Ramadan*.
tariqat (A), *tarikat* (T)	Sufi 'way' or order.
tasawwuf (A), *tasavvuf* (T)	Islamic 'mysticism,' i.e., Sufism.
tauba estağfurullah (T), *astaghfirullah* (A)	I ask forgiveness of God.
tawheed (A), *tevhid* (T)	Literally, "unity;" specifically, the unity or oneness of God.
tekke (T), *takkiyah* (A)	Gathering or dwelling-place of adherents of a Sufi order.
teleferik (T)	Cable car.
terbiye (A,T), *terbiyesiz* (T)	Upbringing, manners; *terbiyesiz* = mannerless, without training.

tesbih (A)	Literally, "glorification of God;" as used in the text, a string of beads used for counting while reciting the glorification of God *(dhikr),* each phrase being repeated thirty-three times.
teşekkür ederim (T), *shukran* (A) *muteshekkur* (P), *shukria* (U)	Thank you.
teyze (T)	Maternal aunt.
thoup (A)	Outer covering of Muslim women, worn in various parts of the Arab world.
T.L.	Turkish *lira.*
tola (U)	A very small measure of weight for weighing gold, etc.
tonga (U)	The two-wheeled, horse-drawn taxi of West Pakistan.
touman (P)	Unit of Irani currency.
tsharchaf	*Çarsaf*

U

'ulema (A), plural of *'alim*	Islamic scholars.
'ummah (A), *ümmet* (T)	Community or nation, specifically the Muslim community or nation.

Urdu

The language of West Pakistan and some parts of India.

V

vatan (T), *watan* (A)

Fatherland.

ve aleyküm selam (T), *wa alaikum salaam* (A)

"And on you be peace." said in response to "*Esselâmün aleyküm*"(*Assalamu alaikum*).

veli (T), *wali* (A, T, U)

See '*wali*.'

vezir (T), *wazir* (A)

Chief minister.

W

wa alaikum salaam (A), *ve aleyküm selam* (T)

See *ve aleyküm selam*.

wali (A), *veli* (T)

Saintly Muslim to whom great respect is accorded.

wudu (A), *wuzu* (U), *abdest* (T)

Ablution for prayers.

Y

Yılbaşı (T)

Literally, "year's head," i.e., new year.

yogurtcu (T)

Yogurt seller.

Z

Zakat (A), *zekat* (T)

The obligatory poor-due, the fourth 'pillar' of Islam.

zakat al-fitr (A)

The obligatory charity of *'Eid al-Fitr*, a nominal amount to be given to some needy person before the *'Eid al-Fitr* prayer on behalf of each member of the family.

ANNOTATED BIBLIOGRAPHY

[1] THE HOLY QUR'AN.

It should be noted that all attempts to 'translate' the Qur'an are at best an effort to convey the meaning rather than a translation in the accepted sense of the word, particularly as it is impossible to recapture either the Qur'an's pristine simplicity and directness, and at the same time its beauty, majesty and rhythm, in another language. Arabic is a language in which a single word often conveys a highly complex meaning or several meanings, which in English and other languages can only be rendered by many words, producing an extreme lengthening of phraseology in translation, while often failing to reproduce the exact meaning, for which there may be no single equivalent word or concept. For this reason I have retained many Qur'anic terms in the text for which there are no simple English equivalents. Most translations resort to Biblical language which does not exist in the Arabic, primarily in order to make clear the distinction between the singular 'thou' and the plural 'you' or 'ye.' The translations used here are based on that of Yusuf Ali, with some modifications.

[2] A. Afetinan. THE EMANCIPATION OF THE TURKISH WOMAN, UNESCO, Paris, 1961.

Written by a noted Turkish woman professor, a member of Kemal Atatürk's own household and an outspoken Kemalist, this volume is a short and obviously very much biased survey of women in Turkey from Hittite times to the present.

[3] Henry Elisha Allen. THE TURKISH TRANSFORMATION.
Greenwood Press, New York, 1935.

The author was associated with the Department of
Religion, Lafayette College. He views the decline of Islam in
Turkey in terms of how it will benefit Christianity, and at the
same time, as Christianity has to a considerable degree ceased
to provide meaningful guidance, he rejoices in the loss of
meaning of Islam for Turks.   He appears to take at face
value and cites quotations from government-authorized textbooks and *khutbas* put out by the puppet *Diyanet Işleri*
(Religious Affairs Department) of Atatürk's regime, which make
very interesting reading.

[4] A.J. Arberry, SUFISM. George Allen and Unwin, Ltd.,
London, 1969.

This is a short but adequate and informative account of the
genesis of Sufism and its later developments, with a discussion
of many of the prominent Sufis and their movements.

[5] H.C. Armstrong. GRAY WOLF, The Life of Kemal Ataturk.
Capricorn Books, New York, 1933 (a reprint is now available
from AMS Press, New York).

It is stated on the cover that "Nasser said of this book specifically 'This has been the most important book in my life.'"
Without knowing whether or not this statement is true and without commenting on its obvious implications, I found this book
to be highly sensational in style and content, with many inaccu-
racies and glib oversimplifications, hardly qualifying as a serious
biographical work. No documentation nor references are given,
and the rapid staccato style and heavy lurid portrayal of the extreme corruption of Atatürk's personal life, although the facts
may be correct, produces an impression of inaccuracy and exaggeration. At the end the author, after endless descriptions of
Atatürk's drunken orgies, gambling, promiscuity, venereal disease, ruthless liquidation of his opponents, hatred for religion,

etc., discusses his "greatness" and opines that perhaps he is the the voice of one "inspired by the Great Architect of the Universe"!

[6] Niyazi Berkes. THE DEVELOPMENT OF SECULARISM IN TURKEY. McGill University Press, Montreal, 1964.

This volume covers the entire period of Turkish secularism from the early eighteenth century through the Kemalist period. Although the author dwells on intellectual movements from the Tanzimat period until the emergence of Atatürk in considerable detail, what emerges strongly from Berkes' material is the fundamental difference between the discussion, debate, soul-searching and gradual reform employed by earlier reformers and the arbitrary and dictatorial methods employed by Atatürk. In fact, Berkes' discussion of Atatürk and his reforms is quite brief and sketchy in comparison with his thorough treatment of earlier developments, and it is obvious that, although a convinced secularist and Kemalist himself, it is no easy matter even for him to justify and explain Atatürk's devious and autocratic methods of enforcing his will.

[7] Selma Ekrem. TURKEY, OLD AND NEW. Charles Scribner's Sons, New York, 1947.

Written by the grand-daughter of Namık Kemal, who recalls her girlhood during the last days of the Ottoman Empire, the author is an outspoken Kemalist whose work is marred by her defense of Atatürk's dictatorial and oppressive methods of 'reform' and by her naive and inaccurate presentation of Islam as a matter of mere personal 'belief.' Written in a simplistic manner, this book is an interesting study of the confused type of thinking of the contemporary westernized Turk, and I have included some excerpts from it side by side with more objective accounts to show the manner in which the supporters of Atatürk are able to rationalize the policies and actions of their hero.

[8] Lord Kinross. ATATURK. William Morrow and Company, New York, 1965.

A very interesting, well-written volume. The author is quite objective about the personality and weaknesses of his subject, and, on the whole, except in relation to Islam and its exponents, which he does not understand very adequately, it is a balanced and objective account.

[9] Bernard Lewis. THE EMERGENCE OF MODERN TURKEY. Oxford University Press, London, 1961.

   Although in many respects a thoroughly researched and well-thought-out presentation of the subject, this book suffers from the twin evils which almost invariably characterize the works of orientalists—that of an obvious innate bias against Islam coupled with an ignorance of many of its vital aspects, which often (particularly in this instance) takes the form of confusing Islam with what Muslims past or present have done.

[10]Dagobert von Mikusch. MUSTAPHA KEMAL. Doubleday, Doran and Company, Inc., New York, 1931.

   Written by a German Contemporary of Atatürk, this biography is marred by a considerable degree of subjectivity and romanticism. The preface begins with what is in fact a very dubious compliment to Atatürk. "The history of our times," writes von Mikusch, "abounds in outstanding men. Mustapha Kemal, the creator of modern Turkey stands alongside Lenin, the great revolutionary, and Mussolini, who has given actual form to a new conception of the State." Here one sees the difficulty of any biographer of Atatürk at its height: to present the actual accomplishments and outstanding better qualities of his subject simultaneously with his personal vices, his autocracy, and his ill-conceived efforts at reform. As is common, this work suffers greatly from the author's abysmal ignorance of Islam.

[11]Irfan Orga, PHOENIX ASCENDANT. Robert Hale Ltd., London, 1959.

   This is probably the only existing biography of Atatürk written in English by a Turk, an ex-officer who was Atatürk's junior contemporary and obvious admirer. Despite this, the author has managed to maintain a fair degree of objectivity.

Once again, however, this book's validity is considerably weakened by the author's manifest ignorance of Islam and his parroting of the same old slogans of the imperative need for drastic reform. Here too the burden of depicting a great national leader and the savior of his country side by side with the Atatürk whose unlimited power was such a corrupting influence and whose personal immoralities reached such a height is a heavy one for the author, but his effort is admirable. I have not quoted extensively from his book, since to my thinking the scholarship of Lord Kinross' biography is unquestionably superior.

[12]Ferenc A. Váli. BRIDGE ACROSS THE BOSPORUS. Johns Hopkins Press, Baltimore, 1971.

An interesting exposition of the multi-faceted aspects of Turkish foreign policy, which up to the present has represented a studied attempt to maintain and strengthen its alliance with the West, both because Turkey wants to be considered a part of the West and also as a defense against the ever-present threat of Soviet aggression. Turkey has also attempted to mend its relations with the Muslim world, marred by the attempt to secure itself against the Soviet threat. The author's comments at the conclusion of the volume concerning Islam and its place in Turkish society are typical of the common lack of understanding of the real nature of Islam and its significance for the Muslim individual and society.

NOTES

TURKEY

1. Early Movements Toward Nationalism and Westernization

(1) "Until the nineteenth century the Turks thought of themselves primarily as Muslims; their loyalty belonged, on different levels, to Islam and to the Ottoman house and state. The language a man spoke, the territory he inhabited, the race from which he claimed descent, might be of personal, sentimental, or social significance. They had no political relevance. So completely had the Turks identified themselves with Islam that the very concept of a Turkish nationality was submerged—and this despite the survival of the Turkish language and the existence of what was in fact though not in theory a Turkish state. They had not even retained to the same degree as the Arabs and Persians an awareness of their identity as a separate ethnic and cultural group within Islam.

"The Turkish national idea, in the modern sense, first appears in the mid-nineteenth century...

"At first these ideas were limited to a small circle of intellectuals, but gradually they spread far and wide, and their victory was finally symbolized by the official adoption, for the first time, of the names of Turkey and Turk for the country and people of the Republic. The growth of the sentiment of Turkish identity was connected with the movement away from Islamic practice and tradition, and toward Europe. This began with purely practical short-term measures of reform, attempted to accomplish a limited purpose; it developed into a large-scale deliberate attempt to take a whole nation across the frontier from one civilization to another." ([9], pp. 2-3)

"The general feeling of Europe was that the ancient institutions and structure of the [Ottoman] Empire were barbarous and irretrievably bad, and that only the adoption, as rapidly as possible, of a European form of government and way of life would admit Turkey to the rank and privileges of a civilized state. This view was urged on Turkish statesmen with considerable vigour by the governments and embassies of the European powers, and eventually came to be accepted, at least tacitly, by a larger and larger proportion of the Turkish ruling class, which was deeply aware of the power, wealth, and progress of Europe as compared with its own backwardness, poverty, and weakness." ([9], 124)

"The difficulties facing the nineteenth-century reformers were enormous. ...There was much about the reforms to arouse resentment and dislike. The political, social, and economic changes they involved seemed to offer some kind of threat to the interests of almost every group in Turkish society; to almost all they appeared as a triumph over Islam of the millennial Christian enemy in the West. For the reforms were basically the forcible imposition, on a Muslim country, of practices and procedures derived from Europe, with the encouragement, if not the insistence, of European powers, and with the help of European experts and advisers." ([9], 127)

2. Atatürk: His Reforms and Character

A. Ankara as Capital

(2) "Angora was in fact hardly more than a large village, its population reduced to a mere 20,000... The citadel [the castle at Ulus] looked out to all points of the compass over the naked treeless plain, snowbound in winter, sunbaked in summer, waterless but for the rainfall and a few scattered wells.

"From a distance a low ridge of undulating hills, rough and

colourless, half embraced the site. And 'site' it still was. The city—still to become a city—had begun to spill itself down onto the plateau but had yet to spread far across it, obstructed largely by a stretch of wasteland which in the winter became a marsh. Here stood the railway station and a few public buildings which the Young Turks, remedying Ottoman neglect, had erected. Here was also a small and unkempt municipal garden." ([8], 247)

(3) "...On 9 October [1923] Ismet Paşa, at a meeting of the People's Party, moved a constitutional amendment, in the form of 'Ankara is the seat of government of the Turkish state.' Four days later the Assembly formally decided on its adoption.

"The decision meant a new breach with the past—a logical sequel to the abolition of the Sultanate. The Emperor [*Sultan*] had gone; the Imperial City was ill adapted to house the government of revolutionaries that had overthrown him. For nearly five centuries Istanbul had been the capital of an Islamic Empire;...these [old associations] were too intimately associated with the past, in fact and in the mind of the Turkish people, to provide a centre for the new Turkey that Kemal wanted to build. And so a new capital was chosen, symbolizing and accentuating the changes that were taking place. The new state was based not on a dynasty, an empire, or a faith, but on the Turkish nation—and its capital was in the heart of the Turkish homeland." ([9], 260-261)

B. *'Hat Reform'*

(4) "The Turks did not only lack political freedom under the Sultans but they could not even decide what to put on their heads!... No Turk could appear in public without this peculiar headdress [*fez*] and if anyone had been bold enough to wear a hat he would have been dragged to the nearest police station. The hat was considered the symbol of Christianity and utterly unfit to grace good Moslem heads. The wearing of the hat was considered sinful and was prohibited severely. This attitude was fostered and encouraged by many of our *hodjas* who looked at all the ways of the West as the very work of Satan.

"The Turks were far from suspecting that the fez, which was almost part of their makeup, was threatened. But Mustapha Kemal had decided that the best way to usher in his program of modernization was by breaking up prejudice. The government had to tread cautiously, as it was felt that many people would highly resent the adoption of the hat. [Mustafa Kemal appeared at Kastamonu, a 'conservative' Anatolian town, wearing a hat.] ...He told them that the fez was not even Turkish in origin but had been borrowed from the Greeks. He went on to explain that the headgear did not make the man and could never influence his religion. He abused the fez as unhygienic and ugly and fit only for backward people. Turkey, the Gazi went on warmly, had decided to change her ways, to become modern and take her place among the civilized people of the world. But how would the West accept us if we persisted in wearing that ridiculous headgear, symbol of a degrading past?

"It soon became clear that important events were in store for the country. The Gazi had laid his plans and he had talked about them with members of the government. He was now ready to translate them into action. On Nov. 25, 1925, the Grand National Assembly forbade the wearing of the fez or any form of headdress without a vizor, and anyone breaking the law could be arrested or imprisioned." ([7], 54-55)

This sort of discussion is typical of those who are ready to defend any extreme to which westernization is carried, regardless of the methods used for its imposition. Note also the comparison between the 'autocratic' rule of the sultans and the 'democratic' rule of Atatürk. During the time of the later sultans people were quite free to criticize the *fez* (see for example [6], p. 404), but those who criticized Atatürk's Hat Reforms got up to five years' imprisonment and it is said that some were even hanged. As this book is being written, fifty-five members of the Nurcu movement are being tried in Isparta; one of the specific charges against them is that they are against the Hat Reforms.

(5) "The climax was reached on the third day, when he [Atatürk] delivered a long oration to a dazed and respectful audience, variously clad, in the club-room of the Turkish Hearth.

" 'Gentlemen,' he said, 'the Turkish people, who founded the Turkish Republic, are civilized; they are civilized in history and reality. But I tell you... that the people of the Turkish Republic, who claim to be civilized, must prove that they are civilized, by their ideas and their mentality, by their family life and their way of living... They must prove in fact that they are civilized and advanced persons in their outward aspect also... I shall put my explanation to you in the form of a question.

" 'Is our dress national?' Cries of 'No!'

" 'Is it civilized and international?' Cries of 'No, no!'

" 'I agree with you. This grotesque mixture of styles is neither national nor international... A civilized, international dress is worthy and appropriate for our nation, and we will wear it. Boots or shoes on our feet, trousers on our legs, shirt and tie, jacket and waistcoat—and of course, to complete these, a cover with a brim on our heads. I want to make this clear, This head covering is called "Hat." ' "

"...Towards the end of November 1925, when Kemal judged that public opinion was ripe, a new bill was passed by the Assembly which obliged all men to wear hats and made the wearing of the fez a criminal offense. ... For the masses there were produced cloth caps with a peak [vizor] designed to prevent the wearers from touching the ground with their heads as they prayed, but easily reversible and often reversed." ([8], 471-473)

(6) "It was at this time, and in this context, that Kemal made the first of his great symbolic revolutions—those dramatic changes of outward form which expressed in a manner at once vivid and profound, the forcible transference of a whole nation from one civilization to another ...To the Muslim [the enforced replacement of one form of headgear by another] was a matter of fundamental significance, expressing—and affecting—his relations with his neighbors and his ancestors, and his place in society and history. Islam was a faith and a civilization, distinct from other faiths and civilizations, uniting the Muslim to other Muslims... Dress, and especially headgear, was the visible and outward token by which a Muslim indicated his allegiance to the community of Islam and his rejection of others. During the past century modernization and reform had made great inroads into Muslim exclusiveness in matters of dress, and had created a new social gulf between the Western and un-Westernized..." ([9], 267)

"On 2 September [1925] a group of new decrees directed against the theocracy included... an order to civil servants to wear the costume 'common to all civilized nations of the world'—that is, the Western suit and hat. At first ordinary citizens were free to dress as they pleased, but on 25 November 1925 a new law required all men to wear hats and made the wearing of the fez a criminal offense.

"...There were new disturbances in the [eastern part of Turkey as a result of this law], and ominous stirrings elsewhere. The emergency 'Law for the Maintenance of Order', passed in March 1925 to deal with the Kurdish rebellion, was still in force, and the government was able to impose and enforce its will through the armed forces and the 'independence tribunals'. As Kemal grimly remarked:

"'We did it [the abolition of the fez] while the Law for the Maintenance of Order was still in force. Had it not been, we would have done it all the same, but it certainly is true for the existence of the law made it much easier for us. Indeed, the existence of the Law for the Maintenance of Order prevented the large-scale poisoning of the nation by certain reactionaries.'" ([9], 269-270)

C. Change of Calendar and Rest Day

(7) "Once the Turk donned the western hat, it was easier for him to accept changes no less drastic. One by one, the old calendar, the old way of telling time, and the weekly rest day were changed... The adoption of the western calendar hardly caused a ripple.

"On the other hand, the change of the rest day from Friday [the day of obligatory collective worship for Muslims] to Sunday aroused criticism from the old-school Turks... The republic decided that there were not enough working days left and declared Sunday the official day of rest despite the objection of the few." ([7], 58)

D. Change of Legal Code

(8) In discussing the draft of a new family law in 1925, Mustafa Kemal said: "The important point is to free our legal attitudes, our codes, and our legal organizations immediately from principles

dominating our life that are incompatible with the necessities of the age... The direction to be followed in civil law and family law should be nothing but that of Western civilization. Following the road of half measures and attachment to age-old beliefs is the gravest obstacle to the awakening of nations." ([6], 469)

"Two excerpts from the Preamble [to the new Civil Code, taken from that of Switzerland] answered in advance the major objections to its reception." These excerpts affirm that there is no basic difference in the needs of nations in relation to contemporary civilization. What is needed and desired is that the new Turkey conform itself to "contemporary civilization" without reservation, and in the process do away entirely with adherence to religious laws and customs which do not serve this purpose.

"We see, therefore, that the aim of the makers of the Code was not to establish and regulate the civil relations of the people according to existing customs and mores, or religious provision. On the contrary, it was to shape these relations according to what the makers of the Code believed they should be. Here lies the revolutionary character of the Code. Its approach differed radically from the Mecelle, as well as from the two previous family codes, in that it was not a codification bringing together different traditions for the purpose of their reconciliation, but rather one establishing a new system to the exclusion of the provisions of the religious and customary legal systems..." ([6], 471)

E. Alphabet and Language Reform

(9) "Reform followed reform so rapidly that we felt we were living in a laboratory and taking part in numerous interesting and essential experiments. ...Soon the newspapers started on a campaign against our alphabet and our language, which, they argued, needed renovation. It was also rumoured that the President [Atatürk] with a commission of experts, was drawing up a new alphabet." ([7], 61)

"Our newspapers wrote long articles explaining that the percentage of illiteracy was due to the difficult Arabic alphabet and the many 'foreign' [Arabic and Persian] words which our writers used.

It was not enough to build new schools; a new alphabet was needed and the language had to be cleansed of the Arabic and Iranian words which most people in Anatolia did not know and could not understand.

"Commissions headed by the President went into feverish action. The Hungarian and other alphabets were studied and from these a new Turkish Latin alphabet was finally evolved. Another commission studied hundreds of manuscripts in ancient dialects and words found in early inscriptions and documents discovered in Central Asia. A list was then compiled, giving the Turkish equivalent of the Arabic and Iranian word which long ago had been incorporated into the language. For the one word Allah (God) seventeen Turkish equivalents were found. Most people now use the Turkish word *Tanrı* instead of the Arabic Allah [a statement which continues to be wishful thinking on the author's part, rather than fact]." ([7], 62)

"The language reform for the time turned our newspapers into Chinese puzzles. They adopted a policy of writing several articles a day, using the old Turkish words long in disuse in order to teach them to the public. A glossary was added to each article giving the Arabic and Iranian equivalent of these outlandish words which were as difficult to use as the foreign [Arabic and Persian] ones. To read and write became a painful task for a while. Just recently the government changed the names of four of our months and is constantly introducing new words not only from the old Turkish but from French as well. But it is hard for people to change and when they speak, they invariably slip into the old way and the Arabic and Iranian words so long familiar to them tumble out, as of old." ([7], 64)

(10) In introducing the new script, Kemal said: "Our rich and harmonious language will now be able to display itself with new Turkish letters. We must free ourselves from these incomprehensible signs [the Arabic alphabet] that for centuries have held our minds in an iron vise... " ([8], 503)

"In November 1928 the new script became law. Introducing it into the Assembly as the 'key which would enable the people of Turkey to read and write easily,' the Gazi artfully referred to it not as the Latin but as the Turkish script, thus pointing up its distinction from the Arabic, whose use was prohibited from the end of the year onwards." ([8], 505)

It should, however, be noted that after about fifty years of combating illiteracy by means of this 'simplified' Latin alphabet, the literacy rate in Turkey is still only about fifty percent, and I have commented in the text on some of the uses of this literacy.

(11) "Various arguments have been put forward to explain and justify the revolution in the alphabet. ...The basic purpose of the change was not so much practical and pedagogical, as social and cultural—and Mustafa Kemal, in forcing his people to accept it, was slamming a door on the past as well as opening a door to the future. The way was now clear to a final break with the past and with the East—to the final incorporation of Turkey into the civilization of the modern West." ([9], 279)

"By learning a new script and forgetting the old, so it seemed, the past could be buried and forgotten, and a new generation brought up, open only to such ideas as were expressed in the new, romanized Turkish.

"The new script was officially adopted in November 1928, and the old Arabic script outlawed from the New Year. The erection of this great barrier against the past obviously created a new and unprecedented opportunity for linguistic reform, and from the first there seems to have been a clear intention of exploiting it.

"...The first task was the completion of a process already begun by earlier literary reformers—the reduction and eventual elimination of the Arabic and Persian grammatical and syntactical forms, many of which still remained embedded in Turkish literary usage. This was followed by a more radical step—the assault on the Arabic and Persian vocabulary itself. For more than 1,000 years the Turks had been a Muslim people, sharing the common Islamic civilization of the Middle East. Arabic and Persian had been their classical languages, and had made a contribution to their vocabulary comparable in scale and content with the Greek, Latin and Romance elements in English. The earlier language reformers had been content to remove foreign constructions, and foreign words that were rare, learned, or archaic. The radicals of the Linguistic Society [founded by Atatürk] were opposed to Arabic and Persian words as such, even those that had formed an essential part of the basic vocabulary of everyday spoken Turkish. On the one hand, the Society prepared and published an index of alien words, condemned to deportation; on the other search parties collected and examined purely Turkish words, from dialects, from other Turkish languages, and from ancient texts, to serve as replacements. When no suitable words could be discovered, resuscitated or imported, new ones were invented.

"This planned exchange of lexical populations reached its height during the years 1933-4, when it coincided with a general movement of secularization and Westernization. It is significant that the hue and cry after alien words affected only Arabic and Persian—the Islamic, Oriental languages. Words of European origin, equally alien, were exempt, and a number of were imported, to fill the gaps left by the departed.

"Some pruning of the exuberant verbiage of late Ottoman style was certainly necessary; ...reform was needed—but not all would agree with the wisdom and success of the reforms accomplished. The attempt of the reformers to strip away the accretions of 1,000 years of cultural growth seemed at times to bring impoverishment rather than purity, while the arbitrary reassignments of words and meanings have often led to confusion and chaos."* ([9], 433-434)

Since 1935, the author continues, there has been alternation between the continued reform of language and the halting of such reform, as demonstrated by the four different versions of the Turkish constitution: the 1924 original, using the common language of the day; the second in 'pure Turkish,' using only words of Turkish origin and stripped of the classic Arabic and Persian terminologies which had been used for hundreds of years; the third, the repromulgation of the 1924 document, whose wording, under the impact of all this reform, was by now quite archaic; and finally a fourth version which avoided both the incomprehensible, artificial 'purified' Turkish and the now-archaic language of the original document. He goes on to say:

---

* "A parallel movement in English might have imposed folk wain for omnibus, revived ayenbite and in wit for remorse and conscience, and renamed Parliament the Witenagemot."

"A comparison between the text of the 1924 constitution and the current language of Turkish literary, journalistic, and official usage will reveal how much the reform really accomplished. To the Turk of the present day, this thirty-five year-old document, with its numerous Arabic and Persian words and constructions, bears an archaic, almost a medieval aspect. Though certainly more intelligible than the 'pure Turkish' version of 1945, it contains many expressions that are now obsolete, and must be explained to the Turkish schoolboy or student of the new generation. Even the famous speech of Mustafa Kemal, delivered in October 1927, has become a difficult and archaic text, requiring notes and explanations for the children of the new Turkey. The written language of today is unmistakably different from that which was used before the reform, and books a bare half-century old, even when translated into the new script, are as difficult for a Turkish schoolboy as Chaucer or even Langland for his English contemporary." ([9], 436)

The romanization of the Turkish alphabet, it may be added, has no doubt contributed to the variant pronunciation of Persian and Arabic, especially Qur'anic, words in Turkish. For example, in romanized Turkish, Khadijah is Hatice, *Allahu Akbar* is *Allahüekber*, etc., the romanized spellings thus permanently reinforcing and retaining the variant pronunciation.

F.   *Emancipation of Women*

(12) "During the national emergency the Turkish woman had made enormous strides on the road to freedom. Would the new republic force her back into the harem* and the era of the veil? But Kemal Ataturk realized that the country needed free, educated women if it ever would assimilate the changes he had in mind. Women must assume their rights.

"He toured the country again, urging women to throw off their veils, to take part in national affairs and step into their rightful places. He said in one of his speeches that no country could advance with half of society free and the other half lacking all free-

* The portion of a Muslim's house for the use of women, into which outsider males do not come. M.K.

dom. The President was diplomatic too. At one of the numerous balls given at Ankara, he saw an elderly lady wearing a black kerchief over her head. Approaching the woman, Ataturk told her:

"You have beautiful hair. Why do you hide it under this ugly veil?"

"Kemal Ataturk used persuasion to free the women; no laws were passed forbidding the tsharchaf or the veil. The seclusion of women was also bound up with religion and there were many men who objected to seeing their wives or their daughter appearing in public without the traditional costume. Kemal Ataturk showed us the way, and those who wanted to follow could do so.

"The emancipation of women has changed the face of Turkey just as the hat and the Latin alphabet did. The curtains [in trolleys] are gone and women now sit side by side with the men. They stand up, too, hanging to a strap when the trolleys are crowded ...Out in the tennis courts, young women play a vigorous game of tennis and their partners are often young men." ([7], 80-82)

(13) "Democracy won Turkish women the freedom to dress as they pleased [i.e., Western style]. Among other social reforms, the introduction of western costume for men and women gave Turkey a new appearance. It no longer looks like an eastern country. The dress of male citizens was changed by legislation passed in 1925. There is no law affecting women but the tradition which forced them to veil themselves disappeared. It may be possible to see some women in certain parts of Anatolia who still wear veils but they are the exceptions. Generally speaking, Turkish women have said goodbye to the veil and secluded life of their ancestors. In some parts of Anatolia our national costumes are still in use; but they are just historical relics and are valuable in so far as they show the richness of our folklore. As a race Turkish people look very much like Western people. The change in their costume makes it impossible to tell Turkish women from the women of the West. Whereas, in the old days their ways of dressing and living prevented women from advancing, the changes in their outlook gave them the self-respect and increased the confidence which they needed to succeed." ([2], 60)

(14) "Soon after his visit to Kastamonu in 1935 Kemal proceeded

to the more sophisticated city of Izmir (Smyrna). Here he presided over an entertainment which was in effect the first Turkish ball. Only Moslems and their ladies were invited. An orchestra played Western music, and they were expected to dance together—an ordeal which they faced with reluctance, even after the Gazi himself had opened the ball by performing a correct fox trot with the governor's daughter. Never until this moment had a Turkish woman, in her own country, danced with a man in public.

"In Istanbul the habit soon caught on. Elsewhere Kemal had to use all his talents of persuasion to make dances accepted social functions...

"In Ankara he gave a ball in honor of the foundation of the Republic. It went well enough but late in the evening the Gazi noticed a group of young officers, none of whom was dancing. They explained that the ladies had refused their requests for a dance. Kemal immediately addressed them for all the guests to hear: 'My friends, I cannot conceive that any woman in the world can refuse to dance with a Turk wearing an officer's uniform. I now give you an order. Disperse through the ballroom. Quick march! Dance.' " ([8], 478)

G. Secularism

(15)   "Article 9 of the Law of Associations (Cemiyetler Kanunu), promulgated in 1938, prohibited the 'formation of societies based on religion, sect and *tariqa*,' Forming societies for the purpose of religious prayer and practice was not prohibited. The same law prohibited political parties as such from engaging in religious activities and from making religious propaganda. Propaganda against the principles of secularism was prohibited by Article 163 of the Penal Code adopted in 1926. Article 241 of the same law made religious functionaries liable to prosecution for speaking derisively of the laws and public authorities in the course of their ministrations." ([6], 466)

(16) "Within four years, in a series of swift and sweeping changes, Kemal repealed the Holy Law [the *Shari'ah*, as it still applied to family and civil law in Turkey] and disestablished Islam. The stages are well known—the restriction and the prohibition of religious

education, the adoption of European civil and penal codes, the nationalization of the pious foundations [evkaf], the reduction and eventual elimination of the power of the ulema, the transformation of social and cultural symbols and practices, such as dress and headgear, the calendar and the alphabet. The coping-stone of the edifice of legal secularism was laid in April 1928, when Islam was removed from the constitution [as the official state religion of Turkey]." ([9], 404)

"The basis of Kemalist religious policy was laicism [secularism], not irreligion; its purpose was not to destroy Islam, but to disestablish it—to end the power of religion and its exponents in political, social, and cultural affairs, and to limit it to matters of belief and worship..." ([9], 412)

"During the 1930's the pressure of secularization in Turkey became very strong indeed. Although the regime never adopted an avowedly anti-Islamic policy, its desire to end the power of organized Islam and to break its hold on the minds and hearts of the Turkish people was clear. The prohibition of religious education, the transfer of mosques to secular purposes reinforced the lesson of legal and social reform. In the rapidly growing capital, no new mosques were built. Most striking and most symbolic, was the fate of the great basilica of Santa Sophia in Istanbul. Sultan Mehmet the conqueror, in the moment of triumph over Byzantium, had made it a mosque; the Republic made it a museum." ([9], 416)

H. Manipulation of Religion by the Government

(17) A sermon (Khutba) by Ali Vahit: "O Moslems, the greatest worship is obedience to God. God in His Koran says... obey God and His Prophet and your masters. Our Master is the Republican Government.

"If there is no obedience to the Government, then the discipline of the world is broken. All of our affairs become mixed; all those who depend on their strength become rulers. Justice, security and tranquility will be ended. No one° will have surety of his life and property. Then there will not be obedience to God and His Prophet.

"That is why God commanded us to obey our government with equal emphasis. Especially the Government which has the authority today, since it is not the same government of the old times... Today's government is made up from the hearts of a nation and it is the Government of the nation itself. Let us love our Government, and let us obey it. Because God commands us to obey our government.

"O Moslems, if you want to reach happiness and salvation in this world and the next, obey the commands of God; and to be happy in the world and to have comfort and security, we must obey those who work for us day and night, and who perform their duties. Those who do not obey their masters dig their own graves, and with this behavior they rebel against God and will be punished severely in the next world.

"O you creatures of God, I advise you to obey the rules of God and keep away from rebellion. This advice is given to you for your own good in every way." First Sermon—from the Pulpit of Hadji Bairam Mosque. ([3], 223-224)

From Yusuf Ziya: "The decisions of the National Assembly have a religious importance. If the responsible persons come together and make a decision regarding some problems then it becomes *farz* [obligatory] on all Moslems to obey that decision." From Islam Dini, First Book. ([3], 224)

Such distortions of the basic teachings of Islam regarding obedience to the government or ruler can only be imposed on those who do know what Islam enjoins. The Qur'an states, "Obey God and His Prophet and those in authority among you. If you differ in anything refer it to God and His Messengers" (*al-Nisa* 4:59). God and His Prophet are to be obeyed not only by the Muslim citizen but first and foremost by the ruler and members of government. Abu Bakr Siddiq, the first Caliph of Islam, himself told the Muslim Muslim community, "Obey me as long as I obey God and His Messenger. When I disobey Him and His Prophet, then do not obey me," and this is the only correct and acceptable attitude for both the government and people of a Muslim country, whose only master is God Himself, not the ruler or the government.

I. Changes in Religious Affairs and Religious Education

(18) "The Caliph was deposed and his office abolished; the members of his dynasty were forever forbidden to reside within the frontiers of the Turkish Republic; the Ministry of Religious Affairs was disbanded, the historic office of Sheikh of Islam ceased to exist, the revenues of th Pious Foundations were confiscated; and all religious schools were transferred to the secular arm. By a further decree a month later the religious courts of the sheriat, which still administered the laws relating to such matters of family and personal status as marriage, divorce, and inheritance, were closed, and a Civil Code based on that of the Swiss was planned to prevail over all." ([8], 439)

(19) "The bureaucratization of the ulema, begun by Mahmud II, had reached its logical conclusion [in Atatürk's religious 'reforms', by which the control of most religious affairs became a function— and tool— of the government]. Islam had been made a department of state; the ulema had become minor civil servants. General education had already been taken out of the hands of the ulema. There remained the question of religious education, which the state now prepared to take over.

"By the laws of 1924 the *medresses*—the old theological seminaries—were closed. The state did, however, make some attempts to provide for the further training of religious personnel. At the lower level, the Ministry of Education established some training·schools for imams and preachers; at the higher level, the old Süleymaniye *Medrese* was reconstituted as a faculty of divinity in the University of Istanbul—also, therefore, under the ultimate control of the Minister of Education of the Republic in Ankara.

"This new faculty of divinity was intended to serve as the centre of a new modernized and scientific form of religious instruction, more appropriate to a secular, Westernized republic. In 1928 the faculty appointed a committee to examine the problem of reform and modernization in the Islamic religion, and to make proposals through the University to the Ministry of Education. The chairman of the committee was Professor Mehmet Fuad Köprülü; its members included professors of psychology and logic as well as a number of theologians." ([9], 413-414)

This committee, the author continues, published its report in June 1928, stating that since religion is a social institution, it must meet the needs of social life and keep pace with change and development. The report continues:

"It is almost impossible with the modern views of society, to expect such a reform, however much the ground may be ready for it, from the working of mystic and irrational elements. Religious life, like moral and economic life, must be reformed on scientific lines, that it may be in harmony with other institutions..." ([9], 414)

The recommendations for changes in religious observance to suit this purpose were four-fold: (1) Clean, orderly mosques, with pews and cloakrooms, were needed; people should enter them with clean shoes. (2) The language of worship, that is, prayers and sermons, should be in Turkish, which of course meant reciting the Qur'an in translation rather than in Arabic, so that it was in fact no longer the Qur'an, that is, God's word. (3) The character of worship should be beautiful, inspiring and spiritual, and for this purpose mosques should have musical instruments and trained musicians; 'modern and sacred' instrumental music was urgently needed. (4) Real religious guidance, which only preachers with the necessary philosophical training were competent to give, should replace the printed, set sermons. The author continues:

"It was possible to turn the Ottoman Sultanate into a national republic, with a president, ministries and parliament. It was not possible to turn the mosque into a Muslim church, with pews, organ, and an imam-precentor... Only one of the recommendations of the 1928 committee had any practical consequences—that of the Turkicization of worship. Attempts were made to translate the Koran and the Traditions of the Prophet into Turkish, and in 1932 the Assembly voted a sum of TL 4,000 for the preparation and publication of such a translation. It was not completed. An attempt to translate the mosque service into Turkish was abandoned in the face of opposition. In one respect, however, the government held firm. Even if Arabic were still to be used inside the mosque, it could not be tolerated in public places... On 30 January 1932 the cry 'God is great' resounded from the minarets of Santa Sophia, for the first time, in Turkish, and shortly afterwards a version of the call, in 'pure' Turkish, was prepared by the Linguistic Society and published by the Presidency of Religious Affairs.* A Turkish melody was ordered from the Conservatory in Ankara. Muezzins all over Turkey were instructed in the new version, and an order issued early in 1933 superseded, though without actually banning, the call to prayer in Arabic. 'It seems that this one act of government interference in the ritual caused more widespread resentment than any of the other secularist measures.'" (quoted from Rustow, 'Politics and Islam,' p. 84) ([9], 414-416)

As for the faculty of divinity, the author states that it proved to be premature. "The teachers, themselves of the *medrese* tradition, did not take kindly to the task assigned to them, and the atmosphere of the time was not conducive to its realization. The abolition, in 1939, of Arabic and Persian as subjects of instruction in the secondary schools reduced both the numbers and the competence of the students. After some abortive attempts at reform, the faculty was finally suppressed in 1933, and replaced in due course

---

*For the reader's interest, I have given below the *adhan* in Arabic, and 'pure' Turkish, with the English translation, and he is free to draw his own conclusions.

Arabic

Allahu Akbar, Allahu Akbar, Allahu Akbar, Allahu Akbar.
Ashadu an la ilaha illa Allah, ashahadu an la ilaha illa Allah.
Ashadu anna Muhammadu Rasul Allah, ashadu anna
   Muhammadu Rasul Allah.
Hayya 'alas salah, Hayya 'alas salah.
Hayya 'alal falah, hayya 'alal falah.
Allahu Akbar, Allahu Akbar.
La ilaha illa Allah.

'Pure' Turkish

Tanrı uludur, Tanrı uludur, Tanrı uludur, Tanrı uludur.
Suphesiz bilirim bildiririm Tanrıdan başka yoktur tapacak,
   suphesiz bilirim bildiririm Tanrıdan başka yoktur tapacak.
Suphesiz bilirim bildiririm Tanrının elşisidir Muhammad.
   bilirim bildiririm Tanrının elçisidir Muhammad.
Haydin namaza, haydin namaza.
Haydin felaha, haydin felaha.
Tanrı uludur, Tanrı uludur.
Tanrıdan başka yoktur tapacak.

(continued on the following page)

by an Institute of Oriental Studies attached to the faculty of arts. During the nine years that the faculty of divinity existed, the number of its students dropped from 284 to 20. In the same period there was a parallel decline in the schools for imams and preachers, and the last two such schools were closed in 1931. Except for the comparatively unimportant schools for Koran-readers, formal religious education disappeared in Turkey, and the attempt to form a new class of modern religious guides was completely abandoned." ([9], 415)

(20) Concerning religious education for children, "Opening religious schools or schools for the purpose of religious instruction was not prohibited (although no one appears to have exercised this freedom until recently). This freedom was not unlimited; the constitutional provision that every Turkish citizen had the right to free primary education and the subsequent educational laws making secular primary education compulsory to the age of twelve were active deterrents to the opening of religious schools in competition with the primary schools administered by the Ministry of Education. Further, teaching of the Arabic script in unauthorized schools was prohibited when the Latin script was adopted in 1928. Parents were free to provide religious instruction privately in out-of-school time or in collectively established classes, provided that these did not interfere with regular schooling, that they were authorized by the Ministry of Education, and that they were competently supervised with regard to public health and the qualifications of the instructor." ([6], 466-467)

"When the clause stating that Islam was the state religion was dropped from the Constitution in 1928, the Ministry of Education

---

God is the Most Great, God is the Most Great, God is the Most Great, God is the Most Great.

I bear witness that there is no deity except God, I bear witness that there is no deity except God.

I bear witness that Muhammad is a messenger of God, I bear witness that Muhammad is a messenger of God.

Come to prayer, come to prayer.

Come to good, (success, felicity), come to good.

God is the Most Great, God is the Most Great.

There is no deity except God.

took steps to drop classes in religion from the school curricula... Classes in religion were dropped in the urban schools in 1930; the change was effected in the village schools in 1933. In 1933 a law specifying the organization and function of the Ministry of Education confirmed secular education and abolished earlier provisions concerning religious teachig in schools." ([6], 476)

For a brief and partial review of developments in Islam and Islamic education in Turkey since Atatürk's time, see ([9],472-473).

J. Turkish Cultural Nationalism

(21) "The growth of cultural nationalism since 1908 had accustomed the new generation of Turks to the idea of Turkishness—of identity and loyalty based on the Turkish nation. The Kemalist Republic brought a new idea—that of Turkey—the land of Turks. So new was this idea, that the Turkish language even lacked a name for it." ([9], 353)

"The term *vatan,* fatherland, had had a chequered history in modern Turkey. In the mid-nineteenth century, according to Cevdet Pasa, it would have meant, to a Turkish soldier, no more than the village square; by the late nineteenth century, to Namik Kemal, it suggested the whole Ottoman Empire, including—perhaps especially—the Holy Cities of Arabia. For the pan-Turkish Ziya Gökalp in 1911, it was neither Turkey nor Turkistan but the vast land of Turan. Yet as late as August 1917, the Grand Vezir Mehmet Said Helim Pasa could still firmly assert that 'the fatherland of a Muslim is the place where the Şeriat prevails.'

"It was against this variegated background of traditions and ideas that Kemal sought to inculcate the new idea of an Anatolian Turkish fatherland. His aim was to destroy what remained of the Islamic and Ottoman feelings of loyalty, to counter the distractions of pan-Islamic and pan-Turkish appeals, and to forge a new loyalty, of the Turkish nation to its homeland. His chosen instrument was history. The Ottoman Historical Society had been wound up. A new Turkish Historical Society was founded in 1930, to serve as the medium of state policy for the imposition of certain historical theories. Its tasks included the drafting of new historical syllabuses and textbooks, on patriotic lines, for use in schools and universities." ([9], 358-359)

(22) "A common heritage of past experiences and shared traditions is one element in forming a nation. But for the Kemalists, who wanted to speed the development of Turkish national sentiment, eliminating the Ottoman past, or rather degrading it in the minds of the Turkish people, was the primary endeavor. Turkish youth were to be divorced from the Ottoman historical and cultural heritage. Their interest was to be focused on pre-Islamic Turkish precedents and on a language cleansed of non-Turkic grammatical forms, as evidence of Turkish national identity. School children learned of the legendary Turkish kingdon along the Orkhon River in Central Asia but very little about the conquests of the Ottoman sultans in three continents. For them, Turkish history began with the arrival of Mustafa Kemal to Samsun in 1919. To ignore, however, long historical heritage proved in the long run to be inconsistent with the idea of genuine nationalism.

"Since 1946 the possible traditional historical contributions to national consciousness have become more acceptable, although the evaluation of the Ottoman past remains a controversial question between the strict Kemalist positivists and the conservative traditionalists. After the revolution of 1960, the controversy became even more exacerbated when linked with a foreign policy orientation." ([12], 59)

L. *Atatürk's Character and Actions*

(23) "Since childhood, in defiant reaction against his mother's beliefs and devotional practices, he [Kemal] had been developing subconsciously into an agnostic. Now his disbelief was conscious and militant... In public Kemal still had to tread warily, conforming outwardly to the traditions of Islam, mentioning the unmentionable only in the company of his most intimate friends.

"...The bulk of his own associates, the literate elite, were still religious conformists who had carried out their Revolution within the framework of Islam. The reactionaries might cry against their officers as godless. But they were in fact good Moslems, to whom Kemal was the godless one. He drank, he sought to shock, he was promiscuous with women, he scorned moral principles. He was a social *arriviste* who offended against the conventions of the decent middle-class Moslems which they smugly saw themselves to be. It was this, as much as his political views and military ambitions, that caused them [the leaders of the Committee of Union and Progress] to side against him." ([8], 55-56)

"Psychologically, Kemal's emergence as a 'hanging dictator' was rooted in two other factors. The first was an obsessive suspicion of all who had spurned and obstructed him... The second impulse behind his drastic actions was a fear of what he did not understand—the forces of religion. Agnosticism was born in him early and grew in him with time... In his rationalism he understood little of the spiritual concept of Islam, which represented an inner need for the mass of his people and which a mere social philosophy, however enlightened, could not easily replace. He saw it as mere superstition of a dark and primitive kind. But he did not underrate its force. It was a secret weapon liable to be used against him by the peasants and the 'priests' who controlled them, a 'hidden hand' wider in its reach and stronger in its grip than that of any mere rival political party. He understood little, whatever he might say in his speeches, of the social and political principles of Islam as the Prophet had seen them, and as the liberal reformers of the past century had been striving to regenerate them. For Kemal Islam and civilization were a contradiction in terms. 'If only,' he once said of the Turks, with a flash of cynical insight, 'we could make them Christians!' His was not to be the reformed Islamic state for which the faithful were waiting: it was to be a strictly lay [secular] state with a centralized government as strong as the Sultan's, backed by the army and run by his own intellectual bureaucracy." ([8], 496-497)

(24) "...Before the final offensive...Kemal had undertaken to relinquish his extraordinary powers once peace was signed. It was now signed; but he showed no disposition to do so. On the contrary, he planned to reinforce these powers by becoming head of the new People's party, and thus, in Rauf's [Orbay's] view, prejudicing from the outset the democratic development of the new Turkish state. In his usual frank manner he spoke to Kemal of these misgivings, saying that he envisaged the Gazi's position as that of an impartial arbiter, a head of state above all parties and individuals. But now he was involving himself in day-to-day politics.

"Ali Fuad shared these views, which he had voiced at the time of the party's conception, arguing that Kemal's association with it would prevent the free growth of political parties in a country committed to popular sovereignty. So indeed it was to prove in the elections, when Kemal intervened actively, using his commanding position as both head of the party and commander-in-chief of the army to preclude the emergence of any Opposition group.

"This was the dominating issue in the new political phase which now followed the peace. It was the struggle for power between the Gazi in person and the forces of democracy as seen by Rauf and others..." ([8], 424)

"The issue between Kemal and his old friends [the four cofounders of the Revolution, Rauf Orbay, Refet Bele, Ali Faud and Kazim Karabekir] had now to be joined. ...Kemal's own ideals were tempered by expediency and above all by his ruthless sense of realities. His head ruled his heart. He had a colder, more penetrating intelligence than they.

"Their differences now proved fundamental. Kemal was embarking on a social revolution. Rauf and his friends, at this stage, preferred social evolution. What need was there for hurry, for sudden and radical change? Give the people time to settle down after their ten-year upheaval. Give them security from brigandage and aid in recultivating their lands. Let social reforms come gradually in response to their needs and demands. Sovereignty was theirs. Let them exercise it through their own representative institutions, as it was exercised in the democratic countries of Europe. They had an honorable peace. Let them now have two or three years of good government and after that decide, through a referendum, what kind of regime they would prefer. Thus spoke the voice of the liberal Turkish gentleman.

"Kemal knew his people too well to have any illusions as to their political maturity. They were still an oriental people culturally backward and temperamentally unfitted for the literal application of Western democracy. They could not yet rule; they required to be ruled. The strong religious authority of the Sultan-Caliph needed to be replaced by an equally strong secular authority; and this for the present only Kemal himself, by his personal manipulation of Parliament, could provide. Rauf and the rest, by the integrity of their principles and moderation of their outlook, threatened to undermine it and thus to prejudice that process of reform which no one else but he, as he saw it, had the foresight to plan and the capacity to execute. Here was a struggle for power, with his friends as with his enemies, which in alliance with Ismet [Inönü] and Fevzi [Çakmak]—the two latecomers to the Revolution—and his less scrupulous henchmen, must soon be fought out. It was a struggle between the forces of a liberal democracy, literally interpreted, and those of a democratic structure conditioned by one-party government and personal rule." ([8], 445-446)

"While the army completed its preparations Ismet clinched his hold over the country with the introduction into the Assembly of a drastic Law for the Maintenance of Public Order. This was to give the government wide dictatorial powers. For a period of two years (in the event to be extended for a further such period) the Cabinet was accorded the right to forbid and suppress any organization, any attempt, or any publication which might encourage 'reaction and rebellion.' The law was to be enforced through Independence Tribunals. Most of these would be in the region of military operations, where they would replace the courts-martial and have the power to carry out death sentences instantly, without seeking the Assembly's approval. There was to be one additional tribunal in Ankara, with jurisdiction over the rest of the country to suppress reactionary propaganda and punish actions threatening to disturb the peace, but requiring the Assembly's approval for death sentences." ([8], 454-455)

"This policy of suppression was championed by the Ankara press with the reiteration of such words as Law, Order, Unity, and above all Strength. It was illustrated in terms which were often macabre... Thanks to their [the Independence Tribunals' judges] labours, the new Turkish Republic was able, within eighteen months of its proclamation, to boast that it had effectively silenced all political opposition." ([8], 458-459).

In 1925 an attempt was made on Kemal's life. Although the plot had clearly been the work of a few individuals and could easily have been handled by an ordinary criminal prosecution, Kemal

grasped at "the chance which it offered of implicating and
eliminating at one stroke all his opponents... The Independence
Tribunal was at once summoned by special train from Ankara to
Izmir." This body ordered a large number of arrests which included not only the known conspirators but, without respect for
parliamentary immunity, some twenty-five deputies, former
associates of the Union and Progress Party and leading members of
the moderate Progressive Party.

For their alleged responsibility for the plot, "They were to be
tried by a tribunal which placed itself above the law of the country
and above such constitutional trifles as the privilege of members of
the Assembly, to which it was in theory responsible. They had
neither counsel for defense nor the right of appeal. They were
assumed guilty unless they proved themselves innocent. They were
at the mercy of flimsy and arbitrary evidence, obtained by
methods... which Kemal had always so outspokenly deplored. Wit-
nesses were largely dispensed with, and the accused were treated
simply to an interrogation and an arraignment by the judge. Faced
with this mockery of justice, the generals and other Progressive
[Party] leaders took the only course consistent with their honour.
They refused to plead. Asked if they had anything to say in their
defense, they replied, 'No.' " ([8], 486-488)

" 'It was the people that I was afraid of.' Thus did Kemal, in a
remark to a friend, seek to justify afterwards the liquidation of his
opponents and his assumption of supreme dictatorial powers. It was
the people, he was forever telling them, who had saved Turkey. Yet
ironically it was for fear of them that he now pursued a policy contrary to all his professed democratic principles. In fact his prestige
with the people had never been higher than in the first years of the
Republic. They were more securely under his control than they had
been under that of any Sultan. Moreover, theirs was now a personal
loyalty, based on the fact that he had led them personally in war,
saving their lands from the enemy, making his capital in their midst,
and as no• Sultan had done moving continuously among them as
though he were one of them. His hold over the army was unchallenged. Communications, to say nothing of secret service tech-
niques, were now so developed that no centralized administration
need fear serious local unrest. Kemal knew better than most of the
congenial inertia of the Turkish people, whom he alone, at Galla-

poli and later in the War of Independence, had known how to gal-
vanize into action; and now, throughout Anatolia, there was no
other potential national leader able to do so and thus to threaten his
power.

"Paradoxically Kemal had become a dictator not in order to obtain power but after he had done so already. ...This might well
have been the moment for an experiment in some kind of liberal
democracy, whose principles were after all inherent in the new
Turkish Republic. This would have been a fitting culmination to
that movement of reform which had been born in the Ottoman Empire a century earlier. The Young Turks, giving it a new brief lease
of life, had lapsed from parliamentary democracy into a dictatorial
triumvirate at a time of crisis when the foreigner was threatening
the empire from every side, and when a parliamentary Opposition
has shown signs of endangering the unity of the country. But Kemal
had surmounted these very obstacles; he had no need for a dictatorship—for the duumvirate which, with Ismet [Inönü] as his reliable
factotum, he had now set up. Extraordinary measures might have
been necessary to deal with such local outbursts as the Kurdish rebellion and the subsequent hat riots. But there was no need to extend these over the whole country, and above all no need to use
them for the suppression of a parliamentary Opposition of an essentially moderate kind.

"But he had decided otherwise. His decision was firstly a matter
of temperament. By nature and training a soldier, he might delegate
his authority but he could not tolerate the idea of any threat to it;
he might plan his campaigns in cooperation with others but he must
have sole control of their execution. And what was the transformation of Turkish society but another campaign in which, as he saw
it, a rapid decision must be reached?" ([8], 494-495)

(25) "...He brought military tactics into his everyday affairs, insisting on being the Commanding Officer, engendering jealousy,
hatred, and a great deal of opposition. His greatest failing was his
ego-centricity; convinced as he was that only he could save the
nation (despite the nation's obvious reluctance to be saved by him),
he could not bear to see anyone else assuming popularity or getting
too much attention. He could not govern alone but he distrusted
everyone around him. The Assembly, as the voice of the nation,

was often vociferous in its untimely demands; many of the deputies were right thinking, level headed men and they resented his appropriation of power. He detested criticism, feeling that those who criticized had the least ability to do so. By foul means or fair he had set his foot on the nation—plotting intrigues against the popular, persecuting the ascendant... Mustafa Kemal was a man of iron. He stamped on the intrigues ruthlessly, hanging twenty-five insubordinate officers on the way, and brought Parliament sharply to heel. 'Until I have done what I set out to do, pulled the Turks into a nation, I shall continue to be master. Let none of you mistake the compliancy of my actions.' But still the deputies howled for their rights, insisting that Supreme Command should now be taken from him. He told them laconically that none of them could do the job as well as he." ([11], 111)

(26) "His other method of seeking to calm [his nerves] was through alcohol. Kemal had been drinking freely all his life. In his early youth, less sure of himself than he liked to appear, he had drunk to gain confidence, to impose himself the better on others. As his brain developed, he drank to relax it. At night his thoughts denied him peace; in the daytime they drove him like a dynamo. In the evening—but seldom before sundown—he would drink to release nervous tension. Kemal drank not from weakness but deliberately, because he enjoyed alcohol and needed it. He made no secret of the practice, preferring to flaunt it without hypocrisy.

" . . . A French journalist wrote that Turkey was governed by one drunkard, one deaf man (Ismet), and three hundred deaf mutes (the deputies). At this Kemal commented, 'This man is mistaken. Turkey is governed by one drunkard.' " ([8], 298)

"It was a habit which did not endear him to his more strict Moslem deputies. One of the Assembly's first actions had been the passage of a bill against the import and general sale of spirituous liquors. The consumption of alcohol, contrary to the laws of Islam, was alleged to be paralyzing the armed forces, ravaging the population with illness, dragging the country to the edge of an abyss. It was now punishable by heavy fines, flogging, or imprisonment. When, however, an emissary was sent to Kemal in his office, begging him to abstain from the practice, he was laughed out of the door." ([8], 299)

(27) [As a young military attache in Sofia, Bulgaria, about 1913, one night Kemal was taken by a friend] "to a gala performance at the opera. It was a smart social occasion, and the glitter and elegance of the audience made a deep impression on Kemal. In the interval he was presented to King Ferdinand, who asked him for his impressions. He could only reply, 'Wonderful!' Afterwards the two friends took a party to supper at the Grand Hotel de Bulgarie. When their guests had left, Kemal poured out his enthusiasm to Shakir [Zümere]. This was Western civilization. There was nothing like it in Turkey. Constantinople had barely a theatre, far less an opera house. One of these days his country must enjoy these amenities."* ([8], 72-73)

3. Islam in Turkey since Atatürk

A. Religious Education

(28) "At the beginning of 1949 religious education was reintroduced to Turkish schools. It consisted of two hours' instruction on Saturday afternoons, and was only to be taken by children whose parents specifically asked for it. The overwhelming majority did. The textbook was prepared by a joint committee of representatives of the Ministry of Education and the Presidency of Religious Affairs, and presents a modernized version of Islam which Muslims in, say, Mecca or even Damascus would probably have some difficulty in recognizing.

"The next step came in October 1950, when it was decided to make religious education compulsory—or rather, when parents were required to opt out instead of in, as previously. This applied only to fourth and fifth classes of the primary schools. For the rest of the school years religious instruction remained optional.

"These changes, together with the growing interest in religious matters and the increase in public worship, raised the question of religious higher education. For many years there had been no higher religious instruction, and the religious revival therefore revealed an acute shortage of people competent to teach religion, even in schools, and to undertake the various religious functions in mosques. This lack of men with a serious religious education gave scope to fanatics and illiterates in the religious revival, often with

---

* The plans for a New Ankara, fifteen years later, allowed for a large modern opera house.

unfortunate results. It was no doubt for this reason, at least in part, that the government decided to restore the faculty of divinity [*Ilâhiyat Fakültesi*], which opened its gates to students in October 1949. Several features of the new faculty strike the outside observer. Unlike its predecessors, it was not in Istanbul, the old religious centre, with its great mosques, libraries, and tradition, but in Ankara, the new city, the heart of republican Turkey and the seat of the government. Unlike the old *medreses,* it was part of the University, and therefore ultimately under the control of the Ministry of Education. The first chairs to be established included Islamic Art and History of Religions." ([9], 418-419)

B. *Religious Revival*

(29) "After the war there were a number of signs of increasing religious activity, and one of the most striking was the growing self-assertiveness of religious functionaries. For a long time they had been very quiet and did not dare to raise their voices, not in the towns and hardly even in country places. Now they began to be much more in evidence... Some of them openly demanded control of religious education, and they began, in a tentative way, to intervene [sic!] in politics. In about 1950 they started a demand for the return of the *evkaf* to the Presidency of Religious Affairs...

"Mosque attendance rose considerably. Many of the mosques were now equipped with amplifiers; inscribed Arabic texts appeared on the walls in cafes, shops, taxis, and in the markets, and were offered for sale in the streets. Religious books and pamphlets were written and published on an ever-increasing scale. Besides a great number of pamphlets of popular piety, there were books on Islam, biographies of the Prophet and other figures, works on Islamic history, theology, and mysticism, translations of and commentaries on the Koran.

"Quite a considerable number of Turks began to make the pilgrimage to Mecca. In 1950 there were nearly 9,000, in spite of the fact that the government gave no allocation of foreign exchange for the purpose. Three of the major Istanbul dailies sent special correspondents to cover the pilgrimage, and the popular press in general gave increased attention to religious matters." ([9], 419-420)

" . . . Islam has profound roots among the Turkish people.· From its foundation until its fall the Ottoman Empire was a state dedicated to the advancement or defence of the power and faith of Islam. Turkish thought, life, and letters were permeated through and through by the inherited traditions of the classical Muslim cultures, which, though transmuted into something new and distinctive, remained basically and unshakeably Islamic.

"After a century of Westernization, Turkey has undergone immense changes—greater than any outside observer had thought possible. But the deepest Islamic roots of Turkish life and culture are still alive, and the ultimate identity of Turk and Muslim in Turkey is still unchallenged. The resurgence of Islam after a long interval responds to a profound national need." ([9], 424)

ACKNOWLEDGEMENTS

Material from THE TURKISH TRANSFORMATION by Henry Elisha Allen used with the agreement of the reprint publisher, Greenwood Press.

Material from THE EMANCIPATION OF THE TURKISH WOMAN by A. Afetinan, (C) UNESCO 1962, reprinted by permission of UNESCO.

Material taken from ISLAM AT THE CROSSROADS by Muhammad Asad used by permission of the author.

Material taken from THE DEVELOPMENT OF SECULARISM IN TURKEY by Niyazi Berkes used by permission of the author and publisher, McGill-Queen's University Press.

Material taken from TURKEY, OLD AND NEW by Selma Ekrem used by permission of the publisher, Charles Scribners' Sons.

Material taken from ATATURK by Lord Kinross used by permission of the publisher, William Morrow & Company, Incorporated.

Material taken from THE EMERGENCE OF MODERN TURKEY by Bernard Lewis, published by Oxford University Press for the Royal Institute of International Affairs (1961), reprinted by permission of the publisher.

Material from BRIDGE ACROSS THE BOSPORUS by Frenc A. Váli, Copyright 1971, used by permission of the publisher, Johns Hopkins University Press.

Printed by
INTERNATIONAL GRAPHICS PRINTING SERVICE
4411, 41st Street, Brentwood, Maryland 20722